GADAMER

GADAMER

A Philosophical Portrait

Donatella Di Cesare

Translated by Niall Keane

Indiana University Press

Bloomington and Indianapolis

This book is a publication of

Indiana University Press
601 North Morton Street
Bloomington, Indiana 47404-3797 USA

iupress.indiana.edu

Telephone orders   800-842-6796
Fax orders   812-855-7931

©2007 by Società editrice Il Mulino, Bologno
© English translation 2013 by Indiana University Press

Manufactured in the United States of America

Cataloging information is available from the Library of Congress.

ISBN 978-0-253-00763-6 (cloth)
ISBN 978-0-253-00768-1 (ebook)

1 2 3 4 5   18 17 16 15 14 13

Contents

Abbreviations

The following abbreviations will be used throughout the text. Citations from Gadamer's writings will be given with the English translation and, where available, followed by the corresponding text in his collected works, *Gesammelte Werke* (GW). Translations from other writings will be referred to in the same manner. Where no translation exists, reference is made to the German original and the translation is my own.

Primary texts by Gadamer

DD   *Dialogue and Deconstruction: The Gadamer-Derrida Encounter*. Ed. Diane Michelfelder and Richard Palmer. Albany: SUNY Press, 1989.

DDP   *Dialogue and Dialectic: Eight Hermeneutical Studies on Plato*. Trans. P. Christopher Smith. New Haven, Conn.: Yale University Press, 1980.

EE   *Das Erbe Europas*. Frankfurt am Main: Suhrkamp, 1989.

EH   *The Enigma of Health: The Art of Healing in a Scientific Age*. Trans. J. Gaiger and N. Walker. Stanford, Calif: Stanford University Press, 1996.

EPH   *Hans-Georg Gadamer on Education, Poetry, and History: Applied Hermeneutics*. Ed. Dieter Misgeld and Graeme Nicholson. Albany: SUNY Press, 1992.

GC   *Gadamer on Celan: "Who Am I and Who Are You?" and Other Essays*. Trans. and edited by Richard Heinemann and Bruce Krajewski. Albany: SUNY Press, 1997.

GR   *The Gadamer Reader: A Bouquet of the Later Writings*. Ed. and translated by Richard E. Palmer. Evanston, Ill.: Northwestern University Press, 2007.

GW1   *Hermeneutik I: Wahrheit und Methode: Grundzüge einer philosophischen Hermeneutik. Gesammelte Werke, Band 1*. Tübingen: J. C. B. Mohr, 1986.

GW2   *Hermeneutik II: Wahrheit und Methode: Ergänzungen/Register. Gesammelte Werke, Band 2*. Tübingen: J. C. B. Mohr, 1986.

GW3   *Neuere Philosophie I: Hegel—Husserl—Heidegger. Gesammelte Werke, Band 3*. Tübingen: J. C. B. Mohr, 1987.

GW4   *Neuere Philosophie II: Probem—Gestalten. Gesammelte Werke, Band 4*. Tübingen: J. C. B. Mohr, 1987.

GW5   *Griechische Philosophie I. Gesammelte Werke, Band 5*. Tübingen: J. C. B. Mohr, 1985.

GW6   *Griechische Philosophie II. Gesammelte Werke, Band 6.* Tübingen: J. C. B. Mohr, 1985.

GW7   *Griechische Philosophie III: Plato im Dialog. Gesammelte Werke, Band 7.* Tübingen: J. C. B. Mohr, 1991.

GW8   *Ästhetik und Poetik I: Kunst als Aussage. Gesammelte Werke, Band 8.* Tübingen: J. C. B. Mohr, 1993.

GW9   *Ästhetik und Poetik II: Hermeneutik im Vollzug. Gesammelte Werke, Band 9.* Tübingen: J. C. B. Mohr, 1993.

GW10   *Nachträge und Verzeichnisse. Gesammelte Werke, Band 10.* Tübingen: J. C. B. Mohr, 1994.

HD   *Hegel's Dialectic: Five Hermeneutical Studies.* Trans. P. Christopher Smith. New Haven, Conn.: Yale University Press, 1976.

HE   *Hermeneutische Entwürfe. Vorträge und Aufsätze.* Tübingen: Mohr Siebeck, 2000.

HW   *Heidegger's Ways.* Trans. John Stanley. Albany: SUNY Press, 1994.

IG   *Idea of the Good in Platonic-Aristotelian Philosophy.* Trans. P. Christopher Smith. New Haven, Conn.: Yale University Press, 1986.

LL   *Language and Linguisticality in Gadamer's Hermeneutics.* Ed. Lawrence K. Schmidt. Lanham, Md.: Lexington Books, 2000.

LP   *Literature and Philosophy in Dialogue: Essays in German Literary Theory.* Trans. Robert H. Paslick. Albany: SUNY Press, 1994.

LT   *Lob der Theorie: Reden und Aufsätze.* Frankfurt: Suhrkamp, 1983.

PA   *Philosophical Apprenticeships.* Trans. Robert Sullivan. Cambridge, Mass.: MIT Press, 1985.

PD   *Plato's Dialectical Ethics.* Trans. Robert Wallace. New Haven, Conn.: Yale University Press, 1991.

PH   *Philosophical Hermeneutics.* Trans. and edited by David E. Linge. Berkeley: University of California Press, 1976.

PL   *Philosophische Lehrjahre. Eine Rückschau.* Frankfurt am Main: Klostermann, 1977.

PT   *Praise of Theory.* Trans. Chris Dawson. New Haven, Conn.: Yale University Press, 1998.

RAS   *Reason in the Age of Science.* Trans. Frederick Lawrence. Cambridge, Mass.: MIT Press, 1981.

RB   *Relevance of the Beautiful and Other Essays.* Ed. Robert Bernasconi. Cambridge: Cambridge University Press, 1986.

RPJ   "Reflections on My Philosophical Journey." In *The Philosophy of Hans-Georg Gadamer.* Library of Living Philosophers 24. Ed. Lewis Edwin Hahn. Chicago and La Salle, Ill.: Open Court, 1997, 3–63.

TM   *Truth and Method.* 2nd rev. ed. Trans. Joel Weinsheimer and Donald Marshall. New York: Crossroad Publishing, 1989.

UVG   *Über die Verborgenheit der Gesundheit: Aufsätze und Vorträge. Frankfurt: Suhrkamp, 1993.*

VZW   *Vernunft im Zeitalter der Wissenschaft: Aufsätze. Frankfurt: Suhrkamp, 1976.*

WBI   *Wer bin ich und wer bist Du? Kommentar zu Celans Atemkristall.* Frankfurt/M: Suhrkamp, 1986.

Secondary Texts

BT   Martin Heidegger. *Being and Time.* Trans. Joan Stambaugh. Albany: SUNY Press, 1996.

SZ   Martin Heidegger. *Sein und Zeit.* 7th ed. Tübingen: Niemeyer, 1963.

GADAMER

Introduction

THE NAME HANS-GEORG GADAMER is intimately bound up with philosophical hermeneutics. Like only a few other contemporary currents, hermeneutics has exerted a widespread influence that goes well beyond the limits of philosophy and that has a depth and range difficult to evaluate. From aesthetics to literary *criticism*, from theology to jurisprudence, from sociology to psychiatry, there is almost no area of the "humanities" without a hermeneutic substratum. Not even epistemology has remained neutral. Assessing the widely differentiated, international effects of hermeneutics within philosophy is still more difficult. Gadamer was not only a witness of, but also an interlocutor for, the most important philosophical trends in the last century. Beyond the consequences of the many debates, his openness promoted the spread of hermeneutics in Europe and across North America. By virtue of this success, philosophical hermeneutics has become synonymous with "continental philosophy" in general.

A great number of books, essays, dissertations, conferences, debates, and films have been dedicated to Gadamer. His principal work, *Truth and Method,* has been translated into thirteen languages, including English, French, Spanish, and Italian, in addition to Russian, Chinese, and Japanese. Few other philosophers have been so present on the public stage, and few have spoken so often on the most varied and topical issues. In an era that is becoming less and less philosophical, Gadamer bore witness to the necessity of philosophy as a critical vigilance and the unconditional freedom of questioning.

The difficulty of writing a monograph about Gadamer lies not only in giving an account of all this. In the course of his long life Gadamer wrote a great deal, as the ten volumes of his *Collected Works* indicate. Even his well-known book *Truth and Method,* a goal that he reached with difficulty, represents only one stage on his way from phenomenology to dialectics. The fullness of what he went on to produce, over more than forty years, should be neither neglected nor ignored, for if it is, the rich unfolding and differentiation of his philosophical perspective will be overlooked.

The importance usually attributed to *Truth and Method* has overshadowed not only the later writings, but also the earlier ones. Hence the decisive role that Greek philosophy plays for hermeneutics has not been sufficiently noted. There are only a few traces of Greek philosophy in *Truth and Method,* where the main concern is to outline a hermeneutic philosophy against the background of both classical hermeneutics and Heidegger's hermeneutics of facticity. Nevertheless, Gadamer himself judged his work on *Plato's Dialectical Ethics,* as well as his studies on Greek thought, as "the best and most original part" of his philosophical activity.[1] Considering the entire history of his work, it could be said that Gadamer's magnum opus is perhaps the book he never wrote on Plato.

Gadamer would certainly also have wished to publish a more complete volume than the one that appeared in English under the title *Hegel's Dialectic: Five Hermeneutical Studies,* and to elaborate on the many essays—more than twenty—that he dedicated to Heidegger, only some of which were included in the volume *Heidegger's Ways.*

There is a further difficulty that a monograph on Gadamer should not avoid, and that is his tormented relationship to writing. In order to get around his Socratic resistance to writing, he preferred the form of the lecture, the talk, or the debate. It is not an exaggeration to say that almost everything he wrote is based on dialogue.

This inclination is also reflected in Gadamer's style. His texts, above all those of the last period, are written in lucid and striking prose, which makes them accessible to a broad audience. Undoubtedly his texts suffer in the transition from the oral to the written form. However, his way of writing is always careful to interrogate everyday language and to avoid rigid terminology. Without being conceptually imprecise: everything Gadamer said could have been said differently; his texts remain evidently incomplete and open-ended.

Yet this open-endedness, which may cause irritation, is not a flaw for Gadamer. On the contrary, he justifies it theoretically. On closer inspection, the difficulty is not really a difficulty: his impatience with writing is dictated by both personal and philosophical motivations. It is impossible to say where the personal strays into the philosophical, since his philosophy bears the stamp of his individuality. The choice of dialogue is thus not at all arbitrary.

One cannot speak of "philosophical texts" in the same way one speaks of "literary texts." The philosophical text, whose conceptual fixity may tend toward metaphysical rigidity, begins to speak anew through the word that, by questioning, interprets it. Hence dialogue becomes the form of philosophy for Gadamer. Here *the Socratic inspiration of philosophical hermeneutics* comes to light.

Gadamer remained faithful to this inspiration, not only for the sake of coherence but because it would not have been possible for him to be any other way. If, in order to philosophize, Heidegger needed to withdraw to the Black Forest, then Gadamer needed to go to the *agorá,* to let himself be overtaken and surprised by the encounters with others. Gadamer could not think without an interlocutor, without the dialectic of question and answer. The labor of the concept was unimaginable for him without the word of the other. That is why his philosophy shows the traces of the dialogue from which it sprang, and differs according to the interlocutor, situation, and theme. "'Hermeneutic' philosophy"—Gadamer points out—"does not understand itself as an 'absolute' position, but as a path of experiencing." For it "there is no higher principle than this: holding oneself open to the conversation" (RPJ 36/GW2 505). This is possible only for a philosophy of finitude that is aware of its finitude, yet does not renounce the infinite and makes infinite dialogue the very form of its philosophizing.

Without reducing the significance of *Truth and Method* or diminishing the value of the published writings, it is necessary to emphasize that Gadamer's philosophy does not exhaust itself in its written form. This does not mean that there are esoteric doctrines. However, what he says of Plato can also be said of Gadamer himself: everything in his philosophy is *protreptic;* everything points beyond itself. Since nothing can be definitive, philosophical research must remain open and should neither become fixed nor find systematic form, at least within the limits of a written text. Philosophical research points back to dialogue, but also to the philosopher's decisions and lived experience.

Whoever met Gadamer knows how true this description is, but also how difficult and yet necessary it is to render all of this in a monograph. Philosophy was never merely a profession for him. According to the close connection between theory and practice that guides hermeneutics, everything that Gadamer said and did, along with how he acted, formed a unity. This monograph will presume the Socratic harmony of *logos* and *érgon,* word and deed—in order to let the unity of his philosophy emerge—with the awareness that, despite the intervening distance, every portrait is an idealization.

Notes

1. Hans-Georg Gadamer, "Preface to the Italian Edition," in *Studi platonici,* ed. Giovanni Moretto (Torino: Marietti, 1983), 11.

1 Living through a Century

He who philosophizes is not at one with the previous and contemporary world's ways of thinking of things. Thus Plato's discussions are often not only directed *to* something but also directed *against* it. (*DDP* 39/*GW*5 187)

1. The Sky Over Breslau

Hans-Georg Gadamer was born in Marburg on February 11, 1900. His father was a well-known professor of pharmaceutical chemistry; deeply convinced of scientific progress, he was, according to his son, authoritarian "in the worst way but with the best of intentions" (*PA* 3/*PL* 9). In 1902 he was called as a full professor to Breslau, in today's Poland, where Gadamer spent his entire childhood and adolescence. At the age of only thirty-five, Gadamer's mother, Emma Caroline Johanna Gewiese, died in the spring of 1904. Her son, who barely knew her, always remembered her fondness for music, her passion for art, and her love of literature.

In the gray atmosphere of his paternal home the years in Breslau were gloomy and oppressive, marked by the technological advances that heralded the new century. On the city's streets the first cars mingled with horse-drawn carriages. Gas lanterns were slowly replaced by electric lights, movie theaters opened their doors, and telephones were installed. The zeppelin flew across the Breslau sky, but the sinking of the *Titanic* in 1912 shocked contemporary culture and began to undermine the optimistic faith in technology (*EPH* 221/*EE* 8).[1] Although Breslau was a quiet provincial city far removed from the front, the effects of the First World War soon made themselves felt. Germany emerged from the chaos of war economically broke, politically unstable, disillusioned, and disoriented by a deep need for direction.

In the spring of 1918 Gadamer enrolled in Breslau University. During his first semester he studied some of the most disparate topics in the humanities: German, art history, psychology, history, and Asian studies. In his second semester he began to follow the lecture courses of the Neo-Kantians Eugen Kühnemann (1868–1946), Julius Guttmann (1880–1950), and Richard Hönigswald (1875–1947), and it was Hönigswald who urged him toward philosophy. Admitted to a seminar on the philosophy of language that Hönigswald held for advanced students, Gadamer asked a question about the difference between signs and words that brought him unexpected praise, strengthened his self-esteem, and in a sense opened his path to philosophy.[2]

As with many of his generation, the encounter with new ideas in those years occurred through the reading of the *Betrachtungen eines Unpolitischen* (*Reflections of a Nonpolitical Man*) by Thomas Mann (1875–1955) and through the cultural criticism exerted by the *George-Kreis,* the circle around Stefan George (1868–1933).

2. Marburg and Philosophy

In October 1919 Gadamer moved with his family to Marburg, where his father, Johannes Gadamer (1867–1928), had received a new chair and where he became rector in 1922. Through a lucky coincidence the best of German intellectual culture had converged on this university town. It suffices to mention a few names: Ernst Robert Curtius (1886–1956) in Romance studies, Rudolf Bultmann (1884–1976) in theology, Richard Hamann (1879–1961) in art history, and Paul Natorp (1854–1924) and Nicolai Hartmann (1882–1950) in philosophy. Gadamer would take advantage of this constellation through his ability to listen to and learn from different points of view, which distinguished him even then. The twenty years spent in the university town—from 1919 to 1938—were important for his intellectual formation and decisive for his philosophical thought.

His involvement with the George-Circle also dates from his time in Marburg. Gadamer was introduced to the Circle by the Romanist Curtius, who strongly influenced his reading in those years. The Circle was distinctive for its scornful detachment from the decadent civilized world; dominated by the charismatic "leadership" of George, it was governed by ironclad, esoteric rules.[3] The Circle's activity in Marburg revolved around the historian of economics Friedrich Wolters (1876–1930), who taught there from 1920 to 1923; together with his friend, the poet Oskar Schürer (1892–1949), Gadamer attended Wolters's seminars for a time, where he also became acquainted with Hans Anton. Gadamer later witnessed the relationship between Anton and Max Kommerell (1902–44), the writer and literary critic, which came to a tragic end. Gadamer was attracted to the group only by the privilege given to the poetic experience of truth; however, he was driven out of the Circle, where not only science but also philosophy began to be disliked. An even harder destiny befell Kommerell, who, by trying to keep his distance, showed that George and his poetry could also be admired outside the *Kreis.*

When Gadamer started studying philosophy, Marburg was famous above all for Neo-Kantianism. Its founder, Hermann Cohen (1842–1918), having worked for decades in Marburg with the rallying cry "Back to Kant," moved to Berlin in 1912 and left the hard-won fate of the "Marburg School" in the hands of two other proponents: Natorp and Hartmann. Both men, but especially Nicolai Hartmann, would guide Gadamer's initial steps.

Though considered the last representative of Neo-Kantianism, it was actually Hartmann who declared its end by distancing himself in the name of "critical realism."

Still relatively young, he was a teacher, a friend, and, in a sense, a father for Gadamer, supporting him with affection and esteem. Despite the appearance of being cold and distant, Hartmann was very close to his students. He knew how to alternate between intensive and focused work and evenings animated by his affable and energetic personality. His influence on Gadamer should not be underestimated (RPJ 7/*GW2* 483).[4] It was Hartmann, after all, who convinced him to complete his dissertation with Natorp. Entitled "The Essence of Pleasure according to Plato's Dialogues" (*Das Wesen der Lust nach den Platonischen Dialogen*), the dissertation remained unpublished; yet already in those 116 badly written pages, with only five footnotes, there appears the idea of the "good" that, as a bridge between Plato and Aristotle, would guide Gadamer's future reflections.[5] Even if Hartmann and Natorp wrote two diametrically opposed reviews of the work, they both agreed to give it the highest mark.

3. A Demanding Teacher: Heidegger's Example

Immediately after his graduation in August 1922, Gadamer contracted a severe form of infantile paralysis: poliomyelitis. The illness marked a profound break in his life. He had to live in quarantine while his convalescence stretched throughout the entire winter. In those long months he read, among others, the literary work of Jean Paul and the *Logical Investigations* of Edmund Husserl (1859–1938). Yet something new occurred during the time of his illness: Natorp lent Gadamer a manuscript on Aristotle written by Husserl's young assistant in Freiburg, Martin Heidegger (1889–1976).[6]

Heidegger's name had been discussed for a long time, and Gadamer had already heard of him. Surrounded by an aura of fame, Heidegger was regarded as the "secret king" of German philosophy—as Hannah Arendt would later describe him in her memoirs.[7] However, since Heidegger had not yet published anything, this fame was based only on the suggestive power of his lectures. That was precisely why Natorp, who wanted to appoint him to a professorship at the University of Marburg, asked him for a report on his work on Aristotle. Gadamer, perhaps influenced by Natorp's positive evaluation, decided to go to Freiburg as soon as his strength would allow him. In a letter dated September 27, 1922, he communicated his decision to Heidegger, who answered quickly with a card.[8] This was the beginning of a relationship that lasted a lifetime, and the encounter with Heidegger left an indelible mark on Gadamer. Not only were the results Gadamer had achieved by that time in his study of philosophy put into question, but the initial doubts about his self-confidence, which may have been gained too early, started to emerge (*PA* 14/*PL* 23).

In April 1923, not yet having recovered fully from his illness and having just married Frida Kratz (1898–1979), a native of Breslau, Gadamer moved to Freiburg. The small-town university scene was dominated by Husserl, and so Gadamer felt almost obliged to attend his lectures and seminars. For Husserl, it was clear that the young student, recommended by Natorp, should write on Aristotle, while the name of Aristotle seemed the only link that, beyond the label of "phenomenology," still connected Husserl and Heidegger. Yet Gadamer's enthusiasm for Heidegger soon mirrored his disappointment in Husserl, who indulged in long didactic monologues during his lectures—Gadamer would later speak of the "seduction of the podium" (*GW2* 212).[9] Fjodor Stepun (1884–1965), one of his fellow students, described Husserl as a "watchmaker gone mad," because during his explications he turned his right hand in the left, a movement of concentration that had something of a craftsmanlike, ideal descriptive technique to it (*PA* 35/*PL* 31). Thereafter, for Gadamer, phenomenology remained above all that of Max Scheler (1874–1928), whom he had already met in 1920 in Marburg and whom he never ceased to admire.

Heidegger had prepared a course on logic for the summer semester of 1923, but when he learned that a colleague was to offer the same course, he decided to change the topic and announced a new title: "Ontology." A little later the title was stated more precisely: "The Hermeneutics of Facticity."[10] Thus Gadamer's first encounter with Heidegger took place under the banner of hermeneutics. But during that summer semester Gadamer was almost more attracted to another topic.[11] Heidegger held a lecture and gave four seminars, one of which dealt with the sixth book of the *Nicomachean Ethics*. The concept of *phrónesis,* discussed in those pages by Aristotle, would accompany Gadamer into his final years.[12]

The seminar on Aristotle marked the beginning of an even closer relationship between the two that went far beyond academic boundaries: Heidegger invited Gadamer to read the *Metaphysics* with him, and this work stretched unexpectedly into the summer vacation. From July 29 to August 23, 1923, Gadamer and his wife spent four weeks in Heidegger's hut, or *Hütte,* in Todtnauberg. Following his teacher, Gadamer learned how to read Aristotle "phenomenologically," but at the same time he also learned from Aristotle how to address philosophical questions to his own time (*GW10* 31–45). Along with the seminars in Freiburg, this reading experience was his first practical "introduction to the universality of hermeneutics" (*RPJ* 10/*GW2* 486).

Heidegger, for his part, also needed an introduction. The philosopher from the Black Forest, who had never left Freiburg and Baden, had just been invited to Marburg by Natorp and hence took advantage of Gadamer to learn more about that philosophers' stronghold. He was inspired by anything but peaceful intentions: even before his official entry to Marburg, Heidegger took an almost aggressive posture toward his Neo-Kantian colleagues. Hartmann was his main target. On July 14, 1923, he wrote to Karl Jaspers (1883–1969), with whom he had developed a philosophical kinship, about his combat plans: he would "make things hot" for Hartmann, supported by the "shock troops" of sixteen students he would bring with him from Freiburg, some of them just hangers-on, others serious and capable collaborators.[13]

Among the latter was also Gadamer, who left Freiburg reluctantly. The summer semester distanced him once and for all from the "abstract exercises in thinking led by Nicolai Hartmann," and drew him onto Heidegger's paths (*PA* 37/*PL* 34).

His very earliest writings testify to this change. In a contribution to the *Festschrift* for Natorp published in 1924, Gadamer revealed his perplexities about the idea of a philosophical "system," which in Neo-Kantianism was almost a dogmatic principle.[14] In his review of Hartmann's *Metaphysics of Knowledge* (*Metaphysik der Erkenntnis*) for the distinguished journal *Logos,* the place where the text was written appears very clearly: Freiburg im Breisgau.[15] Although he viewed Hartmann's rapprochement with phenomenology positively, Gadamer did not consider his Aristotelian realism radical enough. He pointed to the unavoidable task of a "critical destruction of the philosophical tradition," thus revealing Heidegger as the source of his reflections.[16] At issue in the long debate with Hartmann was the purely descriptive attitude, free from every point of view: according to Gadamer, there was "no way to approach a thing that would not be decisively determined by the peculiarity of one's own position."[17] Though the word "hermeneutics" does not appear, its seeds are clearly recognizable in his critique of the theory of knowledge and his doubts about the very idea of a system.

All beginnings bring significant difficulties. When Gadamer returned to Marburg in the winter semester of 1923–24—this time with his new teacher, whose assistant he had become—he encountered the problem of finding his own place within the complicated academic landscape. He tried to mediate in the relationship between Hartmann and Heidegger, which was steadily worsening. Whereas the majority of students went to the lectures of the latter, the lectures of the former remained poorly attended.[18] When Heidegger stepped up to the podium, he impressed everyone with his energy, his power of concentration, and his radicalism. "It is impossible to exaggerate the drama of Heidegger's appearance in Marburg," Gadamer recalled (*PA* 48/*PL* 214; *GW*10 16). An entire generation was mesmerized by him: along with Gadamer there were such philosophers as Hannah Arendt (1906–75), Karl Löwith (1897–1973), Gerhard Krüger (1902–72), Jacob Klein (1899–1978) and Hans Jonas (1903–93).

But Heidegger was a demanding teacher, especially once he had freed himself from the dominant figure of Husserl and gained a new self-confidence, not only in his self-worth but also in the possibility that he could shape the future of German philosophy. He also owed his confidence to the work that was slowly taking shape through his lectures, namely, *Being and Time.* Gadamer, who had produced only a little, had to bear the consequences. Despite everything, in Heidegger's eyes he remained a follower of Hartmann. For the philosopher from the Black Forest, who in this way revealed his petit bourgeois revanchism, Gadamer was the son of that academic aristocracy, which he could barely tolerate. He bluntly expressed his doubts about Gadamer's philosophical talent in a letter to Löwith from March 27, 1925, using words similar to what he had written to Gadamer himself in a letter from 1924: "If you cannot summon sufficient toughness toward yourself, nothing will become of you."[19] Gadamer, who had decided to write his *Habilitation* with Heidegger, bore his genial teacher's lack of trust with a scarcely concealed bitterness. In truth, he was deeply disappointed. His inner self-certainty, which had already been sorely tested by the figure of his father, was once again powerfully undermined.

4. Plato in the Future

Thus began the years that Gadamer called in his autobiography his "no one's years" (*PA* 35/*PL* 30). He describes them accordingly: "These were years of deep doubt about my intellectual gifts, but they were also years in which I finally began to work seriously. I became a classical philologist under the friendly guidance of Paul Friedländer" (*PA* 37/*PL* 34). For Gadamer, the study of classical philology was his way of liberating himself from Heidegger. After Easter 1925, he started up his new studies and attended the classes of Paul Friedländer (1882–1968) as well as of Ernst Lommatzsch (1871–1949) and Paul Jacobstahl (1880–1957). What he was looking for, after the encounter with Heidegger, was a solid "ground": "I actually became a classical philologist because of the feeling that I would simply be crushed by the dominance of his thinking, unless I found my own ground on which I could stand more firmly than this powerful thinker himself."[20]

A solid ground meant first of all material security. These were the years of the great inflation, the ruin of the middle class in Germany. Gadamer's situation was no different from that of his friends and colleagues in Marburg: all of them barely managed to get by with the help of a fellowship from the Emergency Association of German Science (Notgemeinschaft der Deutschen Wissenschaft).[21] Philology also undoubtedly offered him more security: it would not necessarily facilitate a university career, but it would at least give Gadamer the chance to become a high school teacher of ancient Greek. A solid ground also meant the grounding of textual knowledge: Gadamer moved from the slippery territory of contemporary philosophy to the stable and solid ground of the classics. He would respond to those who asked him about his studies thusly: "I basically only read books that are at least two thousand years old" (*PA* 72/*PL* 47).

Gadamer felt encouraged in his decision by Bultmann, the Protestant theologian who had found in Heidegger's philosophy a framework for critical exegesis, whereby he read the New Testament as a text like any other classic. Gadamer was admitted into Bultmann's famous *Graeca*—in academic terms the *Graeca* meant a circle of docents and students who interpreted the texts of classical literature together—and he took part in it for fifteen years. This was one of his most deeply formative experiences.

Yet Gadamer's initial passion for literature did not diminish during this time. Every week he met with his closest friends, including Löwith and Krüger, to read the great novels by Balzac, Tolstoy, Dostoevsky, Gogol, and Gontcharov, while not overlooking modern authors such as Joseph Conrad, Knut Hamsun, and Andre Gide (*PA* 41/*PL* 39).[22]

Gadamer's main reference point in those years, however, was Paul Friedländer, who was engaged with the first of the three volumes of his magnum opus on Plato (*GW*10 403). Besides attending his lectures and seminars, Gadamer also took part in Friedländer's *Graeca*.[23] This intensive collaboration was productive for both: Gadamer's interpretations may have helped to form Friedländer's image of Plato, while Friedländer's minute textual exegeses not only of Plato and Aristotle, but also of the poets, especially Pindar, deeply influenced the development of Gadamer's philosophical hermeneutics. At that time Gadamer discovered that dialogue was not merely an artistic expedient but a leading motif of Plato's philosophy; the idea of a "dialogical ethics," which would later form the basis of his *Habilitation,* arose in those years.

In Friedländer's seminar Gadamer presented his work on Aristotle's *Protrepticus,* which would be published in 1928 in the prestigious journal *Hermes.*[24] The famous philologist Werner Jaeger (1888–1961) believed that the *Protrepticus* is a text from Aristotle's youth that, in its conception of ethics, retains traces of Platonism. Jaeger wanted to establish a "genetic" interpretation of Aristotle, according to which at least three phases in his philosophy could be distinguished. Gadamer was able, however, through his attentive and bold philological reading of both the text and the context, to show that the *Protrepticus,* as its title would suggest—*protréptein* means "to stimulate" or "to awaken"—does not contain a conception of ethics but rather a call to philosophize. On the invitation from Friedländer, Gadamer took part in the meeting of classical philologists from July 10 to 12, 1930, in Naumburg, where among others he met Karl Reinhardt (1886–1958), for whom he formed a lasting appreciation. On this occasion he also met Jaeger personally, and they remained in contact until his emigration to America in 1936.[25] In the Greek ideal of education Jaeger saw the basis of a "Neo-Humanism," which would emerge later in his *Paideia,* a work published clandestinely in the thirties in Germany. Though Heidegger found humanism to be naïve and bloodless, Gadamer campaigned in *Truth and Method* for a rehabilitation of humanistic concepts.[26]

On July 20, 1927, Gadamer passed the state examination in classical philology with less than brilliant results. He had already decided to continue his studies and to write his *Habilitation* with Friedländer. But the day after the examination Gadamer received a short and peremptory letter from Heidegger, urging Gadamer to write the *Habilitation* with him in philosophy. Despite the strenuous path he had taken to achieve self-confidence and autonomy, Gadamer was surprised and flattered, and could not say no. Once again, Heidegger marked a turning point in his life, bringing him back to philosophy.

Yet time was short: Heidegger was on the verge of returning to Freiburg in order to become Husserl's successor. For Gadamer, there was another even more pressing issue: for some months his father had lain seriously ill in the Marburg University clinic. He died on April 15, 1928, full of concern about his son's future, before it was possible for Gadamer to receive the *venia legendi,* the teaching certification. Even in this difficult situation Gadamer was able to concentrate once again on Plato and to write his *Habilitation* within one year. Its first title, which did not correspond entirely to its contents, was: "Phenomenological Interpretations of Plato's *Philebus.*" Later, however, it was changed to *Plato's Dialectical Ethics: Phenomenological Interpretations Relating to the Philebus,* the final title of the book published in 1931. The work, which remained largely inconclusive, was conceived as a preliminary study of the *Nicomachean Ethics.* It was assessed positively by both Friedländer and Heidegger, and Gadamer graduated on February 23, 1929.

5. "A Terrible Awakening"

A great goal seemed to have been reached. Yet the years immediately following became even more difficult. Gadamer remained a private docent (*Privatdozent*) for almost a decade, so that the thirties would be the hardest and most critical years of his life. His working activity and financial situation did not improve, even after he received the *venia legendi*. He worked at the Philosophical Seminar in Marburg as a *Privatdozent* alongside Löwith and Krüger, with whom he developed an enduring friendship and a deep solidarity. After Heidegger's departure his three students, who had finally become docents, felt much freer and much more responsible. They formed a joint front and in a very short time gained an outstanding reputation. But *Privatdozenten* were not paid and survived in the most humble conditions, supported only by either occasional fellowships or the compensation they received, according to the number of their students, at the end of their courses. Competition was terribly keen. Löwith impressed everyone with his competence, his irony, and his personal charm. Krüger was brilliant and logical in the construction and exposition of his lectures. Gadamer, by contrast, was the youngest and the least confident, and he felt uncomfortable at the podium. The saying was among the students in Marburg that whatever Krüger would distinguish clearly and precisely, Gadamer would turn into a muddle. Soon a new scientific unit of measurement was discovered: the "Gad," which designated "a settled measure of unnecessary complications" (*PA* 71/*PL* 46). In this precarious situation, it was almost impossible to find enough time to devote to research. After having completed his *Habilitation* Gadamer had not published anything else; the project of an edition with a commentary on Aristotle's *Physics* was never carried out.[27] However, these were not the actual reasons that prevented him from receiving a chair.

In 1933 Adolf Hitler seized power in Germany. The political events that followed very rapidly upset the life of the country and did not stop at the gates of the universities. Although many of the docents and students were critical of the Weimar Republic, the seizure of power by the National Socialists brought surprise, bewilderment, and astonishment. The German intelligentsia awoke as if from a long slumber:

> It was a terrible awakening, and we could not absolve ourselves of having failed to perform adequately as citizens. We had underrated Hitler and his kind, and admittedly we made the same mistake as the liberal press in doing this. Not one of us had read *Mein Kampf*. (*PA* 75/*PL* 51)

Inside the university, all or nearly all were convinced that the "nightmare" would soon be over. The deep contempt for the National Socialists, mixed with a foolish arrogance, led to a false estimation of the political reality. Even the anti-Semitism, which seemed far too primitive to be true, was misunderstood as a campaign slogan in a time of serious economic crisis. But the events, which with considerable blindness could be misinterpreted as isolated occurrences, took quite a different course: they proved to be the long-planned and state-sanctioned persecution of Jews, communists, political opponents, and all those taken by the Nazi regime to be foreigners and enemies. The Nuremberg Laws finally left no more room for illusions. All *Dozenten* of the Jewish "race" were forced to quit teaching, and Marburg University was emptied by this decree. Whereas some, such as Erich Frank (1883–1949), were able to withdraw, even after *Kristallnacht* in 1938, and continue to live in Germany, most left the country—among the first to leave was Löwith. He was joined by Strauss, Friedländer, Spitzer, Klein, Auerbach, Kroner, and Jacobsthal, to name just a few. "One felt ashamed to remain," Gadamer later remarked (*PA* 77/*PL* 54).

6. Germany during National Socialism

Gadamer remained. But remaining did not mean joining National Socialism. Various questions arise at this point. How did Gadamer live in those years? What did he think? How did he act? These could be summarized in the one question that everyone confronted at that time: what should be done in the face of National Socialism? If those are exempted who were forced into emigration, for the most part because of racist discrimination, or the minority who chose exile, then it is extremely problematic to evaluate by today's criteria the behavior of those who remained during the Third Reich. Nevertheless, this difficulty does not free us from the task of judging.

The case of Gadamer is not a "case"—as some have attempted to argue in recent years. The accusations, which range from opportunism to complicity or participation, demand a response. Hence it is necessary to show first of all where the accusations arise and what the motivations are behind them. In 1995 a book was published by Teresa Orozco, whose goal was to prove Gadamer's involvement in National Socialism on the basis of his publications from that time.[28] Four years later, in 1999, Jean Grondin published his biography of Gadamer, an extensive collection of materials that are nonetheless insufficiently elaborated; the work achieves precisely the opposite effect from the one the author presumably intended.[29] The way in which Grondin defends Gadamer, especially where no defense is required, gives rise to doubts and suspicions among even the most supportive readers. So he causes irritation and delivers above all a pretext to those who actually, beyond Gadamer, take aim at hermeneutics. In 2000 an essay appeared in English by Richard Wolin, who speaks in the most aggressive tones of Gadamer's "complicity" with National Socialism.[30] The essay was also published in German in an edition of the *Internationale Zeitschrift für Philosophie*.[31] The editors chose to limit themselves to managing the spectacle, so to speak, and declared that their actual goal was in no way to solve the "case" of Gadamer, but was to bring to light the "continuity" between "'political' hermeneutics" in the Third Reich and the subsequent "philosophical hermeneutics."[32] Their attempt is obviously not to prove Gadamer's possible complicities, for these in fact do not exist, but to discredit hermeneutics. Yet what evidence are these accusations based upon? What are the arguments that have been brought forward?

To begin, three clarifications are necessary. First, Gadamer was no National Socialist—in contrast to Heidegger and other "muses called to arms."[33] Gadamer was never a member of the NSDAP (Nationalsozialistische Deutsche Arbeiterpartei), the National Socialist German Workers' Party, and never a supporter of National Socialist ideas. His position did not change after the Röhm Putsch of June 30, 1934, when there was no longer any doubt about the totalitarian violence of the Nazi dictatorship and no further dissent allowed. Not being a party member was no mere bagatelle: one's life was at risk.[34]

Second, Gadamer was no anti-Semite. In those years this was far from obvious, since anti-Semitism had deep and widespread roots. It is worth citing the significant example of Gottlob Frege in this regard. The founder of modern logic and the father of analytic philosophy sympathized with the extreme political right and wished for a logical "Third Reich" that would also lead the way to the new, political Third Reich.[35] Several times he stressed his contempt for every form of democracy, which should undermine the naïve and dangerous belief that logical reason necessarily leads to political insight. On April 30, 1924, he wrote in his diary: "One can recognize that there are highly respectable Jews and still consider it a disaster that there are so many Jews in Germany and that they have the same political rights as the citizens of Aryan descent."[36] Just a few days earlier, on April 22, 1924, he had recorded his attitude in black and white: "Only in recent years have I learned to understand anti-Semitism well. If one wants to make laws against the Jews, one must create a sign by which a Jew can quickly be recognized. This is the difficulty I have always seen."[37] There is not even the shadow of such statements by Gadamer. More importantly, however, his friendships remained unchanged with those Jews from whom many had broken off contact.[38] In difficult conditions, in which any contact with Jews was scarcely tolerated and was already a form of resistance, Gadamer sheltered his friend Klein in his house for almost two years, from 1933 to 1934. Similarly, he supported Frank until the latter's departure from Marburg in 1939, and above all he maintained a steady connection with Löwith during the Nazi period and after, as their correspondence proves.[39]

Finally, Gadamer was in no way "unpolitical"—and certainly not after 1933. This point may seem less relevant when compared to others. Yet Gadamer's allegedly unpolitical attitude has brought the charge that he observed the events around him from a certain "distance," and opportunistically sought only his own interest. But what this claim attacks first is hermeneutics: insofar as it delivers no objective and normative criteria, hermeneutics would only be a philosophy of ambiguity, of ambivalence, and of "non-commitment."[40]

Gadamer belonged to the cultural elite, those who never sided with Hitler and who, even after the initial "terrible awakening," firmly believed that the Nazis would stay in power for only a few months. His position was no different, for example, from that of Löwith.[41] Of course this does not lessen the responsibility of philosophy or philosophers at that time. But the difficulty of reacting immediately to the traumatic reality that had suddenly broken into the Marburg ivory tower cannot even be compared with Heidegger's assent. Heidegger believed he could recognize in the "National Socialist revolution" an answer to the "forgetfulness of Being" in the Western world, and thus felt compelled to "lead the Leader" (*den Führer zu führen*). Like Carl Schmitt he remained loyal to the National Socialist regime, even after he had given up, from 1934 to 1945, all direct involvement.

In order to make this difference still clearer, one must add that Gadamer never succumbed to the fascination that National Socialism had on the second generation of European nihilists, a generation that was on a desperate quest for a way out of the crisis of the bourgeois world. He was, moreover, allergic to the mystical exaltations with which Ernst Jünger described the "storms of steel" in the First World War, just as he was impermeable to the fascistic ideology that in the Hitler regime celebrated the triumph of vitalistic impulses, the victory march of nature and technology, of force and myth. Gadamer was also intellectually immune to the aesthetic attractions of National Socialism that, for example, pervaded the George-Circle.

Certainly one can speak of a "distance" in Gadamer's attitude. But this distance was not the result of cynicism or resignation. Rather it was the distance of irony—which in any case distinguished his manner of thinking and acting. Gadamer was, above all, ironic toward himself; he did not believe that he had been called to a higher mission. This irony marked his entire oeuvre beginning with *Truth and Method*, where his philosophy of play emerges, and for Gadamer guides human practice.[42]

From a political point of view Gadamer always stressed that he was "liberal"—before and after the Nazi period.[43] This position is reflected in both his political thought, which remains insufficiently studied, and his philosophy, which aims for liberation in the sense of going beyond oneself.

This becomes apparent in the difference that exists between Gadamer's philosophical hermeneutics and Heidegger's path of thinking. For Heidegger, *Dasein* in its "thrownness" is imprisoned, without escape, in the facticity of its "there" (*Da*), which subsequently risks becoming ensnared. Levinas very clearly showed the similarity between an ontology of *Dasein*, who only cares about its own modes of being and does not call for *any other*, and the "philosophy of Hitlerism."[44] For Gadamer, the experience of finitude is the collision of *Dasein* against its limits, which indeed, while it reveals its irrefutable ex-centricity, drives *Dasein* at the same time to go outside itself into a beyond that is always the infinite beyond of the other.[45]

Yet even before this difference in their philosophies could emerge, relations broke off between student and master. The news of Heidegger's official entry into the National Socialist Party left everyone in Marburg speechless.[46] Almost no one from his close circle followed him. The new rector of Freiburg was deeply disappointed by the irresoluteness of those "little spoiled professors' sons who never wanted to make a commitment."[47] Beyond the evident political motives, one of the reasons for his resignation in April 1934 may also have been his humiliating isolation.

In 1933 Heidegger sent a folder of various writings to Gadamer, among them his *Rectorial Address,* and signed the package with a "German greeting."[48] Gadamer did not reply.[49] He met Heidegger again only three years later, and art was the pretext for the meeting. The topic that Gadamer had chosen for one of his courses in the summer semester of 1936 was "Art and History (Introduction to the Humanities)." Heidegger, for his part and after the failure of the rectorship, had begun the first of his lecture series on Hölderlin in the winter semester of 1934–35.[50] The echo of these lectures, which were already considered to be a "Hölderlinian philosophy," soon reached Marburg. In November of 1936, news arrived of a three-part lecture series that Heidegger would hold near Frankfurt on "The Origin of the Work of Art." Gadamer, Frank, and Krüger went without hesitation; but even this occasion was not sufficient to break the ice between them. Only Gadamer's visit to Todtnauberg in October of 1937—during which he was accompanied by Krüger and Walter Bröcker (1902–92)—would restore the relationship, which remained unbroken until Heidegger's death in 1976. Yet this relationship was anything but easy or simple for Gadamer, who had to play the role of student, friend, and finally successor: indeed, it was the source of many stimulating ideas but also of many frustrations. "We never had successful conversations with each other," he confessed after Heidegger's death (*GW10* 274).

Gadamer's attitude toward his teacher and his political choices was similar to the responses of Heidegger's other students, both before and, above all, after the war.[51] Apart from a few exceptions—Günther Anders (1902–92) and Herbert Marcuse (1898–1979) should be mentioned—none were intransigent, and, after the break in 1933, all resumed contact. Although they did not follow his path, his students—even the German Jews—were incapable of acknowledging his compliance with National Socialism and the seriousness of his involvement. Löwith himself never broke off correspondence with Heidegger. Hannah Arendt restored her friendship with her former teacher on her return to Germany in 1950, and in an essay that appeared in 1969 to commemorate Heidegger's eightieth birthday, she wrote in a footnote of his attachment to National Socialism as if it were an "escapade."[52]

If one thinks of Heidegger's enormous influence, it is surprising that Gadamer was able to evade it, all the more since in his closest circle, several, from Max Kommerell to Hans Lipps (1889–1941), followed one another to join the National Socialist Party at a dizzying rate. What kept Gadamer from decisions of this kind was his friendship, either casual or not, with many Jews, which became, in various ways, a kind of salvation—as Gadamer later often repeated.[53] Since he experienced the years 1933 to 1934 with his Jewish friends, he inevitably adopted their perspective and saw the events through their eyes. Besides Löwith, it was above all Klein, a passionate reader of newspapers and attentive political observer, who gave the younger Gadamer decisive insights.[54]

7. "Our guilt is that we are alive"

In light of the fact that Gadamer remained in Germany, though he never entered the NSDAP, two accusations have been leveled against him: that he built his career in an opportunistic way and that he held lectures and wrote texts which, through their resonances and indirect references, could be ambiguously in line with the politics of National Socialism. The first charge is directed at the person, the second at his work. However, both charges are aimed at hermeneutics more than at Gadamer.

As for the first charge: not only was Gadamer never a member of the NSDAP, but there is no further documentation that would indicate his involvement. The only exception is his signature on the "Declaration of Support by Professors at German Universities and Colleges for Adolf Hitler and the National Socialist State."[55] At the end of this document there appear twenty-six signatures, among them Heidegger's, but also Krüger's and Werner Krauss's (1900–1976). The latter at that time was a Marxist and later a member of the *Rote Kapelle*.[56] Yet why did Gadamer sign? The document was read at a public meeting, where only those who had opposed it could have refused to sign. To oppose would have meant, in the best case, to pack one's bag. From today's perspective, Gadamer, and not only Gadamer, can be reproached for not expressing his dissent openly. But in Germany at the time there were few alternatives between being a Nazi and keeping silent. The assumption that silence means agreement certainly did not apply in that totalitarian state. One's life was at stake, and those who remained silent simply did not want to risk it. Jaspers wrote in 1946:

> We survivors did not seek death. We did not, as our Jewish friends were led away, go to the streets, we did not scream until someone killed us, too. We preferred to stay alive with the weak but valid reason that our death would not have helped anything. *Our guilt is that we are alive.*[57]

To have remained in Germany and to have remained alive—this is Gadamer's guilt. Still, life at that time was anything but easy; on the contrary, those were years of hardships and obstacles. Gadamer could have spared himself these troubles for the most part if he, like his teacher, had become a member of the party. In any case this would have facilitated his career. Indeed, it is evident that his political position damaged him—how could it have been otherwise? Gadamer completed his *Habilitation* in 1929, but became a full professor only in 1939. At the outset he did not receive a temporary teaching position because of the terrible financial conditions of the university. He had his first appointment in Marburg in the winter semester of 1933–34. In the following two semesters, the summer semester of 1934 and the winter semester of 1934–35, he was called to the University of Kiel, where the chair held by Richard Kroner, who as a Jew was no longer allowed to teach, remained vacant. But since he did not have further prospects in Kiel, Gadamer returned in the winter of 1935 to Marburg, which in the meantime had changed profoundly. The pressure from the National Socialists had intensified. Some months before, the philosophy department had requested a temporary professorial position for him, which was common practice after six years of being a *Privatdozent*. But the Dozentenbund, the Association of National Socialist University Professors, opposed this decision; Gadamer had been stigmatized as politically unreliable. Even the loss of his title of *Privatdozent* was considered.

Gadamer found himself at an extremely difficult crossroads. He would have had to relinquish his academic career, begin another profession (but which?), and perhaps consider emigration—or he could have finally taken the party's membership card. He chose none of these. Instead, he sought another way out of the dilemma. In the fall of 1935 he "voluntarily" put himself forward for a kind of rehabilitation camp (*Rehabilitierungslager*) that had recently been organized to bring docents in line with National Socialism. He went to the camp at Weichselmünde on the Baltic Sea near Danzig, where he spent a few weeks. The "rehabilitation" was primarily a formal matter: besides some "paramilitary nonsense," songs and gymnastic exercises in which all the participants had to engage, no statement of allegiance was required. Along with all the others, Gadamer had to declare publicly what he was working on. The proverbial interest of Germans in philosophy made his life considerably easier (*PA* 79/*PL* 56).

It was during the rehabilitation that all participants at the camp were brought to a ceremony at Tannenberg. On this occasion Gadamer saw Hitler from afar. What struck him was Hitler's small stature and his nervous way of moving his hands, as well as the mediocrity of the person, who even made an "awkward" impression (*PA* 79/*PL* 57).

Back in Marburg, in the winter semester of 1935–36 and in the following summer semester of 1936, Gadamer acted as substitute for the chair held by Frank, who had been "suspended" because of racial discrimination. It had been Frank, a close friend of Gadamer, who had fought for his nomination.[58] But such paradoxical situations had in the meantime become the norm. If not to Gadamer, the substitute position would have been granted to Krüger—who, however, was already committed—or to someone else. Many professorial chairs were vacant, and some of them were canceled. This was the case with Frank's chair, which was eliminated in 1936. Gadamer, who awaited the outcome of an application that had already been lodged in December 1935, received the title of temporary professor on April 20, 1937; one year later he was called to Leipzig as a substitute, where at the beginning of 1939 he finally received a professorial chair.

The "indoctrination" to which he had submitted—not without irony—in order to be "rehabilitated," had probably been decisive in the eyes of the Nazis. If he had not taken this step he probably would have had to give up teaching. But it makes little sense to argue over mere conjecture. Indeed it is questionable to claim that Gadamer promoted his career in an opportune, or even opportunistic, way by profiting from the political conditions of Nazi Germany.[59] The available chairs, which had remained vacant because of the Race Laws, would have certainly facilitated his situation, but his refusal to enter the NSDAP was a major obstacle. How can advantages and disadvantages be weighed up here? Would it not have been much easier to set aside the main disadvantage and declare oneself a Nazi?

Gadamer's decision in those years was to remain in Germany and continue to teach philosophy. However, he published little.[60] From 1933 to 1945, aside from the numerous reviews written mostly in the 1930s (more than twenty can be counted), and his lectures or short talks (about twenty-five), which almost all occurred in the 1940s, Gadamer published only six philosophically relevant works: "Plato and the Poets" and "Ancient Atomic Theory," 1934; "On Kant's Foundation of Aesthetics and the Meaning of Art," as well as "Hegel and the Historical Spirit," 1940; "Hegel and the Dialectic of the Ancient Philosophers," 1940; "Folk and History in Herder's Thought," 1941; and "Plato's Educational State," 1942.[61] Gadamer not only put aside his work on the physics and ethics of Aristotle, but he also avoided all topics that had clearly political echoes. The most telling example is a work on Hölderlin and the repercussions of the French Revolution on German culture: on the one hand, Gadamer did not want to expose himself to attacks, for Nazis liked to speak of Germany's "special path" (*Sonderweg*), and, on the other hand, he feared the exploitation of Hölderlin.[62] His research activity was mostly limited to Greek philosophy. Only at the end of the 1930s did the name of Hegel begin to emerge and, within the context of his philosophy of history, also that of Herder. Even the apparently "safe territory" of Greek philosophy would have been insecure—which confirms that philosophy, in as much as it has its place in the *pólis*, is always already political.[63]

The second accusation leveled against Gadamer concerns the publications from those years. Two texts in particular are controversial: "Plato and the Poets" and the work on Herder. What accusation has been raised against Gadamer's Plato? Undoubtedly Plato's philosophy represents the leading focus of his reflection during those years—and not only of those. What interested him was the "Sophistic and Platonic doctrine of the state"; but, as he remembered later, he had to interrupt his research "for the sake of caution" (RPJ 13/GW2 489). Therefore only two essays, "Plato and the Poets" and "Plato's Educational State," were published.[64] The accusation interprets both essays, especially the first one, against the background of the increasing Nazification of German classical studies, a deep and inexorable process of "ideological transformation." Allegedly this process extends from Jaeger's "Neo-Humanism," whose co-responsibility is particularly emphasized, back to the philology of Ulrich von Wilamowitz-Moellendorf (1848–1931), and finally to the classicism of Winckelmann.[65] The idea of Germany as a new Hellas would have found expression, during the early decades of the twentieth century, in the political relevance attributed to Greek antiquity, which focuses attention on Plato's *Republic*. Gadamer's guilt, presumably, would be his defense of one of the most controversial passages in Plato, namely, the banishment of the poets from the state.

Besides the simplistic reconstruction of the history of classical studies in Germany, there were certainly more than a few philologists and philosophers who in the 1930s drew connections between the Platonic and the National Socialist states. Yet this is not at all the case with Gadamer, who referred to Plato's utopia with the *opposite* aim: to criticize the idea of poetry devoid of all truth and to propose, through the "inner state," an educational model that could suggest a rebirth of the *pólis*.[66] In 1934, exactly one year after the National Socialists seized power, and then again in 1942, Gadamer expressed—*in tyrannos*—his political dissent through the ironic and utopian art of allusion, the only way to criticize the totalitarian state from within.[67] This, and nothing else, is what the motto borrowed from Goethe and appearing at the beginning of the lecture on "Plato and the Poets" means: "Whoever philosophizes does not agree with the ideas of his time." It is not by chance that Gadamer will return to these themes in the development of his political thought in order to show the value of utopia.[68]

Further charges have also been brought against the essay that appeared in 1941, *"Volk und Geschichte bei Herder"* ("*Volk* and History in Herder's Thought"), which is interpreted in the context of German studies at the time. As far as he could be considered a critic of the Enlightenment and a representative of the peculiarity of every culture, Herder was seen in German studies, which was just as assimilated as philology by Nazism, as the prophet of Pan-Germanism.[69] His concept of "folk" seemed to suit this cause.

The text on Herder was the basis of a talk that Gadamer gave in 1941 at the Deutsches Institut in Paris.[70] During the war he undertook two further trips, one to Florence in 1940 and one to Portugal and Spain in 1944. Although he did not have any "political merits," the trips were nevertheless authorized because of the prestige he enjoyed already at that time. Actually these trips were a double-edged sword. On this point he wrote later: "I did not fully recognize that thereby one was being used for purposes of foreign propaganda, for which a political innocent was sometimes suitable" (*PA* 99/*PL* 118). On the one hand, his trips represented the real danger of becoming an instrument of the National Socialist power machine; on the other, they offered the opportunity to make rare contact with the intellectual world outside of Germany. Not least, they were also a way to bring home consumer goods that had become unavailable.

It is not known whether Gadamer lectured in French or in German in Paris, since versions of the text are available in both languages. The German version was revised when the text was published in 1967.[71] But what might be the ideological echoes in this text? The lecture, according to critics, would yield a position favorable to an "ethos of German particularism."[72] In Hegel's wake, Gadamer reflected for some years on the philosophy of history; thus his interest in Herder is not surprising, and even in *Truth and Method* Gadamer continues to refer to his thought.[73] But if, then as now, the concept of "folk" can be used in ambiguous ways, there is not a single passage in the text in which the key words of the National Socialist jargon appear—which in those years was customary and almost required. Against this backdrop, it is rather the lack of such words that is telling. Even more important is Gadamer's insistence on the ideal of the *Bildung* of humanity, in Herder's sense, which would have seemed a provocation to the Nazis.

Gadamer not only republished the writings from those years. After the war he also spoke about both National Socialism and his own life at that time—which distinguishes him from Heidegger's "silence"—in his autobiography, in various essays, and in many interviews.[74] But these reflections and questions about the past reminded Gadamer, as well as those who—from Strauss to Löwith—made National Socialism the turning point of their thinking, of the difficulty of understanding an event experienced as a traumatic laceration.[75]

8. Leipzig, the War, and the Rectorate

On January 1, 1939, after nearly ten years of waiting, Gadamer finally received a chair of philosophy at the University of Leipzig, a university that was considered less politically submissive to the regime. The inaugural lecture that he gave on July 8 had the title "Hegel and the Historical Spirit."

On September 1, 1939, Germany invaded Poland and the Second World War began. Gadamer, who until that point had not imagined the possibility of war, had to change his mind.

> The war news was received in Leipzig like a report of death. Depressed quiet all around, grim faces on the street. . . . I myself was shattered. I still held to the illusion that such an insane thing simply could not happen (*PA* 95/*PL* 113).

Events came to a head. On June 22, 1941, Hitler gave the order to march into Russia. Soon after came the order to begin the *Endlösung,* or the "Final Solution," which had been planned for a long time. Over two days in January 1942, all the remaining Jews in Leipzig were deported by the Gestapo.[76] But the defeat at Stalingrad introduced a new phase of the conflict and gave hope to those who, under the hail of bombs, awaited the end of the terror. *Et illud transit* was the motto that expressed that feeling in Leipzig (*PA* 99/*PL* 118). Gadamer made it his own motto. Life in the city was marked by air raids. On December 4, 1943, the center was nearly completely destroyed, and more than half of the university's buildings were blown up. Yet teaching continued in the remaining rooms or in the air raid shelters. With the few students remaining, Gadamer read Rilke's third "Duino Elegy." Two of his students, Karl-Heinz Volkmann-Schluck (1914–81) and Walter Schulz (1912–2000), were sent to the Eastern Front.[77] At the beginning of 1945, after he had learned of the Allies' landing, Gadamer was called to the *Volkssturm,* the last bastion of the Nazi regime. The Nazis did not hesitate to call in those who had been considered unfit for service, such as Gadamer, the elderly. and children, not least to keep them under control.

On April 18, 1945, American occupying forces entered Leipzig and the almost completely destroyed city capitulated on May 8. Only two months later the Soviets took over political and administrative control from the Americans. By the beginning of 1946 it had become necessary to vote on a new rector for the university. The Russian choice was Gadamer, who had never been a member of the Nazi Party. The reopening of the university on February 5, 1946, was the occasion for Gadamer's rectorial address: "On the Primordiality of Science" (*Die Ursprünglichkeit der Wissenschaft*).[78] Gadamer shared with the Russians the desire for a "democratic renewal" of the German university. It was a matter, he explained, of saving an institution that had been discredited without avoiding the question that would determine the debates of the coming decades: how could the "disfigurement [*Unwesen*] of National Socialism" have arisen among the people of poets and thinkers (*EPH* 15/*GW*10 287)?[79] Gadamer emphasized the role of science, which in its broadest sense could be understood as *epistéme*, as that theoretical knowledge which is primordial and originary insofar as it is the very form of life itself. He described as well a new kind of researcher and, at the same time, denounced the irresponsibility of German scientists: their "alienation from the world," their lack of "decisiveness" and their "immodesty." All this, Gadamer argued, had brought them to "accommodate to the National Socialists' regime," if not to support it (*EPH* 20/*GW*10 293). Precisely during those weeks there occurred the anniversary of Leibniz's birth (1647–1716), which could mark a new point of orientation for the world of science. In his memorial speech Gadamer highlighted the exemplary way in which the great philosopher had found a "path to Europe" among the ruins of the Thirty Years' War.[80] But paradoxically the figure of Leibniz came to represent an obstacle in Gadamer's relationship with the Russians, who called on him to distinguish the academies as pure and free research centers, apart from the universities. Gadamer, by contrast, was convinced that freedom and autonomy should also be given to the universities (*PA* 115/*PL* 131). These differences in conception made a break with the Russian administration unavoidable.

Gadamer began to look for a new position as chair with the intention of settling in the Western sector. Heidegger, who had been suspended from teaching by the Allies, expressed the wish to see Gadamer as his successor in Freiburg.[81] The disappearance of any hope for a reunification of Germany, and the gradual acceptance of the logic of the Cold War, came together to make Gadamer's situation in Leipzig even more untenable. On October 1, 1947, in a climate of suspicion and denunciations, he submitted his resignation as rector.[82] In September he had decided to accept a chair offered to him by the University of Frankfurt. One last event confirmed this decision for him. On November 7, 1947, when he returned briefly to Leipzig for the formal handover of his position, he was arrested by the military police. The reason is not known, and the incident retained a Kafkaesque halo; it was probably a matter of revenge for his resignation (*PA* 111–114/ *PL* 133–135). After four days in prison he was released as a result of protests from the university and the Socialist Unity Party. He immediately left the Eastern sector on a journey that lasted more than five days. After many adventures he reached the metropolis on the Main, which at that time was occupied by Allied troops. He traveled by freight car, on which he had managed to load his books, furniture, and the few things left to him after the war.

During the stormy and grueling period of his rectorate, Gadamer had not been able to devote much time to a philosophical project of any breadth. Nevertheless, the seeds of his interpretations of literary works by Hölderlin, Goethe, Rilke, and Hesse had sprouted, and most appeared together later in the ninth volume of the *Collected Works*. These are not only the seeds of a "poetic hermeneutics." They document the fundamental role of poetry, almost as a kind of "religion of inwardness," in that difficult phase of his life. But these interpretations bear witness above all to Gadamer's public efforts to save whatever was salvageable of German culture from the ruins of war.

9. The Calm of Heidelberg

During the reconstruction Gadamer felt it was absolutely necessary to promote the role of philosophy again. Hence some of his publications from the late 1940s have a pedagogical intent, as for example the new edition of the *Outline of the History of Philosophy* by Dilthey or the translation of book 12 of Aristotle's *Metaphysics*.

The years in Frankfurt from 1947 to 1950 represented for him neither a meaningful nor a happy "intermezzo" (*PA* 117–125/*PL* 139–150), insofar as the living conditions of the postwar period were uncommonly hard. Almost everything was lacking. And while his marriage was coming apart, he had to devote his time entirely to the university, where he had received the only position in philosophy that had been available since 1945 and already had to supervise numerous students. Just as Gadamer applied to leave Frankfurt, Max Horkheimer (1895–1973) and Theodor W. Adorno (1903–69) returned from the United States. Thus there was no opportunity for a debate at that time with the "Frankfurt School," which would only take place much later in the dialogue with Habermas.[83]

In the time of reconstruction, though, contact was resumed with those who had been forced into exile. It was particularly significant for Gadamer to take a trip to Argentina, where from March to April 1948 he took part in the International Congress for Philosophy in Mendoza, the first one that took place after the war. The title of his talk was "The Limits of Historical Reason."[84] The occasion of this congress allowed him to meet with, among others, Helmut Kuhn (1899–1991) and Karl Löwith.[85]

On his return he received important news. Embittered and disillusioned after the publication of his controversial book on the question of German guilt, Karl Jaspers had decided to give up his position in Heidelberg. He felt forced to leave Germany and move to Basel. Gadamer applied for the position, and was called to the University of Heidelberg on September 2, 1949. The small city on the Neckar River became, after Breslau and Marburg, his third hometown, the one with which he was perhaps most tied and where he spent nearly fifty-three years—the last long period of his life became the luckiest and most productive.

After only a short while, Gadamer succeeded in fulfilling a promise he had made to himself: to enable Löwith's return. In April 1951, after decades of exile in Italy, Japan, and the United States, Löwith received a position in the philosophy department in Heidelberg in April 1951. Thus the collaboration between the two philosophers, sustained by a friendship that neither National Socialism nor the war could extinguish, resumed. For the former students, however, the "Heidegger" question remained open, since he was banned from academic circles and lived in isolation in Freiburg. Already at that time there appeared the twofold and almost schizophrenic position taken for years by German—and not only German—philosophers toward Heidegger: servile imitation on the one hand, and exclusion to the point of dismissal on the other. Löwith's attitude toward his former teacher was well known, and marked by a calm but unbending hostility. The surprise was thus all the greater when Löwith took part in the *Festschrift* that Gadamer prepared for Heidegger's sixtieth birthday. Without Löwith's support the *Festschrift*, for which Krüger and Romano Guardini (1885–1968) also contributed articles, would never have appeared.[86] In those years, when Heidegger was far from the fame that would later follow the publication of *Holzwege* in 1950, Gadamer tried to bring him out of isolation by repeatedly inviting him to hold short seminar series in Heidelberg.[87]

In 1953, Gadamer, who had in the meanwhile got married for the second time, to Käte Lekebusch (1921–2006), founded the journal *Philosophische Rundschau* with Helmut Kuhn, a philosophical journal that soon gained a great national and international reputation. Numerous younger philosophers assembled around it, from Jürgen Habermas to Walter Schulz, from Ernst Tugendhat to Wolfgang Wieland. Through this collaboration they received motivations and suggestions that would later help them to choose their own paths.

But Gadamer was not to play only a "protreptic" role. Convinced of the importance of dialogue for teaching, he became known as an attentive, careful, and accessible teacher. His first generation of "students" stretched back to the days in Marburg and Leipzig—the first was Arthur Henkel (1915–2005). In Frankfurt and then in Heidelberg there arose a second generation of students, most of them Germans: Dieter Henrich (b. 1927), Reiner Wiehl (b. 1929), Friedrich Fulda (b. 1929), Wolfgang Wieland (b. 1933), Konrad Cramer (b. 1936), Rüdiger Bubner (1941–2007), and later Gottfried Boehm (b. 1942). Also part of this generation were Valerio Verra (1928–2001), Gianni Vattimo (b. 1936), and the Spaniard Emilio Lledo (b. 1927) (RPJ 17/GW2 493). The *Festschrift* entitled *Hermeneutik und Dialektik*, which was dedicated to Gadamer on his seventieth birthday, testified not only to the resonance of hermeneutics in Germany, but also the work Gadamer had accomplished by teaching so many and such diverse students. In the last years of his life his activity intensified as he continued to teach in North America, in Italy, and finally also again in Heidelberg. In this way Gadamer succeeded in gaining a third generation of students: Günter Figal in Germany, Dennis J. Schmidt in the United States, Jean Grondin in Canada, and Donatella Di Cesare in Italy.[88]

10. *Truth and Method*

His students, for their part, had a positive influence on Gadamer. In the 1950s it was they who pressured him to put into writing everything he had been teaching them in his classes. Since 1931, the year *Plato's Dialectical Ethics* appeared, Gadamer had not published another book. Heidegger, too, poured salt on this wound when he repeatedly insisted: "Gadamer must finally write a book!"[89] Yet Heidegger was precisely the reason why Gadamer hesitated. The critical gaze of the philosopher from Messkirch haunted Gadamer early and late, as he later admitted: "Writing [remained] a torment for me. I had the terrible feeling that Heidegger was standing behind me and looking over my shoulder" (RPJ 15/GW2 491).

Around the middle of the 1950s Gadamer decided to live in a more withdrawn manner and to avoid every distraction. He took out the lecture notes that he had collected over the previous decades. From these materials Gadamer, who was actually a master of the short essay, put together a manuscript of more than five hundred pages.

The title was a problem from the beginning. It could be predicted that it would include the word "hermeneutics." The word had already emerged in its new connotation in Bultmann's book from 1950, *The Problem of Hermeneutics*. Gadamer, for his part, thought of calling what he did "philosophical hermeneutics"; but he always hesitated to speak of "hermeneutic philosophy." He wanted to emphasize the difference of a philosophy that is no longer metaphysical, because it arises from that "middle" to which understanding always refers, and thus renounces a "final foundation."[90] If there is a *prius*, it is hermeneutics, which can also claim philosophical relevance. With the title *Outline of a Philosophical Hermeneutics*, the book was given to the publisher Hans-Georg Siebeck, in Tübingen who, however, expressed his doubts. What was "hermeneutics" supposed to mean? The planned title became the subtitle, and Gadamer's magnum opus became *Truth and Method*. Ironically, this titular "simplification" proved to be the source of many misunderstandings.[91]

Truth and Method, the work Gadamer completed very late, nevertheless became the starting point of all his subsequent thought. The edition of his collected works in ten volumes stretched from 1985 to 1995.[92] But the collected bibliography of his writing compiled by Etsuro Makita (b. 1961) shows that the ten volumes include only a part of his publications. Gadamer loved the form of impromptu speech, which allowed him to dialogue with others, even if the others were a crowd of hundreds. From this untiring activity several further books followed: *Hegel's Dialectics* (1971), *Who am I and Who are You? Commentary on Celan's "Atemkristall"* (1976), *Reason in the Age of Science* (1976), *In Praise of Theory* (1983), *Heidegger's Ways* (1983), *The Inheritance of Europe* (1989), and *On the Enigma of Health* (1993).

11. Hermeneutics in the World

After the publication of *Truth and Method* at the beginning of the 1960s, Gadamer continued his usual life. The book met with only a limited response.[93] This changed with the second edition in 1965. Decisive for the success of the work was, on the one hand, the numerous translations and, on the other hand, the debates it provoked—particularly those with Habermas and Derrida.[94] Especially their questions and criticisms prompted Gadamer to continue to develop his philosophical hermeneutics, to modify and, in some cases, to rethink it in significant ways.

Following the winter semester of 1967–68 he went into retirement, but although he was "emeritus," he held seminars in Heidelberg until 1970. He had already received several invitations to the United States, which he had always declined. Yet unlike Heidegger, for him it was not a matter of preclusion or cautious reserve. The cause of his reluctance was otherwise: Gadamer spoke English very poorly and feared this would be a great obstacle. Tugendhat encouraged him, however, and finally convinced him to travel to the United States. The occasion was a conference on Schleiermacher arranged by Charles Scott at Vanderbilt University in Nashville, Tennessee.[95] In February, 1968, Gadamer embarked on the *Queen Elizabeth* from Hamburg harbor. He wrote to Heidegger:

> In order to bridge the hiatus of becoming emeritus, I have accepted an invitation to the USA and will be abroad from the middle of February until Easter. Over there it is not my philosophy that interests them—for them I am not even an old-timer worth seeing—. But precisely this state of affairs in philosophy there has made my book an unexpected novelty for theologians and people in the humanities (*critics* above all). They see in the book a legitimation of their own needs, which the *philosophy of science* leaves unsatisfied.[96]

Many other travels were to follow this first trip. Gadamer was invited to teach at numerous North American universities: the Catholic University of America in Washington, D.C. (1969), Syracuse University (1971), McMaster University in Hamilton, Canada (1972–74), and Boston College (1974–86). With his teaching in North America a new chapter of his life began, which he described as a "second youth" (*PA* 158/*PL* 198).

His name was indeed completely unknown in the United States—it was as if he were beginning from nothing. Analytic philosophy dominated the "new continent," while all other philosophical movements, which were banished to either departments of literature or theology, were considered "phenomenology":

> That analytic philosophy took up enormous room there, and that so-called continental philosophy was entirely in the shadows was no surprise to me. It was also no surprise that the German philosophy of our time was known only through the phenomenology of Husserl, and that Heidegger and hermeneutics seemed to be completely unknown. However, when I learned to speak English better, it became evident that bridges could be built even from analytic philosophy to hermeneutics.[97]

From the outset Richard Palmer (b. 1933) helped Gadamer to build the initial bridges. Palmer had studied for some years in Heidelberg and in 1969 he published the first introduction to hermeneutics in English.[98] Certainly at the beginning not only the themes, but also his way of conceiving and practicing philosophy, were foreign to the American context. Nevertheless Gadamer did not give up. He continued to teach for two decades, and though at first he had access only to departments of humanities, eventually he was also invited by departments of philosophy. The 1970s were a decisive time, perhaps because Gadamer's presence also coincided in the United States with a kind of critical self-reflection within analytic philosophy. Hermeneutics became both the motivation and the point of reference for a debate. It still seems difficult to evaluate the deep and lasting impact that Gadamer's teaching activity had there on both the spread of "continental philosophy" and the hermeneutization of analytic philosophy. On the other hand, it is necessary to remember that the experiences in the United States considerably expanded Gadamer's own horizon, which until then had been restricted to the German world, and doubtlessly had deep repercussions on the content and manner of his thought.

Gadamer also traveled to South America, Japan, and Africa, without ever neglecting Europe. From the 1980s, for reasons of age, he preferred to avoid trips by air and traveled by train. He concentrated his activity in Italy, the country with which he had felt closely connected for a long time, at least since hearing enthusiastic stories from Löwith—who had been imprisoned in Genoa during the First World War. Gadamer had already been to Italy many times from the 1930s onward; also after the war, in the 1950s, he came back to Italy many times simply as a tourist. In 1961 he was invited to Milan and then to Rome, where he participated in a conference organized by Castelli on "The Problem of Demythologization."[99] His contacts at that time led him above all to northern and central Italy. He went to Naples for a congress organized by the Goethe Institut; on April 22, 1978, he gave his first lecture at the Instituto Italiano per gli Studi filosofici, where Gerardo Marotta had invited him to speak on "Hegel and Hermeneutics."[100] With this talk began a long and intensive collaboration, which continued from 1980 until the last seminar Gadamer gave in Naples, January 6–10, 1997, entitled "From Word to Concept, from Concept to Word."[101] It should be emphasized, though, that this activity was not restricted to individual talks, since he regularly held a series of lectures in Naples, where he received honorary citizenship of the city on November 27, 1990. It is probably not an exaggeration to say that, after Heidelberg and Boston, teaching on the Palazzo Serra di Cassano was Gadamer's last chair. With little regard for his time and energy, he also traveled across southern Italy, where his teaching left deep marks.[102] Numerous connections drew Gadamer not only to Naples but also to the countryside, which for him was still the *Magna Grecia,* Greater Greece. This "intellectual affinity," as Marotta described it, was reciprocal.[103] The status that Naples had always given to German philosophy was matched by the significance that Gadamer found in the names of Pythagoras and Parmenides, but also Bruno, Campanella, and

Vico, not to mention Bertrando Spaventa and Benedetto Croce. The years of teaching in Naples were years of hermeneutic practice in which Gadamer spoke the language of others and learned to listen to their questions and to value their particularities.

12. The Final Years: Between Success and Loneliness

Gadamer's fame, which came only late in life, ultimately became worldwide. From the 1970s on, in Germany and elsewhere, he received honors and prizes that continued to increase until the end of his life.[104] In addition to these came the honorary doctorates from universities in Bamberg, Tübingen, Washington, Hamilton, Ottawa, Boston, Breslau, Leipzig, Prague, and finally, in 2000, St. Petersburg. The honorary doctorate that he received from the University of Marburg on June 24, 1999, brought Gadamer particular pleasure, for it topped off a long career. However, the success became frankly overwhelming. Photographers, journalists, colleagues, and students from all over the world came to his office in the philosophy department at Heidelberg, which he had had for decades. Only with great effort could he satisfy all the obligations that also came, which he nevertheless did not want to refuse because he was convinced of the importance of contact with younger generations. Indeed, these flocked in droves to meet him. With this he had, as he admitted, taken on the role of a "steam engine," and saw himself at times, even if unhappily, forced to reciprocate the strangest requests from many petitioners, including those who wanted to make arrangements for an interview, a dedication, or only a signature, in the hope of basking, however briefly, in his fame. Some only wanted to see themselves in person with the most famous of living philosophers. Thus his public appearances regularly became mass events. All of this distanced him, however, from the gravitational center of his life. With success grew loneliness. For a long time Gadamer had felt himself a "living anachronism," after all his friends and associates gradually disappeared. There was one date that he never forgot, May 24, 1973: the day Karl Löwith died, whom Gadamer cherished as his best friend. At that time Gadamer was convinced that he too would soon die, and he began—so to speak—to prepare himself. Among other things, he sold the greater part of his books to the library at McMaster University in Canada. Loneliness as well as a deep feeling of alienation—the word that he often used was *unheimlich*, "uncanny"—intensified above all in the last years. Furthermore, it did not escape his notice that the philosophical scene in Germany, starting precisely with Heidelberg, had shifted direction; many had begun to work in analytic philosophy, just at a time when American analytic philosophers showed growing interest in hermeneutics.[105]

On February 11, 2000, his one-hundredth birthday, the University of Heidelberg honored Gadamer with a large public ceremony in the "Aula Magna." This event was organized by the Academy of Science, the Department of Philosophy, and the city of Heidelberg. It ended with a philosophical conference in which Gadamer was the central figure.[106]

In the summer of 2001, after the yearly hermeneutic symposium which had been organized since 1989 in Heidelberg by his American students, among others Lawrence K. Schmidt and James C. Risser, it was easy to see that Gadamer was unwell, and this time not only physically.[107] His condition worsened toward the end of August and the beginning of September. He had almost stopped going to the university, as he usually did; his legs simply no longer carried him. Yet there was more than that. He could no longer read for long periods, as he inclined to do, and even conversation exhausted him. His proverbial ability to concentrate, his *Dabei-sein,* his complete absorption in and involvement with everything he did, his attentive dedication, which he had raised to a category of his hermeneutics, had declined. He was no longer able to set himself aside—and precisely that meant the end. He was, by the way, completely conscious of this. To the surprise of those who were close to him, he had even packed his own suitcases since now, as he said, the hour had finally come. In a certain sense he was torn between his strong connection to life and the process of a slow and irresistible alienation. This alienation was not so much from the world of the third millennium, whose events he followed passionately, but from the world immediately surrounding him. Nevertheless, it was enough during those days in March to mention the name of Parmenides, and Gadamer would lift his eyes and begin to speak with enthusiasm. He felt *zu Hause,* "at home," only in philosophy.

Gadamer died on the evening of March 13, 2002, in the University Clinic in Heidelberg. He was buried in the Köpfel cemetery in Ziegelhausen. His gravestone reads: *Hans-Georg Gadamer—Philosopher.*

Notes

1. Compare the account by Ernst Jünger in Antonio Gnoli and Franco Volpi, *Die kommenden Titanen. Gespräche mit Ernst Jünger* (Vienna: Karolinger, 2002), 17–20.
2. See Gadamer, "Zu einem Brief von Hönigswald an Gadamer vom 22.12.1919" ("On a Letter from Hönigswald to Gadamer from December 22, 1919"), in Wolfdietrich Schmied-Kowarzik, ed., *Erkennen—Monas—Sprache,* Internationales Richard-Hönigswald-Symposium (Kassel 1995), Studien und Materialien zum Neukantianismus Band 9 (Würzburg: Königshausen & Neumann 1997), 455–461 at 455.
3. There is still no study that traces the influence of the George-Circle on philosophy. An important testimonial is Gadamer's "Die Wirkung Stefan Georges auf die Wissenschaft" (1983), in *Ästhetik und Poetik* II. *Hermeneutik im Vollzug,* GW9 258–270; see also Stefan Breuer, *Ästhetischer Fundamentalismus. Stefan George und der deutsche Antimodernismus* (Darmstadt: Wissenschaftliche Buchgesellschaft, 1995); Carola Groppe, *Die Macht der Bildung. Das deutsche Bürgertum und der George-Kreis 1890–1933* (Köln u.a.: Böhlau 1997), 395–399.
4. On Gadamer's relation to the Marburg School, see Mirko Wischke, *Die Schwäche der Schrift. Zur philosophischen Hermeneutik Hans-Georg Gadamers* (Köln u.a.: Böhlau, 2001), 61–71. On Gadamer and Natorp, see Jürgen Stolzenberg, "Hermeneutik und Letztbegründung. Hans-Georg Gadamer und der späte Paul Natorp," in István M. Fehér, ed., *Kunst, Hermeneutik, Philosophie. Das Denken Hans-Georg Gadamers im Zusammenhang des 20. Jahrhunderts,* Heidelberg, Universitätsverlag: Winter 2003, 63–74.

5. Dissertation accepted on May 15, 1922, by the philosophical faculty of the University of Marburg. Compare in this volume chapter 6, part 2, and chapter 7, part 5.

6. The manuscript was long considered missing, but was luckily found in 1989 in the estate of Josef König, a student of Georg Misch. See Martin Heidegger, *Phänomenologische Interpretationen zu Aristoteles (Anzeige der hermeneutischen Situation)*. *Ausarbeitung für die Marburger und die Göttinger Philosophische Fakultät* (1922), in *Phänomenologische Interpretationen ausgewählter Abhandlungen des Aristoteles zur Ontologie und Logik*, Gesamtausgabe (*GA*), vol. 62, ed. Günther Neumann (Frankfurt am Main: Klostermann, 2005), 341–415. See also Gadamer, "Heideggers theologische Jugendschrift," in *Dilthey-Jahrbuch für Philosophie und Geschichte der Geisteswissenschaften* 6 (1989): 228–235.

7. Rüdiger Safranski, *Martin Heidegger: Between Good and Evil*, trans. Ewald Osers (Cambridge, Mass.: Harvard University Press 1998), 121; *Ein Meister aus Deutschland. Heidegger und seine Zeit* (Munich: Hanser, 1994), 166.

8. Gadamer, *Sechs Briefe an Martin Heidegger aus der Marburger Zeit. Hans-Georg Gadamer zum 100. Geburtstag, 11 Februar 2000*, Jahresgabe der Martin-Heidegger-Gesellschaft (Messkirch: Martin-Heidegger-Gesellschaft, 1999), 13.

9. Compare Gadamer, "Erinnerungen an Edmund Husserl," in Hans Rainer Sepp, ed., *Edmund Husserl und die phänomenologische Bewegung* (Freiburg/Munich: Alber, 1988), 13–16 at 14.

10. See the editor's afterword in Martin Heidegger, *Ontologie (Hermeneutik der Faktizität)*, *GA* 63, ed. by Käte Bröcker-Oltmanns, 2nd ed. (Frankfurt am Main: Klostermann, 1995), 113; *Ontology— Hermeneutics of Facticity*, trans. John van Buren (Bloomington and Indianapolis: Indiana University Press, 1999), 88.

11. Gadamer, "Sechs Briefe an Heidegger aus der Marburger Zeit," 27–32.

12. See in this volume chapter 6, part 2.

13. See *The Heidegger-Jaspers Correspondence, 1920–63* (Amherst, N.Y.: Humanity Books, 2003), 36; *Martin Heidegger/Karl Jaspers, Briefwechsel. 1920–1963*, ed. Walter Biemel and Hans Saner (Frankfurt am Main: Klostermann/Munich: Piper, 1990), 41.

14. See Hans-Georg Gadamer, "Zur Systemidee in der Philosophie," in *Festschrift für Paul Natorp zum 70. Geburtstag* (Berlin: de Gruyter, 1924), 55–75.

15. Gadamer, "Metaphysik der Erkenntnis. Zu dem gleichnamigen Buch von Nicolai Hartmann," in: *Logos* 12 (1923/1924): 340–359. Gadamer had not wanted to publish these two works in the edition of his *Gesammelte Werke*, since he took them as "premature stuff" (RPJ 8/ *GW*2 483). In my opinion this judgment is not right, especially concerning the essay "Zur Systemidee in der Philosophie," so I suggested to him that he should have it republished in the collection *Hermeneutische Wege*.

16. Gadamer, "Metaphysik der Erkenntnis," 350.

17. Gadamer, "Metaphysik der Erkenntnis," 341.

18. See Karl Löwith, *My Life in Germany before and after 1933: A Report*, trans. Elizabeth King (Urbana: University of Illinois Press, 1994), 61; *Mein Leben in Deutschland vor und nach 1933. Ein Bericht* (Stuttgart: Metzler, 1986), 65.

19. Both letters are preserved in the German National Archive in Marbach am Neckar.

20. Gadamer, "Von Lehrenden und Lernenden" (1986), in *Das Erbe Europas*, 158–165 at 159; see also Gadamer, "Paul Friedländer" (1993), *GW*10 403–405 at 403. See in addition: "A Conversation with Hans-Georg Gadamer" (with Alfons Grieder), in: *The Journal of the British Society for Phenomenology* 26 (1995): 116–126 at 119.

21. Gadamer mentions this in his letters from March 15, 1928; October 2, 1928; October 18, 1928; and April 17, 1929. See Gadamer, "Sechs Briefe aus der Marburger Zeit," 17, 21, 25 and 29. The Emergency Association of German Science was a government-sponsored agency to support academic research, the predecessor of the Deutsche Forschungsgemeinschaft (German Society for Research).

22. Compare Löwith, *My Life in Germany*, 60; *Mein Leben in Deutschland*, 64.

23. See the letter to Heidegger from April 17, 1929, in Gadamer, "Sechs Briefe an Heidegger aus der Marburger Zeit," 27–32.

24. See Gadamer, "Der aristotelische 'Protreptikos' und die entwicklungsgeschichtliche Betrachtung der aristotelischen Ethik" (1927), *GW*5 164–185.

25. See Gadamer, "Sechs Briefe an Heidegger aus der Marburger Zeit," 21–25.

26. See in this volume chapter 2, part 3.

27. See the letters to Heidegger from October 2, 1928; October 18, 1928; and April 17, 1929, in Gadamer, "Sechs Briefe an Heidegger aus der Marburger Zeit," 21, 23, and 29.

28. See Teresa Orozco, *Platonische Gewalt. Gadamers politische Hermeneutik in der NS-Zeit* (Berlin: Argument, 1995; 2nd ed. 2004). The archival material on which Orozco bases her argument is actually quite negligible. For an initial review of this book, see Stefan Breuer, "Mit Platon in den Führerstaat? Teresa Orozcos Analyse von Gadamers Wirken unter dem NS überzeugt nicht," *Frankfurter Allgemeine Zeitung*, December 4, 1995, 4. Grossner had already discussed the possibility of Gadamer's entanglement in National Socialism: see Claus Grossner, *Verfall der Philosophie. Politik deutscher Philosophen* (Reinbek bei Hamburg: Wegner, 1971), 234–237 at 234. More detailed information about philosophy in Germany in the Weimar Republic and the Third Reich is given in Stefan Tilitzki, *Die deutsche Universitätsphilosophie in der Weimarer-Republik und im Dritten Reich*, 2 vols. (Berlin: Akademie-Verlag, 2002). After the book by Orozco there appeared a number of more polemical, rather than documentary, articles on this topic: Jan Ross, "Schmuggel: Gadamers Geheimnis," *Frankfurter Allgemeine Zeitung*, February 11, 1995, 27; Christian Delacampagne, "Questions d'interprétation. L'ouvre du dernier des disciples de Heidegger est enfin largement disponible en français. Avec ses silences," *Le Monde*, May 17, 1996; Robin May Scott, "Gender, Nazism and Hermeneutics," in Lewis E. Hahn, ed., *The Philosophy of Hans-Georg Gadamer*, Library of Living Philosophers 24 (Chicago and La Salle: Open Court, 1997), 499–508. The political and philosophical relevance of Gadamer's writings on Plato during the Nazi period had already been highlighted by Dallmayr and Sullivan in an entirely different way. See Fred Dallmayr, "Hermeneutics and Justice," in Kathleen Wright, ed., *Festivals of Interpretation* (Albany: SUNY Press, 1990), 95–105; Robert R. Sullivan, *Political Hermeneutics: The Early Thinking of Hans-Georg Gadamer* (University Park: Pennsylvania State University Press, 1990); see also Sullivan, "Gadamer's Early and Distinctively Political Hermeneutics," in Hahn, *The Philosophy of Hans-Georg Gadamer*, 237–255, and Gadamer, "Reply to Robert R. Sullivan," 256–258. A further discussion of Orozco's thesis took place in the section "Gadamer in Question," in the book edited by Bruce Krajewski, where Geoff Waite wrote to support Orozco. Catherine H. Zuckert wrote an answer to Orozco and Waite in her article "On the Politics of Gadamerian Hermeneutics," in Bruce Krajewski, ed., *Gadamer's Repercussions: Reconsidering Philosophical Hermeneutics* (Berkeley: University of California Press, 2001), 229–243.

29. Jean Grondin, *Hans-Georg Gadamer. Eine Biographie* (Tübingen: Mohr Siebeck, 1999); *Hans-Georg Gadamer: A Biography*, trans. Joel Weinsheimer (New Haven, Conn., and London: Yale University Press, 2003).

30. Richard Wolin, "Nazism and the Complicities of Hans-Georg Gadamer: Untruth and Method," in *New Republic*, May 15, 2000, 36–45, republished in "Fascism and Hermeneutics: Gadamer and the Ambiguities of 'Inner Emigration,'" in Wolin, *The Seduction of Unreason: The Intellectual Romance with Fascism from Nietzsche to Postmodernism* (Princeton, N.J.: Princeton University Press, 2004), 89–127; see too the review of Grondin's book: Richard Wolin, "Socratic Apology: A Wonderful Horrible Life of Hans-Georg Gadamer," *Book/Forum* 2003, Summer, http://www.bookforum.com/archive/sum_03/wolin.html. Unfortunately, because of the dearth of factual content, Wolin's contribution ultimately turns into mere slander of Gadamer. See in response, Richard E. Palmer, "A Response to Richard Wolin on Gadamer and the Nazis," *International Journal of Philosophical Studies* 10 (2002): 467–482.

31. See Richard Wolin, "Unwahrheit und Methode. Gadamer und die Zweideutigkeiten der 'inneren Emigration,'" in *Internationale Zeitschrift für Philosophie* 2001/1 ("Hermeneutik und Politik

in Deutschland vor und nach 1933"), ed. Andreas Graeser, Dominic Kaegi, André Laks und Enno Rudoph, 7–32.; "Untruth and Method: Nazism and the Convenient Complicities of Hans-Georg Gadamer," *New Republic*, no. 4452 (May 15, 2000): 36–45. The only one of the editors who writes anything in the German edition is Graeser. Yet the *ressentiment* and animosity of the editors are clearly expressed in the foreword to this edition. Günter Figal immediately distanced himself from this publication and removed himself from the editorial board of the journal, which from then on remained in Rudolph's hand. Against the presumed intentions of the editors, the polemical debate about the issues scarcely continued after the publication. Several others participated in this edition of the *Internationale Zeitschrift*, including Frank-Rutger Hausmann, Robert R. Sullivan, Micha Brumlik, Georgia Warnke, and Gabriel Motzkin, with various perspectives and points of emphasis. A further essay by Wolin formed the conclusion. Recently Delannoy has contributed a more balanced appraisal to the discussion, concentrating above all on the interpretation of Gadamer's texts. See Franck Delannoy, "Gadamers frühes Denken und der Nationalsozialismus," in Marion Heinz and Goran Gretic, *Philosophie und Zeitgeist im Nationalsozialismus* (Würzburg: Könighausen & Neumann, 2006), 327–351.

32. See the editors' foreword in: *Internationale Zeitschrift für Philosophie* 2001/1, 4.

33. Whoever begins from an "existential anti-Nazism," which might even spring for example from one's own Judaism, can clearly see the danger that a charge applied to anyone as a Nazi might bring. Gabriel Motzkin makes this point explicitly in his "Comment on Richard Wolin's 'Untruth and Method,'" in *Internationale Zeitschrift für Philosophie* 2001/1, 78–85, 78. The line about "muses called to arms" comes from Philippe Burrin, *La France à l'heure allemande* (Paris: Seuil, 1995), chapter 22.

34. As is well known, this was one of the reasons why there was so little opposition in Germany, except for rare and marginal cases. The members of the "White Rose" or the "Red Chapel" were conscious of heading toward certain death.

35. On the connection between these apparently unrelated points see the important essay by Gottfried Gabriel, "Reich, Drittes," in *Historisches Wörterbuch der Philosophie*, ed. Joachim Ritter and Karl Gründer, vol. 8 (Darmstadt: Wissenschaftliche Buchgesellschaft, 1992), 496–502.

36. "Gottlob Freges politisches Tagebuch. Mit Einleitung und Kommentar herausgeben von Gottfried Gabriel und Wolfgang Kienzler," *Deutsche Zeitschrift für Philosophie* 42 (1994): 1057–1098 at 1092. The diary has not been included in the edition of Frege's posthumous writings (*Nachgelassene Schriften*). Today is not a question of whether to take Frege's comments in his diaries seriously. But it does mean that analytic philosophy cannot make—any more than can continental philosophy—the claim of being immune to ethico-political errors.

37. "Gottlob Freges politisches Tagebuch," 1087. See the outrage of Dummett to this, who however obviously takes this naïve supposition as self-evident. Michael Dummett, *Frege. Philosophy of Language* (London: Duckworth, 1973), XII.

38. It suffices at this point to mention the tragic epilogue in the friendship between Husserl and Heidegger, which in no way honors the latter.

39. This chapter of Gadamer's life has not yet been fully explored. Grondin included a few letters from the correspondence with Löwith, but only those that had been written before the war. The entire correspondence is preserved in the German National Library in Marbach am Neckar. I would like to thank Klaus Stichweh for the chance to see the material. Löwith had a completely different attitude toward Heidegger. In a letter addressed to Gadamer from September 2, 1933, he writes: "Heidegger's evasiveness disgusts me, even if nothing else was to be expected." On Löwith see the monograph by Enrico Donaggio, *Una sobria inquietudine. Karl Löwith e la filosofia* (Milan: Feltrinelli, 2004).

40. This is the thesis of Andreas Graeser, "Philosophische Hermeneutik. Ein Plädoyer der Unverbindlichkeit?" *Internationale Zeitschrift für Philosophie* 2001/1: 86–92.

41. Löwith wrote to Paul Tillich on April 16, 1933: "What might happen to me is still unknown to me—politically I stand neither to the left nor to the right but more than ever in the middle of philoso-

phy, with Hegel and his followers." The outline of this letter is preserved in the University Library in Marburg.

42. See Motzkin, "Comment on Richard Wolin," 75–85. Motzkin correctly identifies this characteristic of Gadamer's, and emphasizes that the question posed by his work consistently focuses on the play between "tradition and subversion," and between "authority and irony."

43. "Liberal" in the German context means neither national-liberal nor conservative. Gadamer said: "I never thought of myself as a conservative. . . . I have always been a liberal from early times to today" (*EPH* 140). Compare "Hans-Georg Gadamer in conversation with Dörte von Westernhagen: 'Die wirklichen Nazis hatten doch kein Interesse an uns . . . ,'" in *Das Argument. Zeitschrift für Philosophie und Sozialwissenschaften* 182 (1990): 543–555 at 546.

44. Compare Emmanuel Levinas, *Die Unvorhersehbarkeiten der Geschichte* (Freiburg/Munich: Alber, 2006). For the argument that the other is beyond Being, see also Emmanuel Levinas, "La trace de l'autre," in *En découvrant l'existence avec Husserl et Heidegger*, 3rd ed. (Paris: Vrin, 1982), 187–202, 189–191. Compare Adriaan T. Peperzak, "On Levinas's Criticism of Heidegger," in *The Philosophy of Emmanuel Levinas* (Evanston, Ill.: Northwestern University Press, 1997), 204–217. In this context Bruns writes: "the relation between Gadamer and Levinas is not so much one of disagreement as one of mutually illuminating differences." See Gerald L. Bruns, "On the Coherence of Hermeneutics and Ethics. An Essay on Gadamer and Levinas," in Bruce Krajewski, ed., *Gadamer's Repercussions* (Berkeley: University of California Press, 2004), 30–54 at 41. On Gadamer and Levinas, also compare James Risser, "Shared Life," *Symposium* 6, no. 2 (2002): 167–179.

45. I will later go more fully into the differences between Heidegger and Gadamer; on this point, see in particular the discussion in chapter 9, parts 4–6.

46. See among others the account by Löwith, *My Life in Germany*, 26; *Mein Leben in Deutschland*, 33.

47. Gadamer, "Breslauer Studienjahre. Hans-Georg Gadamer im Gespräch (mit Roswitha Grass)," in *Schriften des Forschungsprojekts zu Leben und Werk Richard Hönigwalds an der Universität Mannheim*, ed. Georg Groth, 1/40 (1996); republished in *Pädagogische Rundschau* 51 (1997): 115–139 at 124. See also Gadamer, "Erinnerung," in *Jahrbuch der deutschen Schillergesellschaft* 34 (1990): 464–468 at 465.

48. Martin Heidegger, "Die Selbstbehauptung der deutschen Universität," in *Reden und andere Zeugnisse eines Lebensweges: 1910–1976, GA* 16, ed. Hermann Heidegger (Frankfurt am Main: Klostermann, 2000), 107–117; "The Self-Assertion of the German University," in *The Heidegger Controversy: A Critical Reader*, ed. Richard Wolin (Cambridge, Mass.: MIT Press, 1993, 29–39).

49. By contrast, Gadamer remained in contact with Jaspers during these years—as the Jaspers collection in Marbach documents.

50. Martin Heidegger, *Hölderlins Hymnen 'Germanien' und 'Der Rhein,' GA* 39, ed. Susanne Ziegler, 2nd ed. (Frankfurt am Main: Klostermann, 1989).

51. These comparisons should be kept in mind when evaluating more or less explicit claims that charge Gadamer with not having broken off all contact with his teacher. The claim is mentioned by, among others, Grondin in his *Gadamer: A Biography*, 189; *Eine Biographie*, 195.

52. Hannah Arendt, "Martin Heidegger ist achtzig Jahre alt," *Merkur* 10, no. 258 (1969): 893–902; reprinted in: Günther Neske and Emil Kettering, eds., *Antwort—Martin Heidegger im Gespräch* (Pfullingen: Neske, 1988), 232–246.

53. The importance that Gadamer ascribed to friendship should not be underestimated. See in this volume chapter 8, part 7. The inaugural lecture that he gave on February 23, 1929, in Marburg, had the title "The Role of Friendship in Philosophical Ethics."

54. The relationship between Gadamer and Klein has not yet been sufficiently researched. It was important on both levels: the personal and the philosophical. Recently, Burt Hopkins has contributed a great deal in opening new ways into Klein's philosophy, in particular his critique of Hus-

serl's phenomenology. See Burt Hopkins, "Meaning and Truth in Klein's Philosophico-Mathematical Writings," *St. John's Review* 48, no. 3 (2005): 57–87. For more on this issue, see chapter 7, part 4.

55. Submitted by the National Socialist Society of Teachers, Germany/Saxony, Dresden 1933.

56. See "Gadamer in conversation with Dörte von Westernhagen," 548; see in addition George Leaman, *Heidegger im Kontext. Gesamtüberblick zum NS-Engagement der Universitätsprofessoren* (Berlin/Hamburg: Argument, 1993), 40. Krauss was sentenced to death in 1943. Gadamer intervened immediately with a letter, which helped at least somewhat by transmuting the death sentence into imprisonment, which then ended with the war. The letter on behalf of Krauss is published in *Lendemains* 18 (1969–70): 147–148.

57. Karl Jaspers, *The Question of German Guilt*, trans. E. B. Ashton (New York: Fordham University Press, 2001), 59; *Die Schuldfrage. Ein Beitrag zur deutschen Frage* (Heidelberg: Schneider, 1946), 64.

58. Despite Gadamer's concerns it is easily imaginable that it was less bitter for Frank to know that his chair was in the hands of a friend, which may also be why he continued to support Gadamer.

59. See Grondin, *Gadamer. Eine Biographie*, 206, and *A Biography*, 199, as well as Wolin, "Untruth and Method," 10.

60. Above all he did not want to struggle with the National Socialist censorship officials. Gadamer was also very sick during these years and suffered considerably from the diatribes against him from the *Dozentenbund*.

61. Apart from the writing on Kant's aesthetics, which is taken further in *Truth and Method*, and with the exception of the essay on Herder, all of these works were published again unchanged. "Plato and the Poets" and "Plato's Educational State" are in *Dialogue and Dialectic: Eight Hermeneutical Studies on Plato*, trans. and ed. P. Christopher Smith (New Haven, Conn.: Yale University Press, 1980); "Hegel and the Dialectic of the Ancient Philosophers" is in *Hegel's Dialectic: Five Hermeneutical Studies*, trans. P. Christopher Smith (New Haven, Conn.: Yale University Press, 1976).

62. The work was only resumed in the 1980s: Gadamer, "Die Gegenwärtigkeit Hölderlins" (1983), GW9 39–41.

63. See "Gadamer in Conversation with Dörte von Westernhagen," 549.

64. Gadamer, "Plato und die Dichter," GW5 187–211; "Plato and the Poets," *Dialogue and Dialectic*, 39–72; "Platos Staat der Erziehung" (1942), GW5 249–262; "Plato's Educational State," *Dialogue and Dialectic*, 73–92.

65. See Wolin, "Untruth and Method," 18; Teresa Orozco, "Die Platon-Rezeption in Deutschland um 1933," in Ilse Korotin, ed., *Die besten Geister der Nation: Philosophie und Nationalsozialismus* (Vienna: Picus, 1994), 141–185. Jaeger had been forced to immigrate in 1936 and taught at first at Chicago, then at Harvard. In light of his ideal of *paideia*, which Heidegger not coincidentally scorned, one should guard against the overly hasty judgment that would equate Neo-Humanism with National Socialism.

66. The dismissal of poetry, as well as of every kind of art, which serves only self-forgetfulness, prefigures the critique of an "aesthetic consciousness." See in this volume chapter 2, part 5.

67. Orozco misses this significance of the allusion. See Teresa Orozco, "Die Kunst der Anspielung. Hans-Georg Gadamers philosophische Intervention im Nationalsozialismus," *Das Argument. Zeitschrift für Philosophie und Sozialwissenschaften* 37 (1995): 311–324. In the summary review, which appeared in 1933 and which included Gadamer's "Die neue Plato-forschung" (1933), GW5 213–229, the concepts of "utopia" as well as the "educational state" also appear.

68. See in this volume chapter 6, part 5.

69. See Jost Schneider, ed., *Herder im "Dritten Reich"* (Bielefeld: Aisthesis, 1994).

70. The assumptions by Orozco and Wolin regarding the conditions under which the lecture took place have proven to be historically false. For a thorough discussion, see Frank-Rutger Hausmann, "Unwahrheit als Methode? Zu Hans-Georg Gadamers Publikationen im *Dritten Reich*," *Internationale Zeitschrift für Philosophie* 2001/1: 33–54.

71. For a comparison of the passages, see Orozco, "Platonische Gewalt," 235–239.

72. See Richard Wolin, "Gadamer und der deutsche Sonderweg," *Internationale Zeitschrift für Philosophie* 2001/1: 93–103 at 99.

73. See in this volume chapter 4, part 3.

74. See the carefully compiled list by Richard E. Palmer, "Published Interviews and Archival Tapes," in Hahn, *The Philosophy of Hans-Georg Gadamer*, 588–599.

75. The perspective of the exiles was decisive for the small group of German Jews who were among the first to recognize in Auschwitz a "break" in Western history.

76. See David Cassidy, *Uncertainty: The Life and Science of Werner Heisenberg* (New York: Freeman, 1992), 430.

77. Volkmann-Schluck was not only the first, but also the favorite student of Gadamer's. See Gadamer, "Gedenkreden auf Karl-Heinz Volkmann-Schluck (1914–1981)," *Kölner Universitätsreden* 59 (self-published) (1982): 8–17.

78. See Gadamer, *Über die Ursprünglichkeit der Wissenschaft* (Leipzig: J. A. Barth, 1947), now "Über die Ursprünglichkeit der Wissenschaft" (1947), *GW10* 287–294; "On the Primordiality of Science: A Rectoral Address," in *Hans-Georg Gadamer on Education, Poetry and History: Applied Hermeneutics*, ed. Dieter Misgeld and Graeme Nicholson, trans. Lawrence Schmidt and Monica Reuss (Albany: SUNY Press, 1992), 15–21; as well as Gadamer, *Über die Ursprünglichkeit der Philosophie. Zwei Vorträge* (Berlin: Chronos, 1948).

79. *PA* 99/*PL* 118.

80. Gadamer, "Zum 300. Geburtstag von Gottfried Wilhelm Leibniz. Festrede an der Universität Leipzig" (1946/90), *GW10* 295–307 at 297.

81. See the letter from Heidegger to Stadelmann from September 1, 1945: "In the first place I recommend Gadamer (Leipzig); I have no idea where he is at the moment. He is, according to intellectual format, the most valuable as teacher and colleague. I would like to see him as my successor, if that were possible" (Heidegger, *Reden und andere Zeugnisse eines Lebensweges: 1910–1976*, 395).

82. The chapter of his autobiography dedicated to these years is entitled "Leipzig Illusions." Compare *PA* 103–115 and *PL* 122–138.

83. See in this volume, chapter 10, part 2.

84. See Gadamer, "Die Grenzen der historischen Vernunft" (1949), *GW10* 175–178.

85. See "'. . . nein, das letzte Wort will ich gar nicht haben.' Ein Gespräch mit dem Philosophen Hans-Georg Gadamer über die gewaltlose Macht der Sprache," in *Frankfurter Rundschau*, February 11, 1995, 8.

86. The *Festschrift* appeared with the title *Anteile* (*Participations*) in 1950, about one year later, from Klostermann. It had no dedication and did not include the name of the editor, who was obviously Gadamer.

87. Gadamer also succeeded in having Heidegger chosen as a member of the Academy of Sciences in Heidelberg.

88. The memories of Gadamer from these students have been gathered in a volume, edited by Günter Figal: *Begegnungen mit Hans-Georg Gadamer* (Stuttgart: Reclam, 2000). Carsten Dutt worked with Gadamer in his later years in the philosophy department, and he among others should be thanked for perhaps the most successful interview with Gadamer: Carsten Dutt, ed., *Hans-Georg Gadamer im Gespräch* (Heidelberg: Winter, 1995).

89. See "Gadamer im Gespräch," February 11, 1995. Interview with Austrian radio.

90. See in this volume chapter 9.

91. See in this volume chapter 2, part 1.

92. Gadamer was personally involved in the publication of his works. One of his intentions was to avoid the publication of his lectures. In March 1997, he wanted to clear his office at the university and threw a great number of papers away, among them the manuscripts of the lectures he had held in

the United States. On that day, unfortunately, I got to the university later than usual, and so many of the papers had already been lost. I was able, however, to save a few significant exchanges of letters, including those with Löwith and Klein as well as the exchange with Heidegger, which had just recently reappeared. I brought the documents at that time to the university archive in Heidelberg, together with all the other materials that were preserved in the department of philosophy. Today they can be found in the German National Library in Marbach am Neckar, where in the meantime a Gadamer archive has been opened.

93. See the list of reviews in this volume, chapter 10, part 1.

94. See chapter 10 in this volume for all discussions of Gadamer's works.

95. See Gadamer, "The Problem of Language in Schleiermacher's Hermeneutic," trans. David E. Linge, in *Schleiermacher as Contemporary: Journal for Theology and the Church* 7, ed. Robert W. Funk (New York: Herder and Herder, 1970), 68–84; "Das Problem der Sprache bei Schleiermacher" (1968), in *Neuere Philosophie II. Probleme—Gestalten, GW4* 361–373.

96. Letter to Heidegger from February 3, 1968, in the German National Library in Marbach.

97. "Mit der Sprache denken" (1990), *GW10* 346–353 at 346–7.

98. Richard E. Palmer, *Hermeneutics: Interpretation Theory in Schleiermacher, Dilthey, Heidegger, and Gadamer* (Evanston, Ill.: Northwestern University Press, 1969).

99. See in this volume chapter 10, 5.

100. The lecture was slightly revised by Gadamer and given again when he received the Hegel Prize from the city of Stuttgart on June 13, 1979. See Gadamer, "Das Erbe Hegels," in Hans-Georg Gadamer and Jürgen Habermas, *Das Erbe Hegels* (Frankfurt/Main: Suhrkamp, 1979), 33–84, republished as "Das Erbe Hegels" (1980), *GW4*, 463–483; "The Heritage of Hegel," in *Reason in the Age of Science*, trans. Frederick G. Lawrence (Cambridge, Mass.: MIT Press, 1981), 38–68. See in this volume chapter 7, part 6.

101. Antonio Gargano gives an overview of Gadamer's seminars in "Hans-Georg Gadamer e l'Istituto Italiano per gli Studi filosofici," *Sophia* 4 (2002): 151–155.

102. It is for example due to an initiative in those years of the Istituto Italiano degli Studi filosofici in Naples, as well as RAI Educational, that Gadamer taped a series of twenty-seven video cassettes for the series *Enciclopedia multimediale delle scienze filosofiche*, which deals with the history of philosophical thought. The series bore the title *Il cammino della filosofia* ("The Way of Philosophy"), and went back to an idea from Gerardo Marotta (see www.emsf.rai.it).

103. See Gerardo Marotta, "Mit Gadamer für ein Europa der Kultur," in Günter Figal, ed., *Begegnungen mit Hans-Georg Gadamer* (Stuttgart: Reclam, 2000), 21–32 at 25.

104. Compare the "Chronology" at the end of this volume.

105. See in this volume chapter 10, part 1.

106. See Rüdiger Bubner, ed., "Sein, das verstanden werden kann, ist Sprache," in *Hommage an Hans-Georg Gadamer* (Frankfurt/Main: Suhrkamp, 2001).

107. The first unofficial meeting actually took place in the summer of 1988. The participants at that time were Lawrence K. Schmidt, James C. Risser, Brice Wachterhauser, and Joel Weinsheimer. This first group then arranged the symposium for 1989 in the "Wissenschaftsforum." After 1989 the symposium was to be held in the philosophy department in Heidelberg every two years; in light of its success it was held every year after 1991. Many renowned American philosophers, such as John Sallis, and many important representatives of philosophical hermeneutics in the United States, for example Richard E. Palmer, P. Christopher Smith, and Charles Scott, regularly took part in the symposium. This was also a valuable opportunity for a conversation between American and European philosophers. After Gadamer's death in 2002 the symposium was moved to Freiburg, where it still takes place every year in the philosophy department.

2 The Event of Truth

What the tool of method does not achieve must—and really can—be achieved by a discipline of questioning and inquiring, a discipline that guarantees truth. (*TM* 491/*GW1* 494)

1. Against Method?

What does *Truth and Method* mean? The significance of the conjunction "and" has almost turned this title into an enigma. If "method" has a negative value in the title, then the "and" does not connect, but rather represents an alternative. The title could be revised accordingly as *Truth or Method*.[1] In an even more radical version, one could think of the formulation: *Truth against Method*.[2] If "method" is taken as a model and metaphor for the natural sciences, then truth occurs *outside* method. Thus it is possible to speak of "extramethodical" experiences of truth.

Yet it is necessary to address a misinterpretation. Certainly Gadamer no longer understands hermeneutics in a traditional sense as a doctrine of interpretation, and thus he aims to free it from the burden of methodology. But he does not want to put method as such into question altogether. The title implicitly contains a tension between "method" and "truth." When he considers this tension later in greater detail, Gadamer admits that he had sharpened it in a polemical sense (*RHT* 317/*GW2* 238). This was indispensable to show the limits of science to an age in which the faith in science borders on superstition. In the "Afterword to the Third Edition" of *Truth and Method*, Gadamer writes: "Ultimately, as Descartes himself realized, it belongs to the special structure of straightening something crooked that it needs to be bent in the opposite direction. But what was crooked in this case was not so much the methodology of the sciences as their reflexive self-consciousness" (*TM* 555/*GW2* 453). If philosophical hermeneutics highlights the tension between truth *and* method, its aim is not to enter into conflict with science and its method, but to offer an occasion for critical reflection on the truth implied by science. The "and" in the title points to this critical reflection. Hence the epistemological relevance of hermeneutics, according to Gadamer, should be seen as an attempt "to mediate between philosophy and the sciences" (*TM* 552/*GW2* 450).[3] The polemical tension in the title should be read neither as an antithesis nor as a hiatus: "It was, of course, a flat misunderstanding when people accused the expression 'truth and method' of failing to recognize the methodical rigor of modern science"

(*TM* 551/*GW*2 449). It is not that hermeneutics disallows or dismisses method. It would be absurd not to recognize the need for a method when, for example, a mathematical problem is being solved, a skyscraper is being built or a vaccination against a disease must be found. Yet hermeneutics does not allow the imposition of a method—because of its fascinating and enormous results—in a mechanical way everywhere. A method presupposes that the object can be definable and the subject can define it objectively with a scientific demonstration; it proceeds from an instrumental conception of knowledge in which the subject is confident that it can dispose of the object. But if the method is adequate for scientific projects it cannot be for all others; on the contrary, it may bring a reduction or even a distortion of the experience of truth.

Husserl had already opposed the tendency to reduce our experiential world—the world that precedes all scientific research, our everyday "lifeworld" (*Lebenswelt*)—to mathematics. Gadamer follows in Husserl's wake, but takes the truth claim of the lifeworld more strongly into account. For Gadamer, a method can be a valid and legitimate procedure for gaining knowledge.[4] It remains, nevertheless, secondary and derivative when compared to all those experiences of truth that do not fall under its logic, for example those that remain outside of methodical logic and in some cases precede it. Here, "outside of" means "before." The extramethodical experiences of truth that hermeneutics aims to bring to light have a priority that signifies autonomy as well. To put it differently: the truth that precedes method is autonomous, because it does not need a method to be verified, validated, or founded. On the contrary, in any method there is always already a hermeneutic pre-understanding at play. Its application begins with our linguistic orientation, which "is and remains the vehicle of all understanding," just as every specialized language stems from a common language, from which it is inseparable (*TM* 561/*GW*2 459). "Thus all science involves a hermeneutic component" (*TM* 559/*GW*2 458). If there is a foundation here, it is that of hermeneutics and its truth.

2. Understanding Is Like Breathing

Yet what does "hermeneutic truth" mean? Is this not a *contradiction in adjecto*, if truth is supposed to be objective, verifiable, and indubitable? The point is that philosophical hermeneutics does not think of truth in terms of the scientific doctrine of knowledge. Thus hermeneutics does not aim for a cognitive method from which a new theory of truth would be derived. The expectation of finding such a theory in *Truth and Method* is necessarily disappointed.

Understanding, not knowing, is at stake in hermeneutic truth. Hermeneutics interrogates neither the conditions for the possibility of knowledge nor what kind of a method should be followed. Instead it asks what *happens* when one understands (*TM* 5/*GW*1 3).[5] This is the new question that hermeneutics poses. It concerns what occurs in understanding, the *event of truth*. Hermeneutics strives for nothing other than *to* *understand understanding.* But understanding is neither a process nor a cognitive procedure, and knowing is rather a modality derived from understanding.

What is the understanding? It is a capability that is less active than passive. In this sense one can speak of the *experience* of understanding. Understanding means not conceiving, dominating, or controlling. *Understanding is like breathing.* And one does not decide not to breathe any more. Understanding is not a matter of knowing, but of being. Thus it is the understanding that supports and grounds us. The great mistake of modern methodology is that it allows us to forget this supporting ground.

But should the foundation of understanding be founded in turn? "Does what has always supported us need to be grounded?" (*TM* xxxvii/*GW*2 447). Gadamer's position is not simply anti-foundationalist. His intention is to allow the ground to emerge from forgetfulness in order to bring it to light *as* ground, that is, so fundamental that it escapes all foundations. Thus hermeneutics proves to be, in Plato's sense, anamnetic.

If truth is an event of understanding, then it can neither be deduced nor theoretically conceived, but only shown each time at the place where it happens. Hermeneutics aims to describe the event of truth. Although it confronts the most significant philosophical and scientific theories of truth, it avoids all temptations to define its own theory of truth. This corresponds to its conviction that truth, including its own truth, is an event (*TM* 5/*GW*1 3).[6] Hermeneutics seeks to let those experiences of truth reemerge that even the humanities, with their mania for method, have driven into hiding: for example, the study of art, history, and language.

3. The Rediscovery of Vico:
Humanistic Culture and Hermeneutic Meaning

To this end, it is indispensable to consider the place where the humanities arise, as suggested by their ancient name of *humaniora*. It becomes necessary, in other words, to rediscover the humanistic tradition, which today is either repressed or even at times openly dismissed. Especially striking is the case of Heidegger, who, above all in his famous *Letter on Humanism,* decisively distances himself from the humanistic tradition.[7] Gadamer, by contrast, suggests a rediscovery of humanism, and this difference between the two philosophers should not be overlooked.

From the constellation of humanism Gadamer chooses a few "leading concepts" that could shed light on a model of knowledge as an alternative to the methodical one: culture, the community's sense, judgment, and taste. These concepts point to each other and delineate the stages of his important rediscovery.

The first concept is that of *Bildung,* which could be interpreted as "education" or "formation," but also as "culture" (*TM* 9–19/*GW*1 15–24). In the final years, Gadamer returned again and again to the question of *Bildung,* which for him is one of the most urgent of our time.[8] But what does *Bildung* mean? In order to clarify this concept, he interrogates the history of the word.

Following the work of Wilhelm von Humboldt (1767–1835), the word *Bildung* gained a complex meaning. On the one hand it corresponds to the Latin *formatio;* on the other hand *Bildung* contains *Bild,* or image, which points back to the old mystical tradition and ultimately to Genesis 1:26: if the human being was created in the image of God, then humans must develop this likeness. Here *Bildung* does not suggest a being, but a becoming; it is not the result of a process but rather the process itself of constant and further development (*TM* 11/*GW1* 17). It does not involve something given, as when a talent is cultivated or material is assimilated. *Bildung* means to form oneself.

At this point it is necessary to follow Hegel, who recognized in the concept of *Bildung* the prerequisite for philosophy itself. *Bildung* meant for him "rising to the universal," a movement that demands "sacrificing particularity for the sake of the universal" (*TM* 12/*GW1* 18). Another way of saying *Bildung* is "the capacity for abstraction" or *the detachment from oneself.*

How is the cultivated person to be distinguished from the uncultivated person? "Whoever abandons himself to his particularity is *ungebildet* [unformed]—e.g., if someone gives way to blind anger without measure or sense of proportion" (*TM* 12/*GW1* 18). The uncultivated ones are those who cannot look away from themselves, who cannot distance themselves from their own immediate experience and are incapable of raising themselves to a universal standpoint from which to see their own particularities in a new and different way. If culture means detachment, then each form of detachment from oneself and hence each practical behavior, beginning with work, is itself already culture, because it forces individuals to go beyond their own limits.

This becomes more evident with theory, which requires an effort to deal with things that do not exist immediately but are rather distant and strange. It is also similar to the study of ancient languages and the ancient world. Here the greatest distance from oneself is reached. It is the foreignness that provokes it. To recognize oneself in the other: that is culture. Thus the cultured person is not the one who is cultivated, who has gathered a manifold erudition. The cultured person is the one who knows in the Socratic sense about their own not-knowing, who recognizes the limit of their own finitude. By recognizing this limit one recognizes the other and the standpoint of the other. This is the ideal of humanistic culture, which begins with the *condition humana.* Hence Gadamer wrote in his last years: "*Bildung* means to be able to look at things from the standpoint of another" (*GW8* 349). This also means to see oneself with the eyes of the other and from their standpoint.

It appears then that the universality to which one raises oneself is "not that of the concept," it is not the methodological subsumption of the particular under the universal (*TM* 17/*GW1* 23). Here Gadamer follows the lead of Hermann L. F. von Helmholtz (1821–94), who, although he characterized the model of the humanities negatively, saw induction as the basis of the humanities. Instead of a "logical" induction, the humanities employ an "artistic-instinctive" induction, which he characterized as a "kind of tact" (*TM* 5/*GW1* 11).[9] The universality reached along this path is neither abstract nor forever fixed and everywhere valid. It is, by contrast, the universality of the standpoint that the cultivated person leaves open to the extent that he or she recognizes the standpoint of the other. This universality is so concrete that cultivated consciousness can be compared to one of the senses. Yet it is not a matter of a sixth sense that might be added to the others, but a *universal,* or more precisely, a *common sense (TM* 17/*GW*1 23).[10]

With the *sensus communis,* the notion of a communal or common sense, the core of humanism is reached. The name encountered in *Truth and Method* is, not coincidentally, Giambattista Vico (1668–1744) (*TM* 19–24/*GW*1 24–29). It is not necessary to agree with Gadamer's interpretation of Vico here, which he derives primarily from a single work, *De nostri temporis studiorum ratione* (*On the Study Methods of Our Time*), Vico's first Latin work from 1701. But it is significant that Gadamer writes an important chapter on the Italian philosopher, which represents one of the few exceptions in the realm of German philosophy.[11]

In his "pedagogical manifesto," which contains *in nuce* many elements of his later *scienza nuova,* his "new science," Vico revaluates the rhetorical tradition (*RHT* 48/ *GW*2 280). The theme of his work is the opposition between *topic* and *critique.* Against the Cartesian method, which starts from an initial truth and by proceeding deductively reduces everything "true" to a "mathematical truth," Vico develops the new concept of "verisimilitude," which would legitimize not only the dignity, but also the autonomy, of the *artes* or the *humanities.* The critical-deductive method, which is fully self-enclosed, cannot discover anything new and can only make explicit whatever is already contained in its premises. These premises have not been established by critique, but by topic and the ability of topics to reveal something new. Critique is thus dependent on topic, just as *ratio* or reason is dependent on *ingenium* or disposition. Topics actually require the art of discovering *tópoi,* the "commonplaces" from which all argument proceeds. Whereas Descartes had criticized these as the mere accumulation of prejudices and pseudo-truths, which cannot be traced back to a clear and distinct foundation, for Vico the commonplaces of rhetoric are the places of inductive and creative knowledge. Without being founded on something else, they are for their part foundational: the places where "common sense" gets articulated. With a connotation that already suggests communication and language, the word *communis* or "communal" in the sense of "common," points to what can be communicated and shared with one another. The same can be said for that concrete, temporary, and historically valid universality that substantiates common sense. Here it becomes clear why Gadamer's interpretation of Vico had precisely this common sense in mind: it should not be interpreted as an ability that can be shared by all, but as "the sense that founds community" (*TM* 21/*GW*1 26). Vico's appeal to common sense, in which Gadamer finds the recuperation not only of the Latin *sensus communis* but also of the Aristotelian *phrónesis,* is an appeal to that sense which lives in all of us and can be gained only by living together: the sense of the common good. *The cultivated person is the one who has a sense of community.*

What corresponds to common sense in the German language and the German tradition? In the Latin, Italian, and French traditions, as well as in the English tradition, *common sense* indicates the general quality of citizens. An example of this is the "common sense" that Shaftesbury (1671–1713) had understood as the social virtue of *sympathy;* from this would arise the doctrine of *moral sense* (*TM* 25/*GW1* 31). In the German tradition, by contrast, which takes shape first through reflection on the humanities, common sense was intellectualized, robbed of its political and social content, and reduced to a mere corrective, the faculty of judgment (*TM* 30/*GW1* 36).

Common sense can also be called the *Urteilskraft* or faculty of judgment, because this sense cultivates the ability to judge what is convenient and right. The faculty of judgment is not merely a formal ability, but an exigency that arises from social and moral solidarity: it manifests itself from case to case. Thus it is not possible to refer to it by a principle or a method. Hence the dilemma felt by those who judge. *Judging,* which goes together with the sensory ability to differentiate, is more like *tasting,* as in the immediate rejection or acceptance of things. *Taste,* which has a more moral than aesthetic value, is another way to say judgment, common sense, and culture (*TM* 34/*GW1* 40).

In all these ways, that sense can be described which can be neither taught nor learned, which is the result of neither rules nor contents, but which is instead a practical wisdom of living that can only be cultivated and refined, and would be unthinkable without human social life. The *hermeneutic sense* gains a more precise contour from the rediscovery of humanism, as a kind of knowledge completely different from the exact and methodical knowledge of the sciences. If the hermeneutic sense were measured by the natural sciences, it would have to be excluded from the realm of knowledge or be reduced to an aesthetic function. With this not only would the entire heritage of humanistic study be lost, which is based on the hermeneutic sense, but a humane conception of knowledge as well.

4. Kant's "Caesura":
From the Aesthetics of Taste to the Aesthetics of Genius

For Gadamer, the slow but inexorable darkening of the humanistic tradition is closely bound up with the name of Kant; yet Kant, for his part, had recognized the value of this tradition. So how could Gadamer charge Kant with this responsibility?

The humanities, which came to exist as such only with Kant, were from then on faced with a radical alternative: to become either a method or aesthetics. In other words, either they would have to measure themselves as a method in relation to the exact sciences and risk disappearing, or they must submit to aestheticization. The starting point for the discussion is in both instances Kant's *Critique of Pure Reason* from 1781. Kant perceives the need to redefine metaphysics with the intention of saving it. The result of his project, however, is quite the opposite: by measuring metaphysics against the pure science of nature, metaphysics becomes discredited forever. This condemnation also falls on all forms of knowledge that do not follow the criteria and methods of the sciences, so that the latter will be identified exclusively with exact science.

At this moment the fate of the "humanistic" sciences is sealed, especially those in which any echo of the humanistic tradition can still be heard, and which in Germany are given the name of "the Arts" (*Geisteswissenschaften*). These "sciences," or better, "arts," are negatively defined. From the beginning they have been characterized by a lack. Thus Kant's "caesura" discredits every form of nonmethodical knowledge that had developed in the humanistic tradition (*TM* 41/*GW1* 46).[12] How could culture, common sense, judgment, and taste be grounded and legitimized now? Obviously, taste has nothing to do with science. But if it is not a science, then what is it? Taste is aesthetic. This is the answer introduced by Kant and radicalized after him. Indeed today the culture of taste or of good taste falls entirely within the realm of aesthetics. As this realm is more clearly profiled, two phenomena emerge that are closely bound up with one another. On the one hand, the humanities are separated from the humanistic tradition, forced to be measured against the monopoly of truth held by the exact sciences, and obliged to understand themselves from the standpoint of a completely different identity (*TM* 41/*GW1* 46). On the other hand they find the possibility of surviving, with the loss of their identity and origin in this aestheticization, at the price of losing all cognitive value. A source as untrustworthy as judgment can be entrusted with nothing or next to nothing.

In this sense Gadamer can say that the Kantian foundation of aesthetics is "epoch-making" (*TM* 41/*GW1* 47).[13] After the first *Critique* and the *Critique of Practical Reason* from 1788, Kant laid the foundation of the new aesthetics in an autonomous domain, beyond knowledge and beyond morality, in his *Critique of Judgment* from 1790. His central question concerns the possibility of discovering an a priori in taste that would legitimize his requirement of universal validity. In order to understand better the drastic reduction that this question implies, it is important to remember that everything which was aesthetic, above all aesthetic judgment, had belonged to the realm of taste, and that taste, which was almost a synonym for common sense, also had a moral and political connotation. After Kant, taste was abstracted from this connotation, aestheticized, subjected to critique, and required to meet a criterion of validity that ultimately is that of science. Obviously it will not be able to respond. So it is robbed of all "significance as knowledge" and reduced to a subjective principle (*TM* 43/*GW1* 49). Indeed, one cannot know anything cognitively from objects judged to be beautiful. With great effort Kant attributes to taste a "subjective universality," a paradoxical formulation meant to show the free play of the faculties. This free play is the source of aesthetic pleasure, and, although it is purposively subjective, it is nevertheless identical in every subject and universally communicable.[14]

In the complex interpretation that he gives of Kantian aesthetics, Gadamer highlights a distinction that remains somewhat secondary in the third *Critique*, yet is indispensable if the autonomy of the aesthetic is to be understood in Kant's sense. It is the distinction between "free" and "adherent" beauty.[15] This topic represents one of the core issues of Gadamer's Kant interpretation; he returned to it many times, as for example in his essay "Intuition and Vividness" ("Anschauung und Anschaulichkeit") from 1980 (RB 155–170/GW8 189–205). But what makes this distinction possible? Free beauty, or authentic beauty for Kant, may become the object of a "pure judgment of taste," where neither intellectual nor moral factors intervene. Kant's examples include pure music, or music without content, arabesques, and floral ornaments. These objects are beautiful because they have no other purpose than pure beauty. Less pure, by contrast, is the beauty of "adherent" objects, which are called this because they adhere to a concept. Their purpose is no longer purely aesthetic. Examples of this beauty are the beauty of a human figure, of an animal, or of a building. Here a further purpose is presupposed. Indeed, a building should also be useful. In these cases a pure judgment of taste becomes impossible, since it is compromised by the representation of the purpose. Gadamer calls this doctrine "particularly dangerous," because it marks the moment from which the aesthetic judgment is robbed of all cognitive value. From this point on, aesthetics survives only by delimiting itself in a negative way from both knowledge and morality (TM 44/GW1 50).

At the same time Gadamer is aware that aesthetics did not reach the climax of this development with Kant, for whom the beautiful was nevertheless a "symbol of the moral good."[16] The beautiful in this context is "natural beauty." It is as if nature itself were to contribute to aesthetic pleasure. The "wonderful purposiveness [Zweckmässigkeit] of nature for us" indicates that we are the ultimate goal of creation and reveals our moral destiny (TM 50–51/GW1 56). While this destiny reduces the moral significance of aesthetics, it also explains the priority Kant grants to natural beauty over artistic beauty.[17] If the "products of art" speak to us through something that is already a language of the spirit, then natural objects do not exist to speak to us; but precisely because they do not assert anything determinate, they are even more eloquent: they remind us of our moral destiny by the accord they excite in us (TM 53/GW1 57). Yet however much it pretends to be autonomous, the Kantian founding of aesthetics requires a further ground, which is that of a teleology and theology of creation.

It is this further ground that is called into question in the post-Kantian era. Beginning with Schiller, the preoccupation with safeguarding the autonomy of aesthetics becomes dominant. This is expressed in a new distancing from the humanistic tradition, to which Kant, who still conceives of taste and natural beauty in a moral framework, nevertheless remained bound. In his famous work from 1795, Letters on the Aesthetic Education of Man, Schiller speaks of an "education" that is nevertheless still aesthetic. Thus he prepares the turn to Romanticism, which consistently gives preference to artistic beauty and consistently, by emphasizing creativity, privileges genius over taste. The transition from taste to genius appears symptomatic in many respects (TM 55–57/GW1 59–61). If aesthetics occupies an autonomous realm outside knowledge and morality, a realm characterized by the free exercise of subjectivity, then it should allow room for that subjectivity which expresses itself in the artistic creation of the genius. The opposition between genius and taste becomes unavoidable: taste, another name for common sense, becomes the discipline imposed on the invention of the genius. After Kant it is thus the revolt of the genius, with the originality of his production, which will prevail. In the nineteenth century one can speak with Gadamer of a "true apotheosis" of genius and creativity (*TM* 59/*GW*1 65). This "apotheosis" is promoted by irrationalism and the cult of unconscious production, which will contribute to separating the world of art from the world of knowledge and morality.

The protagonists of this turn are, above all, Goethe and Rousseau, both of whom merge aesthetic experience with personal and autobiographical experience. It suffices to think of Goethe's *Poetry and Truth* (*Dichtung und Wahrheit*), and Rousseau's *Confessions*. Following these works, art appears more and more bound up with *Erlebnis*, with "lived experience." The theorist of this connection was Wilhelm Dilthey (1833–1911), who made *Erlebnis* a key concept not only of aesthetics, but also of hermeneutics and indeed of all the humanities.[18]

As far as it seems to originate from lived experience, art becomes increasingly separated from truth and marginalized by reason. Gadamer documents this process with his account of the development of the concept of *Erlebnis* (*TM* 64–70/*GW*1 70–76). In the course of the nineteenth century the concept followed two apparently contrary, but actually complementary, lines of development. On the one hand, in the *Erlebnis* a certain givenness is discerned that would counterbalance the "fact" of the empiricists. On the other hand, the cult of lived experience declines into a "pantheistic" horizon, which—precisely because of its unfathomable many-sidedness—escapes all rational knowledge (*TM* 64/*GW*1 69). *Erlebnis* finds its last instance in the "philosophy of life." Yet positivism and pantheism are, ultimately, two sides of the same coin. In the age of "science," which dominates reason, the humanities search indefatigably for an ultimate givenness that could legitimate them, and inevitably fall into an irrationalism that confirms their marginality.

5. The Superiority of Science and the Unreality of Art: Aesthetic Consciousness

Hence a new realm for aesthetic experience takes shape: the realm of appearance *alongside* the real world. Throughout the entire nineteenth and twentieth centuries it becomes accepted that art has nothing to do with knowledge. From this perspective, and on the basis of the Kantian and Romantic concepts of genius, *aesthetic consciousness* develops.

In order to show the limits of this consciousness, Gadamer dwells on *allegory* (*TM* 70–81/*GW*1 76–87).[19] Why did the extension of aesthetic consciousness correspond simultaneously to a dismissal of allegory? More than a form of visual art, as for example with allegorical painting, allegory is a rhetorical and exegetical form. To give just one example: the allegorical representation of justice is a goddess with blindfolded eyes who holds a pair of scales in her hand. The image suggests that allegory is not only the work of a genius, but rests on consolidated traditions (*TM* 79/*GW1* 85). It is a kind of cryptic script that points beyond what it expresses to a determined reality. In this sense, it is an experience of reality (*TM* 76/*GW1* 82). But this claim, which makes it suspicious for aesthetic consciousness, lets allegory appear all the more interesting for Gadamer. In fact, he proceeds toward a "rehabilitation of allegory." His intention underlines the necessity of recovering a relationship between art and reality (*TM* 70/ *GW1* 76).

With regard to the fatal separation of art and reality, Gadamer speaks of the *abstraction* of aesthetic consciousness. This has been the price for the autonomy of the aesthetic. Schiller already had to pay that price. Although he wanted to overcome Kant's dualisms, Schiller created a deeper abyss between art and reality (*TM* 81–88/ *GW1* 87–94). Yet the abyss is actually made possible and consolidated by the scientistic reduction that limits reality more and more to the spatiotemporal matter investigated and controlled by science. Everything else for science is appearance, or even fiction. It is no coincidence that the Anglo-Saxon world uses the word "fiction" to designate literature (*LL* 36/*GW8* 424).

Through "aesthetic differentiation," art is made unreal (*TM* 85/*GW1* 91). Aesthetic consciousness, which recognizes only the "aesthetic quality" of the object, separates and abstracts it from the real world in order to transpose it into the realm of beautiful appearance (*TM* 85/*GW1* 91). This could happen only because science has already appropriated authentic being. The abstraction of aesthetic consciousness is the product of the occult empire of science. Art gains its autonomy, to be sure, but this is merely imaginary. The clearest proof of this imaginary autonomy is those places that, though they are destined for art, ultimately marginalize it. There is no city that does not have theaters, concert halls, or museums. But these places banish art from reality—which is different and elsewhere—where it can be managed and dominated by the economy and by science. For Gadamer the museum functions as the place of this marginalization par excellence. In contrast to the older collections, which reflected a taste or contained the works of a single school, today's museum is a "collection of such collections" that hides its own origin, even through its historical disposition (*TM* 87/*GW1* 92). Here aesthetic consciousness celebrates its unreality.

In this context it is not surprising that such de-realization also has consequences for the artist, who "loses his place in the world" because he falls under the illusion that he can produce art in complete independence. He becomes an outsider, someone allowed to live as a bohemian. The desacralized and secularized world of science, through its relentless search for new myths, turns the artist into a kind of "secular savior," on whom the world's salvation would depend. The artist's tragedy is that he can accomplish only a particular redemption, which is actually the negation of redemption. In the attempt he merely experiences, through the public around him, the failure of this particularity (*TM* 88/*GW1* 94). Gadamer's point is that, historically, works of art were generally commissioned. From Mozart's *Requiem* to the Sistine Chapel, it would be difficult to find an exception. What aesthetic consciousness calls inspiration, geniality, and creativity, is for the artist in a very prosaic way a matter of career and work, above all commissioned work.

In the end, however, the abstraction of aesthetic consciousness abstracts from art itself, which must therefore be recovered in its relation to reality. This relation is not a relation of discontinuity. Art interrupts, but does not cut off, the hermeneutic continuity of our existence. Far from a kind of experience that ends only in disenchantment, the encounter with the work of art can impact life so profoundly that it can be the beginning of a renewal, of an entirely new way of living in the world (*TM* 99/*GW1* 105). Since art is not an unreal reality, but on the contrary a reality elevated to a higher power, it can be said that being increases, strengthens. Gadamer speaks of an *"increase in being"* (*TM* 140/*GW1* 145). Art is then an *experience of truth*. But wherever the conception of art changes, the conception of truth will change as well.

Notes

1. See Gianni Vattimo's introduction to the Italian edition of *Truth and Method* (*L'ontologica ermeneutica nella filosofia contemporanea*).
2. This is the interpretation of, for example, Rorty. See Richard Rorty, *Philosophy and the Mirror of Nature* (Princeton, N.J.: Princeton University Press, 1979), 358n1: "Indeed, it would be reasonable to call Gadamer's book a tract against the very idea of method, where this is conceived of as an attempt at commensuration. It is instructive to note the parallels between this book and Paul Feyerabend's *Against Method*." See Paul Feyerabend, *Against Method* (New York: New Left Books, 1975). Habermas, too, had interpreted the title in a polemic sense, as "truth against method," though in a way his reading is much closer to Gadamer's intention than Rorty's reading. On Gadamer's discussion with Habermas and Rorty, see chapter 10 in this volume, parts 2–3.
3. See Michael Kelly, "On Hermeneutics and Science: Why Hermeneutics is Not Anti-Science," in *Southern Journal of Philosophy* 25 (1987), 481–500. For a study on this topic that is still important, see Wolfgang Wieland, "Möglichkeiten der Wissenschaftstheorie," in Rüdiger Bubner, Konrad Cramer, and Reiner Wiehl, eds., *Hermeneutik und Dialektik. Hans-Georg Gadamer zum 70. Geburtstag*, 2 vols. (Tübingen: Mohr, 1970), 1:31–56.
4. See Tuan A. Nuyen, "Truth, Method and Objectivity: Husserl and Gadamer on Scientific Method," *Philosophy of the Social Sciences* 20 (1990): 437–452.
5. On the conception of understanding, see Damir Barbaric, "Event as Transition," in Günter Figal, Jean Grondin, Dennis Schmidt, eds., *Hermeneutische Wege. Hans-Georg Gadamer zum Hundertsten* (Tübingen: Mohr Siebeck, 2000), 63–83.
6. See Jean Grondin, *Hermeneutische Wahrheit? Zum Wahrheitsbegriff Hans-Georg Gadamers* (1982), 2nd ed. (Weinheim: Belz-Athenäum, 1994).
7. Martin Heidegger, "Brief über den 'Humanismus,'" in Wegmarken, *GA* 9, ed. Friedrich-Wilhelm von Herrmann, 2nd ed. (Frankfurt/M: Klostermann, 1996), 313–364; "Letter on Humanism," in *Basic Writings*, ed. David Farrell Krell (New York: Harper Collins, 1993), 217–265.
8. See Gadamer, *Erziehung ist sich erziehen* (Heidelberg: Kurpfälzischer Verlag, 2000).

9. See Reinhard Schulz, "Helmholtz und Gadamer: Provokation und Solidarität. Über den Ursprung der philosophischen Hermeneutik im Geist der Naturwissenschaft," in *Philosophia naturalis. Archiv für Naturphilosophie und die philosophischen Grenzgebiete der exakten Wissenschaften und Wissenschaftsgeschichte* 32/I (1995): 141–153.

10. See Allen Hance, "The Hermeneutic Significance of the Sensus Communis," in *International Philosophical Quarterly* 2 (1997): 133–148.

11. See Donald P. Verene, "Gadamer and Vico on Sensus Communis and the Tradition of Humane Knowledge," in *The Philosophy of Hans-Georg Gadamer,* ed. Lewis Edwin Hahn, *Library of Living Philosophers* 24 (Chicago: Open Court, 1997), 137–153. A critique of Gadamer's interpretation was formulated by John D. Schaeffer, "'Sensus Communis' in Vico and Gadamer," *New Vico Studies* 5 (1987): 117–130, and by Christoph Jermann, "Gadamer und Vico. Zwei Modelle philosophischer Hermeneutik," *Wiener Jahrbuch für Philosophie* 25 (1993): 145–161.

12. See Istvan M. Fehér, "Gadamers Destruktion der Ästhetik im Zusammenhang seiner philosophischen Neubegründung der Geisteswissenschaften," in Dietmar Koch, ed., *Denkwege. Philosophische Aufsätze* (Tübingen: Attempto Verlag, 1998), 25–54.

13. See Dennis J. Schmidt, "Aesthetics and Subjectivity. Subjektivierung der Ästhetik durch Kantische Kritik (GW 1, 48–87)," in Günter Figal, ed., *Hans-Georg Gadamer—Wahrheit und Methode* (Berlin: Akademie Verlag, 2007), 29–43.

14. See Immanuel Kant, Kritik der Urteilskraft, in *Werkausgabe,* ed. Wilhelm Weischedel (Frankfurt/M: Suhrkamp, 1978), vol. X, #6, B 18–19/A 18/19, 124–125.

15. Kant, *Kritik der Urteilskraft,* #16, B 49–50/A 49–50, 146–147.

16. Kant, *Kritik der Urteilskraft,* #59, B 257/A 254, 297.

17. Kant, *Kritik der Urteilskraft,* #42, B 166–173/A, 163–171, 231–236.

18. See in this volume chapter 4, part 3.

19. See on this Joel C. Weinsheimer, *Gadamer's Hermeneutics: A Reading of Truth and Method* (New Haven and London: Yale University Press, 1985), 89–90.

3 Lingering in Art

Our experience of the aesthetic too is a mode of self-understanding. (*TM* 97/*GW1* 102)

The essence of temporal experience in art is that we learn to tarry. That is perhaps the finite equivalent given to us of what we call eternity. (*RB* 50/*GW8* 136)

1. Toward a Phenomenology of Play

It may seem surprising—and Gadamer himself admits this in retrospect—that *Truth and Method*, despite the title's promise of a close examination of truth, begins with an extensive discussion of art (*GR* 195/*GW8* 373). However, art in particular plays a key role in philosophical hermeneutics, and this is because a new experience of truth can be achieved only from art; thus the need arises to free aesthetics from the quarrel with modern science. The modern scientific demand for objectivity forces aesthetic experience to understand itself merely subjectively, as if we were dealing with a form of subjectivity that is engaged in a frivolous, self-referential play. The abstraction of aesthetic consciousness underwrites the triumph of science.

How can this dead end be avoided? Gadamer does so by conceiving of art as the experience of being, or better, an "increase in being," in which subjectivity plays a secondary role (*TM* 140/*GW1* 145). Against the rigid dichotomy of subject and object, he offers the dynamic model of an encounter that has the character of an event: "*all encounter with the language of art is an encounter with an unfinished event and is itself part of this event*" (*TM* 99/*GW1* 105). The "ontology of the work of art" will clarify this new model.

Gadamer's ontology of the work of art unfolds through the theme of *play*. More generally, play is the guiding thread of Gadamer's entire oeuvre. It is play or game that unites art and language (*RPJ* 41/*GW2* 5), insofar as play belongs to the concepts that fundamentally undermine, unhinge, and call the metaphysics of subjectivity into question. In fact, Kant and Schiller had already discussed play, and precisely in an aesthetic sense. Whereas Kant refers to the free play of our faculties, Schiller sees in art the play that frees us from the constraints of knowledge and morality. In opposition to the seriousness of knowledge and morality, the play of art unlocks the aesthetic space of *enjoyment and entertainment*. Even prior to asking whether art is a serious matter, Gadamer first asks whether play is a serious matter. Hence, he draws on the categories of aesthetic consciousness in order to overturn them. The play of subjectivity turns into the play of art, which limits and calls subjectivity into question; while unreality, that is, the beautiful appearance of aesthetic consciousness, becomes the reality of art, which is more real than reality itself.

Far from being mere leisure, play demands to be taken seriously. Play occurs when the player is drawn into and captivated by the game, when the player becomes completely immersed in the game. As Gadamer has it, "Someone who doesn't take the game seriously is a spoilsport" (*TM* 102/*GW1* 108). The game does not allow the player to remain outside, or to address the game as if it were an object. Gadamer follows the allusions offered by language, which speaks of the play of lights, the play of waves, of forces, of colors, even of words. The German terms *Spiel/spielen* indicate, much like the English cognates, a semantic field that includes the playing of an instrument, acting, and the performance of a musical or theatrical piece. If play has a subject, as these examples show, it is not the player but the game itself. Gadamer refers to the "primacy of the game over the players engaged in it" (*TM* 106/*GW1* 111), insofar as to play means to let oneself be taken by the game; for it is the game that asserts itself and takes hold of the player with its rules, its movement, and its primacy. It is the game that entices the player, holds him or her captive and at play—not the other way round. The player cannot but give himself or herself over to the game, to bend to "a reality that surpasses him," which thereby raises the player beyond his or her own limits (*TM* 109/*GW1* 115). The player should not claim to dominate the game, to rule, or to lead it. Indeed, players should not even believe they are the active components. Gadamer speaks of the "medial sense" of play, referring to the character of the Greek verb indicating an activity that involves the subject in such a way that he or she crosses over into passivity (*TM* 105/*GW1* 111). In this sense it can be said that "all playing is a being-played" (*TM* 106/*GW1* 112). Hence playing is not simply an activity that the subject does for him- or herself. It requires *reciprocity*: even in solitary games it is necessary for something to correspond to the player's movement with a symmetrical countermovement. This happens when a child plays with a ball, or a cat plays with a ball of wool. It happens, too, when one plays with life's possibilities.

The *phenomenology of play*, which runs through and connects concepts such as art, festival, ritual, and language, acquires an importance in Gadamer's hermeneutics that should not be underestimated. But what status does play have in an ontology of the work of art? Play brings to light two contradictory and yet correlated aspects of aesthetic experience. On the one hand, it can be said that subjectivity, as it bends itself in play to the autonomous reality of the game, also accepts the *transcendence of art*. On the other hand, it must be added that this transcendence is neither indifferent nor detached, since it calls subjectivity into play, entices it, and holds it captive. Being held captive is another way of saying understanding. The poem speaks to me, the painting looks at me. Subjectivity that plays the game of art is raised to a higher reality, but does not cease to be addressed in the process. Insofar as it responds to the demand of art, subjectivity remains secondary. This demand resembles a decree, a kind of injunction that points to the sacred character of art, to its absoluteness or its majesty (*Hoheit*).[1] Gadamer insists on this theme, most of all in his later works.

Absoluteness evokes a "distinction." Indeed, Gadamer uses the word *Auszeichnung*, "distinction," many times. But if this is the case then perhaps we risk falling back into the "aesthetic differentiation" that separates the work of art from the real world and transports it to the realm of beautiful appearance. Hence it is necessary to follow Gadamer in his subtle differentiation. The work of art distinguishes itself from reality, but never separates itself from reality. Consequently, Gadamer speaks of an "*aesthetic non-differentiation*" because non-differentiation presumes a differentiation that should not be read as a distinction, but rather as a distinguishing trait (*TM* 117/ *GW* 1 122). Art is more real than reality; it is an excess of reality, an increase in being. In this way, it can claim a "rightness" for itself that no scientific rightness can challenge: the rightness of an astronomical discovery will fade away sooner than that of the *Mona Lisa*. Art can claim a truth that makes it an *assertion* (*Aussage*). Indeed, *Art as Assertion* (*Kunst als Aussage*) becomes the title of volume 8 of Gadamer's *Collected Works,* a volume dedicated entirely to aesthetics. The concept of the "assertion" is taken in a polemical sense from that logic which would reduce truth to propositional truth. Gadamer argues that, in light of its truth, art is more of an assertion than every other assertion. However, it never ceases to concern us and awaits our response. This response will be a *playing along with,* a *Mitspielen,* playing along with the play of art. In this playing along with, the work of art enacts itself.

2. On Transformation

It remains to be clarified, however, how the work of art, understood as play, is more than a fleeting event, acquiring consistency and autonomy as a work. Gadamer speaks of the ontological process of art as an emanation or presentation (*Darstellung*). If play's manner of being is that of self-presentation, insofar as it does not refer to a finalistic context, art's way of being is that of presentation, because the closed space of the world of play, letting down one of its walls, points beyond itself to those who share in the event as spectators (*TM* 108/*GW*1 114). Art is both the presentation *of* something and presentation *for* someone. With this the being of the artwork is structured. In this respect, Gadamer speaks in *Truth and Method* of the "transformation into a structure" (*Verwandlung ins Gebilde*). But what might this mean? "Transformation means that something is suddenly and as a whole something else, that this other transformed thing that it has become is its true being, in comparison with which its earlier being is nil" (*TM* 111/*GW*1 116). First of all, Gadamer means that the play of art condenses itself into a structure in which it reaches its own "ideality" (*TM* 114/*GW*1 119). Yet the word "transformation" (*Verwandlung*), which should not be confused with change, and which can also be translated as "metamorphosis" or "transfiguration," has numerous resonances that need to be further determined in order to clarify such a complex concept.

What is presented is *structured* by way of transfiguration as a work of art, and as a result it gains an increase in being, or better—in order to avoid the mistake to which the idea of quantity could lead us, it acquires its own true being. Transformation in this sense is "transformation into the true" (*TM* 112/*GW1* 118). What is presented does not change its identity. Think for example of a portrait. It can be said, in the case of a successful portrait: "there she is," or "she is exactly like that"; in the case of an unsuccessful portrait, by contrast, it is said: "she is not like that," or "she is not like that at all." In both cases it is a matter of the same person: only the successful portrait enables her being to become knowable or recognizable. Here lies "the ontological valence" of the image (*TM* 134/*GW1* 139).[2] This valence comes to light even more when art presents what does not exist in reality. The religious image is paradigmatic—for example, the icons of the Eastern churches—since it is "in ontological communion with what is copied" (*TM* 143/*GW1* 147). Transformation as transfiguration thus also has a religious dimension and, in the sense that it recalls an epiphany, points to an elevation to a rank of being that sheds new light on what the one presented once was. But transfiguration is a process that not only involves the one presented. Art also transforms the ones it comes into contact with. Whoever takes part in the play of art cannot avoid the transfiguration of his or her very being. While it reveals the transfigured being of what is presented, at the same time art uncovers our being, our entire being-in-the-world, that Being of our world which is suddenly transfigured.

Another way of saying transfiguration is "mediation" (*Vermittlung*), which also has the twofold sense of performance and interpretation. It refers, on the one hand, to the staging or the performance of a work, as for example a piece of music, and on the other hand, to the way in which the spectator interprets it. One could speak here of "total mediation," which means not only that art merges with its interpretation, but also that "the medium as such is superseded" (*TM* 120/*GW1* 125). An interpretation is successful when it is not noticed, when it lets the work of art speak.[3]

3. Between *Mimesis* and *Anamnesis*

When *Truth and Method* states that art should be conceived as a happening of Being, as the opening of world, or as the event of truth, one would expect to encounter the name of Heidegger; yet his name does not appear once in Gadamer's ontology of the artwork. This absence is actually quite surprising, especially if one listens to the unmistakable echoes: the transfiguration into the work reminds us for example of the "setting-into-work of truth," which Heidegger discusses in his famous essay on "The Origin of the Work of Art" from 1935–36. This absence is even stranger if one thinks that Gadamer had written in 1959, on Heidegger's invitation, an important afterword entitled "The Truth of the Work of Art" for the Reclam edition of Heidegger's essay.[4] Gadamer's debt to Heidegger is unquestionable, and it should be traced back to Heidegger's way of understanding art as an experience that reveals Being.

Notwithstanding these affinities, however, there are a number of differences between the two philosophers that gradually emerge. Most importantly, the philosophical contexts in which Being, truth, and the work are embedded are completely different—as are their positions on the "question of Being," metaphysics, and its overcoming.[5] Gadamer shares neither Heidegger's idea of the forgetfulness of Being, which characterizes the history of Western metaphysics, nor the need to overcome metaphysics. Instead, Gadamer insists in a simply a-metaphysical way on the reminiscence of Being, where this reminiscence is understood as that which always goes beyond subjectivity (*TM* 103/*GW1* 108). In such a way, in art subjectivity captivated by the play is drawn beyond itself until it experiences its own limits, that is, it remembers Being. Art is this very reminiscence of Being for Gadamer, and the encounter with the work of art is *an anamnetic recognizing*. In a word, art is *mimesis* insofar as it is always *anamnesis*.

Gadamer distances himself from Heidegger by retrieving two concepts from Plato. The concept of mimesis, which was abandoned with the affirmation of the aesthetics of genius and the dominance of science, both of which deny the epistemological value to art, is taken up again and rehabilitated by Gadamer. Already for Aristotle *mimesis* is not a mere repetition or copy, which would end up duplicating the real. "In imitating, one has to leave out and to heighten" (*TM* 115/*GW1* 120). However, if Plato's doctrine of *mimesis* offers important hints, it also presents some difficulties. In the *Republic* (595a–608c) Plato famously bases his argument on ontological difference, not only to distinguish between the image as copy (*Bild*) from the image as original (*Urbild*), but also to relegate to a third level the image as a copy of a copy (*Abbild*). Gadamer begins here and in a certain way plays Plato against Plato.[6] At first he reverses the relation between the image and the original, since the original is always only given in the image. Then he argues that this is even truer for the artistic image, which, far from being a loss, is rather an increase of Being. Only here, in the artistic image, does the original become knowable and recognizable. This recognizing, provoked by *mimesis,* is always a knowing "more" than one knew before (*TM* 114/*GW1* 119). His point becomes easier to understand in light of what Plato says in the *Phaedo* about *anamnesis,* where recognizing is not a simple knowing but rather a remembering of innate ideas.[7] Due to their higher ontological status, *anamnesis* is already concerned with an increase in Being.

In his essay "Art and Imitation," Gadamer again corrects the Platonic doctrine of *mimesis* through the Pythagorean (*RB* 92–104/*GW8* 25–36). This new aspect of *mimesis* should not go unnoticed, because the recollection of the original model might give the impression that it is a matter of a realistic imitation aiming at an essence. Pythagorean *mimesis* introduces the idea of a cosmic order—*kósmos* is the order of the starry skies, which for the Greeks is the shining of the beautiful itself. According to the ancient meaning of the word, *mimesis* means "chosen from the dance of the stars" (*RB* 40/ *GW8* 127). And the stars represent pure mathematical laws and proportions. No less than the heavenly harmonies, the stars are constant and unfailing in contrast to the inconstancy of human life. In art a need for order finds expression, which distinguishes art from the chaos in which the world's relations commonly appear. Such a conception of *mimesis* draws less on an "original image" (*Urbild*) and more on an "original relation" (*Urverhältnis*), in which everyday disorder is transfigured into a cosmic order; it is especially the contemporary arts, from absolute music to abstract painting, that correspond to such *mimesis*. These arts can be called mimetic insofar as by holding together what is divided and fragmented, they evoke the possibility of an order. This does not mean, however, that the new establishment of an order does not challenge what was previously accepted: "The intimacy with which the work of art touches us is at the same time, in enigmatic fashion, a shattering and a demolition of the familiar" (*PH* 104/*GW8* 8).

The order-generating *mimesis* of art is thus an anamnetic recollection, because it wakes us from the ontic sleep in which we, bewildered, confused, and consumed in the chaos of the beings of everyday life, have lost the sense of Being. It is the event of art that reminds us of this. In the work of art we recognize the world in which we live, as if we knew it for the very first time, and in recognizing what was already known we say gratefully, though not without surprise: "so it is," "it is just so," to affirm its rightness. Here aesthetic experience reveals its continuity with existence, which encounters itself in art.

4. The Time of Art

Yet what does "presence" (*Gegenwart*) mean in relation to art? The concept of presence is closely bound up with the concepts of "presentation" or "representation." In *Truth and Method* Gadamer uses the word *Darstellung*, which is gradually replaced by the word *Vollzug*, "enactment," which has a clear Heideggerian provenance. "Hermeneutics in its Enactment" is the title of volume 9 of the *Collected Works*, which is dedicated to poetic hermeneutics. It could also be said that the work of art exists only in the setting-into-work of its enactment, that is, the being of the artwork lies in its presentation. Emphasizing a further affinity between art and literature, Gadamer states: "Art as art is in *Vollzug*, just as language *is* in conversation" (*GR* 220/*GW8* 395).

What distinguishes the artistic image, as well as the poetic word, is its "presentness" (*Gegenwärtigkeit*). The work of art reaches us by bridging all distance. It is "absolute" in the Hegelian sense of the word because it can claim absoluteness despite the differences and distances of history, but "despite" here means "throughout." Art runs throughout history, though not as an essence that survives all changes unchanged and thus remains victorious over history. Rather, it is an event in which the times of history encounter each other. In the presentation, where the artwork is called to a new life, the past becomes present. Art—Gadamer writes in his article on the "End of Art?"—is the "presence of the past" (*GW8* 208). He is referring here to Hegel's famous thesis on the "past character of art" (*Vergangenheitscharakter der Kunst*) or on the "death of art," a thesis that Gadamer often considers in order to emphasize that it should not be conceived in a banal way as the mere end of art, just like when one speaks of the end of philosophy. The character of art as past means that art for Hegel will no longer be understandable; it will require justification, since the divine we revere no longer exists in the work of art (*RB* 6/*GW8* 97). For Hegel, art appears "past" in comparison to the concept.

Thus to speak of the end of art is to affirm, in a speculative way, both its contemporaneity, because art is not subject to any progress, and its sovereignty in relation to history.[8] In this sense, the past presence of art is an absolute present and an absolute presence, which can be fruitfully compared to the Christian *parousia* (*TM* 127/*GW1* 132).

To clarify the time of art, that "present time sui generis," Gadamer introduces explicitly theological concepts. For him the concept of "contemporaneity" (*Gleichzeitigkeit*) plays a key role, which he adopts from Kierkegaard by way of the dialectical theology of Karl Barth and Rudolf Bultmann (*TM* 127/*GW1* 132). For Kierkegaard, the Christian message of salvation retains its contemporary urgency: far from being a story from past centuries, it appeals to us here and now. Gadamer relates this appeal to the aesthetic experience in order to show that the temporality of art is not one of distance—marked by both aesthetic consciousness and historicism. Art is always *contemporaneous.* Yet what does this mean? To understand this it is necessary to distinguish the concept of *contemporaneity* (*Gleichzeitigkeit*) from that of *simultaneity* (*Simultaneität*). When walking through a museum, for example, in which works are exhibited according to epochs and styles, there is the experience of simultaneity. Aesthetic consciousness moves from one room to another, from the Renaissance to the Baroque, from Impressionism to Expressionism, where the different works simultaneously become the object of a single aesthetic experience. Though historicizing is unavoidable—well before we look at a Braque, we know that he is a cubist—the temporality of an artwork cannot be reduced to such historical distance. Not even aesthetic simultaneity can dispel the original contemporaneity that radiates from the truth of art. There is always something appealing in a work of art, something that removes it from historical research and lets it appear present and contemporaneous (*GR* 199 /*GW8* 377). This time is a *present* (*Gegenwart*) in which there comes, from the past, a future that is waiting and for which we are waiting. It is in this space of time, this *Weile,* which is neither long enough for boredom nor brief enough for recreation, that art invites us to linger (*Verweilen*) (*GR* 211/*GW8* 392–393).[9]

5. The Example of Tragedy

It is not surprising that Gadamer finds an excellent example of contemporaneity in tragedy. The complexity of tragedy has long posed a problem for aesthetics, and led theorists such as Hamann and Scheler, who were important interlocutors for Gadamer, to view the tragic as an ethical-metaphysical, and thus extra-aesthetic, phenomenon (*TM* 129/*GW1* 134). With respect to the differentiation that characterizes aesthetic consciousness, here we have an "aesthetic non-differentiation." The tragic work of art refers directly to the tragedy of life, which drives Gadamer to think of tragedy as a fundamental aesthetic phenomenon. This is so not only because tragedy has its being in presentation, and not only because the spectator is involved in the performance of the tragedy, but especially because in tragedy there is a continuity with life that cannot be found elsewhere.

Even if contemporaneity is more than evident here, what interests Gadamer is another aspect of art that Aristotle reveals in the *Poetics*.[10] It involves the famous definition, whereby tragedy produces a *kathársis,* or purification, of the passions of *éleos,* or sadness, and *phóbos,* or fear. This definition can be interpreted in various ways, depending on whether the genitive is meant in the objective sense, as liberation from the passions, or in the subjective sense, as purification of these passions (*TM* 130/*GW1* 135). Gadamer chooses the second interpretation, but for him the key to this phenomenon is found elsewhere. Aristotle himself provides the key, when he stresses that the effect on the spectator belongs to the essence of the tragedy. The spectator becomes involved to the point where he or she experiences the cleansing of his or her own passions. Tragedy becomes exemplary because it dramatizes what actually happens in every art: the spectators' encounter with themselves. Though participating in tragedy may appear to mean stepping out of everyday life, in reality it deepens the spectator's *"continuity with himself"* (*TM* 133/*GW1* 137, emphasis added). Whoever is present at the tragedy discovers himself and the tragic nature of his finite existence. Participation becomes an experience of truth.

6. The Event of Being in Presentation

More than merely an example, tragedy constitutes an exceptional case for Gadamer, both for its continuity—it is after all a small step from the tragic work to the tragedy of life—and for its staging, or better, for its presentation. Tragedy clearly confirms his thesis: "we must recognize that 'presentation' is the mode of being of the work of art" (*TM* 115/*GW1* 121).[11] To put it differently, once play (*Spiel*) has been transformed into a structure (*Gebilde*), and despite the ideal unity it has reached, which can be presented and understood repeatedly, its form remains nonetheless a play and reaches its full being only when it is "played" (*gespielt*), that is performed, presented, and staged (*TM* 117/ *GW1* 122). Gadamer speaks in this context of a "double *mimesis,*" as for example that of the poet and the actor (*TM* 117/*GW1* 122). Yet what comes into being in both mimetic processes is the same, namely, the work of art. In short, the work of art cannot be separated ontologically from its presentation. Whereas in his later writings Gadamer focuses more on the process of understanding, that is, of listening to and answering the appeal of art, in *Truth and Method* he concentrates on *"the event of being that occurs in presentation"* (*TM* 116/*GW1* 122).

The so-called transitory arts show this most clearly. It suffices to think of a piece of music, which does not exist as long as it is not performed. In fact, the example of music is the most telling. But the same could be said for the recitation of a poem or the staging of a theater piece. Each presentation brings the work into being; it lets the work be in a certain way. The presentation is also an interpretation, and the work achieves its being only insofar as it is interpreted. One should not think here, however, of an interpretation that remains locked within the subjectivity of the interpreter, mainly because the work must be performed for others. In the process we do not arrive at a merely subjective multiplicity of interpretations, but rather at possible ways of Being for the work (*TM* 118/*GW1* 123). This ontological inseparability of the work and its performance does not prevent us, however, from distinguishing them. Thus a staging of Anton Chekhov's *Cherry Orchard* can disappoint us because the performance of the piece goes too far. We might say that the staging does not seem to have done justice to the work, and hence does not appear "right" to us. We can assert this because we have in mind another performance that seems more right. But "more right" here does not mean "right" in an absolute sense: the idea of a single right presentation for all occasions contradicts our finitude. It is not that there is one right presentation fixed for all time, but neither is there an arbitrariness of reproduction (*TM* 120/*GW1* 124). We would never allow a violin player to produce all possible random effects from a piece by Mozart. This means that all the possible presentations of a work remain subject to the criterion of a "right" presentation, even where the criterion is changeable. Although the work of art is distinguishable from its performance, the work cannot be separated from the performance and remains dependent upon it.

While this happens in the transitory arts, which hold the identity and continuity of the work open to the future, it is less clear what happens in the other arts. Can similar claims be made for painting, architecture, or literature? Gadamer believes that his thesis can be extended to all art forms. It should be emphasized, however, that the sections on art in *Truth and Method* do not intend to provide a comprehensive and integrated account of aesthetics. Gadamer is interested in recovering a truth *from art* that puts the methodological concept of truth into play: beyond art, he points to a hermeneutics that would be revealed as universal according to the guiding thread of language. The truth derived from art is that of transformed and presented Being, recognizable as a "heightened truth" (*TM* 137/*GW1* 142). This truth is at the same time, however, the truth of the encounter with oneself in art.

If the performing arts are particularly relevant in this respect, it does not exclude the possibility that the event of Being in presentation would also occur in the pictorial and plastic arts. Gadamer uses the example of painting. Enclosed by its frame, the painting proves to be completely autonomous and independent from every location, so that it can be moved from one gallery to another. The painting presents itself in this way as a prime example of aesthetic consciousness. Nothing about the painting seems to refer to either mediation or presentation, and the difficulty of showing how the painting cannot but offer itself in its presentation forces Gadamer to state his concept of presentation more precisely. In the first place it is important to remember what was said for all works of art: the painting presents something or someone, and it presents this for someone.

Although the picture, as an image (*Bild*), cannot be reduced to a mere copy (*Abbild*), the painting nevertheless does not have an autonomous reality and refers to an original (*Urbild*). The relation Gadamer seeks to draw between these concepts had already appeared in his reversal of Platonic *mimesis*. Thus this picture further confirms his theory of the "ontological valence of the picture" (*TM* 134–144/*GW1* 139–149). There follows an answer to the question of presentation. The first step is to distinguish the image of the painting from a mere copy. The copy has no other purpose than to resemble the original. The criterion used to measure the copy is one of adequacy. In this sense the ideal copy would be the mirror image, since one sees the being itself in the mirror. Strictly speaking it is not a question of a copy, because it does not exist in itself. The copy wants to be seen. Yet the copy is only instrumental: it points back to the original, but as soon as its purpose has been achieved, it no longer has reason to exist and is destined to cancel itself out. On the contrary, the image of the painting does not cancel itself out, because it does not relate to the original as a means to an end. Here the picture "points by causing us to linger over it" (*TM* 153/*GW1* 158). Its purpose is not *what* is presented, but *how* it is presented. The how of the presentation is one and the same as what is presented.

This ontological inseparability, which also justifies its sacred character, refers already to the ontological status of the picture, which comes further to light through its particular relationship to the original. The picture is, indeed, more than a simple copy, for it "says something about the original" (*TM* 140/*GW1* 145). The relationship to the original is no longer one-sided. The original needs the picture that presents it in order to present itself in it. This does not mean that it needs this particular picture; it could just as well come to presentation in another picture. But the mode of presentation is not accidental for the Being of what is presented. Rather, each presentation changes the ontological condition of what is presented, so that it gains an "*increase in being*" (*TM* 140/*GW1* 145).[12] The ontological relationship between the original and the copy reverses itself: "For strictly speaking, it is only through the picture [*Bild*] that the original [*Urbild*] becomes the original [*Ur-bild*; also, ur-picture]—e.g., it is only by being pictured that a landscape becomes picturesque" (*TM* 142/*GW1* 146). This is also true for the most banal objects of everyday life, those that are most quickly forgotten, or least observed and considered, which suddenly, through their presentation in a picture, reach a new ontological level. This is the case, for example, in still-life painting. One could also mention numerous examples from contemporary art, from van Gogh's shoes to Matisse's stool. Yet Gadamer's thesis is directed at a different subject, on the basis of which it can be radicalized in a way that could perhaps appear strange but that shows, on the contrary, it relevance. What is presented in a painting already tends toward presentation because it fulfills a representative function. This is the case of the sovereign, the statesman, or the hero. Such a representative picture seems to lose a certain amount of status, because it presents the need of the one presented to present him- or herself. Considered more closely, the one presented should correspond to the expectations aroused by his picture. The paradox lies in this: if the picture is the manifestation of the original, then the original becomes an original only in the picture. Whoever is in need of showing themselves no longer belongs to themselves, and "must ultimately show himself as his picture prescribes" (*TM* 142/*GW1* 147).

7. The Occasionality of Art

The presentation, which turns out to be equally constitutive for both the plastic and performing arts, seems to bind the work of art to the world depicted in it. The portrait, but also the poem dedicated to someone or something and the comedy, can be seen as telling examples of this.[13] The portrait, for example, even if drawing attention to itself, conceals in the content of the picture a reference to the original. This very referring, however, seems to belong to every work of art that for this reason is embedded in the horizon of life. This means that the artwork is situated because it has been occasioned. One can speak of "occasionality" in relation to every artwork, even if it does not appear at first to have been occasioned: "Occasionality means that their meaning and contents are determined by the occasion for which they are intended, so that they contain more than they would without this occasion" (*TM* 144/*GW1* 149). The occasionality of art, which for Gadamer can also be found in language, forms an additional argument against the abstraction of aesthetic consciousness. It could also be interpreted as a historical or historicizing perspective, as though one would have to begin with the historical context to interpret a work. But Gadamer wants to avoid both aesthetic consciousness, which abstracts art from the continuity of life, and historicism, which willingly forgets that the work is a work of art. In order not to be misinterpreted in a historicizing sense, he speaks of a "universal occasionality" (*TM* 148/*GW1* 153). With this he makes clear that it is not necessary for the interpretation of a work to solve the problem of references in the work; that is, it is not a matter of reconstructing the entire historical context. It is not necessary to know all the references to understand a satire by Horace, for example. On the other hand, Picasso's *Guernica* will preserve its references to the context of the painting, even when these references are no longer known. Occasionality is hence nothing other than the work referring to the original for its meaning. Its occasionality is also ours, that of our world.

The occasional meaning of the work is also the meaning it gathers for us in the course of its effective history. Hence, this occasional meaning constantly determines itself anew. Sculpture and architecture offer examples of this. Statues and monuments, for example, regularly acquire new functions and new tasks. But architecture is even more significant. For aesthetic consciousness, architecture is an art form that, because of its practical dimension, has only marginal value and nearly falls outside of aesthetics. Yet architecture is also a problem for historical consciousness, because a building can actualize itself only in responding to the changing requirements of its environment. In this sense, too, the work lies in its presentation, and its ontological valence is not static. The work does not remain fixed in its original world, thereafter living in a kind of alienation (*TM* 157/*GW1* 162). Rather, it demands the mediation between past and present. Well-known examples of this include the Musée d'Orsay in Paris and the Tate Gallery in London, a former train station and a former factory, which have been transformed into museums. Their occasionality demonstrates the importance of understanding and situating the works each and every time. From *Truth and Method* to his last essays, architecture has a paradigmatic value for Gadamer, not only due to the character of its enactment, but also for the understanding that it demands of us. "Understanding" here means "visiting," "frequenting," and "occupying."[14]

In his ontology of art Gadamer finally considers the decorative arts, which are normally taken as the opposite of authentic works of art, and hence dismissed from aesthetic consideration. They again offer Gadamer the opportunity to test his concept of occasionality, and to reconsider the concept of presentation. Decoration is not merely external, but belongs to the "self-presentation of its wearer" (*TM* 159/*GW1* 164). It is thus the ornament that brings to expression the Being of its wearer and allows it to be in the first place. This Being is there only in the ontological process of its presentation. Here, too, Gadamer's intention is to show that presentation is essential to all the arts. The presentation points to a Being that occurs only in this process and comes to its truth there. Yet the spectator also takes part in the presentation, and gets drawn from his present into the play of art.

8. Play, Art, and Festival

A question emerges out of the way in which Gadamer outlines the process of presentation, which also emerges in the time of art, that is, in the presence of the past. This question concerns the identity of a structure (*Gebilde*) that runs throughout history and its differentiations. What kind of "identity" is at stake if the work of art is brought to life in a new way by each presentation? And is it even justifiable to speak of an *identity*?

This question is very complex, because it points beyond the context where it is raised to a much more comprehensive philosophical question. It puts in doubt the metaphysical concept of identity, which has already been shaken by the concept of "play." Following the phenomenology of play, the phenomenology of art further undermines the concept of identity. From the experience of art, the need arises for a new understanding of truth and a new conception of identity. In the years following *Truth and Method*, Gadamer speaks of a "hermeneutic identity" (*RB* 23/*GW8* 116), and for him it is "the hermeneutic identity that founds the unity of the work" (*RB* 23/*GW8* 116). It concerns a kind of identity that exists only in its difference, only in its differentiation, or in the radical temporality of its becoming and recurrence.[15] This sense of identity contains the paradox of the repetition of the unrepeatable: "Here 'repetition' does not mean that something is literally repeated—i.e., can be reduced to something original. Rather, every repetition is as original as the work itself" (*TM* 122/*GW1* 127–128).

Any new identity that comes to light is an identity that forms itself only in *difference*. Thus difference becomes indispensable for identity. Even though Gadamer moves from identity to difference, and not the other way round, his proximity to Derrida on this point should not be overlooked.[16]

Gadamer highlights the notion of "festival" in order to illuminate the hermeneutic identity that we encounter in play and art. The themes of "festival" and the festive quality of art extend throughout his entire work, from *Truth and Method* to the article on "Art as Play, Symbol, Festival" from 1974, and his essay entitled "Towards a Phenomenology of Ritual and Language" from 1992. Yet what is a festival? An initial answer might be: "A festival exists only in being celebrated" (*TM* 124/*GW1* 129). To attend a festival, to celebrate it, does not simply mean that one does not work. More than work, the festival founds communal being. A festival occurs when a community gathers, and the community exists as such thanks to the festival. Yet this is something we hardly remember.

"To celebrate is an art" (*RB* 37/*GW8* 130). This art, which was well known in antiquity and is the art of being together, has become increasingly rare today. To understand the multilayered temporal experience of festival, the word "celebration" or "procession" (*Begehung*) becomes important, since it points to "walking" or "going" (*Gehen*) (*RB* 38/*GW8* 131). But this is not the kind of movement to reach a goal. Rather, the goal has already been reached in the moving. The festival is there, it has its existence in the time in which it is celebrated. Yet the present time of the festival is not simply present; it is rather a present time in which the past returns and recurs. Hence one speaks of the recurrence of the festival. The recurrence belongs to the festival no less than the community who celebrates it. To "recur" means that a past event repeats itself in the present, despite its unrepeatability. Thus every festival is always identical and always different. It is identical because it is a festival that recurs, as for example that of Easter. And it is different, because it is always celebrated in different ways. It does not refer to an original historical event that becomes present in commemoration. Even if a major part of the festival refers back to an event, there are also festivals that exist only in the ritual enactment of their celebration. This is shown to be the case, for example, in that no one thinks back to the original event anymore. Every summer in Heidelberg the castle is illuminated and everyone takes part in the festival, but only a few remember, when celebrating it, that it is in memory of the great fire that destroyed the old city during the French retreat in the seventeenth century (*LL* 31/*GW8*, 415). Hence the recurrence of the festival has its "own time" (*RB* 40/ *GW8* 133). "It is the celebration. The calculating, dispensing character with which we otherwise manage time is brought to a standstill in the celebration" (*RB* 40/*GW8* 133).

The time of the festival is very important for Gadamer. It is important in the first place because recurring festivals cannot be put in a temporal order, but rather the reverse: the temporal order emerges only in accordance with the festivals—beginning with the year itself. Secondly, the primacy of the festival's recurrence is the primacy of an event that comes into its time and has its own time; it can be neither calculated nor filled out. The practical experience of time is the experience of time that is at our disposal, the time one has or thinks one has for something. But this is an "empty time," which can be filled out by being busy or can remain empty in boredom. The time of the festival is, by contrast, a "fulfilled time," which brings the time of calculation to a standstill and brings a halt to it. It is a time of celebration, which is the celebration of time itself.[17]

The experience of the festival resembles the experience of art, because it invites us to linger, to participate and be present. As in play, however, so too in art and in festival: whoever participates in the presentation, whoever plays together with (*mitspielt*) and celebrates the event, is changed, transformed, and raised from his or her subjectivity to a higher reality, the reality of a nearly "sacral" commonality that seizes everyone (*TM* 124/*GW*1 129).

9. "That's it!" Art and Its Truth

Lingering with the work of art, for Gadamer, has a great significance that goes beyond aesthetic experience itself. Yet what does it mean to linger? Mere amusement, in the sense of entertainment, is quite different from lingering, which appears to be closer to contemplation. Already in *Truth and Method*, Gadamer brings the Greek word *theoría* into connection with the sacral communion of festival and art (*TM* 124/*GW*1 129). *Theoría* here means not being merely spectators but rather participating in a festive act and being entirely immersed in it.[18] "Theoria is a true participation, not something active but something passive [*páthos*], namely being totally involved in and carried away by what one sees" (*TM* 124–125/*GW*1 130). The *théoros*, who is present at and participates in the ritual of the festival, is outside of himself. This being outside of himself, however, is nothing other than that self-forgetfulness which results when one is entirely swept away and taken in by something. "In fact, being outside oneself is the positive possibility of being wholly with something else" (*TM* 126/*GW*1 131). Thus the state of being there alongside (*dabeisein*) requires devoting one's attention to the matter at hand, and corresponds to a continuity with oneself (*TM* 125–126/*GW*1 130). Already through culture, one learns to forget one's own immediate interests.[19] Thus, beyond the aesthetic experience, it is in such a way that the hermeneutic approach to oneself and toward others comes to be characterized.[20]

Yet lingering as waiting and attentiveness has a further meaning for Gadamer, which comes to light in the important essay from 1992, "The Artwork in Word and Image: 'So True, So Full of Being!'" (*GR* 192–224) ("*Wort und Bild—'so wahr, so seiend,'*" *GW*8 373–399). This essay marks the final stage of Gadamer's aesthetic thought. Whoever is swept away, whoever participates, for example in worship, enables the divine to "come forth" (*GR* 212/*GW*8 389). Lingering is associated here with the emergence of the divine in the case of worship, and with the "emergence" of truth in the case of art. To clarify this association Gadamer refers especially to Plato's *Philebus,* in which becoming is interpreted as a coming into Being that leaves something in Being of its having become. "Being emerges from becoming" (*GR* 209/*GW8* 386).[21] From this coming into Being Aristotle in his *Physics* makes the transition to the Being of becoming, and in that context introduces the concept of *enérgeia.* This concept suggests "contemporaneity," which characterizes the temporal structure of those activities that have no goal beyond themselves, like seeing and having seen, observing and having observed. At the same time, this Being also characterizes the lingering that is a kind of being-present in which we are immersed and absorbed. Aristotle mentions life as an example, and Gadamer returns to this example. To linger in this sense is another way of saying "that one 'is alive'" (*GR* 211/*GW8,* 387).[22]

Yet what happens if one accepts the invitation of art and lingers over the image or the word? To linger does not mean to achieve something, to do this or that, but to be completely absorbed, so as to let the work of art emerge—as if it were a making (*GR* 211/*GW8* 389). Such an *emergence* distinguishes the experience of art. "We are there—and at the end the impression grows on us: 'That's right!'" (*GR* 211/*GW8* 388). We say, "That's it," or "That's right," to the emergence of art, to the "shining forth" of the beautiful, which has the perfection of the starry skies above.

The truth of art is thus not only that of *alétheia.* In contrast to Heidegger, the truth of the artwork for Gadamer does not so much occur in the ontological entwinement of unconcealment and concealment. The truth of art is not only the unconcealment of something that emerges from concealment, but rather, and above all, this emergence itself (*GR* 211/*GW8* 388).[23] Even if the work is always the same, it emerges differently in every encounter (*GR* 214/*GW* 8 390). It is in this differing emergence that each work exists as true. For those who experience it, it has neither the ontological status of a created object nor the ontological status of a reproduction. It happens only in the fulfillment of its emergence. It would be difficult to imagine this emergence other than as an encounter, or better, with Gadamer, as a *dialogue.*

It is necessary at this point to question the distinction between word and image. Neither here nor elsewhere does Gadamer grasp this distinction in a theoretical manner. Yet the proximity to poetry and *poíesis* indicates that writing poetry, too, no less than painting or sculpting, is a kind of making. In these latter cases, to be sure, the making is a "real making," because material, for example, colors or stones, is needed for production. In the case of poetry, by contrast, it is "almost more than making," because poetry enables entire worlds to arise from the lightness of breath and the miracle of memory (*GR* 201/*GW8* 378). Here, on the strength of the ontological status of the word, Not-Being becomes Being.

10. The Transcendence of the Beautiful

Gadamer evokes religious overtones when he describes the majesty or solemnity of art, the way in which art "emerges" like the divine, the event that resembles that of worship, the contemporaneity that distinguishes it and the ecstatic immersion of those who are swept away by it, as well as the sacred communion that art founds. This correspondence is obviously no coincidence. In several essays from different periods, which are gathered together in volume 8 of his *Collected Works* under the title *The Transcendence of the Beautiful,* Gadamer explicitly insists on the proximity between art and religion—indeed, even on the *religious dimension of art.*

This religious dimension can be traced back to myth. But what is myth? The concept of *mythos* from antiquity appears to be indissolubly linked to the divine, even if *mythos* occurs only in narration. The myth is what is said, the saga that must be taken as it is because it allows no other possibility of experience. It is content from tradition that can only be believed.[24] In the 1981 essay "Mythology and Revelatory Religion" ("Mythologie und Offenbarungsreligion"), Gadamer distances himself from Bultmann who, in the context of "demythologization," which he applies to the biblical tradition, sees myth as the polar opposite of reason, something that can be no longer believed. Yet for Gadamer, it is precisely in relation to *logos* that myth becomes relevant. In this context he turns above all to the work of Max Weber (1864–1920), and especially to his famous thesis on the "demystification of the world," which was developed in his 1919 work, *Science as Vocation.* The demystified world for Weber is the world that no longer believes in magic; indeed it believes in nothing outside of science. It is the world of the Enlightenment and of scientific atheism, which so rationalizes life that it excludes everything from discussion that cannot be verified by method. Myth is seen here in opposition to the *logos* of reason. "Demystification," according to Weber, would be the result of a universal law development. This development is summarized in the title of a work by Wilhelm Nestle from 1940, called *From Myth to Logos (Vom Mythos zum Logos).* For Gadamer, it is a matter of revising this paradigm. Far from a universal law of development, it is rather a "historical fact," to which the secularization produced by Christianity contributed, by destroying the worldview dominated by myth and pagan gods:

> From myth to *logos,* the de-mystification of reality would only be the single clear direction of history if demystified reason were certain of itself and realized itself with absolute determination. What we see, however, is the actual dependence of reason on a superior economic, social and state-supported power. The idea of absolute reason is an illusion." (*GW8* 167)

The paradigm, "from myth to logos," arises from the opposition of myth to reason and from reason's claim to absoluteness. Reason tries to bring myth back under its rule or to diminish it, which means to overcome or even to extinguish it. Yet precisely because reason is not absolute, but real and historical, it fails to abolish myth or other nonscientific experiences of truth, which may have been driven to the margins of our world, but which still bear witness to the limits of reason. Gadamer inquires into the consequences of this opposition, especially in light of the fruitful bond between myth and *logos* in Greek culture, whose highest expression is to be found in the Platonic dialogues.[25] What remains from this culture is the word *mýthos* itself, which points to a realm "beyond" knowledge and science (*GW8* 170). It is this very "beyond" that is denied today. The current situation is quite different from the one described by Weber, who still recognized the limits of science. This situation is singular and unprecedented because access to a beyond is considered closed off for the first time. In its planetary extension, science leaves no room for the beyond. Similarly, the atheism of indifference no longer recognizes the religious question. Is this the end of an illusion?—Gadamer asks. Or should we not consider the rejection of a *beyond* as an illusion?

The more the beyond is denied, the more strength it gains, in the process not only revealing the impossibility that reason could occupy all areas of life, but also pointing to the possibility of a "more reasonable" reason, which, proceeding from the experiences of the beyond, both in art and in religion, could understand itself better (*GW8* 168). The essential proximity of religion and art can be seen in the beyond of transcendence. The aesthetic and religious experience awaken us from an ontic sleep, and point us toward Being. The proximity between them is such that, even when religion seems to disappear, art rushes in to fuse with myth: in this way "the poetic experience of the world sees mythically" (*GW8* 168). It is no coincidence that Gadamer mentions Rilke's angel in this context. In another passage, too, this figure indicates for him the movement of transcendence, which is so indispensable for life.[26] The beauty of art is also crucial for life since, like the sacred in its truth, it is simply *there*. "The beautiful is something about which it is never appropriate to ask what it is 'for'" (*GR* 203/*GW8* 380). At the same time, the beautiful is always the evocation of a possible sacred order (*RB* 15/*GW8* 123).

11. Literature and Reading

The final art form that Gadamer considers in *Truth and Method* is literature, to which only five pages are dedicated (*TM* 159–164/*GW1* 165–169). This is particularly surprising considering the role literature will later play in Gadamer's thought, which ultimately confirms the importance of literature more fully. Volumes 8 and 9 of the *Collected Works* gather together the numerous essays in which hermeneutics is applied, not only and not so much to the pictorial arts, but especially to literature and poetry. From Goethe to Hölderlin, from Rilke to George, and the lyric poetry of the twentieth century, above all the works of Hilde Domin (1909–2006) and Paul Celan (1920–70), poetic hermeneutics acquires a significance that goes far beyond the act of application and has an effect on fundamental philosophical concepts, including the conception of language itself.

The role of literature in his later work makes it all the more important to ask why literature is dealt with so briefly in *Truth and Method*. Clearly Gadamer thought that this case, too, would verify his theory of presentation. Yet it is just as evident that the milieu of 1960 was not yet ready for such an argument, and thus Gadamer clashed with a conception whereby the literary work is a closed form, a form that exists only in the ideality of the text. Presentation with an ontological import seemed to be excluded from literature (*TM* 160/*GW*1 165). After all, what would constitute presentation? Gadamer's answer is that presentation in literature lies in reading. Reading a book is "an event in which the read content brings itself to presentation" (*TM* 160–161/*GW*1 166). From today's perspective it seems nearly self-evident that the literary work realizes itself in reading, which in some ways contributes to the meaning of the text. But this is the case only because philosophical hermeneutics has had considerable influence on literary criticism, in particular on Jauss and Iser.[27]

Perhaps influenced by these developments, Gadamer paid more and more attention to *reading,* since for him it characterizes the event in which the work, including the literary work, but also the musical, pictorial, and even architectural works, realize themselves. Consequently, what does reading mean? It means to decipher the ciphers of the work, to give them back a voice and hence a life. Especially if we consider the sense of reading as "gathering," or "gathering oneself" in listening, which is part of the German word "Lesen," then reading means giving voice to, that is, letting speak. "In this way reading is a genuine universal: All our experience is reading" (*GW*8 178). The expansion of this concept for Gadamer connects with the recognition of the universality of language: for the later Gadamer, reading, that is, *giving voice,* expands until it coincides with hermeneutics itself.[28]

12. Aesthetics and Hermeneutics

It is therefore unavoidable that the question of the relation between aesthetics and hermeneutics should be asked in *Truth and Method.* Yet what kinds of aesthetics, and what of hermeneutics? It can no longer be a matter of aesthetics as aesthetic consciousness conceives it. Truth is at stake in art. And truth can not be dominated, controlled, or possessed, since it emerges only in an encounter: in the encounter with art that, because it speaks to us and invites us to linger, demands to be understood. It also becomes clear that the encounter with art is for each of us an encounter with ourselves. The understanding of this truth always implies an understanding of oneself, and from this event we constantly emerge transformed. With this transformation the *transition from aesthetics to hermeneutics* is completed. This transition shows itself as necessary in the light of art and its truth, which at the same time brings a critical revision of aesthetics and an expansion of its range. "*Aesthetics has to be absorbed into hermeneutics*" (*TM* 164/*GW*1 170). But hermeneutics, too, must for its part broaden its horizon in order to do justice to the experience of art. As Gadamer emphasizes in his essay "Aesthetics and Hermeneutics," it is crucial that hermeneutics, which had acquired a certain relevance in the human sciences but nevertheless remained marginal and limited in its impact, should now conceive of itself differently and in a new way, on the basis of the central question of understanding (*PH* 95–104/*GW*8 1–8).

Notes

1. See João Manuel Duque, *Die Kunst als Ort immanenter Transzendenz. Zu einer fundamental-theologischen Rezeption der Kunstphilosophie Hans-Georg Gadamers* (Frankfurt/M: Knecht, 1997).

2. See Guy Deniau, "Bild und Sprache. Über die Seinsvalenz des Bildes. Ästhetische und hermeneutische Folgerungen (*GW1*, 139–176)," in *Hans-Georg Gadamer. Wahrheit und Methode*, ed. Günter Figal (Berlin: Akademie Verlag, 2007), 59–74.

3. See in this volume chapter 8, part 11.

4. Now in Gadamer, "Die Wahrheit des Kunstwerks (1960)," in *Neuere Philosophie I—Hegel, Husserl, Heidegger, GW3* 249–261; "The Truth of the Work of Art," in *Heidegger's Ways*, trans. John W. Stanley (Albany: SUNY Press, 1994), 95–109.

5. See in this volume chapter 4, part 5, and chapter 9, part 2.

6. See in this volume, chapter 6, part 5.

7. Plato, *Phaedo*, 72e–73b; Plato, 63–64.

8. See Valerio Verra, "L'esthetique hégélienne dans l'interpretation de Hans-Georg Gadamer," in Pierre Osmo, ed., *Autour de Hegel* (Paris: Vrin, 2000), 417–427.

9. See chapter 3, part 8, in this volume.

10. Aristotle, *Poetics*, 1449b 24–28.

11. On the multiple connotations of "presentation" in Gadamer, see Jean Grondin, "L'art comme présentation chez Hans-Georg Gadamer. Portée et limites d'un concept," *Études Germaniques (Hans-Georg Gadamer—Esthétique et herméneutique)*, ed. Frank Delannoy, 62 (2007): 337–350.

12. See on this Gottfried Boehm, "Zuwachs an Sein. Hermeneutische Reflexion und bildende Kunst," in Hans-Georg Gadamer, ed., *Die Moderne und die Grenze der Vergegenständlichung* (Munich: Klüser, 1996), 95–125; see also Boehm, "Das Bild und die hermeneutische Reflexion," in Günter Figal and Hans-Helmuth Gander, eds., *Dimensionen des Hermeneutischen. Heidegger und Gadaner* (Frankfurt a/M: Klostermann, 2005), 23–35 at 29–30.

13. On the portrait as an "iconic logos," see Gottfried Boehm, *Bildnis und Individuum. Über den Ursprung der Porträtmalerei in der italienischen Renaissance* (Munich: Prestel, 1985).

14. Gadamer, "Über das Lesen von Bauten und Bildern" (1979), *GW8*, 331–338 at 334.

15. For more recent reflections on this theme see Béla Bacsó, "Die 'Wiederholung' als ästhetische und existenzielle Kategorie," in *Die Unvermeidbarkeit des Irrtums. Essays zur Hermeneutik* (Cuxhaven/Dartford: Junghans, 1997), 57–66.

16. See in this volume, chapter 10, part 4.

17. On this distinction, see Gadamer, "Concerning Empty and Ful-filled Time," trans. R. P. O'Hara, in *Martin Heidegger: In Europe and America*, ed. Edward G. Ballard and Charles E. Scott (The Hague: Martinus Nijhoff, 1973), 77–89; "Über leere und erfüllte Zeit" (1969), *GW4* 137–153.

18. On the question of *théoros*, see Guy Deniau, *Cognitio imaginative. La phénoménologie herméneutique de Gadamer* (Brussels: Ousia, 2002), 159–320.

19. See in this volume chapter 2, part 2.

20. See in this volume chapter 9, part 5.

21. See Plato, *Philebus*, 27b 8.

22. For a discussion of art as *enérgeia*, see Dieter Teichert, "Kunst als Geschehen. Gadamers anti-subjektivistische Ästhetik und Kunsttheorie," in István M. Fehér, ed., *Kunst, Hermeneutik, Philosophie* (Heidelberg: Universitätsverlag, 2003), 193–217, 211–212.

23. On Gadamer's distance from Heidegger in relation to the truth of art, see John Sallis, "The Hermeneutics of the Artwork. Die Ontologie des Kunstwerks und ihre hermeneutische Bedeutung (GW 1, 87–138)," in Günter Figal, ed., *Hans-Georg Gadamer—Wahrheit und Methode*, 45–57, 55–56.

24. Gadamer, "Mythos und Vernunft" (1954), *GW8* 163–169 at 162 and 165.

25. Gadamer, "Mythos und Logos" (1981), *GW8* 170–179 at 173.
26. See in this volume chapter 8, part 6.
27. See in this volume chapter 10, part 1. Compare on this also Joel C. Weinsheimer, *Philosophical Hermeneutics and Literary Theory* (New Haven: Yale University Press, 1991).
28. See in this volume, chapter 8, part 2.

4 On the Way to Philosophical Hermeneutics

Schleiermacher's idea of a universal hermeneutics starts from this: that the experience of the alien and the possibility of misunderstanding is universal. (*TM* 179/*GW*1 182)

What one now calls *hermeneutical philosophy* is based to a large extent on a phenomenology. (*HW* 51/*GW*3 214)

Facticity refers, after all, to the fact in its being a fact, i.e., precisely the thing back of which and behind which one cannot go. In Dilthey (as early as volume XIX of the new edition of his works) we find life characterized as such an irreducible fact. (*RHS* 24/*GW*3 422)

1. A Discipline in Retrospect

The importance of the question of understanding in the aesthetic realm requires a redefinition of hermeneutics, or a critical reconstruction of its history, which in the end amounts to its actual construction. It is not an exaggeration to say that hermeneutics, in a certain sense, was *constructed* in the middle of the 1950s. Those are the years in which, while Heidegger inquires into the meaning of the word "hermeneutics" in his famous essay "A Dialogue on Language," from 1953–54, Gadamer is working on his project of a philosophical hermeneutics.[1] The discipline, which only from the seventeenth century on is called *hermeneutica,* the ancient methodical doctrine of interpretation, actually exhibits an extremely fragmented form. Especially because of this, and not simply because it is an "auxiliary discipline," and is not very visible from without, hermeneutics lacks autonomy and unity. Only on the basis of a new self-understanding, achieved through a sort of autobiography, almost an *anamnesis* of its genesis, can hermeneutics present itself as an autonomous and unified discipline. The reconstruction accomplished in retrospect, or in other words the post-construction, first constructs the discipline. Thus the history of hermeneutics brings hermeneutics into the world.[2] It is no wonder, then, that hermeneutics has been reconstructed according to the model of a linear and teleological process. Its birth act is Dilthey's short essay "The Rise of Hermeneutics," from 1900.[3] Today this essay would hardly have any resonance at all if Gadamer had not returned to it in his section on "Historical Preparation" from *Truth and Method* and had not thereby confirmed the historiographical paradigm, in light of which the genealogy of hermeneutics is usually read (*TM* 173–218/ *GW1* 177–222).

The paradigm, which is repeated in almost all subsequent reconstructions of hermeneutics and is typically understood in a singular form, can be easily summarized according to its stages. The ancient *hermeneía*, which in the Greek world was the art of saying, announcing, explaining, and translating, produced only dispersed and disconnected rules. An initial turn is represented by Martin Luther (1483–1546) who, with the principle of *sola scriptura*, "by scripture alone," defends a form of exegesis freed from all authorities. Sacred hermeneutics intertwines with secular hermeneutics, and above all with humanistic philology, which reopens critical access to the classics.[4] The second turn, which marks the transition from the "prehistory" to the actual "history" of hermeneutics, is represented by Friedrich D. E. Schleiermacher (1768–1834), who is credited with having unified hermeneutics as the universal art of understanding. If Dilthey expands this art to a methodology of the human sciences, Heidegger frees hermeneutics from method and plants it in the ground of human facticity. Finally Gadamer establishes the foundation of a philosophical hermeneutics, which makes a claim to universality.

This paradigm not only presupposes a prehistory and a history, but also distinguishes between a "classical" and a "philosophical" hermeneutics, in Heidegger's and Gadamer's sense. This is certainly contradictory: on the one hand the history of hermeneutics finds its *telos* in philosophical hermeneutics, but on the other hand the latter takes shape only through its break with classical hermeneutics. Against this background it is easy to see why Gadamer's reconstructions in *Truth and Method*—for example of Schleiermacher and Dilthey—are often deconstructions.

After criticisms were raised against him, Gadamer weakened the contrast between classical and philosophical hermeneutics.[5] Even in his later works, though, he continued to follow this same paradigm, as for example in the anthology *Seminar: Philosophische Hermeneutik*, which he published together with Gottfried Boehm, and in the article "Hermeneutik," written in 1974 for the *Historisches Wörterbuch der Philosophie.*[6]

2. The Congeniality of Understanding: Which Schleiermacher?

The dispute with classical hermeneutics begins with the reconstruction of Schleiermacher's project (*TM* 184–197/*GW1* 188–201). It is necessary to stress two important limits of the reconstruction: on the one hand it returns to the image of the Romantic philosopher already developed by Dilthey; on the other hand it does an injustice to Schleiermacher, by criticizing him as if his approach were dominated by an "aesthetic metaphysics of individuality," which would mean that he loses sight of the hermeneutic problem (*TM* 190/*GW1* 193). In short: the founder of modern hermeneutics would have—so to speak—failed to construct hermeneutics.

Such a critical reconstruction obviously supports Gadamer's strategic goal of lending a sharper profile to his own turn. He has two ways of reaching this goal: either make Schleiermacher into a kind of anti-Hegel, that is a philosopher of empathy, of sympathy, and of psycho-genial understanding, from whom he must take a distance; or recognize the importance Schleiermacher attributes to the grammatical aspect of interpretation, in order to point out the balanced, insightful way he describes the relationship of interdependence between language and the individual. In this last case Gadamer may have found a model for the third part of *Truth and Method,* where he focuses on language. Indeed, an indirect recognition of this is Schleiermacher's sentence that Gadamer takes as a motto for his chapter on language: "Everything presupposed in hermeneutics is but language" (*TM* 381/*GW1* 187). Yet Gadamer follows the first way, and this has brought him numerous criticisms.[7] In his defense it can be said that Gadamer, despite his often repeated solidarity with Romantic hermeneutics, uncovers the aporias that arise in both Schleiermacher and Dilthey from their overly methodical ways of approaching the hermeneutic question. One should also not forget that, without Gadamer's reconstructions, hardly anyone today would be speaking about Schleiermacher's or Dilthey's hermeneutics. Schleiermacher would perhaps be known only as an important Protestant theologian, famous in Germany for his Plato translations; Dilthey would probably be recognized for his studies on the history of philosophy and the methodology of the human sciences. Though often unjustly critical, Gadamer's reconstructions have in both cases been rediscoveries.

In his interpretation of Schleiermacher, Gadamer connects hermeneutics with aesthetics, and not with dialectics and ethics. Hence he privileges the "psychological" over the "grammatical" interpretation, even though the one appears close to the other in Schleiermacher. How does Schleiermacher characterize the hermeneutic act? To him it seems possible to bridge the gulf between the author and the interpreter psychologically, "by *feeling*, by an immediate, sympathetic, and con-genial understanding" (*TM* 191/*GW1* 194). Understanding for Schleiermacher involves the imitation of an original production. Thus it became important for him to return to that "germinal decision" at the "vital moment of conception," to that living and absolutely individual moment from which the genial product emerged (*TM* 187/*GW1* 191). The imitation should also be genial and creative, like the creation itself. For Gadamer's Schleiermacher, understanding is an art no less than speech. In this sense "hermeneutics ... is for Schleiermacher the inverse of an act of speech, the reconstruction of a construction" (*TM* 188–189/*GW1* 192). A text or speech is not understood on the basis of its "subject matter but as an aesthetic construct, as a work of art or 'artistic thought'" by a singular individuality (*TM* 187/*GW1* 191). From this there arises the *divinatory* character of hermeneutics. The divinatory act of understanding depends for Gadamer on the immediacy of feeling—though for Schleiermacher, interpretation depends on a comparative procedure even prior to the divinatory one.[8]

This psychologization of Schleiermacher's hermeneutics coincides with its aestheticization, since what is understood is actually the *expression* of an *individuality* that is always free of rules.[9] By casting the shadow of the Kantian aesthetics of genius on this hermeneutics, it is easy for Gadamer to charge it with subjectivism. On this reading, Schleiermacher would focus our attention on the expression of the individual subject, namely the author.

It would probably have been much more fruitful to stress another feature of Schleiermacher's hermeneutics, where his distance from philosophical hermeneutics appears more sharply. Gadamer himself points to this feature at the beginning of his reconstruction, but drops the issue and refers to the context in which he develops his own hermeneutics (*TM* 184–190/*GW1* 188–189). Schleiermacher marks a turn in the history of hermeneutics because he poses the question of understanding in its full radicality. Following the lead of Friedrich Schlegel (1772–1829) and Humboldt, understanding is no longer assumed to be evident, since it is compromised from the outset by misunderstanding and nonunderstanding. One does not always and everywhere understand, and misunderstanding occurs not only in borderline cases or in the obscure passages to which hermeneutics is applied. On the contrary, Schleiermacher says that "misunderstanding arises on its own and understanding must be wanted and sought after at every point."[10] Misunderstanding, which may seem inevitable in the interpretation of sacred texts written in strange, old, and difficult languages, is actually only a symptom of the much more comprehensive misunderstanding that occurs repeatedly in the conversations of everyday life. In this reversal of our conventional perspective, which unifies the specific practices of hermeneutics with the more general practices of understanding, Schleiermacher also sheds light on the universality of hermeneutics. Ever since Schleiermacher, misunderstanding and nonunderstanding, even if conceived in different forms, have remained in the constellation of hermeneutics. Understanding will never again be taken for granted. Schleiermacher begins with misunderstanding and nonunderstanding, and he sees the task of hermeneutics in the transition to understanding. But there will never be a point at which the transition will be complete and the understanding will be perfect. The hermeneutic task is infinite. There is neither empathy nor sympathetic understanding in Schleiermacher.[11] Even if there were they would not be the goal of interpretation, for interpretation maintains its critical vigilance in order to go beyond every form of identification. Hence one must "understand the discourse just as well, at first, and then even better . . . than its creator."[12] With these words Schleiermacher reformulates an old hermeneutic principle—for Gadamer, "the whole history of modern hermeneutics can be read" in this formulation—which, considered closely, can be traced back to Kant (*TM* 192/*GW1* 195). In the *Critique of Pure Reason* Kant writes, in regard to Plato's "idea," that it "is not unusual at all" to understand an author better "than he understood himself, because he had not determined his concept sufficiently."[13] Schleiermacher thinks, too, that understanding is a productive reconstruction that can say better what the author had said—if only because it is being said again. To understand better, for Schleiermacher, already points to understanding differently.[14]

In the "Afterword" to the third edition of *Truth and Method*, Gadamer acknowledges "a certain one-sidedness" in his reconstruction of hermeneutics; yet he still insists that Schleiermacher's most characteristic contribution is his psychological interpretation (*TM* 564/*GW*2 462). Even later, in his "Attempt at Self-Criticism" from 1985, which leads to a debate with Manfred Frank (b. 1945), he emphasizes again the relevance of the psychological view though he also sees that he had neglected aesthetics and dialectics in his account (RPJ 43–44/*GW*2 14–15). Gadamer refers to his important text from 1968, "The Problem of Language for Schleiermacher," in which he corrects his own position by more sharply outlining the process of mediation, which is never dialectically concluded between language and the speaker.[15]

3. The Sickness of Historical Consciousness and Dilthey's Aporias

Hermeneutics after Schleiermacher was expanded by the "Historical School," whose greatest representatives were the philologist August W. Boeck (1785–1867) and the historians Leopold von Ranke (1795–1886) and Gustav Droysen (1808–84). For Gadamer, who had already shown the limits of aesthetic consciousness, the debate with the Historical School and subsequently with Dilthey offered the opportunity to explore the question of historical consciousness, which had already occupied him in the years before *Truth and Method*. If history has a goal and an end, whether in divine or human completion, then its course runs consistently in a positive direction. This metaphysical-Christian conception has also been secularized in the Enlightenment belief in progress and the Hegelian philosophy of history. Once the metaphysical background crumbles, however, the question of historical consciousness appears in its abyssal gravity. There is neither a goal nor an end to history; there are only the finite purposes of mankind, which recognizes its own finitude in its historicity—this is the tragic truth of historical consciousness. In a few works from the 1940s, particularly in the essay on "The Limits of Historical Reason" from 1949, Gadamer lets Nietzsche unmask a "historical sickness,"[16] which marks the emergence of European nihilism. Has historical consciousness taught the modern human to view the world with a hundred eyes, or has it dissolved the world into the vertigo of perspectives? And what does the world of history, in all of its infinite variety, mean to the human who now sees herself or himself as historical and finite? This question had already been asked by Herder in his text on "Another Philosophy of History for the Education of Humanity," from 1744. The ironic title, according to Gadamer, shows his intention to take a distance from every philosophy of history that is guided by the pretension of the enlightened man to become a mirror of the past.[17] Since all progress involves a loss at the same time, the idea of perfectibility wanes. Only a few years later, Humboldt will warn that being in time is merely a creating and a declining. Not at all linear, the course of history appears as a chaotic wavering, in which there is neither an overcoming on the way to harmonic perfection nor an absolute synthesis. History has "no fixed goal that can be discovered outside itself" (*TM* 203/*GW1* 207).

How should one orient oneself in this chaos? How should one still find meaning in the drama of glittering victories and sad ruins? The Historical School tries to answer these questions by contrasting Herder's and Humboldt's conceptions to Hegel's philosophy of history, since Hegel's model, with its a priori teleology, does violence to historical facts. It is hence no wonder that *hermeneutics* becomes the path of orientation for *historicism*. But historicism is, according to Gadamer, an aestheticizing hermeneutics that takes on positivistic connotations, not only because it commits to facts, but also because it seeks objectivity. The criterion of interpretation that it applies is the relation between the parts and the whole. In secret it postulates that history is like a great book that must be deciphered. Yet only the text of the philologists encompasses a self-enclosed whole. By contrast, "the book of history is a fragment that, so far as any particular present time is concerned, breaks off in the dark" (*TM* 199/*GW1* 203). How could the interpreter have the entire book before them without distorting their own historicity? And how could the interpreter, on the other hand, renounce the whole that is ultimately the whole of world history?

These are the two aporias that the Historical School cannot overcome. The great question of world history must therefore remain open. Nevertheless it becomes clear that it may not be a question of whether and how humans understand history, but whether and how humans see themselves historically, each time modifying one's understanding of history.

What becomes decisive at this point for Gadamer is the confrontation with Dilthey, though Gadamer's interpretation is itself debatable.[18] It is important from the outset to distinguish Gadamer's reading from Heidegger's reading of Dilthey. Whereas Heidegger breaks with the tradition of the human sciences and also with Dilthey, Gadamer prefers dialogue. Gadamer's works from the 1950s bears witness to this, as well as the lectures he gave in Leuven in 1957.[19] It is no accident that the confrontation with Dilthey opens the text of *Truth and Method*.[20] It is just as true, however, that over the following decades the figure of Dilthey becomes increasingly less present in Gadamer's work. Gadamer did not devote many essays to him: apart from the first, which he had written in 1933 for Dilthey's one-hundredth birthday, all the others go back to the 1980s and are mostly reworkings of the chapter in *Truth and Method*.[21] An exception is the essay on "Hermeneutics and the Dilthey School" from 1991, in which Gadamer answers the criticisms from Frithjof Rodi and partially modifies his own interpretation.[22]

The word "hermeneutics" appears very rarely in Dilthey's writings. From the outset it is his aim to free himself from the impasses that had stranded the Historical School, halfway "between philosophy and experience" (*TM* 219/*GW1* 222). Dilthey's era is marked by the collision between Romantic culture and the rise of positivism. The rejection of Hegel's philosophy enabled a return to Kant. Just as Kant had grounded the natural sciences in the *Critique of Pure Reason,* Dilthey plans to ground the human sciences through a "Critique of Historical Reason"—a promising formulation as a possible title for a book that, however, he was unable to publish because, according to Gadamer, he was never able to reconcile the particular aporias that cripple his thought.[23]

The question that occupies Dilthey is one of historical consciousness in the form it takes after Nietzsche. If every person, every epoch, and every manifestation of spirit is to be conceived historically, how is it possible to guarantee a universally valid knowledge of history? To give universal validity to historical knowledge means to measure history in terms of scientific knowledge. Dilthey's intention—already in the *Introduction to the Human Sciences* from 1883—is to use hermeneutics to raise the human sciences to the status of the natural sciences. Though he wavers between a unified and a complementary model, Dilthey ultimately tends toward the latter, which reserves the hermeneutic approach for the humanities. Gadamer's critical interpretation begins at this point. He shows how Dilthey's oscillation derives from an inner contradiction in his thought: the contradiction between positivism and Romanticism, between the methodological claim to objective knowledge and the Romantic insight into the historicity of thought. If we are historical beings, how could we ever reach a universal knowledge that reaches beyond our historicity? Isn't any fixed certainty, the *fundamentum inconcussum* that Dilthey wants to reclaim for the human sciences, already compromised by their fundamental historicity? And isn't there a danger in projecting the model of the natural sciences onto the human sciences?

In contrast to the Neo-Kantians, Dilthey distinguishes clearly between historical knowledge and knowledge in the natural sciences. For this he returns to the principle of *verum-factum,* or truth and fact, which Vico had applied to the "civilized world": the human being recognizes as true only what he has made in history, not in nature. In such a way the possibility of historical knowledge is justified (*TM* 222/*GW1* 226). Just like in Romantic hermeneutics, the solution lies in the congeniality of the subject and the object. For Gadamer, however, this is precisely the problem. How can the transition from the individual historical experience to the general experience of history be explained? Doesn't Vico's principle simply transpose an experience from the world of art onto the world of history? Does it make sense, with regard to the human conditions within the course of history, to speak of a "making"? These questions reveal one of Gadamer's most important objections to Dilthey. Historical consciousness is, for Dilthey, consciousness conditioned *by* history, and on the other hand it is also consciousness *of* history, the consciousness of the historical character of everything human. This consciousness distinguishes our epoch from all preceding ones. Historical consciousness would amount to a remedy for its own, self-created, ills. Since we are conscious of our historicity, we should be able to take that distance which allows us to know it an objective way. Consciousness crosses over into knowledge, self-consciousness into wisdom. But with this transition it is taken as self-evident that consciousness is "*a mode of self-knowledge*" in the Cartesian sense (*TM* 235/*GW1* 239). In short, Dilthey's historical consciousness deceives itself—no differently than aesthetic consciousness—about its own possibilities. In contrast to this historical consciousness, which is confident of its ability to reach a transparent knowledge of itself, Gadamer proposes a "historically effected consciousness."[24]

Yet Dilthey made several attempts to anchor consciousness to its historical being. To do this he introduced the concept of "life," which he advanced as the cornerstone of his hermeneutics. Even before one realizes it, he or she already understands the lifeworld by articulating connections or structures of sense that can, as a result, be understood again. The process by which sense arises is life articulating itself: "Here life grasps life."[25] Or, in Gadamer's words: "Life interprets itself. Life itself has a hermeneutical structure" (TM 226/GW1 230). Understanding represents the opposite process to that in which the lived experience expresses itself in understandable figures of sense. Life, by articulating itself, returns to itself in reflection; this becomes the hermeneutic principle that would clarify the transition from individual to general experience, ultimately from psychology to hermeneutics. It should then be able to specify the way the individual is bound to the objective spirit (TM 224/GW1 228–229). On the one hand the life of each individual has the character of historicity; on the other hand history is nothing other than life viewed from the standpoint of all humanity. Life proves to be the a priori that guarantees the possibility of understanding all individual and historical manifestations, whereby history structures itself as a text. Through hermeneutic circularity, which moves from the whole to the parts and from the parts to the whole, always broader connections in the direction of universal history are achieved with a movement that can never complete itself in the absolute (TM 236/GW1 240–241).

Nevertheless for Gadamer this concept of life, in which the moment of self-reflection is sharply accentuated, is still burdened with Cartesian presuppositions—beginning with the proximity of methodical doubt to the doubt that torments human existence. Dilthey does not see that the search for certainty in science, and in life, goes two very different ways. The doubt of the first, Cartesian kind, doubts in order to reach an unassailable certainty; the latter, existential doubt, doubts the very possibility of such certainty. Far from being an extension of existential doubt, the methodological doubt of scientific reflection is "a movement that is directed against life" (TM 238/GW1 242). Here Gadamer polarizes the opposition between science and life in Dilthey: scientific knowledge offers certainty in the sense of protection against the "incomprehensibility" of life (TM 239/GW1 244). But the certainty that life seeks is not the certainty that can be derived from a final principle; more than a foundation, life seeks forms of belonging and community. The program of a philosophy of life remains active, though it must be freed from the epistemological impasse in which Dilthey remains entangled. This liberation happens through phenomenology.

4. Husserl and the Hermeneutic Turn in Phenomenology

Contrary to the conventional view, the relation between Gadamer and Husserl should not be underestimated. In the first place, their relation should be valued because of the theoretical relevance that phenomenology obviously had for hermeneutics, which

Gadamer frequently emphasized. His encounter with Husserl was not decided in the few months that he spent in Freiburg in 1923. In addition to the passages in *Truth and Method,* Gadamer wrote two essays on Husserl in the 1970s: "The Science of the Life-World" in 1972, and "On the Relevance of Husserl's Phenomenology," in 1974 (*TM* 242–254/*GW1* 246–258).[26] Particularly important, however, is the essay already published in 1963, "The Phenomenological Movement," in which he took stock of the debate over phenomenology and at the same time clarified and defined his own position (*PH* 130–181/*GW3* 105–146).

What connects Gadamer to Husserl, and what separates them? Husserl's maxim "Back to the things themselves!" had a liberating function. With these words he showed philosophy the way to escape the impasse of formulas and theories, precisely by returning to the "things themselves."[27] In short, for Husserl philosophy should no longer merely occupy itself with scientific theories, establishing itself as "meta-theory" or a secondary science. Nor should philosophy limit itself to the history of philosophy. Rather, Husserl recommended a return to "things themselves," in order to begin philosophizing from that point. Erudition has little to do with the practice of philosophy. What is necessary is philosophical conversion, a suspension or *epoché* of the natural attitude. This should be conceived as a phenomenological "reduction," which would provide an *"entirely new point of departure"* for philosophy.[28] The first effect of this approach, which had an immediate fascination for both Heidegger and Gadamer, is the liberation from the technical vocabulary of Neo-Kantianism and more generally the paradigm of scientific objectivism. The hermeneutic significance of Husserl's appeal should not be unacknowledged. Philosophy should leave behind all theories that are not grounded on a visible phenomenality shared by all, and proceed from things as they make themselves known through "intuition." This resonates as a call to philosophy to be vigilant against all metaphysical constructions and to hold fast to what is given through intuition—a call that points from the beginning to the possibility of overcoming metaphysics. The "things" Husserl wants to return to are not things in themselves, independent from consciousness; rather they are only given thanks to the intentionality of consciousness. "Intentionality" in this sense means that every object has the way of being of consciousness. It is intentionality that allows the real to appear to consciousness, and it can therefore be understood as a hermeneutic category: there is no objectivity without the constitutive intentionality of consciousness. But it is Husserl's great merit to have seen that this "constitution" is not simply to be attributed to the accomplishment of a transcendental subject. Considered more closely, the subject contributes to the constitution of sense that arises together with the subject itself—without ever being fully able to control this sense. The constitution is the "movement of reconstruction" of intentionality, which unfolds in a horizon of sense that always lies beyond the limits of the subject (*PH* 165/*GW3* 135).

In *Truth and Method,* Gadamer returns to this concept of "horizon." By inscribing itself into a horizon, intentionality is destined to move as the horizon moves.[29] On the other hand, Gadamer also refers to the implicit horizon of understanding, which emerges from the subterranean temporality of conscious life that Husserl had spoken of as "absolute historicity"—an expression Gadamer mentions twice (*TM* 243, 255/*GW1* 248, 259). Even more important for Gadamer is the "lifeworld." Gadamer repeatedly returns to this concept, in order to emphasize its productivity and its "astounding resonance" in the philosophy of the twentieth century (*PH* 151/*GW3* 123). The "lifeworld" is an expression that Husserl had probably coined in contrast to the "world of science."[30] Intentionality itself needs the lifeworld, because the *ego* is no longer the source of the constitution of sense and so it becomes necessary to return to another source, indeed to the anonymous but intersubjectively understood source of the *lifeworld*.

Yet for Gadamer, Husserl was not radical enough. In the lifeworld thus conceived, it appears as if one might recognize the finitude of the ego. But Husserl still seeks to ground the lifeworld by tracing it back to the transcendental subjectivity of "the Ur-Ich ('the primal I')" (*TM* 248/*GW1* 252). This means that, in spite of everything, Husserl remains caught in a Cartesian conception of philosophy, which as an apodictic science aims for an ultimate foundation (*letzte Begründung*).

This is the point where hermeneutics is furthest from phenomenology, or where the *hermeneutic turn* takes place within phenomenology. In phenomenology—as in large parts of the philosophical tradition—language has played only a secondary role; though it is precisely with language that a critique of Neo-Kantianism could have developed. Although it marked a turn from the "facts" of science to the lifeworld, phenomenology did not go further, since it did not recognize the role of language in the lifeworld. Phenomenology never relinquished the idea of an ultimate foundation. But one motive points to another: the idea of a ultimate foundation leads to forgetting language, whereas language puts all foundations into question (*GW8* 401, 418, 435). On the contrary, hermeneutics tries to find a place in philosophy for the mysterious proximity of language and reason. The *hermeneutic turn in phenomenology* is a *turn toward language*.

5. The Hermeneutics of Facticity: Beyond Heidegger

It was only with the turn Heidegger took in phenomenology that the ontological presuppositions of any ultimate foundation were first uncovered. Heidegger's work makes clear that the *fundamentum inconcussum* is actually, if considered more closely, *concussum*, namely temporal and finite. It is "*the whole idea of grounding itself*" that "*underwent a total reversal*" (*TM* 257/*GW1* 261). Gadamer's hermeneutics in *Truth and Method* begins after a long section dedicated to Heidegger's project (*TM* 254–264/*GW1* 258–269). In spite of all the inspiration from Schleiermacher, from Dilthey, and finally also from Husserl, it was after all Heidegger who provided the decisive impulse for Gadamer's philosophical hermeneutics.

Yet which Heidegger? This question is of considerable importance. With the answer one can not only clarify the section devoted to Heidegger in *Truth and Method*, but also illuminate Gadamer's entire interpretation of Heidegger. To begin it must be emphasized that the Heidegger to whom Gadamer refers is not the one from *Being and Time*, but rather the one from the *Hermeneutics of Facticity*. This is the "early" Heidegger, whose lectures Gadamer had heard in the 1920s—even though, according to Gadamer, it is misleading to speak of the "early" and the "late" Heidegger, because it risks obscuring the continuity of his thought. This continuity should be seen precisely between the hermeneutics of facticity and the "turn" of the late Heidegger; it was simply interrupted by the interlude of *Being and Time* (*TM* 257–258/*GW*1 261–262). Later, in an essay from 1986 with the telling title "Martin Heidegger's One Path," Gadamer will speak of "the turning before the turning" in order to underline Heidegger's coherent development (*RHS* 26/*GW*3 423). Gadamer saw, from very early on, a unity in Heidegger's path and was able to stress such a continuity in both his interpretation of Heidegger and his own philosophy. Since he continued to speak of hermeneutics, even when other interpreters had long ceased to do so, Gadamer was able to rejoin the end of Heidegger's path back to its beginnings.

Of course such a claim is really possible only today, on the basis of Heidegger's more recently published manuscripts from his lectures and seminars. In 1960, at the time of *Truth and Method*, the Heidegger of *Being and Time* was still seen as the early Heidegger, from whom the later one, the thinker of poetic thought, had distanced himself. This way of reading Heidegger's work was shared by most of his interpreters. The "hermeneutics of facticity" was for the most part unknown, though traces of it remained in Gadamer's memory, in his notes, and in Heidegger's manuscripts. After these had been published, Gadamer had not only the texts but also the necessary distance to be able to write. The collection *Heidegger's Ways* from 1983 was the result. In addition to these essays, which had been revised for publication, more than ten later ones appeared. Seven of these are in the tenth volume of the *Collected Works*, which was published in 1995.

It is clear that if Heidegger's lectures had been published earlier, the section in *Truth and Method* would have had a different content and perhaps even a different character. But when Gadamer wrote this section he could rely on only *Being and Time* to underline the significance of Heidegger's thought for hermeneutics. In order to make his argumentation more convincing, and to show the radical change made to the conception of understanding, Gadamer appeals, perhaps surprisingly, to Count von Yorck (1835–97). Yorck had become known both because of his critical letters to Dilthey and because Heidegger had reproduced a part of this correspondence in paragraph #77 of *Being and Time*. For Gadamer, Yorck becomes a key figure in overcoming the epistemological paradigm represented by Dilthey. Yorck not only points to Dilthey's aestheticism, which falls prey to an objectivist world view, but also shows that Dilthey is not aware that the interpreter belongs to what is interpreted, and that he had not understood the historicity of life, but thought of it only in a very Cartesian way (*TM* 248–254/*GW*1 255–258). Yorck's alternative model remains a bit obscure, however, as do Gadamer's own remarks. In any case, Gadamer later no longer refers to Yorck.

The concept of "belonging" first is clarified by Heidegger and then becomes decisive for hermeneutics in *Truth and Method* (*TM* 262/*GW*1 266). Yet this is only possible thanks to a completely new way of conceptualizing *understanding*. Although he did not have access to the published materials, Gadamer explicitly refers to the "hermeneutics of facticity" (*TM* 254/*GW*1 259).[31] What does the *hermeneutics of facticity* mean? At first it should be said that "facticity" does not mean an ultimate given, or a new positivity. According to Heidegger in his 1923 lecture, facticity must be understood as the ontological character of our *Dasein,* which gives itself differently than any other being; for "*Da-sein*" means to fulfill this facticity.[32] To put it differently, in this facticity that I am, what is at stake is me, what I make of myself. So why should one speak of "hermeneutics?" It is because hermeneutics, according to Heidegger, is understood as a way of gaining access to facticity.[33] Even more: *Dasein* is or it exists only insofar as it understands. Hermeneutics attributes facticity to the body and articulates it, expresses it, understands it. Without hermeneutics, there would be no facticity of *Dasein* and *Dasein* would not exist in the first place. *Facticity can only be hermeneutic.* For the first time hermeneutics dealt not only with texts, but also with existence.[34] The break Heidegger accomplishes here is radical. It means that one has no choice whether to understand or not to understand. *To exist is to understand—to understand is to exist.* Gadamer expresses the point effectively: "*Understanding is . . . the original form of the realization of Dasein*" (*TM* 259/*GW*1 264).

This *fundamental* transition carries many philosophical implications with it. *Dasein,* with its way of realization, or its understanding that is also always a self-understanding, reveals its ineluctable temporality, its inescapable finitude. The idea of an ultimate foundation seems more doubtful and problematic than ever. Because the unshakable ground proves to be shakable, this shows that it had been the dream of metaphysics to overcome finitude with a secure, fixed, and unchanging position: an absolute foundation on which everything else could be grounded, a *subjectum* or *hypokéimenon* to which humans had elevated themselves in modern thought. But is this *Dasein* really the foundation of all that is, or is it not for its part "thrown" into being, and only for a brief period of time? The hermeneutics of facticity cannot retreat from the "thrownness" of *Dasein.* Precisely because our thrownness indicates the nonavailability of the "there" in which our *Dasein* always exists, one would have to speak of a hermeneutics of thrownness or, with Gadamer, even of a *hermeneutics of finitude.*[35]

If one considers not only *Truth and Method,* however, but also the collection *Heidegger's Ways* as well as the many later essays, including the book about Heidegger that Gadamer never wrote, then it is not an exaggeration to say that Gadamer did pay his debt to his teacher, above all in the new way that *understanding* is brought into connection with the *finitude* of existence. Thus it is much easier to say what connects the two thinkers than what divides them. But the image of Gadamer limiting himself to the "urbanization of the Heideggerian province" would have to be revised.[36] Certainly Gadamer himself contributed to this picture, by suggesting to many inattentive readers that his thought is a continuation of, rather than a break from, Heidegger's. Perhaps he himself did not want to recognize this break entirely, let alone emphasize it. Nevertheless, the filiation is much less direct than has often been thought.[37]

Gadamer does not share the radical as well as solipsistic disquiet of Heidegger, his concerns about existence, his striving for authenticity. Heidegger's analytic of *Dasein* is foreign to Gadamer, for it contains a "transcendental" residue (*TM* 257, 263/*GW*1 261, 268). Above all Gadamer does not follow the development in *Being and Time*, where the hermeneutics of facticity is in the service of the question of Being. Today this is no longer a question for hermeneutics, since hermeneutics makes no claim to found any ontology. This explains why Gadamer is not concerned with the "overcoming" of metaphysics, and why he shows so little interest in the "history of metaphysics" or, even less, in a new "beginning."[38] But what should be said about the way in which Gadamer, through a phenomenology of understanding, interprets finitude and the limit that is always the beyond of the other? What about his attempt to put all ultimate foundations into question, through the dialectics of language and dialogue? At the watershed of the hermeneutics of facticity, one must finally follow Gadamer on the path of his philosophical hermeneutics.

Notes

1. Heidegger, "A Dialogue on Language," in *On the Way to Language,* trans. Peter D. Hertz (San Francisco: Harper & Row, 1971), 1–54 at 28–34; "Aus einem Gespräch von der Sprache," in *Unterwegs zur Sprache, GA*13, ed. Friedrich-Wilhelm von Herrmann (Frankfurt/M: Klostermann, 1985), 85–155 at 90–94.

2. See Jean Grondin, *Introduction to Philosophical Hermeneutics,* trans. Joel Weinsheimer (New Haven, Conn.: Yale University Press, 1994, 1–15; *Einführung in die philosophische Hermeneutik* (Darmstadt: Wissenschaftliche Buchgesellschaft, 1991), 1–20. For the break in the tradition of hermeneutics and its questionable "identity," see John Wrae Stanley, *Die gebrochene Tradition. Zur Genese der philosophischen Hermeneutik Hans-Georg Gadamers* (Würzburg: Königshausen & Neumann, 2005), 11–112. See especially Günter Figal, "Die Komplexität philosophischer Hermeneutik," in *Der Sinn des Verstehens* (Stuttgart: Reclam, 1996), 11–31.

3. Wilhelm Dilthey, "The Rise of Hermeneutics," in *Hermeneutics and the Study of History,* vol. 4 of *Selected Works,* ed. R. A. Makkreel and F. Rodi (Princeton, N.J.: Princeton University Press, 1996); "Die Entstehung der Hermeneutik" (1900), in *Gesammelte Schriften* (hereafter *GS*), vol. 5, ed. Georg Misch, 4th ed. (Göttingen: Vandenhoeck & Ruprecht, 1964), 317–338.

4. It is important to note that hermeneutics has in the past often proven to be antidogmatic and antitraditional. It frequently played a role when religious, cultural, or political conflicts arose.

5. See in particular Emilio Betti, *Allgemeine Auslegungslehre als Methodik der Geisteswissenschaften* (Tübingen: Mohr Siebeck, 1967) (in Italian, *Theoria generale dell'interpretazione,* 1955); Eric D. Hirsch, *Validity in Interpretation* (New Haven, Conn.: Yale University Press, 1967); Thomas M. Seebohm, *Zur Kritik der hermeneutischen Vernunft* (Bonn: Bouvier, 1972).

6. Hans-Georg Gadamer, "Hermeneutik," in *Historisches Wörterbuch der Philosophie,* ed. Joachim Ritter and Karl Gründer (Darmstadt: Wissenschaftliche Buchgesellschaft, 1974), 3:1061–1973. See also "Klassische und philosophische Hermeneutik" (1968), *GW*2 92–117.

7. Szondi initiated these critiques: Peter Szondi, *Einführung in die literarische Hermeneutik* (Frankfurt/M: Suhrkamp, 1975). There followed Manfred Frank, *Das individuelle Allgemeine. Textstrukturierung und -interpretation nach Schleiermacher* (Frankfurt/M: Suhrkamp, 1977); Ron Bontekoe, "A Fusion of Horizons: Gadamer and Schleiermacher," *International Philosophical Quarterly* 27 (1987): 3–16; Christian Berner, *La philosophie de Schleiermacher* (Paris: Edition du CERF, 1995). See also the more recent critical account by Andrea Arndt, "Schleiermachers Hermeneutik im Horizont Gadamers," in Mirko Wischke and Michael Hofer, eds., *Gadamer verstehen/Understanding Gadamer* (Darmstadt: Wissenschaftliche Buchgesellschaft, 2003), 157–168. The book by Gianni Vattimo, *Schleiermacher filosofo dell'interpretazione* (Milan: Mursia, 1986), is by contrast very influenced by Gadamer, but also by Heidegger's existential hermeneutics. This is also the first book on Schleiermacher's philosophy, however, that leaves hidden the connection between hermeneutics on the one hand and on the other hand dialectics and ethics.

8. See Friedrich Daniel Ernst Schleiermacher, *Hermeneutik und Kritik,* ed. Manfred Frank (Frankfurt/M: Suhrkamp, 1977), 325–327.

9. Gadamer developed his critique of the psychological conception of the expression in an appendix that he added to *Truth and Method*. His argument is that the expression relies on the experience of the subject, without however considering its rhetorical-linguistic emergence. See Gadamer, *TM* 494–505 at 503–505; "Exkurse I–VI" (1960), *GW2* 375–386, especially at 384–386.

10. Schleiermacher, *Hermeneutik und Kritik,* 92.

11. Jung asks, correctly, whether there has ever been "such a naïve hermeneutics of empathy." Matthias Jung, *Hermeneutik zur Einführung. Auslegung, Interpretation, Verstehen, Deutung* (Hamburg: Junius, 2001), 63.

12. Schleiermacher, *Hermeneutik und Kritik,* 94.

13. Immanuel Kant, *Kritik der reinen Vernunft,* edited, according to the first and second original editions, by Jens Timmermann (Hamburg: Meiner, 1998), B 370/A 314.

14. See in this volume, chapter 5, part 2.

15. See Gadamer, "The Problem of Language in Schleiermacher's Hermeneutic," trans. David Linge, *Journal for Theology and Church* 7 (1970): 68–84; "Das Problem der Sprache bei Schleiermacher" (1968), *GW4* 361–373.

16. Gadamer, "Die Grenzen der historischen Vernunft" (1949), *GW10* 175–178.

17. See Gadamer, "Herder und die geschichtliche Welt" (1967), *GW4* 318–335.

18. As in the case of his Schleiermacher interpretation, Gadamer's view of Dilthey has received criticism, especially from the figures in the "Dilthey School," which includes such authors as Georg Misch, Hermann Nohl, Josef König, Raymond Aaron, George Gusdorf, Otto Friedrich Bollnow, and Frithjof Rodi. The sharpest criticism has come from Frithjof Rodi. Frithjof Rodi, *Die Erkenntnis des Erkannten. Zur Hermeneutik des 19. und 20. Jahrhunderts* (Frankfurt/M: Suhrkamp, 1990).

19. It suffices to mention the texts by Gadamer, "Truth in the Human Sciences," in *Hermeneutics and Truth,* ed. Brice Wachterhauser (Evanston, Ill.: Northwestern University Press, 1994), 25–32; "Wahrheit in den Geisteswissenschaften" (1953), *GW2* 37–43, and "What Is Truth?" in *Hermeneutics and Truth,* 33–46; "Was ist Wahrheit?" (1957), *GW2* 44–56. See also Gadamer, "The Problem of Historical Consciousness," in *Interpretive Social Science,* ed. Paul Rabinow and W. Sullivan (Los Angeles: University of California Press, 1979), 103–160; 2nd ed. (1987), 82–140; *Das Problem des historischen Bewusstseins,* trans. from the French by Tobias Nikolaus Klass (Tübingen: Mohr Siebeck, 2001); *Le problème de la conscience historique* (Leuven/Paris: Publications Universitaires de Louvain/ Beatrice-Nauwelaerts, 1963); new ed. by Pierre Fruchon (Paris: Seuil, 1996).

20. This text corresponds to the first lecture in Leuven. Gadamer included it in order to prepare the lectures for publication. A shortened version of the original document from 1955–56 is in the archive of the university library in Heidelberg (Heid. Hs. 3913). The opening section has recently been published and edited by Jean Grondin in the *Dilthey-Jahrbuch* (1992–1993): 131–142.

21. See Gadamer, "Wilhelm Dilthey zu seinem 100. Geburtstag" (1933), *GW4* 425–428. See Gadamer, *WM, GW1* 222–246; *TM* 218–242. For later essays see Gadamer, "Das Problem Diltheys. Zwischen Romantik und Positivismus" (1984), *GW4* 406–424; "Der Unvollendete und das Unvollendbare. Zum 150. Geburtstag von Wilhelm Dilthey" (1983), *GW4* 429–435; "Wilhelm Dilthey und Ortega. Philosophie des Lebens" (1985), *GW4* 436–447.

22. See Gadamer, "Die Hermeneutik und die Dilthey-Schule" (1991), *GW10* 185–205.

23. See Gadamer, "Der Unvollendete und das Unvollendbare," *GW4* 431. Dilthey's formulation already appears in a diary entry from 1860. See *Der junge Dilthey. Ein Lebensbild in Briefen und Tagebüchern 1852–1870*, ed. Clara Dilthey Misch (Leipzig: Teubner, 1933; 2nd ed. 1960).

24. See in this volume, chapter 5, part 6.

25. Wilhelm Dilthey, "Der Aufbau der geschichtlichen Welt in den Geisteswissenschaften," *GS 7*, ed. Bernhard Groethuysen, 2nd ed. (Göttingen: Vandenhoeck & Ruprecht, 1958), 136.

26. See Gadamer, "The Science of the Life-World" (1969), in *Philosophical Hermeneutics*, ed. and trans. David E. Linge (Berkeley: University of California Press, 1976), 182–197; "Die Wissenschaft von der Lebenswelt" (1972), *GW3* 147–169; "Zur Aktualität der Husserlschen Phänomenologie" (1974) *GW3* 160–171. See Jérôme Porée, "Phénoménologie, herméneutique et discours philosophique," *Archives de Philosophie* 56 (1993): 389–415; on Husserl and Gadamer, see Guy Deniau, "L'héritage husserlienne de l'herméneutique gadamerienne," *Epokhé* 14 (1994): 211–226, as well as David Vessey, "Who Was Gadamer's Husserl?" in *New Yearbook for Phenomenology and Phenomenological Philosophy 7* (2007): 1–23.

27. Edmund Husserl, *Logische Untersuchungen*, vol. 1, "Foreword," ed. Elmar Holenstein, Husserliana 18 (The Hague: Nijhoff, 1975), 9.

28. Husserl, *The Idea of Phenomenology*, trans. William P. Alston and George Nakhnikian (The Hague: Martinus Nijhoff, 1964), 19; *Die Idee der Phänomenologie*, ed. Walter Biemel, Husserliana 2 (The Hague: Nijhoff, 1950), 44.

29. See in this volume, chapter 5, part 6.

30. It is interesting to note that Gadamer understood the concept of the lifeworld as the result of Husserl's late thought, and at the same time as an answer to Heidegger, whereas the publications from Husserl's posthumous writings have shown that the concept appears very early and that it was rather Heidegger who had made the most of it.

31. But Gadamer had already spoken of the "hermeneutics of facticity" in relation to Heidegger in the essay from 1957, "The Problem of Historical Consciousness" (*PHC* 33).

32. Heidegger, *Ontologie (Hermeneutik der Faktizität)*, 7; *Ontology (Hermeneutics of Facticity)*, trans. John van Buren (Bloomington: Indiana University Press, 1999), 13.

33. Heidegger, *Ontologie (Hermeneutik der Faktizität)*, 14; *Ontology (Hermeneutics of Facticity)*, 14.

34. On this topic, see Ben Vedder, *Was ist Hermeneutik? Ein Weg von der Textdeutung zur Interpretation der Wirklichkeit* (Stuttgart: Kohlhammer, 2000).

35. See in this volume chapter 9, part 3.

36. See Jürgen Habermas, "Hans-Georg Gadamer: Urbanizing the Heideggerian Province," in *Philosophical-Political Profiles*, trans. Frederick G. Lawrence (Cambridge, Mass.: MIT Press, 1983), 189–198; "Urbanisierung der Heideggerschen Provinz," in Habermas, *Philosophisch-politische Profile*, 3rd. expanded ed. (Frankfurt/M: Suhrkamp, 1981), 392–401.

37. Bernasconi had already written on the continuity and discontinuity between Heidegger and Gadamer: see Robert Bernasconi, "Bridging the Abyss: Heidegger and Gadamer," *Research in Phenomenology* 16 (1986): 1–24. But most works on this topic have appeared only in recent years. The relationship of both philosophers to Plato, Aristotle, Hölderlin, and Hegel has been investigated by Coltman. See Rod Coltman, *The Language of Hermeneutics: Gadamer and Heidegger in Dialogue* (Albany: SUNY Press, 1998). See also Walter Lammi, "Hans-Georg Gadamer's Platonic 'Destruktion'

of the Later Heidegger," *Philosophy Today* 41 (1997): 394–404; Sayed Tawfik, "The Phenomenological Motives of Heidegger's and Gadamer's Hermeneutics of the Literary Text," *Analecta Husserliana* 53 (1998): 181–207; Ingrid Scheibler, *Gadamer: Between Heidegger and Habermas* (Lanham: Rowman & Littlefield, 2000); Jean Grondin, *Von Heidegger zu Gadamer. Unterwegs zur Hermeneutik* (Darmstadt: Wissenschaftliche Buchgesellschaft, 2001); James Risser, "From Phenomenology to Hermeneutics and Beyond: The Transformation of Hermeneutics after *Phenomenology*," in István M. Fehér, ed., *Kunst, Hermeneutik, Philosophie*, 75–88; see Damir Barbaric, *Aneignung der Welt. Heidegger—Gadamer—Fink* (Frankfurt/M: Lang, 2007).

38. See in this volume chapter 7, 2; chapter 9, part 2. See also Robert J. Dostal, "Gadamer's Relation to Heidegger and Phenomenology," in Robert J. Dostal, ed., *The Cambridge Companion to Gadamer* (Cambridge: Cambridge University Press, 2002), 247–266 at 260–261.

5 The Constellation of Understanding

It is enough to say that we understand in a *different* way, *if we understand at all.* (*TM* 297/*GW*1 302)

In fact history does not belong to us; we belong to it. (*TM* 276/*GW*1 281)

1. Understanding between Circles and Spirals

Gadamer emphasizes the breaks more than the continuities in his reconstruction of hermeneutics. The decisive break occurs with "Heidegger's disclosure of the fore-structure of understanding" (*TM* 265/*GW*1 270). Heidegger conceives of understanding as the movement of *Dasein* itself, and he uncovers circularity as its basic character. Gadamer begins with Heidegger's view, but reinterprets both the *circle* and *understanding*. He broadens the *hermeneutic circle* so fundamentally that it becomes the guiding thread of the entire middle section of *Truth and Method*.

What does "the fore-structure of understanding," or "fore-understanding," mean? Why does this amount to a new way of comprehending understanding? Romantic hermeneutics starts from the assumption of misunderstanding and nonunderstanding. Understanding, for Schleiermacher, defines itself negatively; it is based "on the fact of nonunderstanding."[1] Understanding becomes for him the overcoming of misunderstanding and nonunderstanding—a kind of overcoming that, however, is condemned to fail unless a chimerical way out is found, such as empathic identification. Beyond such illusory moments of happiness, Romantic hermeneutics appears to stagnate in nonunderstanding.

What distinguishes philosophical hermeneutics, by contrast, is the reversal of these premises. In *Being and Time* understanding is the assumption from which Heidegger starts. Far from a private condition, understanding emerges as the originary phenomenon from which misunderstanding and nonunderstanding derive (*BT* 143/ *SZ* 153). Understanding is always already there, whereas misunderstanding and nonunderstanding occur only within the context of understanding. Only insofar as I understand, according to Heidegger, can I not understand or misunderstand. From this basis, hermeneutics is reformulated, and it takes up the task of reflecting on understanding in a new and more radical way.

Gadamer recalls that the depiction of understanding with the figure of the *circle* "stems from ancient rhetoric" (*TM* 291/*GW*1 296). The figure then made the transition from rhetoric to hermeneutics. The circle describes the movement from the parts to the whole and from the whole to the parts. The parts and the whole necessarily presuppose each other and influence each other reciprocally. Their circular relation is explained by the context, which ties the sentences to the entirety of a text: the understanding of an individual sentence presupposes the understanding of the text, but on the other hand, the understanding of the text can arise only from understanding the sentences. The principle of all understanding concentrates in this circularity, which was formulated for the first time by G. A. Friedrich Ast (1778–1841) during the Romantic period.[2]

Circularity excludes linearity. Circular interwovenness cannot be untied and leveled down. This insight causes Schleiermacher to reconsider the legitimacy of understanding, since the understanding, as the figure of the circle clearly shows, is compromised by the lack of a ground.[3] Even if it proceeds through its parts, and is both motivated and justified by them, the understanding of the whole is groundless from the beginning. Seen in this way, the circle appears to be a methodological obstacle. As a result Schleiermacher wanted to replace the circle with the figure of the spiral—a figure that has recently been taken up again by some interpreters.[4] With the spiral, circularity could resolve itself in linearity. For this, however, one would have to presuppose that the understanding of the whole is adjusted and integrated by the parts in an asymptotic process of approximation. Yet this model of understanding does not acknowledge that groundlessness remains in every turn of the spiral: it is inherent in the structure and thus impossible to overcome. What undoubtedly also contributed to Schleiermacher's negative view of the circle was his way of comprehending nonunderstanding and understanding in dichotomous opposition to each other. Only when this opposition is relinquished can the circle, along with its groundlessness, acquire another meaning.

This is exactly what happens with Heidegger. He describes circularity as the way in which existence, which he calls *Dasein*—understands itself and exists understanding itself. Thrown into the world, *Dasein* projects itself in each case according to the anticipation of its understanding. In this way it cares for its own future, opening up to its own possibilities (*BT* 138/*SZ* 147). "We shall call the development of understanding *interpretation*," Heidegger writes (*BT* 139/*SZ* 148). To interpret means not only to adopt an understanding, but also to develop and articulate it. The hermeneutic circle takes place here between understanding and interpretation: there is no interpretation where there is no prior fore-understanding. This is, however, a traditional example that could be misunderstood. That is why Heidegger says that he wants to move the circle beyond the "philological interpretation." For him it is a matter of giving the circle an entirely new range, one that goes beyond the interpretation of a text, acquiring an "existential" value. Understanding is the way in which *Dasein* enacts its existence.

This view of understanding expands its importance and yields an entirely new reading of the circle. What is a circle, after all? It is well known that in logic, for example, the circle is always a *circulus vitiosus,* whose error is to presuppose what it needs to prove. The circularity of understanding appears to indicate this error directly. But Heidegger meets the logician's objection in advance: he reverses the argument by emphasizing the *circularity* and *primordiality* of understanding, which uncovers the connection between them. Only from the Cartesian perspective of linearity can the circle appear as an "inevitable imperfection" (*BT* 143/*SZ* 153).[5] The epistemological ideal of linear knowledge can be maintained, but only to the extent that one is aware it is secondary, derived from the primordial circularity of understanding. In this sense it would be useless to criticize the circle for its groundlessness and error. It carries its ground in itself and thereby grounds understanding in a figurative way, or better: it manifests the fundamental circularity of understanding. It follows, then, as Heidegger writes: "What is decisive is not to get out of the circle, but to get in it in the right way" (*BT* 143/*SZ* 153). The circle should not be reduced to a vicious circle, nor should it be taken as a mere obstacle, since within the circle there dwells the positive possibility of understanding, that is the primordial way in which *Dasein* enacts its existence.

2. All Understanding Is Ultimately Self-Understanding

Gadamer opens the systematic part of *Truth and Method* with the hermeneutic circle. This section bears the pregnant title: "Elements of a Theory of Hermeneutic Experience" (*TM* 265–379/ *GW1* 270–384). He emphasizes, almost in the words of *Being and Time,* that "this circle possesses an ontologically positive significance" (*TM* 266/*GW1* 271). At the same time he returns to the classical version of rhetoric and hermeneutics, to introduce the movement between the parts and the whole (*TM* 291–295/*GW1* 296–299). Is this a lapse back into a pre-Heideggerian conception of the circle? Or is something new introduced here?

Heidegger's motivation was existential. Gadamer, by contrast, engages in a critique of the methodological ideal of objectivity, which threatens to reduce and distort the value of understanding. This difference also appears with the differences in the examples they give. Heidegger speaks of the interpretation of existence, whereas Gadamer refers to the interpretation of texts. For textual interpretation Gadamer proceeds from our "fore-meanings," which anticipate the meaning of the whole text (*TM* 267/*GW1* 272). It would be a mistake, however, to draw the conclusion of Marquard that Heidegger's "being-towards-death" is simply replaced by Gadamer's "being towards text."[6]

Gadamer is fully aware of the existential breadth that understanding gains in Heidegger's description. But he does not limit himself to describing the structure of *Dasein* in terms of the "belonging" of the interpreter to what is interpreted (*TM* 264/*GW1* 268). Instead he proposes a critical version of "thrownness." In Heidegger's description of *Dasein,* which always understands itself by going beyond itself, the future is particularly emphasized. But the self-projection of *Dasein,* on the basis of its thrownness toward future possibilities, is only one dimension of understanding. The dimension of the past belongs, according to Gadamer, "just as originally and essentially to the historical finitude of *Dasein*" (*TM* 262/*GW*1 266). He elaborates: "*Dasein* that projects itself on its own potentiality-for-being has always already 'been'" (*TM* 264/*GW*1 268). In order to project itself into the future, *Dasein* must proceed from what has already been understood. But what has been understood is past, it has already occurred. We cannot abstract from this dimension. What has been understood also affects the understanding; it is neither neutral and indifferent nor separable. If we try to separate our understanding from the past, then *Dasein* becomes isolated from the community to which it has always belonged. The circle of understanding, as Heidegger characterizes it, is actually much too abstract. This was Gadamer's indirect criticism. The danger in Heidegger's account is that an isolated *Dasein* without a past will emerge, and will approach the future with the same free abstractedness as its predecessor, the phenomenological subject. But the hermeneutics of facticity had already shown that, on the contrary, the boundaries of the "Da," the "there" or the "here," cannot be crossed. In fact, these boundaries both limit and enable the projections of *Dasein*.

The circle thus remains the model for understanding in hermeneutics, but now it is conceived more in terms of *sharing* and *participating*, where the one who understands is always already involved in what is to be understood. Due to the ontological co-belonging of the one who understands and the understood, it is evident within the circularity that the one who understands projects itself onto possibilities that have always belonged to it. Gadamer formulates the point in one of the most significant theses of his philosophical hermeneutics: *"all such understanding is ultimately self-understanding"* (*TM* 260/*GW*1 265).

This thesis had already been suggested in *Being and Time*, where Heidegger argues that *Dasein*, on the basis of its care-structure, cannot help but understand itself (*BT* 53/*SZ* 57). But from Gadamer's perspective it is a mistake to separate the understanding of oneself from the understanding of another, since it is the same process. Already in the everyday understanding of things that are "at hand," as for example when we reach for the doorknob in order to open the door, it is clear that understanding (*Verstehen*) is always a form of "know how" (*Sich-Verstehen-auf*), that is, less a form of knowledge than an ability. Here *Dasein* understands itself by understanding the things it encounters in the lifeworld. These things are never simply given in their naked exteriority, to which our understanding adds a bit of color, but always already exist for our anticipation and are to a certain extent fore-understood. If *Dasein* understands itself by understanding the other, then it cannot understand itself when it does not understand the other or others.

Gadamer follows the way opened by Heidegger, but tries to overcome the duality between oneself and the other. Understanding is always already given in self-understanding. In order to avoid a possible misunderstanding, it is important to emphasize here that "self-understanding" does not mean "understanding oneself as a self."[7] The latter would be the self-consciousness that is unshakably certain of itself—to hermeneutics this is an empty chimera. For hermeneutics there is no self in understanding that would exclude the other. Understanding involves understanding the *self* and *other* simultaneously, since self-understanding can articulate itself only through the understanding of the other. The distinction at stake here is not between self and other, but between what was already understood and what is not yet understood. In this way hermeneutics, following Heidegger's teaching, takes its start from understanding and bypasses the previously insurmountable transition from nonunderstanding to understanding. Yet, following Schleiermacher's teaching, it contains the other within itself from the very beginning.

3. The "Fore-Conception of Completeness"

There are still many open questions regarding the hermeneutic circle and the way understanding enacts itself. Gadamer chooses phenomenological description to address these questions. Rather than formulate normative prescriptions, hermeneutics tries to bring to light what happens in the practice of understanding. But this lack of prescriptions and norms should not be equated with a lack of criteria. Hermeneutics does not encourage interpretive arbitrariness; it insists instead on a critical conception of interpretation. Conscious of its presuppositions, such an interpretation avoids blindly taking up its own assumptions and gives itself over—as Heidegger had already suggested—to the "things themselves" (*BT* 142/*SZ* 152). This last expression, which Gadamer also recuperates, is inherited from phenomenology and needs to be clarified (*TM* 267/*GW*1 272). That the interpreter must give him- or herself over to "the things themselves" does not at all imply the ideal of objective knowledge. One should not confuse the "thing" (*Sache*) with the "object" (*Objekt*). In the context of hermeneutics, the "thing" is neither the "thing in itself" of Kant nor the "thing itself" of Husserl. Following the etymology, "thing," or *Sache* in German, means "the matter for debate" (*Streitsache*), in much the same way as *cosa* does in Italian or *chose* in French, which stem from the Latin *causa*. The "matter" or "issue" (*Sache*) is that which is to be debated, whatever people address and discuss.[8] One is always implied and seized by the matter at issue.

What is important in this dialogical model is that the interpreter legitimizes his anticipations in accord with the issue that concerns him. But he should not let himself be led by his anticipations alone, for this would amount to arbitrariness. Here is an example: I have decided to review a book about Plato. If I write only about my own thoughts in the review, without considering the views in the book, the result will be a bad review. Neither an impossible neutrality nor self-forgetfulness is expected from the interpreter. What is expected is "openness" towards the alterity of the text, in other words the ability to allow the text to speak (*TM* 269/*GW*1 273). In this we can recognize "a hermeneutically trained consciousness" (*TM* 269/*GW*1 273). The interpreter, who is conscious of their own anticipations and their own biases, allows the text to assert its own truth.

This is the only criterion that hermeneutics indicates explicitly. Gadamer calls this the "fore-conception of completeness" (*TM* 294/*GW1* 299). Put succinctly, completeness is projected onto the text to be interpreted. One presupposes, in other words, that the text has a truth and a coherence with which it puts forth its truth. To return to the circle: the coherent unity of the whole becomes the presupposition that guides the understanding of the parts; while the harmony of all the parts with the whole, which bears witness to this coherence, becomes the criterion of correctness. Only when what is interpreted does not correspond to the fore-conception of completeness, when a coherent truth is unable to appear, does the interpretation get displaced from the text to the author and hence become psychological. For Gadamer this is further confirmation that understanding means understanding on the bases of the "thing," and only subsequently does it mean understanding an author.[9]

4. We Are Distorting Mirrors: On Prejudice

The fore-understanding, from which the understanding proceeds, contains the complex of one's own "prejudices" (*TM* 268–271/*GW1* 272–274). With this Gadamer describes the hermeneutic circle more precisely. If Heidegger shows that understanding is based on what is already understood, Gadamer makes clear that what has already been understood, or the fore-understanding, is a *pre-judice*. In order to radicalize the hermeneutic question and develop its ultimate consequences, it is important to recognize that "all understanding inevitably involves some prejudice" (*TM* 270/*GW1* 274).

With this thesis Gadamer wants above all to rehabilitate prejudice, which he pursues through his critique of the Enlightenment. If we look at the Latin word *preiudicium* and its juridical use, then "prejudice" has neither a negative nor a positive meaning. It has acquired a negative connotation only since the Enlightenment, which it still has to this day, indicating an "unfounded judgment" (*TM* 271/*GW1* 275). This semantic passage is important: prejudice is considered false because it has not been legitimated by a secure and objective foundation. But the presupposition that the Enlightenment uses to discredit prejudice is also a prejudice, actually a "'prejudice against prejudices'" (*TM* 272/*GW1* 275). It is completely paradoxical to claim that one can free thought from prejudices by means of another prejudice! Isn't it necessary to clarify and revise this new prejudice?

Still within the spirit of the Enlightenment, Gadamer criticizes Enlightenment prejudice and exposes it as the inheritance of Cartesian doubt. With its devotion to the ideal of scientific knowledge founded on methodological doubt, Enlightenment prejudice distorts the reality of historical understanding. Here there emerges the question of the ultimate foundation, which begins to shows itself as impossible in light of the finitude of human existence. Whether prejudice stems from respect for others' authority or from one's own "hastiness," in any case the Enlightenment demands that tradition should be judged without prejudice before the tribunal of reason. By taking up this abstract alternative between tradition and reason, Romanticism strengthens belief in the overcoming of myth by *logos*, though it does this in an opposite direction, hence traditionalist and conservative.[10]

Historical science, which claims to know the world of the past objectively, takes its start from the Romantic reaction, but ultimately also from the Enlightenment. This convergence "simply indicates that the same break with the continuity of meaning in tradition lies behind both traditions" (*TM* 275/*GW1* 280). One believes in the possibility of a subject who forgets that the interpreter belongs to what is being interpreted and elevates itself above history, above historical tradition, and above its own prejudices. In such a way, the subject, becoming a mirror of itself, would know and judge with objective rationality. Yet this would mean not wanting to admit that human reason—as Kant has had taught us—far from being absolute, is finite and historical.

"Subjectivity is only a distorting mirror. The self-awareness of the individual is only a flickering in the closed circuits of historical life. *That is why the prejudices of the individual, far more than his judgments, constitute the historical reality of his being*" (*TM* 276–277/*GW1* 281).

For Gadamer, rehabilitating prejudice does not mean praising prejudice. We can and should become conscious of our own prejudices. However much consciousness is critically trained, it can never be perfected. If this were not this case, one would fall back into the errors of the Enlightenment. Can a distinction at least be made between true and false prejudices? *Truth and Method* raises this question, but it remains unanswered because it is posed badly and still suffers from the epistemological paradigm of knowledge. If a criterion for distinguishing prejudice can be found, then it follows that prejudice can be eliminated. Ultimately the negative connotation of prejudice has an impact on Gadamer's argument, too, and prevents him from designating it as a positive limit. Although it is a key concept in *Truth and Method* it is scarcely mentioned later, and his treatment of prejudice does not open the way to a radically new interpretation of the limits.

One of the criteria that Gadamer mentions to distinguish between true and false prejudices is "temporal distance" (*TM* 296/*GW1* 301). For him, an interpretation becomes generally accepted over time on the basis of its fruitfulness. How should one distinguish otherwise between authentic art and art that only corresponds to the taste of the moment? But even if temporal distance plays a role in understanding, it cannot be seen as the only criterion of distinction—Gadamer himself later changes his thesis and the text accordingly.[11] What had been overvalued was the filter formed by temporal distance. Gadamer is right when he does not conceive of temporal distance as an abyss to be jumped over, but rather as a type of continuity that makes understanding possible. Temporal distance does not, however, solve the question of the legitimacy of judgments and prejudices regarding contemporary works. Indeed, it can actually have the opposite effect and consolidate the less valid interpretations while obscuring the more valid ones. Thus in past times entire passages were stricken from classical works because they were seen as inappropriate, not to mention the stories of peoples that exist only orally, or generations from which not even a memory remains. Tradition can also have a concealing effect.

5. The Voices of Tradition

What is *tradition* in the first place, and what role does it play in understanding? The rediscovery of tradition is perhaps the most misunderstood chapter of hermeneutics. It is quite possible that the way in which Gadamer describes it in *Truth and Method,* where he connects the concept of "tradition" with "authority" and the "classical," has led to many mistaken misunderstandings (*TM* 277–290/*GW1* 281–295).

In his argument Gadamer further describes the hermeneutic circle. With the term "prejudice" Gadamer names the fore-understanding from which understanding takes its start. It is clear, however, that other fore-understandings must come into play in the circle, not only those of the one understanding, but also those of the one being understood. To be sure, it is not easy to make a clear distinction between the one and the other, because prejudices are for their part a form of tradition, often the very form that tradition takes in understanding.

As is the case with prejudice, the rehabilitation of tradition by no means includes an apology for or a defense of its effects. It would be a grave misunderstanding to take Gadamer's position as mere traditionalism.[12] Rather, by "tradition" one should understand the immemorial present in understanding, and this refers to two meanings that are bound together. On the one hand, it points to the impossibility of the one understanding to freely avail itself of the immemorial, which is made up of all the fore-understandings sedimented in the tradition. On the other hand, it refers to the lack of an ultimate foundation. The very enduring influence of tradition shows how superfluous the notion of an ultimate foundation is outside the framework of logical-mathematical knowledge. "This is precisely what we call tradition: the ground of their validity" (*TM* 281/*GW1* 285). Here Gadamer does not claim that what happens according to tradition has a grounding validity. This would be a traditionalist position. On the contrary, he wants to say that not everything that has been done according to tradition can be brought back to an ultimate foundation. In every founding act tradition always plays a role, insofar as that which belongs to the act has a groundless validity. The foundation presupposes the tradition—not the reverse. As we will see, language, the form in which tradition takes shape and is transmitted, not only shows this clearly but also calls into question every claim for an ultimate foundation.[13]

How can tradition assert itself, though, if it does not have rational validity arising from an ultimate foundation? It is true that tradition can assert itself without being more closely tested by reason—at least not consciously. But it is just as true that it would be a mistake to see tradition as an irrational and authoritarian power. Tradition appears this way only when it is opposed, as in the Enlightenment, to abstract reason. Gadamer disputes precisely this opposition. He disputes it in the first place because such an opposition does not consider how much tradition there already is in human reason, which is finite and historical. In addition, the opposition between reason and tradition does not take into account how much reason flows in tradition. In this regard Gadamer writes of a tradition "freely taken over" (*TM* 280/*GW1* 285). He is not referring to the gesture of a separated consciousness that appropriates tradition, taking it up as an object, and submitting it to the critical examination of instrumental reason. For this kind of reason, which claims it can control and dominate the order of things as well as history, tradition counts as a corrective. And this is because it marks its limits. Considered more closely, however, the one cannot do without the other. Reason cannot do without tradition, because it is precisely tradition that forms the most fundamental ground of all rational projects and all linear foundations. Tradition cannot do without reason, either, because it needs the free assent of reason in order to perpetuate itself. Its "inertia" alone will not suffice (*TM* 281/*GW1* 286).[14] In this sense we should speak of a rationality of tradition, which persists insofar as it renews itself through reason.

Continuity is not at all self-evident and requires confirmation again and again. Many examples of this could be given, yet it should suffice to think of the consent we give to traditional forms of greetings or thanks. When an English speaker says, "You're welcome," he not only uses a formula but carries on a tradition whose rationality he recognizes and supports, even if only unintentionally and almost by chance. It is an exaggeration to speak of this recognition as an "act," since it almost never occurs as a conscious act. Gadamer wants to emphasize that reason has an effect not only by renewing or overthrowing, but also by preserving. Preservation is simply less striking than renewal or overthrow. Thus, for example, whatever is preserved enjoys a certain authority. This is something that, according to Gadamer, neither Jaspers nor Krüger had seen. Just as personal authority is recognized by an act of freedom and reason, so too "an authority that is nameless," that is, tradition, is also recognized (*TM* 280/*GW1* 285). There is no irrationality here: instead the authority of tradition is accepted insofar as the transmission process continues. A tradition whose authority appears to be questionable will soon die out, unless it can maintain itself with repressive restoration or as a kind of folklore.

The importance hermeneutics gives to the concept of "transmission," in relation to "tradition," should be clear. For hermeneutics there is no tradition without transmission, since a tradition that cannot be transmitted will rigidify and perish. Tradition should not be understood as static, because it is the historical process of transmitting the past.[15] The accent lies on the dynamic relationship that binds the past to historical consciousness. Gadamer writes: "we are always situated within traditions" (*TM* 282/*GW1* 286). This means that we partake in an uninterrupted dialogue through which tradition can perpetuate itself; and secondly, that even our Being is defined by this participation, or shown to be finite. What runs through our historical consciousness is a "variety of voices in which the echo of the past is heard" (*TM* 294/*GW1* 289). Our consciousness, as historical, is not intimate and private but deeply foreign, because of the voices from the past that we harbor within. On the other hand, we can participate in the dialogue of tradition only by articulating these voices from the past anew, again and again. In this way we concretize the past, which, according to Gadamer, exists only "in the multifariousness of such voices" (*TM* 284/*GW*1 289). In determining the concept of transmission Gadamer also determines the concept of participating, which he calls "participating in a common meaning," and particularly in terms of a linguistically articulated and articulable meaning (*TM* 292/*GW*1 297). In this way he shows the always open mediation between "familiarity and strangeness," "the play" between familiarity and strangeness, as "*the true locus of hermeneutics*" (*TM* 295/*GW*1 300).

In order to illuminate how the mediation between the past and the present is to be understood, Gadamer chooses the example of the *classical*. The concept of the classical, taken from Hegel but also from Curtius, carries both a normative and a historical value. Classical is what has reached such a perfection that it becomes a model to be imitated. This normative value has to a large extent been erased by historicism, which emphasizes only its historical value. Without adopting the solution from historicism, but also without falling back into an unhistorical way of thinking, Gadamer stresses that a normative element always remains in historical consciousness. Yet the normative value of the "classical" is never "suprahistorical": even if it cannot be identified with an epoch or with a style, what reaches its peak in the classical is "a notable mode of being historical" (*TM* 287/*GW*1 292).

In the destructive passing of time the classical retains something that is not past from the past with an ever-renewing preservation, and raises it to a timeless present that is contemporary to every time. In bearing witness to the past, but also turning to the present, the classical mediates between past and present. Here Gadamer asks whether the classical, beyond the liminal case that it represents, does not reveal the mediation between past and present that lies at the base of all understanding: "*Understanding is to be thought of less as a subjective act than as participating in an event of tradition*, a process of transmission in which past and present are constantly mediated" (*TM* 290/*GW*1 295).

6. *Wirkungsgeschichte:* The Blind Labor of History

The concept of *effective history (Wirkungsgeschichte)* is the central point around which the theoretical part of *Truth and Method* turns. After he overcomes the instrumentalism of historical consciousness, Gadamer spends the rest of the book exploring the consequences for historical and linguistic experience that arise from the new consciousness of effective history.

Yet what does "effective history" mean? The expression was already widespread in the literary criticism of the nineteenth century. It refers to the auxiliary discipline that deals with the reception of a work and, above all, with the interpretations that have arisen in the reception.[16] The various ways in which—in the course of the century—

texts have been read and events interpreted demonstrate the productivity of history. Every text, every event, takes on a new meaning and shows a new side, each time according to the expectations raised by the historical context but also according to the previous interpretations. Let me provide a few examples. We do not know, of course, exactly how Hegel assessed Plato, but we certainly view Plato differently now on the basis of Hegel's readings. And we look with different eyes, more with the eyes of the vanquished than of the victor, on an experience like the conquest of America. In short: in order to study a work or an event it is necessary to take into account its effects in history. Thus historicism has a great interest in the history of effect and its effectiveness. But historicism is led by the naive intention of separating the original work from its reception, in order to study it in a completely objective manner.

Historical consciousness seems more enlightened on this point than the Enlightenment. It renounces the belief in progress and drops the aim of understanding the course of history rationally, since the course of history is to a certain extent foreign to reason. Instead it proceeds from the viewpoint of historical consciousness. Gadamer uses his principle of effective history to criticize the presumptuousness of this way of thinking.

In order to understand this turning point in philosophical hermeneutics, one must dwell on the complex meaning of this phrase, "effective history." It is important in the first place to recognize that "effective history" means not only the "history of effects," or the history of the reception, which is studied and known as such. Gadamer is trying to assert something far more fundamental with his concept. In order to grasp it, one should consider that an "effect" (*Wirkung*) is not only the result of an activity, but also refers to the activity itself. "Effect" is a synonym for "having an effect" or "bringing something about"—in the sense of operating or working (*Wirken*). "Effective history" thus has a double meaning. On the one hand, it points to a product: for example the various interpretations of the Bible, which can be seen as the effects of history or as the product of its work completed over the course of centuries.[17] On the other hand, it also points to an activity, in particular to the blind and quiet workings of history, which has no *telos* and which often remains unnoticed and concealed, nearly unconscious or in any case "more being than consciousness" (*GW2* 247/*RHT* 329). The work of history gathers Hegelian negativity into itself, which is a kind of suffering and undergoing, a labor like that of birth. But from this very negativity, history brings forth unexpected fruits that carry the traces of the negative within them. In its work history is constantly active, writing and inscribing the traces that make the past legible, and nevertheless irrevocably absent.

It is along this path that history reaches us; we do not remain unscathed. The workings of history penetrate us far more deeply than our consciousness can absorb. This is what "effect" means: that history works above and beyond the consciousness we can have of it. To put it differently: history subjects us to its effects and contaminates us in our supposed intimacy, so that what is our own appears foreign, and what is foreign appears to us as our own (*TM* 301/*GW1* 306). Effective history is the constant "interweaving" of history and effects. Consciousness is drawn into and embedded in this process. The web woven by history also works when we neither sense nor even suspect anything. Consciousness will never be able to detach itself from such an impenetrable entanglement, for it actually penetrates consciousness itself and is its substance. For this reason, consciousness is never transparent and pure, but rather opaque and contaminated. It is historically effected consciousness (*wirkungsgeschichtliches Bewußtseins*), that is, a consciousness that knows that it has been produced, worked out, and tormented by history (*TM* 302/*GW1* 307). It cannot withdraw from the multiple effects of history because it can never reach the outside of history, from which it might observe the process. More than acting, it seems to be a suffering, dragged and drawn into that "interplay" which Gadamer has described as the hermeneutic circle (*TM* 293/*GW1* 298).

In order to articulate the concept of historically effected consciousness more closely, it is necessary to distinguish at least two different meanings. The first meaning is determined by the objective genitive. This consciousness knows of its historicity; it knows that it is always situated. It involves a "consciousness of the hermeneutic *situation*" (*TM* 302/*GW1* 307). The existential nuance can be heard quite clearly here and is underscored by the concept of the "situation," which Gadamer adapts from Jaspers's philosophy. Such consciousness knows both that it belongs to the horizon of an epoch and that it finds itself at a particular point in time and space: the site of its own situation, which it can leave only by moving to another situation, without being able to overcome its situatedness. Here it is not a matter of objective knowledge but rather of "illumination," to use another word from Jaspers. Proceeding from its own situation, this consciousness knows that: "*To be historically means that knowledge of oneself can never be complete*" (*TM* 302/*GW1* 307). Complete self-knowledge is impeded by history, since history never lets itself be integrated into an absolute subject. Historically effected consciousness knows, in other words, that in every understanding, especially in all self-understanding, history is at work. It is not only determined, limited, and defined by history, but also delivered over to the infinity of understanding. But what limits consciousness is at the same time its opportunity. The work of history does not lock us into the one-sidedness of an insurmountable point of view. At the same time that it spins us into the web, which it is ceaselessly weaving, it opens consciousness to the possibility of an endless dialogue with tradition.

The second meaning of "historically effected consciousness" concerns the subjective genitive. In this case one can say metaphorically that history has consciousness of itself, in as much as consciousness is the result of its working. Here Hegel's conception of history can be perceived, and has led to the suspicion that Gadamer ontologizes history: as if history were a kind of autonomous power, a gigantic consciousness meant to encompass all other consciousness, like a new version of Heidegger's history of Being. Read this way, the history of effects would be a long monologue, culminating in the absolute spirit. On the contrary, Gadamer would rather "retrace the path of Hegel's phenomenology of mind" (*TM* 302/*GW1* 307). The metaphorical meaning of the genitive refers to a communal consciousness that is produced by the work of history and that, therefore, goes beyond subjective consciousness. To the latter is not denied a dialogical interaction, but its beyond is also its limit. Here is perhaps the most important effect produced by the workings of history: to indicate the limit of modern consciousness, that is, its impossibility of being self-consciousness.

Perhaps one should give this consciousness, which knows less about itself but more about its own limits, another name. This would have the advantage, among other things, of avoiding the idealistic connotations that remain in the concept of consciousness. The name that Gadamer suggests and develops, above all in his later writings, is "vigilance" (*Wachsamkeit*). Instead of being-conscious (*Bewusst-Sein*), philosophical hermeneutics chooses to speak of being-vigilant (*Wachsam-Sein*).[18]

Already in the first edition of *Truth and Method* Gadamer spoke of a "task" that he related to a "process of understanding." It is the task of combining past and future, which occurs in history as the "fusion of horizons" (*TM* 306–307/*GW1* 311–312). Yet the word "task" has given rise to numerous mistaken interpretations. Many interpreters have spoken of a "task of understanding," as if understanding were a methodological exercise or a moral duty for hermeneutics. But in the 1986 edition, Gadamer made a major alteration: the word "task" (*Aufgabe*) is replaced by the word *Wachheit*, or "alertness" (*TM* 307/*GW1* 312; the English retains "task"). Consciousness that knows about the work of history, and knows that history works within it, is alert and awake to the fusion of horizons.

With the concepts of "vigilance" or "alertness" it becomes possible to clarify what Gadamer means by his "fusion of horizons" (*Horizontverschmelzung*). Situatedness means to be bound to a point in time and space, which limits our vision. As Husserl first showed, followed by Heidegger and Jaspers, the word "horizon" from the Greek refers to the movable circle that limits everything that is visible to be seen from a particular point. It characterizes the limit that moves with us when we move. Thus one speaks of more or less limited horizons, the range of horizons, and the opening of new horizons (*TM* 302–307/*GW1* 307–308). Understanding can be seen as the encounter, inscribed into a particular historical constellation, between two horizons. Historicism conceptualizes this encounter as the self-transposition of consciousness into the past. It claims to be able to step out of the horizon of the present, in order to transpose itself into the horizon of the past, and appropriate that horizon to itself. In this way, whoever understands appears to have reached a position of objective neutrality. Gadamer's doubts about such a view concern not only this position but also the very possibility of separating horizons from each other, as if they were closed horizons. For him, all this is nothing more than an abstraction. On the one hand, the horizons move and we move with them, so that even the horizon of the past does not lie fixed but moves in the articulation of a new present. On the other hand, the boundaries between them are certainly not clear. One horizon fades into another and thus forms a movable horizon, which encompasses the depth of history out of which human life is lived and which can be defined as "heritage and tradition" (*TM* 304/*GW1* 310). Thus, horizons are not separable, but simply distinguishable. Their encounter emerges as a "fusing of horizons," which for Gadamer has not only a horizontal but also a vertical dimension (*TM* 307/*GW1* 312). As such, it is a "rising to a higher universality," in which the boundaries of each horizon are surpassed or expanded, and thereby elevated as well (*TM* 305/*GW1* 310). The movement of eyes, which rise from what is close by to look into the distance, exemplify well this rising in which we take up a new point of view. Here both horizons, one's own and the other's, are changed.[19]

7. Understanding Means Application

What role does application play? Gadamer looks to the history of classical hermeneutics for his answer. Prior to Schleiermacher, application was an integrating component in the process of interpretation. Gadamer refers to Pietism, in particular to Johann Jacob Rambach (1693–1735)—where a *subtilitas applicandi* is placed side by side with the *subtilitas intelligenti* and the *subtilitas explicandi*.[20] Gadamer draws attention first to the word *subtilitas*, which can be translated as a "finesse of mind" (*TM* 307/*GW1* 312). With this phrase he wants to emphasize that understanding is not a procedure governed by rules, but rather an ability that in rhetoric might be called subtlety or, better, astuteness. As Vico taught, these qualities of mind go hand in hand with tradition and common sense.[21] In the hermeneutics of sacred texts the moment of understanding requires a moment of interpretation, and interpretation for its part requires application. How would it be possible to understand sacred texts, or even to interpret them, without applying them to the contemporary situation? Is it not precisely the application that provides evidence of the enacted understanding?

Gadamer has a twofold aim: first he would like to recuperate application, which was excluded by Romanticism and even more so by post-Romantic epistemology. Second, he wants to depict understanding, interpretation, and application not as separate but as constitutive moments of a unified process.[22] Application does not simply come after, but is rather the cornerstone of, understanding. "Understanding here is always application" (*TM* 309/*GW1* 314).[23] If it cannot be translated into practice, then the understanding is no understanding at all. Gadamer's return to the concept of *applicatio*, or application, entails a paradigm shift in hermeneutics: the cognitive value becomes secondary, as the practical value of understanding comes to the fore. This paradigm shift also leads to a change in which discipline becomes the paradigm, since it is no longer the historical-philological form of interpretation but the theological and legal forms of hermeneutics that matter. The case of the interpreter who interprets sacred texts by applying them to the present is by no means a limit case. On the contrary, this approach exemplifies every form of understanding. For Gadamer, recuperating the concept of application means to proceed from theological and legal hermeneutics in order to rethink philology and historiography. This new model should show, once and for all, that hermeneutics is not a form of domination or mastery but a form of service. This is shown in the application of the divine word or the will of the law. All these are forms of interpretation in which application involves applying oneself, a concentration or dedication that almost involves a devotional attitude to what ought to be given in its validity (*TM* 311/*GW1* 316).

8. The Exemplary Practice of Legal Hermeneutics

"Practical" hermeneutics makes clear on the one hand the relation between the universal and the particular in the processes of interpretation and application, and on the other hand the value of application. Yet legal hermeneutics has been separated from the other hermeneutic disciplines because—if taken merely as an auxiliary discipline to the law—it has little to do with historical understanding. Gadamer questions this separation. What is the difference between the lawyer or the judge and the legal historian? Gadamer refers here to Betti, who had emphasized the difference between these examples (*TM* 325–328/*GW1* 330–332).

In contrast to the legal historian, whose primary task is to grasp the original meaning of a law, the judge, according to Betti, applies the law to the individual case. The assumption here is that the original meaning is self-evident, and that it is just as self-evident that the meaning could be applied to various circumstances. The starting and end points are, to be sure, different respectively, but the hermeneutic path is the same. The judge begins with the individual case, and operates with practical or normative aims in mind. The historian does not proceed from an individual case, but attempts to capture the meaning of the law with a theoretical or descriptive aim.

At the same time, though, the lawyer should also behave like the historian and the historian like the lawyer. They have in common the understanding of the law, which, on the basis of the historicity of the understanding, always mediates between past and present, in other words always involves an *application*. Even the historian cannot avoid mediating between past and present when studying a law—whether it is in effect or not—simply because the interpreter cannot ignore their own situatedness. Beyond that, the historian cannot avoid the question of application in understanding the law. The so-called meaning of the law is not an abstract, self-identical universal; is the meaning that the law has acquired through the diverse concrete cases in which it has been applied. For this very reason the historian should take into account all the applications of the law, up to and including the present ones. But in applying the law to the present, the historian is doing nothing different from what the lawyer does. For his part, the lawyer, applying the law to the individual case, understands its sense hitherto, thus mediating between past and present. The lawyer also always behaves, in other words, like a historian.

Understanding means "*to concretize* the law," and in this way involves its application (*TM* 329/*GW1* 335). In light of legal hermeneutics it becomes clear that application should not be confused with a "kind of logical technique of subsumption," which would subsume the particular under the universal.[24] It is rather the case of a concretization that amounts to a "creative supplementing of the law" (*TM* 329/*GW1* 335). Because it is not a logical-mathematical procedure, but rather a historical event, the application proves to be productive or creative; it always involves a reproductive overcoming. It moves from the universal to the particular, from the identical to the different, from the abstract to the concrete. Here the application can be seen in close proximity to art, for example music, where the reproductive interpretation is inseparable from the work.[25] It is not by chance that Gadamer introduces in this context a "hermeneutic identity," which is open to the future and occurs only in the temporality of its ongoing self-differentiation. *Application* is thus simply another, more comprehensive, designation for what is called *performance* in art.

9. The Creativity of Application and the Unity of Hermeneutic Disciplines

In these ways Gadamer expands the limits of understanding. His intention is to restore the unity of the hermeneutic disciplines. Where should such a unity be found? It appears neither in the universality of the process of understanding nor in historical consciousness, and even less so in the objective considerations of philology. The application, as the "task of mediating between then and now, between the Thou and the I," is the thread that joins hermeneutic disciplines to each other (*TM* 333/*GW1* 339).[26]

Even in theological hermeneutics the *kerygma*, or the proclamation of the Gospel, must be repeated in order to be effective, just like the concretization of the law. In other words, "the proclamation cannot be detached from its fulfillment." However, there is the important distinction that in the relation of the human to the divine law the latter retains its "absolute priority" in interpretation (*TM* 331/*GW1* 336).

Application is at work in every understanding, even those of philological and historical hermeneutics. From this perspective Gadamer criticizes not only the view of objectivity that dominates the historical-philological realm, but also the claim to universality in historiography. In the course of the nineteenth century, historiography relied on the philological model that understanding could be achieved by moving from the individual to the whole, and as a product of the whole—even though the whole is never given in history. If we can speak of the philologization of historiography, we could just as well speak of the historicization of philology. "The philologist is a historian" (*TM* 337/*GW1* 342). He interprets texts not by following what they want to express, but by looking for what their expression "betrays": the texts are "understood in terms of not only what they say, but what they exemplify." In other words, they are read as the testimonies of a great narrative of history (*TM* 336/*GW1* 342).

The model of objectivity thus becomes inappropriate both for philology and for historiography, because in both cases understanding involves application. The philologist reads texts for what they say to him, and this reading is a reproductive interpretation—just as every reading is always an application. The same goes for the "fact," which the historian examines in its meaning, which obviously arises from its historical effect (*TM* 340/*GW1* 344). In short: the past, which presents itself to the historian, is already the result of the work of history; it is the result of an application that not even the historian can escape. Where would his questions come from, if not from their belonging to a past to which he would like to give voice? The historian, too, performs an application that is not, however, related to the individual text but to the collective unity of historical tradition. Here we might return to the metaphor of reading. The historian reads "the great book of world history" by mediating with the present time of his own life, which is just as understood or transformed as the book itself (*TM* 339/*GW1* 345). "Understanding proves itself to be a kind of effect [*Wirkung*] and knows itself as such" (*TM* 341/*GW1* 346). In the historically effected consciousness common to all understanding, Gadamer sees the possibility of restoring the unity of the hermeneutic disciplines.

10. The Magic Spell of Hegelian Reflection and the Remains of Finitude

When we speak of historically effected consciousness there are many questions that gather around the word "consciousness." Gadamer himself asks: "But what sort of consciousness is this?" (*TM* 341/*GW1* 347). The question inevitably brings up the problem of *reflexivity*, which seems to be implied in every form of consciousness. At this point a confrontation with Hegel and his "reflective philosophy" becomes unavoidable (*TM* 341–346/*GW1* 346–351).

Hegel's particular contribution should be recognized: he saw that history is not only the object of research, but the constitution of consciousness itself. Consciousness develops its own effective history and in the process becomes self-consciousness. Hermeneutics, too, culminates in historically effected consciousness reflecting on itself. Should we thus understand hermeneutic consciousness as a new version of Hegelian self-consciousness? Facing this question, Gadamer is forced to take a decisive position in order to preserve "the truth of Hegel's thought" against the reflexive and totalizing aspirations of his system (*TM* 342/*GW1* 348). In a word, he must break the "magic spell" of reflective philosophy.

The concept of "reflective philosophy" refers to Hegel's claim to cancel, preserve, and elevate history in consciousness. But the expression "reflective philosophy" is ambiguous and says even more. Hegel had already used it to reproach Kant, Jacobi, and Fichte for having remained within the domain of subjectivity. Gadamer, for his part, turns this criticism against Hegel, arguing that Hegel overlooked the effects history has on consciousness. For Gadamer, Hegel resolved history in the truth of absolute consciousness. It is this *"absolute mediation of history and truth"* that hermeneutics wants to escape (*TM* 341/*GW1* 347). The danger lies in the absoluteness of a consciousness whose reflection solves and resolves any immediacy opposed to it, thereby achieving a complete identification of history with historical consciousness. By contrast, the hermeneutic concept of historically effected consciousness avoids such an absolute identification. In historically effected consciousness, the immediacy of historical conditions is never transformed by reflection to the point of transparency. With his description of a consciousness that cannot be self-transparent but must instead remain vigilant, Gadamer develops his effective history as a way of limiting the "omnipotence of reflection" in Hegel (*TM* 342/*GW*1 348).

Here appears the question of the *limit,* which runs through all of philosophical hermeneutics and which makes hermeneutics a philosophy of infinite finitude.[27] The question arises with the search for the "Archimedean point" that allows us to unhinge reflective philosophy (*TM* 344/*GW*1 349). In this respect one should underline the distance separating Gadamer from other philosophers in the twentieth century who pursue a similar aim. It suffices to mention the tradition of Jewish philosophy that runs from Franz Rosenzweig (1886–1929) to Emmanuel Lévinas (1906–95). For Gadamer, the "Archimedean point" does not lie in the difference between "the I and the you" that this tradition emphasizes. According to Gadamer, Hegel had already met the objections later used against him, through the form of Spirit described in the *Phenomenology.* There seems no position that cannot immediately be integrated into the absolute mediation of reflection: none of the examples of immediacy—whether of being, the body, you, or the relations of production—have immediacy in themselves. They all involve a process of reflection. The lever to unhinge Hegel's philosophy would not be, for Gadamer, simply another kind of immediacy. Rather, it would be the remnant that remains unresolved between history and historical consciousness, which arises for finite human consciousness seeking a path to infinity—to that "bad infinity" which Gadamer, who remains true to Hegel here, understands not only as "an untruth" but also as "a truth" (*RAS* 40/*GW*4 465; *TM* 344/*GW*1 350). Here Gadamer must read Hegel against the grain and reawaken a need in Hegelian philosophy that had been silenced by Absolute Spirit. It is finitude that breaks the magic spell of reflective philosophy by introducing a rift into total dialectical mediation. Finitude prevents totalization, blocks perfection, forbids the completion of becoming, and denies both the absolute and absolutism. The concept of infinite finitude is the line that delimits Gadamer's with respect to Hegel's.[28]

11. Relativism and Self-Contradiction: Attempts to Take Philosophy by Surprise

Hermeneutics has drawn two fundamental criticisms: one of relativism and the other of self-contradiction. Taken together, according to Gadamer, both simply represent new forms of the old reflective philosophy. They amount to reflective philosophy in a new guise. This explains, at least in part, why he treats these criticisms with a certain nonchalance. Of course behind this nonchalance there is perhaps irritation, insofar as hermeneutics had already answered these objections. In reality, hermeneutics understands itself as asking the prior question, which aims to dismantle the foundation on which these criticisms have been built.

The charge of relativism can be easily summarized: if historically effected consciousness can never be separated from its own historicity, is it not fundamentally relative? From this position it is a short step to the claim that, for hermeneutics, everything is relative. It would be an even shorter step to the assumption that everything is excusable. According to the charge, hermeneutics exposes itself to a dangerous risk. Yet the real aim of the accusation is to sow anxiety and uneasiness, so that the consequences of abandoning an absolute standpoint might be highlighted over adopting a relative one. Here lies a mistake that hermeneutics cannot accept. The abandonment of the absolute in no way implies the absolutism of the relative. Whoever affirms this view simply proceeds from an absolute and absolutistic conception of truth, which actually derives from an ultimate foundation. The charge of relativism can be raised only from the position of absolute truth. The reason why this is so irritating is because it overlooks the actual hermeneutic project: to call into question the very idea of an ultimate foundation. Whoever does not dispense with a *fundamentum inconcussum* denies finitude, suppresses all its forms, and sees in them only a limit that should be overcome on the way to absolute truth. As against this negative view of the limit, however, hermeneutics posits a positive one. The limit is not only what concludes and brings to a conclusion, but also what opens the horizon of a new truth.[29] It is a grave misunderstanding to take the basic experience of historicity as mere relativism. To put it more radically: the charge of relativism can arise only within reflection. Refuting the charge would already mean buying into the empty dizziness of its mirages. By contrast, hermeneutics opens up a path that leads to the dismantling of the metaphysical idol of absolute truth.

The second charge claims that hermeneutics ends in self-contradiction because it emphasizes the historicity of understanding. Yet this is simply a newer version of the classical argument against the skeptic. The victorious tone of those who raise this objection is just as irritating as the derisory tone of those who level the charge of relativism. In both cases, which are closely linked to each other, one presumes to dispense with a philosophy on the basis of two sentences. The charge of self-contradiction, especially, is raised in a very unphilosophical way that recalls what Heidegger and then Gadamer, too, called an "attempt to bowl one over" (*BT* 210/*SZ* 229; the English has it as "overturn"; *TM* 344/*GW*1 350). It is very doubtful whether philosophy has anything to do with victories of this kind. Although the argument is formally uncontroversial, it rebounds not only on the one who argues this way but also on the truth claim of the corresponding argumentation. In reality, it dispenses with all philosophical development. Gadamer compares such "empty reflection" to sophism, in particular to the plausible but sterile conclusions of the Sophists. It takes refuge in formalism in order to avoid seeing the historical character of understanding. Yet at the same time it fails to notice that, when it negates historicity, historicity is actually being recognized and confirmed in its universality. The ultimate goal of an absolute claim to truth is to cling to a truth outside of time and space, a truth that is absolute because it has been freed from every condition that would condition it, from every limit that would delimit it, and from every barrier that would constrain it or show it to be finite. But the truth that it claims is absolute only because it absolutizes its own limits. It claims its own standpoint as the unconditioned viewpoint: it is the truth of one's reflection that reflects itself to itself, and mirrors itself back to itself.

Hermeneutics certainly does not strive for absolute truth. It insists, rather, on human finitude. Can it really escape its own finite conditionality, by recognizing that it cannot maintain itself without contradiction, as the argument from reflective philosophy would have it? Obviously not. If this were the case, then finitude would have to become a new absolute, an absolute that, however, cannot guarantee absolute truth. But does one really fall into self-contradiction by remembering finitude? Speaking of finitude in no way eliminates the finite. The argument from reflection is not "in place," for it is not a matter of logical relation but of the "relationships of life" (*TM* 448/*GW1* 452). It is precisely for this reason that hermeneutics does not fall into a contradiction: it simply limits itself to speaking of finitude with the finite tenses and words in which the experience of truth occurs for people. A truth that does not satisfy this *condition humana* no longer contains any truth for us. This also holds for the truths of the sciences, for in order to be understandable, even these truths must be articulated in the language of a certain epoch. Hermeneutics, for its part, knows very well that it cannot escape finitude, and it also knows that it is nothing more than a temporary answer to the question of absolute truth posed by its age. Since it does not abstract itself from the constellation in which it was written, and does not look away from its own historical-linguistic context, hermeneutics does not try to formulate this conditionality in theoretically universal assertions. Instead it prefers to unfold itself within the limits of the dialogue in which it takes part. Only dialogue suits a hermeneutic consciousness that does not forget its finitude and holds itself open for what is beyond its own limits, that is, for the other.

12. Experiencing the Limit: The Openness of Hermeneutic Consciousness

In order to clarify the openness that characterizes hermeneutic consciousness in contrast to the closed quality of reflective philosophy, Gadamer devotes many pages of *Truth and Method* to the concept of "experience" (*Erfahrung*) (*TM* 346–362/*GW1* 352–368).[30] Later he repeatedly highlights these pages as offering the "key position" for the entire work (*TM* xxxv/*GW2* 445). Reconstructing the conceptual history becomes for him the occasion for a confrontation with many philosophers: from Aristotle to Bacon, from Hegel to Husserl and Heidegger.[31] But it is a verse from Aeschylus's *Agamemnon* that provides an exemplary model for the hermeneutic concept of experience: *páthei máthos*, "learning through suffering" (*TM* 356/*GW1* 362).[32] What does *experience* mean for hermeneutics? Why does every experience amount to a *hermeneutic experience*?

Experience should first be distinguished from a scientific experiment: to experience does not mean to experiment. An experiment is carried out in a laboratory according to an inductive method and is controlled, verified, and confirmed—until proven otherwise. Its success lies in its confirmation, which depends on the possibility of repeating it, but which also suppresses all historicity. The enforcement of the scientific paradigm has relegated experience to an experiment, and it is precisely this relegation that Gadamer criticizes. Husserl had already grasped the idealization of the experiment, but he then outlined a genealogy of experience within the lifeworld that comes very close to the scientific experiment. At least since Bacon and his experimental method, scientific experience has been seen from a teleological perspective: the *télos*, the goal of experience lies only in whether "it ends in knowledge" (*TM* 350/*GW1* 355).

In order to escape this perspective, one has to look for other philosophical models. Gadamer finds them in Aristotle and Hegel. When Aristotle describes experience, *empeiría*, he uses the famous image of a fleeing army that gradually comes to a standstill and listens again to the *arché*—here one should bear in mind the dual meaning of the Greek word: as "principle" and as "command."[33] Our perceptions form a river like the fleeing army. Although they are fleeing and isolated at first, they repeat themselves, finally coming to a standstill and unifying themselves around the new command that science represents. This image illustrates the transition from perception to the universal truth of the concept. Experience plays a mediating role between perception and concept, and it is experience that ultimately leads to the transition. Experience retains perceptions on the basis of what they have in common—the *empeiría* is always bound up with the *mnéme*, which is in turn linked to the *lógos*. Experience unifies perceptions and concepts into universality, which actually foreshadows the universality of science. But it differs from the universality of science, too: it is a universality at once open to and inseparable from experienced perceptions. This universality, which must be distinguished from the abstract, universal concept of science, shows the constitutive openness of experience, which is always changing and transformable (*TM* 350–353/ *GW1* 356–358).[34]

Yet this image has one defect: it proceeds from the assumption that, before fleeing, the army had been standing still. It does not account, however, for the process of experience. Aristotle describes it this way because he has in mind not the process but the final result, or in other words: science. This defect can be turned into an advantage, because it allows a previously overlooked particularity of experience to emerge, namely, its unpredictability. Experience is an event that nobody can control, and that happens in a sudden and inexplicable way.

Here Gadamer introduces his new conception of experience, which is not to be understood as a positive development, neither affirming nor confirming, but as a "negative process" (*TM* 353–354/*GW1* 358–359). Experience for him is negation. In the first place, it is the negation of our expectations. Of course this does not mean that there cannot be experiences that meet our expectations, by for example correcting false generalizations. Incidentally, this is the basic principle of *trial and error* that Karl Popper (1902–94) formulated. Gadamer seems quite close to Popper in this regard; but the distance between them, and this should not be overlooked, lies in the voluntaristic character of Popper's concept of experience, which robs experience of its "impassioned" and rebellious side.[35] Negative experience, which for Gadamer is the "actual" one, is quite different (*TM* 353/*GW*1 359). Instead of mastering our experiences we are mastered by them, and in the end we are not so much deranged by them as disoriented. Thus we say, for example: "I had to go through this experience, too." This means: "I did not expect it and I had to learn." Perhaps I have learned that things were not quite the way I believed them to be. In a moment everything is changed—and I, too, am changed. I became different in a world become different—I am somewhere else. The etymology of the German word *Erfahrung,* or "experience," includes the word *Fahrt,* or "journey," which points to this meaning. To have an experience, in German, implies a sort of journeying. Heidegger already identified this connection when he wrote: "To undergo an experience with something—be it a thing, a person, or a god—means that this something befalls us, strikes us, comes over us, overwhelms and transforms us."[36]

The negativity that constitutes experience in this sense is radically different from theoretical knowledge. In order to make this clear, it was necessary for Gadamer to come to terms with Hegel. In the *Phenomenology of Spirit,* experience is famously described as a "reversal of consciousness itself."[37] Here it is precisely a matter of the transformation produced by an unexpected experience. Hegel views the reversal as a dialectical movement in which consciousness, after it has recognized itself in the other, returns to the certainty of itself. Experience is thereby transcended in absolute self-consciousness. Even when Gadamer, with Hegel, thinks of consciousness dialectically, he cannot follow Hegel's way, which would bring experience to an end. Gadamer remains consistent in his defense of bad infinity and holds fast to the moment of negativity that translates for him into the constant "openness" (*Offenheit*) of experience. Precisely because it manifests a constitutive negation, experience remains open and can never, so long as it does not become annulled, end in scientific knowledge (*TM* 355/*GW*1 361).[38]

On the one hand the openness is the site where experience fulfills itself, but on the other hand it is experience that reestablishes openness: the negative character of experience necessarily brings forth new experiences. "That is why a person who is called experienced has become so not only *through* experiences but is also open *to* new experiences" (*TM* 355/*GW*1 361). Experience is certainly nothing one can withdraw from in life. Nevertheless, different forms of comportment can be adopted: there are those who will shy away from their experiences by closing off their own horizon; there are others who will accept their experiences, abandon themselves to them, and affirm their situation with the openness to which their finitude has determined them.

Yet if experience is negative, what does one learn? The answer lies in the dictum of Aeschylus: we learn our own limits from experience; we learn to see the limits of our own finitude. "Thus experience is experience of human finitude" (*TM* 357/*GW*1 363).

Those who are conscious of their own limits know that they are not the masters of their time and future. They know it is not the case that every moment is the right moment, and it is even less the case that everything can be resolved and remedied. They also know that not everything is foreseeable or goes according to plan, because every plan made by a finite being is finite and limited (*TM* 357/*GW1* 363).

The more one opens oneself to experience, the more differentiated the consciousness of one's own finitude becomes, and the more one cultivates one's judgment. Hermeneutic consciousness is nothing more than the consciousness of one's own limits. Those who close themselves off from experience, those uneducated ones who make their own standpoint absolute, become satisfied with their own limited horizons, do not see their own limits, and are thus unable to bring themselves beyond their limits. Such people cannot recognize the other and do not need the other. By contrast, hermeneutic consciousness perceives its own limits and is thereby driven to overcome them, which is possible only in and with the other. Reciprocity is thus indispensable for hermeneutic experience. The close connection between *openness* and *finitude* becomes especially clear from a positive conception of limit, which is always read as the *beyond* of the *other*.[39]

The *experience of the you* that Gadamer describes is thus neither the tragic experience of the failure of human finitude nor the moral experience of accepting the other under a communal law. Rather, openness to the otherness of the you is a necessity for hermeneutic consciousness, since for this consciousness the other is the beyond of its own limit, the way out of its own finitude.

Understanding reaches its greatest extension with the concept of experience after that of application. It is no wonder that experience is also involved with tradition and in this context Gadamer speaks of "*hermeneutical experience*" (*TM* 358/*GW1* 363). To understand the past means to experience it in the event of transmission, as a present that has something to say to the future. Historically effected consciousness articulates itself in the enactment of hermeneutic experience and its openness, which in this case is the openness toward tradition. Just as it is important to give voice to the you, so too is it important to listen to the voices of tradition.

Notes

1. Friedrich Daniel Ernst Schleiermacher, *Allgemeine Hermeneutik von 1809/10*, ed. Wolfgang Virmond, in Kurt-Viktor Selge, ed., *Internationaler Schleiermacher-Kongress*, Berlin 1984, vol. 2 (Berlin/New York: de Gruyter, 1985), 1270–1310, 1271.

2. Georg Anton Friedrich Ast, "Hermeneutik," in Hans-Georg Gadamer and Gottfried Boehm, *Seminar: Philosophische Hermeneutik* (Frankfurt/M: Suhrkamp, 1979), 111–130, 116–117.

3. Schleiermacher, *Hermeneutik und Kritik*, 144.

4. See the essay by Werner Hamacher, "Hermeneutische Ellipsen—Schrift und Zirkel bei Schleiermacher," in Ulrich Nassen, ed., *Texthermeneutik: Geschichte, Aktualität, Kritik* (Paderborn: Schöningh, 1979), 113–148; see also Jürgen Bolten, "Die hermeneutische Spirale," *Poetica* 17 (1985):

355–371; Jean Greisch, "Le cercle et l'ellipse. Le statut de l'herméneutique de Platon à Schleiermacher," *Revue des sciences philosophiques et théologiques* 73 (1989): 161–164.

5. See John Tate, "The Hermeneutic Circle vs. The Enlightenment," *Telos* 110 (1998): 283–296; Jaako Hintikka, "Gadamer: Squaring the Hermeneutical Circle," *Revue internationale de philosophie* 54 (2000): 487–498.

6. See Odo Marquard, *Abschied vom Prinzipiellen* (Stuttgart: Reclam, 1982), 130. Gadamer responded to this position in his essay on "Rhetoric, Hermeneutics, and Ideology-Critique" (*RHT* 313–334/*GW*2 232–250). See also the footnote added later at *TM* 311/*GW*1, 316–317.

7. Gadamer used both "self-understanding" and "understanding oneself as a self," which is "misleading," as he himself admitted. See Gadamer, "Letter to Dallmayr," in *DD* (93–101, 97): "Here lies, it seems to me, a false conception of self-understanding. 'Understanding oneself as a self' is perhaps a misleading expression, which I have used and which I naturally found in connection with Protestant theology—but also in Heidegger's linguistic tradition"; "Dekonstruktion und Hermeneutik" (1988), *GW*10 138–147 at 142. He had already referred to the religious or Pietistic undertones of this conception of self-understanding. See Gadamer, "Zur Problematik des Selbstverständnisses. Ein hermeneutischer Beitrag zur Frage der 'Entmythologisierung,'" (1961), *GW*2 121–132; 125 and 130. The concept of "understanding oneself as a self," which is "inherited from transcendental idealism," does not mean a "sovereign, self-mediated being with itself for self-consciousness"; it is rather based on the fact "that we do not understand ourselves, unless before God." See on this Petra Plieger, *Sprache im Gespräch. Studien zum hermeneutischen Sprachverständnis bei Hans-Georg Gadamer* (Vienna: WUV, 2000), 207–208.

8. Gadamer later made the significance of "thing" or *Sache* more precise. See Gadamer, *Lesebuch*, ed. Jean Grondin (Tübingen: Mohr Siebeck [UTB], 1997), 280–295, 285. See also Pavel Kouba, "Die Sache des Verstehens," *Internationale Zeitschrift für Philosophie* 2 (1996): 185–196; 189–190.

9. See in this volume chapter 4, part 2.

10. See in this volume chapter 3, part 10.

11. In the first edition of *Truth and Method* it reads, "It is only temporal distance . . . ," whereas in the fifth edition from 1986 it says, "Often temporal distance. . . ." (Compare *TM* 298 and *GW*1 304).

12. See in this volume, chapter 10, part 2.

13. See in this volume chapter 8.

14. For some of the problematic contexts in this regard see Bernd Auerochs, "Gadamer über Tradition," *Zeitschrift für philosophische Forschung* 49 (1995): 294–311.

15. See Hans-Helmuth Gander, "In den Netzen der Überlieferung. Eine hermeneutische Analyse zur Geschichtlichkeit der Erkenntnis," in Günter Figal, Jean Grondin, and Dennis E. Schmidt, eds., *Hermeneutische Wege* (Tübingen: Mohr Verlag, 2000), 257–268. See also James Risser, "Interpreting Tradition," *Journal for the British Society for Phenomenology* 34 (2003): 297–308.

16. See Karl Robert Mandelkow, "Probleme der Wirkungsgeschichte," *Jahrbuch für internationale Germanistik* 2 (1970): 69–78, 71.

17. See Jean Grondin, "La conscience du travail de l'histoire et le problème de la vérité en herméneutique," in *L'horizon herméneutique de la pensée contemporaine* (Paris, Vrin, 1993), 213–233.

18. See in this volume chapter 9, part 5.

19. To be sure: the word "fusion" was not a successful choice. It has led to many criticisms—some justified—since it can cause misunderstanding. In particular, the "fusion" of horizons suggests a process of understanding through which the identity of those who understand, no less than those being understood, can be lost—and obviously, too, the difference between them. This paradigmatic criticism was raised by Stanley Rosen, "Interpretation and Fusion of Horizons: Remarks on Gadamer," in Rosen, *Metaphysics and Ordinary Language* (New Haven, Conn.: Yale University Press, 1999), 182–201; see also Marina Vitkin, "The Fusion of Horizons on Knowledge and Alterity," *Philosophy and Social Research* 21 (1995): 57–76.

20. Rambach speaks of *applicatio* only in the last part of his work. See Johann Jacob Rambach, *Institutiones hermeneuticae sacrae*, vol. 4, chap. 3: "De sensus inventi adplicatione" (Jena: Hartung, 1723), 804–805. See also Jean-Claude Gens, "La révaluation par Gadamer du concept piétiste d'application," *L'art de comprendre* 4 (1996): 24–37.

21. See in this volume chapter 2, part 2.

22. Betti, for example, argued that a text would have to be understood objectively at first and could only then be applied. See in this volume chapter 10, part 1.

23. See Joel C. Weinsheimer, "Gadamer's Hermeneutic," 184–199.

24. Gadamer, "Hermeneutics as Practical Philosophy" (*RAS* 88–112, 96); "Hermeneutik als praktische Philosophie," in *Vernunft im Zeitalter der Wissenschaft* (Frankfurt/M: Suhrkamp, 1976), 78–109, 88. See Anthony Kerby, "Gadamer's Concrete Universal," *Man and World* 24 (1991): 49–61.

25. See in this volume chapter 3, parts 6 and 8.

26. Hegel's influence in this context should not be underestimated. Compare Jeff Mitscherling, "Hegelian Elements in Gadamer's Notions of Application and Play," *Man and World* 25 (1992): 61–67.

27. See in this volume chapter 9, parts 3–4.

28. See in this volume chapter 7, part 6; chapter 9, part 4.

29. See in this volume chapter 9, part 6.

30. See his response to the essay by Robert Sokolowski in Lewis E. Hahn, ed., *The Philosophy of Hans-Georg Gadamer* (Chicago: Open Court, 1997), 235. On the concept of "experience," see John Hogan, "Gadamer and the Hermeneutical Experience," *Philosophy Today* 20 (1976): 3–12.

31. For a comparison between the empirical and the hermeneutic concepts of experience, see Friederike Rese, "Expérience et induction chez Aristote, Bacon et Gadamer," in Guy Deniau and André Stanguennec, eds., *Expérience et herméneutique*, Colloque de Nantes, June 2005 (Paris: Le Cercle Herméneutique [Collection Phéno], 2006), 59–78.

32. Compare Aeschylus, *Agamemnon*: "Men shall learn wisdom, by affliction schooled" (v. 177).

33. See Aristotle, *Posterior Analytics*, II, 19.

34. On the complexity of the relation between experience and hermeneutics, see Deniau and Stanguennec, *Expérience et herméneutique*, 191–202.

35. See on this point the remark added by Gadamer at *TM* 353 and *GW1* 359. See also Gadamer, "Philosophy or Theory of Science?" (*RAS* 151–167, 162) and "Philosophie oder Wissenschaftstheorie?" in *Vernunft im Zeitalter der Wissenschaft*, 125–149, 142–143.

36. Heidegger, "The Nature of Language" in *On the Way to Language*, trans. Peter D. Hertz (San Francisco: Harper & Row, 1971), 57–108, 57; *Unterwegs zur Sprach* (Pfullingen: Verlag Günther Neske, 1959), 149.

37. G. W. F. Hegel, *Phenomenology of Spirit*, trans. A. V. Miller (Oxford: Oxford University Press, 1977), 55; *Phänomenologie des Geistes. Gesammelte Werke*, vol. 9, ed. Wolfgang Bonsiepen and Reinhard Heede (Hamburg: Felix Meiner, 1980), 61. On the concept of "experience" between Hegel and Gadamer, see Luis Eduardo Gama, *Erfahrung, Erinnerung und Text. Über das Gespräch zwischen Gadamer und Hegel und die Grenzen zwischen Dialektik und Hermeneutik* (Würzburg: Königshausen & Neumann, 2006), 42–125.

38. In this way we can speak of the tragic element of hermeneutic experience, but only as long as it remains wordless. See Gerald L. Bruns, "On the Tragedy of Hermeneutical Experience" (*RHT* 73–89).

39. This close link has been overlooked, for example, by Bormann. See Claus von Bormann, "Die Zweideutigkeit der hermeneutischen Erfahrung," in Karl Otto Apel, ed., *Hermeneutik und Ideologiekritik* (Frankfurt/M: Suhrkamp, 1971), 83–119.

6 An Ethics Close to Life

Nevertheless, the thought here cannot be that one learns how to live in the right way, and is finally capable of it, in the manner in which one learns how to sing, speak or write. (*IG* 121/*GW*7 196)

The Aristotelian concept of practice has yet another specific emphasis inasmuch as it is applied to the status of a free citizen in the *polis*. This is where human practice exists in the eminent sense of the word. (*RAS* 91/*VZW* 81)

... if the essence of a utopia could be defined other than in the form of a distant longing. (*GW*7 277)

1. Is a Philosophical Ethics Possible?

To understand means to apply; understanding is always put into practice and thus becomes a form of action in itself, in the world, and with others. It should come as no surprise that hermeneutics, as it recuperates the theoretical as well as practical value it has had since antiquity, develops in proximity to *practical philosophy*. Gadamer emphasizes this point in his 1972 essay, "Hermeneutics as Practical Philosophy" (*RAS* 88–112/*VZW* 78–109). Here the *ethical* dimension of hermeneutics becomes clearer: it does not lie in understanding as such, and even less in the alleged task or duty of understanding, but rather in the openness of hermeneutic consciousness, which is pushed to overcome its own limits in the "beyond" offered by the other, and to raise itself to ethical vigilance.

Considered more closely, Gadamer's path of thought was marked by ethics even prior to hermeneutics. The influence of the Marburg School, Hartmann's role in bringing him closer to Scheler's value ethics, and finally Heidegger's famous seminar from 1923 in Freiburg on the sixth book of the *Nicomachean Ethics*—all these contribute to awakening Gadamer's attention to ethics, which never subsided.[1] His writings bear witness to this: his Master's thesis from 1922; the essay "Der aristotelische 'Protreptikos'" from 1927; the important essay "Practical Knowledge," which was long unpublished and goes back to 1930; the 1931 book on *Plato's Dialectical Ethics;* the chapter on Aristotle appended to "The Problem of Historical Consciousness" that is taken up again in the excursus of *Truth and Method;* and the more than twenty essays from his later years on this topic.[2] Finally, in 1998, Klostermann published Gadamer's edition of the sixth book of the *Nicomachean Ethics*.[3]

The rediscovery in recent decades of the relevance of the Greek philosophers' ethics and politics is in large part due to philosophical hermeneutics. In particular, Gadamer's reading of Aristotle brought ethical questions back to the center of philosophical debate, and especially in Germany led to the "rehabilitation of practical philosophy."[4] However, not only his return to Aristotle but also his entire view of ethics has often been misunderstood. Gadamer has been accused of ethical relativism, though this would be a charge more appropriate to "Neo-Aristotelianism." There has even been a certain dismissal of his project because one assumes that Heidegger had already, years before, said everything there was to say about Aristotle and practical philosophy.

In an important 1963 essay entitled "On the Possibility of a Philosophical Ethics," which has probably provoked the greatest reaction, Gadamer plays Aristotle off against Kant.[5] It would be a trivial misunderstanding, however, to read this essay as supporting Aristotelian relativism against Kantian universalism. The primary question addresses the very possibility of a philosophical ethics, in other words the "foundation" of ethics in Husserl's sense, as Gadamer states more precisely later in the 1989 essay, "Aristotle and Imperative Ethics," when he returns to the problem.[6] Here there lies concealed a "nearly indissoluble *aporia*" that appears when ethics, in order to become philosophical, reaches the level of a reflection on the universal (*HRE* 19/*GW*4 176). A philosophical ethics that wants to be unconditional and absolute is, however, an ethics that is at a remove from life—as Kierkegaard showed—and separated from any concrete situation that would call for a decision. Kant made two important contributions: on the one hand he exposed the arrogance of Enlightenment ethics when he showed that the "voice of reason" can be heard by everyone; on the other hand he secured the universal absoluteness of a moral law that is free from all inclinations and interests, and in which good will expresses itself. Thus, what is the trouble with imperative ethics? Certainly not its universality, but rather a kind of intellectualism that makes the rightness of moral action depend on an abstract norm, as if the person acting were always able to recognize the norm objectively and with the necessary detachment. In this way, however, moral action is reduced to the paradigm of a method. And if in contemporary ethics the concept of "norm" dominates, shaped by the model of scientific laws, one reason is because Kant formulated the categorical imperative as a law of nature. Gerhard Krüger clarified this issue: Kant's ethics presumes that the moral law has already been recognized.[7] The example used to discuss this argument is suicide. According to the categorical imperative, in which one's own maxims should be as valid as a universal law, the suicidal person, as long as he is in possession of reason, should not be able to overlook the indefensibility of his decision. This way of looking at things is, however, far too intellectualistic: it is unlikely that anyone haunted by thoughts of suicide will possess sufficient reason to reflect on the unlawfulness of his or her own deed. Kant measures reflection in accordance with the ideal of objective knowledge, which he binds his ethics to when he characterizes the limits of judgment as an index of both the obfuscation of purity and heteronomy. But does one not lose sight this way of the particularity of moral action, when action is not based solely on knowledge, much less objective knowledge? Are there really absolute norms to which moral action must conform, or are we not rather dealing with a kind of lawfulness that, quite different from scientific law, recalls the Jewish Torah or the *nómoi* of the Greeks?

First and foremost, Gadamer's critique of Kant warns against an ethics at a distance from the situation in which the person who must act finds himself, and which subsequently covers over the concrete demands of the situation by abstracting from an "exceptional situation"—which ultimately is no exception if one remembers that "the temptation to consider oneself an exception is a universal human situation" (*HRE* 26/ *GW*4 181). By placing the accent on the situation, from which no one, least of all the philosopher, can claim to escape, Gadamer shows the impossibility of a philosophical ethics that is unaware of its own open-endedness, that refuses to take this open-endedness as its essential content—for only in this way can ethics claim to satisfy the unconditionality of the moral: "This means, however, that philosophical ethics occurs in the same situation where everyone else finds themselves" (*HRE* 28/*GW*4 184).[8] The philosopher who is concerned with ethics is thus not an expert who knows more than others and can give recommendations, construct new laws, or write new stone tablets—on the contrary, he is much more in danger of fleeing the situation.[9] Experts in ethics, bioethics, and business ethics create a problem, as indeed every other "expert" does, too, because ultimately they claim the decision making for themselves and thereby take away responsibility from others. And it is far from evident that they are wiser.

2. *Phrónesis:* Acting Reasonably

We are generally dissatisfied with the definition of the good, because we would want to know what the good is in order to put it into practice. Hence philosophical ethics cannot be separated from practical ethics: it is precisely in ethics where the inescapable transition from theory to practice becomes clear. Here lies the relevance of Aristotle: his entire ethics is predicated by that "other kind of knowing" that is at stake in life (*HRE* 148/*GW*7 388).[10]

In his critique of the "theoretical subject" of metaphysics, which in contrast to *Dasein* is artificially cut off from understanding themselves in their care for the world, Heidegger made a decisive step toward the rediscovery of practical knowledge. Traces of this critique are to be found in his 1921–23 lectures on Aristotle, in the *Natorpbericht*, and in his study of book 6 of the *Nicomachean Ethics*, which was first conducted in 1923 in Freiburg as a seminar and then revisited in 1924–25 in his Marburg lectures.[11] It is therefore certainly true that Heidegger's early phenomenological research led the way to the rehabilitation of practical philosophy; but it is just as true that the ethical dimension of Heidegger's thought, which is much discussed today, leaves the care for others in the dark as it focuses on care for the self.[12] It is no coincidence that after 1945 his closest students turned to ethics: from Krüger, who takes up Kantian morality, and Hannah Arendt, who brings the *vita activa* to its high point, to Leo Strauss, who highlights the Greek natural law, along with those who invoke Heidegger only indirectly, above all Emmanuel Lévinas, who raises ethics to First Philosophy. All of these philosophers begin with the priority of the other and ask less about individual action than about collective and communicative action.[13] Gadamer belongs among these philosophers. His rehabilitation of practical philosophy, even though it was certainly influenced by Heidegger's starting point, follows another path instead, which is clear already in the 1930 essay "Practical Knowledge" (*GW5* 230–248) and which is taken up again later in the chapter on "The Hermeneutic Relevance of Aristotle" in *Truth and Method* (*TM* 312–324/*GW1* 317–329). This chapter, which signals the rebirth of practical philosophy in the twentieth century, outlines in just a few pages at least four key ideas: the autonomy and particularity of practical actions; the value of *phrónesis*, which Gadamer translates as "reasonableness" and which guides human behavior; the necessity of taking *ethós* into consideration, in particular the context in which ethico-political relations orient action; and finally his view of a necessarily dialectical path for ethics, in which the theoretical search for the good, which is articulated in the dialogue with the other, is already in itself a realization of the practical good.

Yet how does Gadamer's position actually differ from Heidegger's? Their perspectives are different and to a certain extent even opposed. Heidegger leaves Plato behind in order to turn to Aristotle, whereby he does not have *phrónesis* in mind as much in mind as *sophía*, which ultimately forms the basis on which he develops his theoretical philosophy.[14] By contrast, Gadamer reads Aristotelian ethics in the light of Plato's dialectic, and Aristotle interests him only to the extent that he can be more Socratic than Socrates himself—as is shown clearly through his entire confrontation with Greek philosophy.[15] Given his Platonic perspective, which also stresses the unity of theory and practice, it is not surprising that Gadamer sees practical wisdom less in its individual and more in its communitarian dimension.[16] Gadamer's attention is not so much turned to the relation between *sophía* and *phrónesis*, but rather to the relation between *phrónesis* and *téchne*. This relationship, which runs through his entire account of Greek philosophy, embodies in a nutshell the distinction between "truth" and "method."[17] Although the chapter on Aristotle deals with philosophical problems of considerable weight, as for example the problem of "application," and hence the problem of a new concept of the "universal" that cannot be imposed on concrete particulars, the "hermeneutic relevance" of Aristotelian ethics lies for Gadamer in the new paradigm offered by *phrónesis*. The core of Gadamer's argument lies precisely in delimiting the practical knowledge of *phrónesis*. Such delimiting creates no difficulties for the theoretical knowledge of *epistéme* or science, which, as mathematics shows, is knowledge of what is immutable and objectively proven. This is all the more true for *sóphia*, which thinks the immutable being of things on the basis of its principles. Those who know a great deal are often not at all wise; they may know "marvelous things" and yet still overlook human goods.[18]

The relationship between *phrónesis* and *téchne* is much more complex: practical knowledge is both the wisdom that guides action (*práxis*) and the skill that guides the craftsman in the production of things (*poíesis*). So what distinguishes the two? For example, what is the difference between the knowledge that guides my behavior and the knowledge that governs the way in which I fashion clay into a vase? In order to create a vase, I must in the first place have learned a *téchne*—otherwise I would not know how to proceed. A *téchne* can be learned, but also forgotten (*TM* 317/*GW1* 322).[19] Ethical knowledge is different. I can of course choose whether I want to learn an art or take up a profession, and I can choose to give up my work, or to interrupt it, in order to rest. But I cannot withdraw from the constitutive human situation that compels me to act, that is, to make decisions. "The human being always already stands within the realm of what is at stake in *phrónesis*" (*GW5* 242). Here it is not a matter of learning or teaching, and also not a matter of training, as in the sense of perfecting technical knowledge. It is senseless to devote oneself to the chimera of a technical knowledge that could lessen or even abolish the toil of a day's deliberation. This toil, this work is so complex because it is not limited to discovering the means useful for reaching some specific end. Here a second important difference comes into view, which concerns the relationship between means and ends. Ethical knowledge is never entirely complete before its application, and thus it is not in any way objectifiable or objectified, so that the appropriate means for reaching an end could be learned or taught. The very choice of means is an ethical question. What is more important is that here one must make a decision about the goal. "There is no pre-existing certainty about what the good life is directed toward as a whole" (*TM* 318/*GW1* 326). This should not mean that ethics does not establish ideal models to show the right mean point or the midpoint we ought to aim for—much as the archer effectively aims at his target by looking at a particular point; but it cannot guarantee that the center will be hit.[20] To hit the center means to apply knowledge to the situation at that moment. Perfection lies in making the right decision at the right moment, without letting the *kairós* slip away. Such a hit is not seeing in the sense of pure seeing, but rather intuiting, through *noûs,* of what the right thing to do would be. What would be the opposite of this? Not error or illusion, but being blinded or dazzled. Whoever is overcome by the passions loses sight of the goal and can no longer keep moving in the right direction (*TM* 319/*GW1* 327).

For Gadamer's argument, however, a further distinction is more significant, that between ethical and technical knowledge, which also bears on the distinction between acting and making. To understand it one must refer back to Aristotle's famous distinction between *érgon* and *enérgeia,* or between the work itself and the activity of working.[21] All human activity can be divided here: either it is a making that has its goal in some external work (*érgon*), or it is an action that carries its goal within itself. The examples Aristotle uses are of building and seeing: whereas the activity of building is completed in the built house, the goal of seeing coincides with the activity itself. When I fashion a vase, my work ends in the product. My ethical action has, by contrast, its goal in itself. More than doing it is Being, indeed it is one's very manner of Being in the world. *You are how you comport yourself.* This perspective brings the distinction between ethical and practical knowledge more clearly into view. According to practical knowledge, the produced object is separate from me. Yet in ethical action, I cannot deal with myself as if I were an object. What is clearly missing here is the detachment that makes it possible to look at myself in the way one looks at an object, for one is always already involved in the situation in which one must act. Practical ethical knowledge is a "self-knowing" that takes the form of neither objectification nor detachment from oneself, but is given rather in the form of "vigilance" (*GW5* 238).

If hermeneutic ethics, which is so close to life and hence fundamentally antinormative, questions every a priori norm, it does not follow that, as a countermove, the situation or even the *éthos* becomes normative, in other words the totality of "those convictions, values, habits we all hold in common" (*GW2* 319–329, 325).[22] Otherwise the role of the *phrónesis* of every individual would be undervalued. The dialogical relation between language and speaker can clarify this ethical model (*EPH* 165–180, 178/*GW2* 155–173, 170). On the basis of the ethical order of the *pólis,* everyone acts in accordance with his *phrónesis* by virtue of articulating the *éthos* in light of the individual situation. One can, by recognizing what is "doable," what is both appropriate and right, take aim at the center, actually find the mean and realize the good, the *prákton agathón.* Thus "the good is in the first place nothing more than the logos shared by the community" (*IG* 147/*GW7* 208).

Our action, the *prohaíresis* or "choice of the better," that self-projection into the future of possibility that defines our Being, always occurs "within the horizon of the polis" (*HRE* 29, 31/*GW4* 185, 188). Or to put it another way: ethical action is also always political action. This explains Gadamer's attention to those "modifications" in Aristotle's discussion of *phrónesis* in the *Nicomachean Ethics* (*TM* 319/*GW1* 328).[23] What becomes more important is the reference to responsibility, not only to oneself, but also to the other, a responsibility included in *phrónesis* when Aristotle speaks of *sýnesis.* *Phrónesis* leads to a decision involving consultation with the self that is always consultation with others. Just as my consultation is never abstract and isolated, *phrónesis* is not individual wisdom, for it is inseparable from *sýnesis,* or sympathetic understanding, which makes it possible for me to grasp the action of the other. The ability to have insight and patience, to discriminate correctly, to enter into the situation of the other and thus to judge correctly (the Aristotelian concepts are *gnóme, syngnóme,* and *epeikeîa*), is possible only on the basis of that "belonging" which always already binds me to the other in the community. On the one hand this "belonging" prevents me from adopting an external, disinterested standpoint, but on the other hand it allows me to give and accept advice—all this in the name of friendship.

3. The Unity of Theory and Practice

Even if his position on an ethics close to life emphasizes the transition from theory to practice, it does not follow that Gadamer agrees with those who denigrate theory.

Rather the opposite is the case. He published *Praise of Theory* in 1983, where he suggests a new way of seeing theory and practice that conceives of their relationship as a substantial continuity. It should also be clear that philosophical hermeneutics, even though it understands itself to be a practical philosophy, in no way relinquishes its claim to be a theoretical philosophy.

The antagonism between theory and practice, which is so widespread today, can be encapsulated in a familiar turn of phrase: "That is all pure theory; but what happens in practice?" Nevertheless the new evaluation of practice brings about a new evaluation of theory. What has happened, instead, over the last centuries? On the one hand theory has lost prestige and been reduced to a purely instrumental concept, used in the service of new scientific insights. On the other hand practice has sunk to the level of mere scientific application. In order to rediscover the value of theory *and* practice, the context of Greek philosophy should be taken into account, in which *theoría* is a form of *práxis*. The most active ones are those engaged in the activity of thinking.[24] Important here is the translation of *theorein,* which has more the meaning of "participating in" than of "looking at," as for example participating in the sacredness of a festival or art.[25] To go beyond oneself and to dwell in or with another means *being-there,* being alive.[26] Thus theory is a form of life; indeed it is the highest form, just as the eye that guides it seeks the highest point. Theory is a way of acting, living, and being there with and through others, an active participation in what suddenly appears and offers itself to everyone as "shared property" (*RAS* 77/*VZW* 64). In contrast to the goods that remain only private and dwindle when they are shared with others, the good that is at stake in theory is never private, but always held in common, and far from dwindling, it becomes greater and grows when it is shared with others (*PT* 31/*LT* 45). If theory is an action that is ultimately a practice, then practice for its part is always already theory. For it is a looking away from oneself in order to turn toward others and, together with them, to strive for what is right or the common good (*PT* 33/*LT* 47–48). "Practice is conducting oneself and acting in solidarity" (*RAS* 87/*VZW* 77). The gesture beyond the self and the participation in what is shared by all mark the continuity between theory and practice.

Gadamer means here the specifics of human practice. Every living being can be described in terms of practice. But in the case of animals, their behavior is bound to nature and the instinct for self-preservation. Human beings can free themselves from the cycle of nature; our actions transgress the immediate requirements of life. Survival is a living beyond oneself that is confirmed in the burial of the dead—a decisive step in becoming human.[27] As Hegel already emphasized, survival manifests itself in the enormous renunciation of work, whose product belongs less to the individual than to the community. Survival is just as evident in language, which, taking distance from what is present, and making present what is distant, allows us to exercise *prohaíresis,* that is, the preliminary choice, and it allows us to deliberate on the realization of future common goals. Here can be grasped the political character of human practice, whose *ethos* is articulated as *lógos* and forms the foundation of the *pólis.*

4. The Technological Rationalization of Life: On the Art of Healing

When practice is reduced to an anonymous application, to *Technik*—mere technique, technology, or method—freedom almost disappears. Not only does production dominate action, but production is no longer oriented toward a naturally given model; instead it aims to replace nature itself with an "artificial counter-reality" (*EH* 6 /*UVG* 18). A totalizing technological civilization not only leads to the artificial transformation of nature and the conquest of space, but brings with it an escalating rational control over ever greater areas of human life. This modification of life has consequences that remain unknown and difficult to gauge. The only certainty is that it favors the "tendency towards conformity" and disadvantages "creative capacity" or the power of judgment (*RAS* 81/*VZW* 60). In the closed laboratory of the earth, space of what is common to all is dwindling. Clearly, the endless search for profit grants priority to private goods. As "if the world was a single, large factory," it should come as no surprise that economic rationality dominates over social rationality (*EPH* 166/*GW2* 156). At the same time, though, a simple critique of technology, like any cultural critique, carries "little conviction," since it enjoys the benefits of what it criticizes (*EPH* 169/*GW2* 159). Emotional resistance to the new and superstition, which often takes the form of a flight from freedom, are extreme reactions that only show how little humanity is prepared for the progress of technology (*EH* 1–30/*UVG* 11–49).

Yet the consequences of this progress should not be blamed on science. Even if science is able to demythologize itself, action is once again the task of politics. For Gadamer this means developing "an awareness out of necessity once again of new normative and common solidarities," the need to generate cohesion precisely where division holds sway, and to show that our very "extant differences" ultimately bring us together (*RAS* 87/*VZW* 76; *EPH* 178/*GW2* 171). It is politics that must show science its *limits,* for whatever the capabilities of science, it "will not be able to exceed a measure which perhaps no one knows and to which, nevertheless, we are all subject" (*EPH* 180/*GW2* 173).

It is also true, however, that while the opposition between political action and technical production has become extremely tense, the realm of action for politics has increasingly narrowed. The technical rationalization of life, which translates into an escalation of the means for exercising control, leads to disorientation and makes the choice of ends superfluous. Moreover, the relationship between means and ends has been entirely reversed. This reversal can be seen for example in the language of computer science, which excludes all ends that cannot be codified by the means at its disposal. According to this view, only that which can be codified and communicated can be thought. This is just one example among many. In fact this reversal has a bearing on all forms of life, where we enjoy the extraordinary powers that technology offers and where, in comparison with the past, we can do more. But this "more" casts a shadow on what we can no longer make, and perhaps it is not even what we wanted to make. The pact we have made with technology forces us to renounce our freedom of action. Often unconsciously we put our choices in the hands of those who know the means better than we do: the experts.

In his 1989 essay "The Limitations of the Expert," Gadamer stresses the irreplaceability of this figure who mediates between scientific knowledge and its social effects (*EPH* 181–192/*EE* 136–157). Nevertheless, he says, the risks of a "society of experts" based on specialization should be discussed. The expert is the one who has a particular knowledge at his disposal and as such must be listened to; but there is no guarantee that he is wiser or more experienced than others. For this reason, it would be a mistake to give him the final decision and the last word. This would have the devastating effect, among others, of the majority relinquishing their responsibility and surrendering their possibilities for action and decision. The result would be a further erosion of the social rationality that should guide us in the choice of common goals, and hence a widespread irrationality.

If the possibilities for action are narrowed, this will also reduce that fragile site equilibrium that enables human life to find a way from destinal "eccentricity" back to its center (*EH* 12/*UVG* 26). It is precisely medicine, because it is concerned with this balance, that shows how important practical experience and judgment are. Gadamer's 1993 book, *The Enigma of Health*, expresses his interest in the "art of healing." It was written not only for doctors and patients but for all, since everyone must learn how to care for themselves. In this book, Gadamer explores the unique ambiguity of medicine from the standpoint of the enigmatic complexity of good health. Despite tremendous technical and scientific progress, medicine still requires practical knowledge and the decision-making prowess of the physician. Medicine's distinctive character lies in the fact that its results do not culminate in a product—although the trend toward hospitalization and the treatment of patients as objects, as sick bodies, grows increasingly stronger. The task of the physician is to heal, that is, to restore the natural balance (*EH*13/*UVG* 26).[28] Medicine is thus the very art of balance that works together with nature and so manifests a clear hermeneutic vocation: not only because the physician is also a patient but because the treatment, like any good interpretation, succeeds only when it withdraws in order to restore that balance (*EH* 31–42/*UVG* 50–64).[29] The disappearance of the physician, who withdraws in order to leave the patient free again, is even more important for psychiatry. In a lecture from 1989 entitled "Hermeneutics and Psychiatry," Gadamer insists above all on the participatory relationship: if the one who heals is himself a patient, then the one who is the patient will not be condemned to the passivity of taking medication, but rather will be called to the active care of the self (*EH* 138–151/*UVG* 201–213). Nothing should be simply and completely entrusted to the expert, least of all the balance of one's life, for action that allows participation in the community is the inalienable right of all.

5. "Thinking in Utopias": The Philosopher and the *Polis*

From the 1930s on, Gadamer's political thinking unfolded with unmistakable continuity within the framework of his engagement with Plato's philosophy, and specifically with the *Republic*. Gadamer's political thinking is closely aligned with his project of a philosophical ethics. The concept of "utopia" is the pivotal moment of this project, and over the years it becomes ever more important in Gadamer's thinking until it ultimately characterizes a way of thought. Hermeneutics, as political philosophy, is necessarily thinking in utopias. But what does *utopia* mean?

A utopia is "far removed from any reality": Gadamer describes it this way already in his 1942 essay, "Plato's Educational State" (*DDP* 73/*GW5* 251), and later he often returns to this designation (*RAS* 80/*VZW* 67). In order to understand the meaning he attributes to "utopia" we should go back to the lecture of 1934, "Plato and the Poets," before looking at the important essay of 1982, "Plato's Thinking in Utopias," in which he defends the critical significance of Plato's utopia in a polemical discussion with Karl Popper.[30]

How was Socrates possible, "the just man in the unjust state?" (*DDP* 76/*GW5* 252). Socrates's condemnation lies at the core of Platonic utopia, which hence does not represent an abstract claim but emerges out of a concrete political context. Though he was directed toward a career in politics, Plato fell silent when faced with the death of his teacher. His philosophy is born from this death, which is why it is spoken through the mouth of Socrates. Even the visits to Syracuse should not be read as deviations from this path.[31] Yet the renunciation of a career in politics by no means signifies a renunciation of politics; quite the contrary: "Plato is no more a statesman than Socrates but no less either" (*DDP* 76/*GW5* 251). What Gadamer writes about Plato in 1942 could equally apply to himself.[32] Plato's utopia arises from the reality of the *polis,* and it refers back to that reality.

Plato's otherwise incomprehensible attitude toward the poets can be explained only if we remember the situation in Athens at his time. In the tenth book of the *Republic,* Homer and the great dramatic poets are excluded from the state.[33] Here it is a matter of neither criticism of mythology nor the ancient hostility between poetry and philosophy. It would be reductive to suppose that Plato was compelled by the ontological presuppositions of his system to see poetry as a representation of reality, in other words as a copy of a copy of the world of ideas. Gadamer suggests we consider the context in which Plato banishes the poets (*DDP* 48/*GW5* 193). This suggestion should obviously be considered relevant for Gadamer himself, who was writing in the years of National Socialism. Poetry was the basis of Greek *paideia,* the ground from which sophism took root and grew. On the one hand, the sophists used the texts of the poets, but at the same time emptied them of their content; on the other hand, they outlined a new ethos, according to which justice was the right of the strongest (*DDP* 50/*GW5* 195). The condemnation poetry in Plato's writing on the state is an attack against sophism and has a twofold aim. First, it is about exposing the dangers of an art that is entirely dedicated to putting people under a spell and forgetting themselves, deprived of all truth-value. The critique of poetry is thus not at all an ontological critique: inasmuch as it concentrates on effects, it is more of "a *critique of 'aesthetic consciousness'*" (*DDP* 65/*GW5* 206).[34] Secondly, with the utopia of an "inner state" Plato wants to suggest a new educative model that could be the prelude to a rebirth of the *polis.* This second aim can be achieved only by a philosophy that promotes the human disposition of "being for others" (DDP 57/GW5 200). Socrates praises the new "educational state" for the kind of justice that begins when everyone watches over themselves, instead of demanding rights over others. This state is founded on the new reformation of the soul. Only a person who is rightly attuned to him- or herself can be in harmony with others.[35] Hannah Arendt, too, emphasizes the Platonic analogy between the parts of the soul and the parts of the city.[36] However, whereas Arendt sees action already integrated in the realm of theoretical cognition, Gadamer takes Plato's main point to be that political action is different from technical production and is bound up inextricably with philosophy as the practice of education. The community of Plato's academy, which aimed at the realization of this practice, stands in sharp relief against the backdrop of the Republic. The utopian state gestures toward an education that is "not authoritative instruction based on an ideal organization at all," but rather the experience of justice itself, which is acquired in the process of dialectical investigation (DDP 52/GW5 197).[37] No political institution can achieve any good end without the philosophical education of its citizens (DDP 52/GW5 197). Philosophy is the tonic against the abuse of power, because it teaches us to keep the common good in view.

It is therefore mistaken to take Plato's "educational state" as a real proposal for reform, as Popper does and as Aristotle had already done.[38] Aristotle grasped just as little of the ideological value of the eîdos in the ideal state as of the theory of ideas. Plato's works, the Republic but also the Laws, belong to the literary genre of utopian writing—this is Gadamer's argument—a genre that was already well represented in ancient Greek literature. Utopias are not concerned with blueprints for the implementation of actual reforms; rather they offer an ironic critique of the present. Nevertheless, with Plato utopia takes on a deeper political and philosophical meaning.

Utopia becomes a cipher of the further and the beyond that thinking of and in the polis cannot dismiss. Utopia becomes a cipher not only of political thinking but also of thinking itself, of that thinking which refuses to come to a standstill, which rejects closure and instead remains open to the further and the beyond. Plato's great achievement lies in transforming the atopia of Socrates, influenced by his peculiarity and strangeness, his being out of place, which forced him to the margin of the polis, to utopia.[39] The philosopher remains on the margin—and Gadamer's Plato emphasizes this especially during the "Third Reich"—but from this non-place, or better this not-yet-place, he gives a sign, an intimation, a gesture from afar (GW7 277). The dialogue that he writes is a speculative signpost, and Socrates is a "utopian figure of thought" (GW7 283). He reflects political reality, sets it in a brighter light, by revealing what the polis is not. From its margins he critically marks the limits of the polis. Hence, Plato's intention is clearly not to introduce some new reform. The "practical" value of utopia, which aims not at action but at critical reflection, lies in the significance not of wishing, but of choosing (RAS 81/VZW 67–69). This does not mean, however, that utopia evaporates into unreality. Instead, it reinterprets the ou-topos, the non-place, as the place that is otherwise and beyond, the place that does not yet exist but will exist and in the unconditionality of the common word, on the basis of which the *polis* can be thought anew. Utopia proves to be a "dialectical concept": thanks to the dialogical carrying-over and the carrying-through into the beyond of the other, utopia becomes for hermeneutics a "way of thinking" (*GW7* 283).

Denken in Utopien, "thinking in utopias," means to think in the endlessly finite process of dialogical and dichotomous dialectics. This form of thinking demands the choosing of a responsible response. It involves "bringing about the possible in the image of the impossible," reaching an opening to the further and the beyond that only the other can offer. Here is where philosophical hermeneutics takes its political stance: without silencing the negative moment of critique of the present, it turns toward the utopian word of the future (*DDP* 72/*GW5* 197).[40]

The dialectic of utopia lies in its speculative character. The ideal city inversely reflects the limits of the real city. Even though it never becomes reality, the "rule of the philosopher" reveals the abuse of power that is a temptation for anyone who exercises power. In his 1978 essay, "The Polis and Knowledge of the Good," which appears in his book *The Idea of the Good in Platonic-Aristotelian Philosophy,* Gadamer insists on the speculative dialectic of utopia (*IG* 63–103/*GW7* 162–185). Here utopia is the political model that Gadamer opposes to planning. With the economic order clearly in mind, Gadamer had warned against the planning, or misplanning, of the political world order as early as 1966 in his essay "Notes on Planning for the Future" (*EPH* 165–180/*GW2* 155–173). Planning seduces us into believing in a normative politics that takes as its task the elimination of disorder, as for example in the disorderly, "underdeveloped" countries. Finally it presents the world as the object of rational scientific production. Order for the sake of order takes over, and the means become ends in themselves: the "perfect administration," whose ideal is neutrality, no longer recognizes any ideal (*EPH* 169/*GW2* 160). Against this backdrop of world planning, the dialectical value of "the game of utopia" stands out more distinctly. In this game—as Plato shows (*IG* 72–73/ *GW7* 168)—reason and wisdom leave room for the disorder of human things, without however ceasing to point toward the further and the beyond that belong to the ideal city of justice.

Notes

1. On the debate with value ethics, compare the essays: Gadamer, "Das ontologische Problem des Werte" (1971), *GW4* 189–202; "Wertethik und praktische Philosophie" (1982), *GW4* 203–215.
2. See Gadamer, "Der aristotelische 'Protreptikos' und die entwicklungsgeschichtliche Betrachtung der aristotelischen Ethik" (1927), *GW5* 164–186; "Praktisches Wissen" (1930), *GW5* 230–248; *TM* 312–324/*GW1* 317–329.
3. See Aristotle, *Nikomachische Ethik VI,* ed. and trans. Hans-Georg Gadamer (Frankfurt/M: Klostermann, 1998).

4. See Manfred Riedel, *Die Rehabilitierung der praktischen Philosophie*, 2 vols. (Freiburg: Rombach, 1972–74); this work signaled the rehabilitation of practical philosophy in Germany. For an overview that includes critical questions, see Franco Volpi, "Praktische Klugheit im Nihilismus der Technik: Hermeneutik, praktische Philosophie, Neoaristotelismus," *Internationale Zeitschrift für Philosophie* 1 (1992): 5–23; and Volpi, "Herméneutique et philosophie pratique," in Guy Deniau and Jean-Claude Gens, eds., *L'héritage de Hans-Georg Gadamer* (Paris: Le Cercle Herméneutique [Collection Phéno], 2004), 13–36.

5. Gadamer, "On the Possibility of a Philosophical Ethics," in *Hermeneutics, Religion and Ethics*, trans. Joel Weinsheimer (New Haven, Conn.: Yale University Press, 1999), 18–36; "Über die Möglichkeit einer philosophischen Ethik," (1963), *GW4* 175–188.

6. See Gadamer, "Aristotle and Imperative Ethics," in *Hermeneutics, Religion and Ethics*, 142–161; "Aristoteles und die imperativische Ethik" (1989), *GW7* 381–395.

7. Gadamer had at hand a copy of the work by Gerhard Krüger, *Philosophie und Moral in der Kantischen Ethik* (Tübingen: Mohr, 1931).

8. See Ronald Beiner, "Do We Need a Philosophical Ethics? Theory, Prudence, and the Primacy of *Ethos*," in Robert Bartlett and Susan Collins, eds., *Action and Contemplation* (Albany: SUNY Press, 1999), 37–52.

9. Compare Gadamer's view of the philosopher in chapter 9, part 1, of this volume.

10. See Aristotle, *Nicomachean Ethics*, 1141b 33, 1142a 30; *Eudemian Ethics*, 1242b 36.

11. The *Natorpbericht* appears in Heidegger's *Phänomenologische Interpretationen*, 341–415. The seminar on book 6 of the *Nicomachean Ethics* is published as the introduction to the lecture on the "Sophists": Heidegger, *Platon: Sophistes, GA* 19, ed. Ingeborg Schüssler (Frankfurt/M: Klostermann, 1992), 21–188.

12. Gadamer also expressed his views on the question of ethics for Heidegger. Compare for example his review on the book by Werner Marx, *Is There a Measure on Earth? Foundations for a Nonmetaphysical Ethics*, trans. Thomas J. Nenon Jr. and Reginald Lilly (Chicago: University of Chicago Press, 1987), in *GW3*, 333–349.

13. The ethics of intersubjective communication was developed by Apel and Habermas.

14. In the afterword to his edition of the *Nicomachean Ethics* Gadamer writes: "Obviously Heidegger is not pursuing an interest in ethics," *Nikomachische Ethik VI*, 61–68, 67. Rather, Heidegger is much more interested in the difference between theoretical and practical philosophy. On this difference see Günter Figal, "Vollzugssinn und Faktizität," in his *Der Sinn des Verstehens: Beiträge zur hermeneutischen Philosophie* (Stuttgart: Reclam, 1996), 32–44. Following Figal, Stolzenberg has emphasized Gadamer's "practical" starting point: Stolzenberg, "Hermeneutik der praktischen Vernunft. Hans-Georg Gadamer interpretiert Martin Heideggers Aristoteles Interpretation," in Günter Figal and Hans-Helmuth Gander, eds., *"Dimensionen des Hermeneutischen": Heidegger und Gadamer* (Frankfurt/M: Klostermann, 2005), 133–152, especially 134–135. For a critical debate with Gadamer, see Enrico Berti, "The Reception of Aristotle's Intellectual Virtues in Gadamer and the Hermeneutic Philosophy," in Riccardo Pozzo, ed., *The Impact of Aristotelianism on Modern Philosophy*, Studies in Philosophy and the History of Philosophy 39 (Washington, D.C.: Catholic University of America Press, 2004), 285–300.

15. See chapter 7, part 7, in this volume.

16. See on this theme P. Christopher Smith, "Phrónesis: The Individual and the Community: Divergent Appropriation of Aristotle's Ethical Discernment in Heidegger's and Gadamer's Hermeneutics," in Mirko Wischke and Michael Hofer, eds., *Gadamer verstehen/Understanding Gadamer* (Darmstadt: Wissenschaftliche Buchgesellschaft, 2003), 169–185.

17. Gadamer, "Natur und Welt: Die hermeneutische Dimension in Naturerkenntnis und Naturwissenschaft" (1986), *GW7* 418–442, 430.

18. Nicomachean Ethics, 1141b 5–7.

19. See Joseph Dunne, "Aristotle after Gadamer: An Analysis of the Distinction between the Concepts of Phronesis and Techne," *Irish Philosophical Journal* 2 (1985): 105–123.

20. Nicomachean Ethics, 1094a 23.

21. Nicomachean Ethics, 1094a 3–6.

22. See Ernst Tugendhat, *Probleme der Ethik* (Stuttgart: Reclam, 1984), 39. Doubts about the call to the human ethos have recently been raised by Ineichen: see Hans Ineichen, "Gadamer über praktische Philosophie. Einige kritische Bermerkungen," in Andrzej Przylebski, ed., *Das Erbe Gadamers* (Frankfurt/M: Peter Lang, 2006), 247–254, 252.

23. "Einführung," in *Nikomachische Ethik VI*, 9–10.

24. Aristotle, *Politics*, 1325b 21.

25. See in this volume chapter 3, part 9.

26. See in this volume chapter 9, part 5.

27. See in this volume chapter 9, part 3.

28. On this topic see Fred Dallmayr, "The Enigma of Health: Gadamer at Century's End," LL 155–169. See also Vittorio Lingiardi, "Hermeneutics and the Philosophy of Medicine: Hans-Georg Gadamer's Platonic Metaphor," Theoretical Medicine and Bioethics 20 (1999): 413–422; Fredrik Svenaeus, "Hermeneutics of Medicine in the Wake of Gadamer: The Issue of Phronesis," Theoretical Medicine and Bioethics 24 (2003): 407–431.

29. On this concept of interpretation see chapter 8, part 11, of this volume.

30. Gadamer, *"Plato and the Poets"* (DDP 39–72/GW5 187–211). "Platos Denken in Utopien," *GW7* 270–289. The work under discussion is Karl Popper's *The Open Society and Its Enemies* (London: Routledge and K. Paul, 1949); *Die offene Gesellschaft und ihre Feinde* (1944), 2 vols. *Gesammelte Werke in deutscher Sprache*, vols. 5–6 (Tübingen: Mohr Siebeck, 2003).

31. See Plato, *Seventh Letter*, 327e; *Plato*, 1649.

32. Grondin's claim that Gadamer's work is "nonpolitical," because Plato's state was not a historical project, fails to see the role that Platonic utopias played in Gadamer's work from the outset. See Grondin, *Hans-Georg Gadamer: A Biography* (New Haven, Conn.: Yale University Press, 2003), 213; *Gadamer: Eine Biographie*, 215. By contrast, Dallmayr lays emphasis on the political dimension of Gadamer's thought. Dallmayr sees the *Republic* as a utopia, a "city in speech." See Fred Dallmayr, "Hermeneutics and Justice," in Kathleen Wright, ed., *Festival of Interpretation* (Albany: SUNY Press, 1990), 95–105, 95–96. On Gadamer and the political scope of poetry see Dennis J. Schmidt, "Wozu Hermeneutik? On Poetry and the Political," in his *Lyrical and Ethical Subjects: Essays on the Periphery of the Word, Freedom and History* (Albany: SUNY Press, 2002), 19–31, 20ff.

33. *Republic*, 595–608c; *Plato*, 1199–1212.

34. Gadamer returns to the aestheticization of art in *Truth and Method* (see chapter 3, part 1, of the present volume).

35. See *Republic*, 434d–445c; *Plato*, 1066–1076.

36. See Hannah Arendt, *Vita activa oder Vom tätigen Leben* (Munich and Zurich: Piper, 1981), 244–245, 260–261. See Lawrence Biskowski, "Reason in Politics: Arendt and Gadamer on the Role of the Eide," in *Polity* 31 (1998): 217–244.

37. See also "Platos Denken in Utopien," *GW7* 284.

38. See Aristotle, *Politics,* B 1; see also Robert R. Sullivan, "Poets, Education and State," in his *Political Hermeneutics* (University Park: Pennsylvania State University Press, 1989), 137–164, 142–143.

39. On the significance of atopos for hermeneutics see chapter 8, part 8, of this volume.

40. In an interview with Dutt, the affinity of hermeneutics with both ideology critique and the Frankfurt School comes to light. *Hans-Georg Gadamer im Gespräch: Hermeneutik, Ästhetik, praktische Philosophie*, ed. Carsten Dutt (Heidelberg: Universitätsverlag C. Winter, 1995), 72–75.

7 The Enigma of Socrates: Philosophical Hermeneutics and Greek Philosophy

But of course Plato was at the center of my studies. (RPJ 12/GW2 487)

1. We Are the Greeks—They Are the Moderns

It is impossible to imagine philosophical hermeneutics without Greek philosophy. Nonetheless, hermeneutics is not a retreat from the questions of contemporary philosophy to the historical-philological study of Greek texts, nor should Gadamer's project be reduced to a mere "application" of Greek ideas. Greek philosophy plays a decisive role for hermeneutics, which has not yet been sufficiently recognized.

There is already an effective history of hermeneutics that must be deconstructed if one wants to avoid leaving *Truth and Method* as its magnum opus, which supposedly contains all of hermeneutics and casts its shadow over all other works, beginning with the studies of Greek philosophy. In this context Pöggeler writes:

> When we read *Truth and Method* we can very well assume (until we reach the third part on being as language) that Gadamer is an Aristotelian, one who takes rhetoric, poetry, and the legal structuring of life as his main themes. The works of volume 7 of the *Collected Works*, however, which certainly form a second highpoint next to *Truth and Method*, prove that Gadamer was a Platonist.[1]

Thus we should ask ourselves: what relation exists between philosophical hermeneutics and Greek philosophy? At the same time we can ask the still relevant question: *do we really need the Greeks for philosophy?* Gadamer's answer is, decisively, yes. Greek philosophy is the constellation for philosophical hermeneutics. Both are bound up with each other through the circularity of understanding. Reading the Greek texts involves a philosophical-hermeneutic reading, whereby Greek philosophy represents a challenge, since it calls into question modern customs and prejudices. Hermeneutics accepts this challenge and lets itself be led by the Greeks in the circular openness of an infinite dialogue. The actuality of Greek philosophy becomes hermeneutics itself, understood as the philosophical reappraisal of the dialogue with the Greeks because, despite the breaks and interruptions, continuity persists.[2] Hermeneutics approaches the Greeks "not from the perspective of the assumed superiority of modernity, which believes itself beyond the ancient philosophers because it possesses an infinitely refined logic, but instead with the conviction that philosophy is a human experience that remains the same and that characterizes the human being as such, and that there is no progress in it, but only participation" (*IG* 6/*GW*7 130). When he speaks of "participation," Gadamer means the Platonic *methéxis*. In this regard he wrote, in the 1972 essay on "The Contemporary Importance of Greek Philosophy," that for us the encounter with the Greeks is ultimately an "encounter with ourselves."[3] Here Greek philosophy, together with hermeneutics, becomes a new paradigm for philosophy, indeed the very one that today is called "continental philosophy." In this regard the relation between "the Greeks and us" takes on a completely different significance: *We are the Greeks— they are the moderns.*

Gadamer stands in the wake of Kant, Hegel, and even Schleiermacher; he follows in other words all those German philosophers who, gripped by "Graecomania," have linked philosophy inextricably to its history.[4] His interest can be seen as part of the rebirth of ancient philosophy in the first half of the twentieth century, in which philology and philosophy cross over and into each other.[5] But Gadamer was driven to the Greeks by his philosophical questions, and hence the huge impression that Heidegger's reading made on Gadamer should not be surprising. It was not only the radicality with which Heidegger questioned Greek philosophy. In addition, his interpretation responded to the necessity demanded by Husserl to free philosophy from the history of philosophy.[6] This phenomenological turn in textual hermeneutics cannot be emphasized enough. *Philosophical hermeneutics is a phenomenological revival of Greek philosophy.* The productivity of this new hermeneutics was soon to deliver important results. Although Heidegger famously concentrated on Aristotle, most of his students preferred Plato: Hannah Arendt, Jacob Klein, Gerhard Krüger, Georg Picht, Leo Strauss, Wilhelm Szilasi. Gadamer's case, in this context, is particularly significant. How would philosophical hermeneutics have been possible without Greek philosophy, in other words without the Socratic dialogue, without the Platonic dialectic of the one and the many, without Aristotelian *phrónesis*?

2. On The Language of Metaphysics

For his phenomenological interpretation of the Greeks, Heidegger is guided by a new watchword: "destructuring." Although he takes up Husserl's demand to show the experiences of the lifeworld directly, Heidegger notes that such immediacy is not possible, since all showing is mediated by language. Thus it becomes essential to destructure, that is, to dismantle, the sedimented layers with which the tradition has domesticated philosophy and covered over the original experiences of thought. It is essential to reveal the origin of concepts, and thereby to bring the language of philosophy back to the life context from which it emerges. Philosophy will be possible again only through the dismantling of the language that has been rigidified by centuries of Western metaphysics. In this way, on the one hand, the confrontation with Greek philosophy is reopened by recognizing the *Seinsfrage,* that is the "question of Being," which has fallen into forgetfulness, and on the other hand, we begin to think again on the basis of our own life experiences. For Gadamer these are one and the same, since philosophy is always a "continuous dialogue with itself" (*LL* 39/*GW8* 430).

The question of Being deepens and intensifies in the question of the *language of metaphysics.* Here Gadamer cannot hide what distances him from his teacher. In both his 1968 essay "The Language of Metaphysics" and his 1990 "Heidegger and Language," Gadamer asks himself what the "language of metaphysics" could actually be.[7] His thesis is that a language of metaphysics does not exist at all. "Language is always only the one that we speak with others and to others" (*DD* 48/*GW8* 144.) This does not rule out the existence of a "metaphysical" tradition, which has consolidated itself through linguistic and conceptual rigidity.[8] Metaphysics is this rigidity. But philosophical language takes root in everyday language—and not even metaphysics can sever these roots. It is not language that is metaphysical but its hardening into concepts, which, however, as soon as they return to the flow of philosophical dialogue—as Wittgenstein suggested[9]—already prefigure the lines of their own overcoming.

In this way hermeneutics limits not only the question of the language of metaphysics, but also the question of metaphysics itself.[10] Gadamer does not at all share the catastrophic view of a history of philosophy condemned to decline. For him there is also no worry about "twisting out" of metaphysics, which he interprets as "a conscious achievement of the suffering" of a past in which we simultaneously "remain," even if we have overcome it (*HD* 81/*GW3* 87).[11] What would be "beyond" metaphysics? Gadamer shares even less Heidegger's project of returning to the history of Western metaphysics in order to prepare a new "beginning" of thought. For hermeneutics nothing is more "metaphysical" than a totally new beginning, since we are always already in the middle of a dialogue.

But Gadamer also dismantles the philosophical tradition and excavates its effective history—which proves moreover that historically effected consciousness is not a parasitical consciousness—in the search for that Socrates who is hidden in pre-Socratic and post-Socratic philosophy. Along a path that goes through Parmenides and Heraclitus, Plato and Aristotle, from the first essays of the twenties to the seventh volume of his *Work* published in 1991, Gadamer engages in a destructuring of the history of Greek philosophy, in order to lead it back to its forgotten, Socratic inspiration.

3. Parmenides and Heraclitus: The *Logos* of Mortals

Heidegger's return to the pre-Socratics, mediated through Aristotle, is determined by the need to open a nonmetaphysical access to *phýsis,* which is thought in its coming into presence. For Gadamer, by contrast, *phýsis* is an Aristotelian and not a pre-Socratic thought, which the "meta-physical" Aristotle had projected back onto the pre-Socratics (*GW7* 43–82, 52). It is a matter, for Gadamer, of freeing ourselves from the Aristotelian construction that reads and forces us to read the entirety of Greek philosophy as a philosophy of nature, in its teleological progress from Thales to Aristotle. What is the picture of Parmenides and Heraclitus that emerges from this reading of the tradition?

Both are far apart from the Ionian philosophy of Thales, Anaximander, and Anaximenes. Parmenides and Heraclitus are not concerned with *phýsis,* or nature understood as the ground or substance of all things; they concern themselves rather with human errancy and human finitude. Their thought has a political, ethical, and ultimately religious inspiration—modern terms that can be used only with caution when talking about philosophers whose *lógos* remains indissolubly bound up with *mýthos* (*GW7* 3–31, 14–15).[12] This first becomes visible in the fragments from the didactic poem by Parmenides. It is quite naive to believe that an ontological doctrine could be found in this poem. According to Gadamer, we should not ignore the literary fiction. After all, the *logos* that claims that Being is, is proclaimed by a goddess.[13] Why is this the case? Because the *logos* that leads to truth, to *alétheia,* which therefore does not mix being and not-being, can only be divine.[14] When mortals speak, by contrast, they cannot avoid saying "is" and "is not" in one breath, that is, contradicting themselves without deciding "between the yes and the no."[15] The divine truth stands opposed to the many "opinions" of mortals, who are "deaf and blind, dumbfounded," unable to avoid the "not" and thus destined to endless error.[16] The goddess describes their world darkened by contradiction; but in doing so she remains "on the way to truth," which is reserved for only the divine dimension (*GW7* 9). Mortal like the others, Parmenides does not speak in the first person but, making use of myth, lets the goddess speak. The *logos* of being is thus a *logos* from the beyond; as such it does not affect mortals, who are plagued by death, by their end, and by their finitude (*GW7* 24). The point that the *logos* of being is from the beyond can be interpreted as a critical rejoinder to Heidegger and his question of Being. In any case the human *logos* remains on "this side of Being"—as the title of the essay "Parmenides or This Side of Being," suggests. According to the traditional reading, Parmenides introduced the separation between the sensual and intelligible worlds. For Gadamer, by contrast, Parmenides is the philosopher of finitude, of the world that exists *on this side,* which is at the same time Being and Not-Being, whereas Being is only of the gods.

It is no different with Heraclitus. If we follow—as Gadamer does—the historiographical paradigm that Reinhard suggests, then Heraclitus lived at the same time as or even later than Parmenides.[17] Heraclitus was no opponent of the Ionian school, and he never sought to erect a cosmology. Even his doctrine of fire, which also confounds Aristotle, is a Stoic reinterpretation (*GW7* 51–52). Heraclitus was able to think the speculative unity of opposites in a "contentious harmony," which is the *logos* of the world.[18] "To attend to the one in all the differences"—that is his contribution (*GW7*

57). Gadamer mentions in this context Hegel's famous words: "there is no sentence by Heraclitus that I have not taken up in my logic."[19] From the oppositions of which Heraclitus speaks, the mystery of the unity is not the passage from the identical to the different, but the sudden change (*GW7* 48). The words often bear witness to this: for example, the word *bios* points both to "life" and to the deadly "bow."[20] The inseparability of life and death begins to emerge in this "as a final, unsolvable, self-solving riddle" (*GW7* 41). Is there a return from death to life, as from sleep to awakening? This question is taken up again later by Plato's Socrates in the *Phaedo*.

Heraclitus looks past multiplicity and discovers unity in the sudden flare-up and extinguishing of life, as if like fire. This is precisely the meaning of the sentence carved over the entrance to Heidegger's hut in Todtnauberg: "Lightning directs everything."[21] But Heraclitus also wants to awaken from the sleep of nonunderstanding. It is thus not difficult to read his famous fragment hermeneutically: "The waking ones have one and a shared world, but in sleep everyone turns from it into their own."[22] The way to emerge from the night of isolation, and to return to oneself, is the way that leads to the other, to "sharing in the days and world we have in common" (*GW7* 78).[23] Gadamer wrote of Heraclitus:

> This philosopher weeps a bit too obviously over humans and their non-understanding and, forgetting himself, reflects on human life, which, stretched out between sleep and waking, death and life, dream and the reason of daytime that everyone shares, is also deeply non-understandable to itself—as truly as it is exposed to the abruptness of change and the riddle of non-being. (*GW7* 38)

In this call to alertness, to wakefulness, to philosophy, his closeness to Socrates becomes visible, and even more so when Heraclitus says: "I have sought myself."[24]

4. Socrates, Philosophy, and Immortality

Yet in the path Gadamer outlines it is Socrates who represents the true turning point. Socrates is the *philosopher* par excellence, because the love of *sophia* for him accomplishes the transition from sleeping to waking, becoming wakeful, and raises itself to that wisdom which knows of its not-knowing from the outset. Even though Gadamer dedicated no more than three essays to him, the figure of Socrates dominates philosophical hermeneutics and forms the model that cannot be imitated, but nevertheless should be imitated. Gadamer's Socrates is above all the one portrayed by Plato in the *Apology*, the *Euthyphro*, and the *Phaedo*—for it is the Platonic Socrates who has effected our historical consciousness (*GW7* 83). Following the way opened by Parmenides and Heraclitus, he disappointedly gives up the inquiry into natural phenomena, the position of the earth, the orbits of the heavens. Socrates fears that if he were to proceed like the natural philosophers, who turn immediately to things and demand to grasp them with their five senses, he would end up blinding his soul altogether. So he prepares himself for a "second journey," a metaphor the Greeks use to designate the extreme case when the wind stops and the ship can be moved forward only by the rowers. The second journey by Socrates is his escape into the *logoi,* which is depicted in the *Phaedo.* For Gadamer this is the epochal turn made by Greek philosophy, which is at the same time a decisive transition for hermeneutics.[25]

We should not overlook the ironic tone with which Plato speaks of this "second" voyage, which is by far superior to immediate experience. It represents the passage from the sensual to the intelligible, which, however, is the intelligible not of the ideas, but rather of the *logoi* (*PDE* 70/*GW*5 53). Gadamer translates as follows the words of Socrates in the *Phaedo:* "So I thought I must take refuge in discussions and investigate the truth of things by means of words."[26] The flight into the *logoi* is the *anamnesis* of language, the anamnetic recognition of the other and the word of the other that articulate shared experience. With Socrates, philosophy no longer boldly presumes to see things in their immediacy. And as philosophy turns its gaze away from things, it listens to the word of the other. It becomes *dialogue.* Here lies above all the Socratic inspiration of hermeneutics. "I am devoted to learning; landscapes and trees have nothing to teach me—only the people in the city can do that"—so Socrates says in the *Phaedrus* (*Plato,* 510; 230d). More than a flight, this is the entry of philosophy into the world of the *polis,* into the community of citizens. With Socrates, philosophy discovers its political and ethical vocation. Philosophy concerns itself with the why of human actions and for the first time asks the question of the "good," which will draw all of classical philosophy, beginning with Plato and Aristotle, under its influence.[27]

But to live with others is no easy matter—at least for a philosopher. In Athens Socrates lives with others, but he does not live like others. Thus his trial and his death sentence for *asebeîa,* "impiety," become unavoidable. Socrates listens only to his own daemon. Precisely this is his *eusebeîa,* his "piety" (*Frömmigkeit*), namely the devout respect with which he "shows his humility in not-knowing" (*GW*7 109). The religious character of Socrates's not-knowing discloses the vanity of the technical-scientific knowledge that spread in the Greek Enlightenment.[28] With his constant questioning Socrates challenges the assumptions of the Athenians, who claimed to know what the good is. The service he accomplished is a divine one. According to the oracle at Delphi, Socrates is the wisest of all humans. Socrates, by contrast, says that he does not know—and with that answer he at once confirms and refutes the oracle (*GW*7 111). The provocation proves to be the divine vocation of philosophy. Thus Socrates does not flee, but accepts his sentence and drinks the hemlock. But even as parts of his body begin to grow cold and stiff, he continues to speak and to question. He reminds his friends that "we owe a cock to Asclepius; make this offering to him": an offering to the god of medicine, in order to say that he is healed and for him a new and true life is beginning (*Plato* 100/ *Phaedo*118a).

The death of the philosopher is the confirmation of his life, and his words are the most convincing proof of the immortality of the soul. In probably one of the most beautiful essays that Gadamer dedicated to Greek philosophy, "The Proofs of Immortality in Plato's *Phaedo*," he has Socrates speak for him (*DDP* 21–38/*GW6* 187–200). On the most extreme outer limits of death, without understanding, or wanting to make understandable, what marks the limit of human understanding itself, the word of the dying philosopher is directed to the others who share in his death, in order to receive an answer that takes the dialogue further—even after death. This is the way in which hermeneutics thinks of immortality.[29]

5. Plato's Aporetic Dialectics: Between the One and the Dyad

Philosophical hermeneutics is a conscious recovery of Platonic philosophy in the twentieth century.[30] Plato shows the way beyond metaphysics toward the openness of philosophical experience: from *dialectics* to the *dialogue*.

Who is Gadamer's Plato? He is not the "metaphysical" philosopher, responsible for the forgetting of Being, as he was depicted by Heidegger and even before that by Nietzsche.[31] As Gadamer put it in 1983, "That Plato did more than prepare in advance Aristotelian 'ontotheology,' which Heidegger saw in him, was certain to me" (*EE* 170). But Plato is also not the founder of a theory of principles, as the Tübingen School interpreted him.[32] It is of course true that without Plato there would never have been metaphysics, but it is equally true that "Plato was no Platonist" (*RPJ* 40/*GW2* 508). This polemical thesis, in which the emancipatory potential of his interpretation begins to emerge, also brings Gadamer close to Schleiermacher, insofar as he rediscovers in Plato the master of dialogue, whose dialectic in its Socratic vocation is a reflection on finitude.[33] Hermeneutics proceeds from this dialectic and unfolds itself in an uninterrupted process.

The unitary conception of Platonic philosophy does not prevent Gadamer from privileging certain texts: the *Phaedo*, the *Symposium*, the *Phaedrus*, the *Philebus*, the *Parmenides*, the *Theaetetus*, the *Sophist*, the *Timaeus*, the *Republic*, and the *Seventh Letter*. As he had already done in the case of the pre-Socratics, Gadamer aims to deconstruct Aristotle's reading and to show that his criticism of Plato is unjustified. On the one hand, there is in Plato no *chorismós*, no ontological separation between the world of ideas and the sensible world, and on the other hand it emerges clearly on the basis of the "*Parmenides*" that what actually interested Plato was the "web of ideas," the *dialectical interweaving* (*DDP* 119/*GW6* 113).[34]

The work by Gadamer that contains *in nuce* the most important features not only of his Plato interpretation, but also of his entire philosophy, is his 1931 book *Plato's Dialectical Ethics*, which focuses specifically on the *Philebus*. Before the connection between ethics and dialectics is articulated, however, it is important to say what is meant by "dialectics," the key term of philosophical hermeneutics. Gadamer writes:

> Platonic philosophy is a dialectic not only because in conceiving and comprehending [*im Begreifen*] it keeps itself on the way [*unterwegs*] to the concept [*zum Begriff*] but also because, as a philosophy that conceives and comprehends in that way,

it knows man as a creature that is thus "on the way" [*Unterwegs*] and "between" [*Zwischen*]. (*PDE* 3–4/*GW5* 5–6)

Gadamer explains that it is important to keep in mind the Greek prefix *día-*, which means "through" (*IG* 98/*GW7* 182), if we are to grasp the Socratic meaning of Platonic philosophy, which unfolds in the dialectical openness *between* question and answer, and which recognizes itself as a kind of *between* that grants the provisionality, indeterminacy, and incompleteness that emerge from it.[35] By knowing itself as *finite*, it accepts *infinite* openness. It is thus no *sophía*, since it does not pretend to be wisdom. Instead it is much more *philo-sophía*, a striving for wisdom (*DDP* 155/*GW6* 153).

This dialectic is dialogical: the "between" is the between of the *dia-logue*. Platonic dialectics arises not only from Socratic dialogue, in which the dialogical character of *logos* comes to light, but unfolds in an exemplary manner with the guiding thread of language. It develops itself in a dialogical form, in which the *logoi* are again and again placed "back within the original movement of the conversation" (*TM* 369/*GW1* 374).[36]

Socrates's "flight" into the *logoi*, which connects not coincidentally with the "hypothesis" of the ideas, becomes more relevant here (*GW7* 335). The idea is anchored to the name and to discourse. In the search for a "ground" of truth, Socrates finds it in that characteristic "*remaining equal to itself*" of the name, even in its self-differentiation, that is, in that "shared substantive understanding" which is articulated here (*PDE* 52/*GW5* 52–53).[37] Philosophy begins with language as the site of unreflective knowledge that through *anamnesis*, which is only linguistic, can become reflective and conscious—albeit always incompletely. But Gadamer's thesis is still more radical: Plato discovers the "dialectical miracle," the possibility of the *one* in the *many* and the *many* in the *one*, because he looks at the structure of the *logos* (*GW6* 20). How is it possible for the one to be the many and the many the one? How is this contradiction possible, against which the Eleatics cautioned and from which the Sophists profited? Is it not perhaps a question here of a contradiction that makes even speaking impossible? For if it is said that the one is the many, that it *is* itself insofar as it is one, and *is not* itself insofar as it is many, then ultimately we are mixing Being and Not-Being with each other.

For Plato the quarrel with the Sophists does not end in "misology," the hatred of "reasonable discourse" (*Phaedo* 89c–d).[38] On the contrary, the Eleatic Stranger in the *Sophist* warns: "If we were deprived of that, we'd be deprived of philosophy" (*Sophist* 260a). If philosophy were a noetic, intellectual intuition of Being, then it would not need to say anything *other* than Being; it could remain with the identical, that is, say nothing, and give up saying altogether. Philosophy would begin and end—in a divine way—in the intuition of Being. Since philosophy cannot, however, be reduced to this it requires the dianoetic, discursive transition to the other of Being, to what is different: this means it needs saying and needs the *logos*. In knowing itself to be dependent on the discursivity of *logos*, philosophy since Plato is aware that it can develop only in that "between" traversed by discourse; it cannot be other than dialectical. In order to save philosophy it is necessary to save or to legitimize the *logos*. But precisely through this view of the characteristic interweaving of the *logos*, being also appears different. Nevertheless, dialectics conceives itself as Being bringing itself to language, it "*does not think in the logos of being* [. . .] *it thinks of being itself as logos*" (GW6 28).

The wonder of the one and the many lies in their "interweaving," their *symploké*. The *logos* is simultaneously the many woven together with the one, and the one that carries within itself the many. The one and the many are concepts that are correlated and fluid. Gadamer writes: "the one is necessarily many and the many, one" (PDE 96 / GW5 90). This is possible because of the "instability" of discourse.[39] Thus there begins to emerge in language a circular movement of ascent and descent that goes from the one to the many and from the many to the one. What counts for the dialectician, in this infinite circularity that articulates itself in the finitude of the *légein*, the saying, is something that escapes most people, namely what lies "in the middle," "the intermediates" (*Philebus* 17a). In this fruitful *between,* in the *dia-* of the *légein,* of discourse that is constantly a *dialégesthai,* a speaking with each other, the tangled web of Being is woven.

The procedure followed here, which constantly runs through discourse, is that of *diaeresis,* which represents for Gadamer "the positive turn of the dialectic, [. . .] the 'euporie' after the 'aporie.'"[40] The dialectician's art is described in the *Phaedrus* (*Phaedrus* 265d) and it consists of pulling apart an idea that appears in its unity and distinguishing it "according to its parts"; here what matters is to follow the natural weave of nerves, as with the cutting up of a sacred offering.[41] *Diaeresis* is thus a dichotomous process. Through differentiation, the characteristic features of what one is seeking are brought to light; what results from this is the diaeretic *logos*. It would, however, be a mistake to believe that this *logos* gives an objective definition of the essence of a thing, since in reality it limits itself to emphasizing new perspectives. The impossibility of reaching a definition—which Aristotle, by contrast, takes to be possible—can be led back to the "irrevocable weakness" of all forms of human knowledge, the names (*ónoma*), discourse (*lógos*), the image (*eidolon*), knowledge (*epistéme*)—which is fundamentally different from intuition (*nous*)—that Plato examines in the famous excursus in the *Seventh Letter* (*Seventh Letter* 342a–344d). But precisely from this weakness—as Gadamer writes in his study on "Dialectics and Sophism in the Seventh Platonic Letter"—the "productivity" of dialectics will emerge (DDP 111/GW6 106). Every diaeretic *logos* always permits its own overcoming, because its unity arises from the interweaving of the many, which can always be dissolved anew. What Gadamer will call the "limits" of language, which we repeatedly run up against in our speaking and thinking, on the one hand reveals the unavoidable failure of any systematic exposition of philosophy, and on the other hand destines dialectical inquiry to infinite progress.[42]

The interweaving of the *logos* plays a decisive role in Gadamer's interpretation of Platonic dialectic. Only in the not yet fully clarified interweaving of the one and the many, the many and the one, is the fate of *logos* and philosophy decided. Another word for interweaving is "mixture"; the one and the many already have history on their side and are derived from two Pythagorean categories: the *péras*, the limit, and the *ápeiron*, the unlimited. According to Gadamer, "the great accomplishment of Plato's thought" was to interpret these two categories anew, as they were developed in the *Republic* and the *Theaetetus* (*DDP* 139/*GW6* 140). Here it is important to emphasize that "limit" in all of pre-Socratic philosophy had a positive significance, that is, an initial and inaugural significance: the limit does not mark an end but opens up or discloses. Thanks to the limit, what *is* emerges from the unlimited. The unlimited thus has a negative significance: it is the incomplete, the imperfect—actually the very opposite of what is typically believed today. Plato preserves the positive significance of limit but rehabilitates the unlimited. This rehabilitation, with which he at the same time commits patricide on Parmenides, is important for philosophical hermeneutics, which develops around the concept of the "limit" as a philosophy of infinite finitude and thereby takes up the legacy of Platonic philosophy.[43]

The interpretation of the *Philebus* takes on a significance that should not be overlooked.[44] According to the Pythagorean doctrine of numbers, the limit is opposed to the unlimited. On the basis of a "naïve ontological identification," as Jacob Klein explains, the Pythagoreans do not distinguish between the "limit" and the "limited."[45] The innovation that Plato achieved lies precisely in the "limited," the "mixed" that arises from the "mixture" of the limit and the unlimited. All that is, all that belongs to this world, is "limited," "mixed," or exists thanks to a *mixture*. Gadamer stresses the point: "So *the ontological 'mixture' of the indefinite and the defining*, producing definiteness, *is the condition of the possibility of the being* and the being unitary, *of (ontically) mixed things*" (*PDE* 142/*GW5* 102). To mix according to proportion, according to *logos*, mean to bring being into Being.[46]

In Plato's philosophy the limit and the unlimited of the Pythagoreans are called the "one" and the "two" or the "dyad" (*dýad*).[47] In his essay on "Plato's Unwritten Dialectics" Gadamer suggests that the problem of multiplicity is from the very beginning the problem of duality (*DDP* 135/*GW6* 137).[48] But what is *duality*, which plays a far more important role in hermeneutics than we typically imagine? The "one" is the limit that unifies by limiting and enclosing. The "indeterminate two" is the way of introducing difference into unity and thus of taking into account the infinite self-differentiation of the many. When Plato prefers, however, to speak of the "dyad" instead of the unlimited, there is a reason for it. As the principle of difference and of differentiation, the dyad also contributes in its unlimitedness to tracing the limits of the order of the world (*DDP* 151/*GW6* 150). The dyad is thus the way in which Plato rehabilitates the unlimited. The unlimited no longer represents the boundless infinity of Not-Being; rather it is Not-Being understood as *being other*; it is the *difference* of Not-Being in its *infinite self-differentiation*. The dyad is another name for the "is not," put forward by the Eleatic Stranger in the *Sophist* (*Sophist* 257b). Only in this way can the *logos* be saved, or the *koinonía* of the highest kinds of Being be demonstrated, and especially the reciprocal participation of Being and Not-Being, of the identical and the different.

For Gadamer, however, the dyad has a still more precise and effective meaning. This is the case in the first place because it refers not only to difference, but also to infinite differentiation. From this view there arises a new conception of being: differentiation sets in motion the being that is coming into Being, in other words Being that occurs only as the interweaving of the limit and the unlimited, identity and difference, the one and the many, as Plato shows in the *Timaeus* (*Timaeus* 37a–b).

Yet the dyad has implications for both philosophy and human life. As the dyad, together with the one, can generate an infinite series of numbers, so it makes possible every *logos* but also destines it to incompleteness. From this point stems the infinite and indeterminate character of the dialectical discourse, or philosophy (*DDP* 151/*GW*6 150).[49] On the other hand, the dyad is also decisive for human life, which is condemned every day to "sink into measurelessness" (*DDP* 155/*GW*6 153). Although human life must balance itself in the middle, in the *mesótes*, it remains constantly exposed to the limitlessness of the dyad, which prohibits all completion and prevents the end coinciding with the goal.

In this intermediacy the ethical dimension of the aporetic dialectic can be grasped. For the dyad leaves open the *aporía*, the difficulty of differentiation, which is also always a decision. The weaving of the *logos* not only points to a new way of thinking Being in mixture, but refers as well to a life that limits itself through measure. Interweaving, mixture, the limited, and the measure become key concepts for hermeneutics and for its way of understanding life as a drink that must be mixed properly, as described in the *Philebus* (*IG* 114/*GW*7 192). At the same time there will be no lack of pleasure, which can also be described as "unlimited," because a life that gives itself over to pleasure knows no limit; similarly, suffering will not be lacking, the "disturbance" of the devotion to pleasure, which can lead *Dasein* back to its own center of gravity (*PDE* 180/*GW*5 130).[50] But the human being realizes and understands itself through the process of constantly reestablishing a center, which is possible only with the other.[51] There is thus no definition of the good, and there also can be none, since it would be absurd to consider the good in its transcendence as one of the highest ideas (*IG* 123–124/*GW*7 198).[52] The idea of the good has the furthermost of a beyond, which likens it to a regulative idea. It gives itself in proper measure and proportion, which cannot but appear as beautiful—here is where the good "has taken refuge" (*IG* 115/*GW*7 192–193) in the beautiful—and it completes itself in the unification of the many, in other words in the one, which is always open and finite. "Consequently, human life is *eo ipso* dialectical" (*IG* 122/*GW*7 197).

6. Hegel, Dialectics, and Hermeneutics

When attempting to clarify the recovery (*Verwindung*) from metaphysics, much like the bearing of a sickness with which one must stay, Gadamer elaborates by saying that this is "particularly appropriate for Hegel, for one must 'stay with' him in a special way" (*HD* 100–101/*GW*3 87).[53] Why does Gadamer *stay with* Hegel and his "inheritance?"

The encounter with Hegel takes place under the sign of Plato—as Gadamer underlines in the lecture on "The Heritage of Hegel" (*RAS* 44/*GW*4 467).[54] No other modern philosopher understood how to develop Greek dialectics to such an extent as Hegel, the last of the Greeks. Heidegger had already expressed the point in a similar way: "With the name of 'the Greeks' we think of the beginning of philosophy, with the name of 'Hegel' we think of its completion."[55] Gadamer sees this proximity too, but his distance from Heidegger's interpretation of Plato, as well as from the entire Western tradition of philosophy, deepens even further in the case of Hegel. Gadamer cannot share the judgment, for example, whereby Hegel would represent the "completion of the metaphysics of subjectivity." As soon as we take into account what Hegel recognizes as "the speculative" in the Greeks and generally, wherever there is philosophy, it is the opposite picture that begins to emerge (*HD* 5–34, 30/*GW*3 3–28, 25).[56]

In his collection *Hegel's Dialectic*, Gadamer explains the complex relationship between Hegel and the Greeks, a relationship marked at the same time by a reciprocal exchange. Precisely this reciprocity does not allow us to speak of a "completion." If Hegel sees in the Greeks what the Greeks themselves did not see, on the other hand it is possible to see Hegel's philosophy in a new way only through the Greeks.

The connection between Gadamer, Hegel, and the Greeks is *dialectics*. The art of the dialectic goes back to those earliest philosophers, who left behind the firm ground of sensible experience and sailed forth for the first time onto the high seas of pure thought (*HD* 74–99 79/ *GW*3 65–86, 69). Hegel's gaze turned toward Eleatic and Platonic dialectics, in particular—as Gadamer elaborates in his essay "Hegel and the Dialectic of the Ancient Philosophers"—to the "speculative" dialogues: the *Sophist*, the *Parmenides*, and the *Philebus* (*HD* 7/*GW*3 4). The *Parmenides*, especially, takes on a decisive role. For here it is shown that truth never clings to an isolated idea, but always lies in the combination of ideas, in the movement that discovers the contradiction and that takes up into itself the antithesis of being and not-being, identity and difference: in a movement that unfolds between the one and the many (*HD* 79, 86/*GW*3 69, 75). Although Hegel believes he can trace this movement in the *Sophist*, it is still especially the Socratic style of the *Parmenides* that shows the self-development of thought in its "immanent formation" (*HD* 7/*GW*3 5).

Where lies, then, *the weakness of this dialectics*? It occurs at first in that "permanent turbulence" in which the one, even if already implicated, has still not been thought as the highest unity, or in Hegel's words, as the totality of the whole (*HD* 86/ *GW*3 75). Platonic dialectics is therefore only *negative* and brings forth nothing positive from its *aporia*. Gadamer states that Platonic dialectics is no method; there is no beginning and even less so a kind of knowledge that would gradually reach absolute completion in the concept (*HD* 81/*GW*3 70). If in the first part of this critique he agrees with Hegel, Gadamer distances himself in the second part, by playing Hegel off against Hegel.

The ancient philosophers wanted to raise themselves from the immediacy of the sensible, in order to reach the universality of thought. The modern age, conversely, in which the individual is already surrounded by abstract forms, is characterized by the effort of making the fixed fluid again. It is in such a way that Hegel describes the quarrel between the ancients and the moderns. On this view, ancient philosophy lacks self-certainty *as* subjectivity, it lacks self-consciousness; but precisely for this reason it is closer to the fluidity in which "'everything that occurs' is thought of in the natural language of natural consciousness" (*HD* 9/*GW3* 6). Here one can see the extent to which the moderns are, as always, dependent on the ancients. Modern dialectics must again take up ancient dialectics, which exhibits the speculative movement of thought (*HD* 33–34/*GW3* 27–28).

What remains to be clarified, however, is not only the meaning of the "speculative," but also its connection with the "logical." This topic is treated in the most important essay in Gadamer's collection: "The Idea of Hegel's Logic" (*HD* 75–99/*GW3* 65–86). After he has explained how the *Phenomenology of Spirit* and the *Science of Logic* are the two great books by Hegel, Gadamer debates the actuality of Hegel's logic (*HD* 76–77/*GW3* 65–66). At the same time, however, he develops a rigorous critique of Hegel that culminates in the thesis: "Dialectics must retrieve itself in hermeneutics" (*HD* 99/*GW3* 86).

Hegel's great discovery is that philosophy completes itself in a speculative movement. Thus the traditional form of the proposition, in other words the "rational proposition" or assertion that combines a subject with a predicate, and that Aristotle had characterized as *lógos apophantikós,* proves to be wholly inadequate. The philosophical proposition, which instead of contenting itself with mere judgment dwells on what is to be thought and forgets itself therein, is a *speculative proposition.* This proposition has one peculiarity: it does not pass from the subject over to the predicate, but *tells the truth about the subject in the form of the predicate.* One could offer an example: "God is one." In this context "one" is not a predicate of "God," but rather his authentic essence. The subject is not determined by the predicate. Instead, the movement of determination "suffers, as we might put it, a counter-thrust" and is halted.[57] It begins precisely from the subject, as if this were its foundation, but then discovers that the predicate is the substance, and the subject, which has become the predicate, is thus sublated in it. The speculative proposition does not, therefore, predicate like a simple assertion, but wavers back and forth—its speculative character is precisely this wavering, in which "the identification of Subject and Predicate is not meant to destroy the difference between them, which the form of the proposition expresses."[58] In short: the speculative proposition does not limit itself to predicating identity, but represents a harmonious unity in which the identity allows difference to exist (*HD* 18/*GW3* 14–16). Its relevance lies precisely in the fact that, before any assertion, the speculative proposition enables the speculative or the dialectical movement of language to be recognized clearly. Gadamer describes this accordingly:

> The speculative statement maintains the mean between the extremes of tautology on the one hand and self-cancelation in the infinite determination of its meaning on the other. Here lies Hegel's great relevance for today: the speculative statement is not so much a statement as it is language. (*HD* 95/*GW3* 83)

In this respect, Hegel speaks also of the "logical instinct" of language. By this he means above all that logical structures are mirrored in grammatical structures, and that the interweavings and correlations of logic are realized thanks to the "vowels of being" of which Plato speaks in the *Sophist* (*Sophist* 253a–b). "Forms of thought are in the first place set out and laid down in the language of humans," writes Hegel in the *Science of Logic*, so that for the human, "language has penetrated into everything [. . .] that he makes his own."[59] To be sure, the logical instinct of language means something more for Hegel, namely the tendency of language toward the "logical," the drive to find its own completion in the idea of logic. The instinctive or natural logic of language would find its goal and end in the elevation to philosophical logic, as the word does in its elevation to the concept. Obviously, Gadamer cannot follow Hegel in this *salto mortale* of thought beyond language. Language is not, in other words, a "transitional form" that thought can leave behind when it reaches transparency in the concept (*HD* 94/*GW*3 82). Hegel does not see that the movement of language, precisely because it is speculative, has a "double direction": whereas language makes the concept present *in the word,* it prohibits the concept at the same time, revokes and retracts it, calls it back. For in the word, which is never isolated but instead always points to a whole and to its relations to the whole, the said always reflects the unsaid.[60] Hegel is right when he recognizes in the "logical" and the "speculative"—which are synonymous here—the very "dialectical articulation" that lies in language itself. But he is mistaken in his assumption that there could be a movement that runs in only one direction and finds its goal outside and beyond language. The triumphal march of self-consciousness fails in its drive to create a stable place to stay with the "appropriation" of the other, which has undermined the Western tradition. The reflection that lies in the movement of the instinctual logic of language is always "homeless" (*unheimisch*), and cannot as such be halted anywhere (*HD* 98/*GW*3 85). But it such a way, also the epic of absolute spirit, which unfolds in Hegel's great monologue, ends in failure (*HD* 7/*GW*3 5; *TM* 369/*GW*1 375).

Just as there is no completion in Hegelian dialectics, so Hegel also shows there is no completion in ancient dialectics. "Were Hegel's idea of logic to include full acknowledgement of its relationship to natural logic [. . .], he would have to draw close again to the classical origin of his idea in Plato's dialectic" (*HD* 99/*GW*3 86). If at first it was necessary to read Greek dialectics through Hegel, in order to discover its still lacking unity, now it is necessary to read Hegelian dialectics through the Greek, in order to realize that no totality can be closed—if it will neither be totalizing nor totalitarian. It holds open the very negativity, the *aporia,* that remains both in the indeterminate dyad of Plato and in the "bad infinity" of Hegel.[61] In the way in which objective spirit articulates itself in language, it limits the subjective spirit on the one hand, and disputes from within the absolute spirit on the other; that is, it makes absolute spirit impossible. Even more: it is language that offers the new model of a whole that is always infinitely open. That dialectics must "retrieve" itself in hermeneutics means that it must retract itself, just as the concept retracts and revokes itself each time in the word. It means that the dual direction must be recognized: from the word to the concept and from the concept to the word (*GR* 108–121/*GL* 100–111).[62] This also means, however, that Hegel's metaphysical dialectics must rely on the contemporary form of the dialogical dialectics of Plato, namely on philosophical hermeneutics.

Hegel himself, though, was of course fully aware of the speculative significance of Platonic dialectics, insofar as he was conscious of all that had been lost in the separation of the dialectic from the analytic, through the closure that the Aristotelian apodictic had established (*HD* 27/*GW*3 22).

7. Apodictics and the Exclusion of the Other: On Aristotle

Although Gadamer is taken for an Aristotelian, if not a Neo-Aristotelian, on the basis of his rehabilitation of *phrónesis,* if we consider his work more closely we will see that the opposite is the case. In order to correct the former impression, we could even describe him as an "Anti-Aristotelian." Gadamer's proximity to Aristotle is ultimately limited to the chapter in which philosophical hermeneutics encounters the practical knowledge of Aristotle, where Aristotle himself returns to Platonic and even Socratic motifs. Gadamer emphasizes this in the 1990 study "The Socratic Question and Aristotle."[63] Otherwise, we should speak rather of the distance between them.

In the first place, Gadamer reads the history of Greek philosophy by demolishing its Aristotelian reconstruction. But this distance from Aristotle also has a considerable philosophical significance. Gadamer is far from the apodictic philosophizing of the Stagirite, and he in no way shares his critique of Plato. In his eyes, Aristotle represents the apodictic closure of Platonic dialectics.

Should Platonic dialectics really be conceived as an intermediate phase on the way to *epistéme,* the apodictic science that Aristotle supposedly achieved? For Gadamer it is important to revise this judgment. It condemns Plato's philosophy for lacking conceptual fixity, which on the basis of its dialectical vocation this philosophy precisely sought to avoid. According to Aristotle, Plato's diaeretic method is unsatisfactory because of this indeterminacy; this is proven for Aristotle by the difficulty of ever choosing the right point in the dichotomous division. Diaeresis could not, therefore, claim a scientific method.[64] The Aristotelian apodictic—and the transition from the literary form of the dialogue to the treatise bears witness to this—tends to overcome Platonic dialectics in the attempt to secure a scientific foundation in the concept, which is the universal and necessary definition of the essence of the object. But "conceptual formation," even if at first glance it seems to bring a gain in clarity, actually reveals itself to be a double loss.

With conceptual formation, in fact, the "inexhaustible ambiguity" of everyday language is lost, whereas philosophical language gets reduced to rigid terminology. Above and beyond that, apodictic discourse extrapolates and isolates its concepts:

téchne, epistéme, sophía, phrónesis, and *noûs* may perhaps gain clearer contours, but the connection that links them to each other and with the context from which they arise is no longer visible. The greatest loss that the Aristotelian apodictic brings, however, since its task consists of separating what is unified, is the hypostatization of the sensible and the intelligible world. The doctrine of two worlds is a consequence of the Aristotelian critique of Plato. For Gadamer it was, paradoxically, precisely Aristotle who, by his renunciation of the Socratic dialogue, initiated Platonism.

In its intention to establish a necessary procedure for evidence, the Aristotelian apodictic must also renounce another moment particular to the dialectic: the consent of the other. The objectivity that is the aim of the definition implies a conclusive understanding. But the other as such is excluded from this understanding. The only role that remains for the other is to confirm the reasonableness of the definitional *logos:* "Thus the other with whom one seeks to reach agreement is *in no way different from any other person,* or better, he is needed only in the ways he is precisely not different from others" (*PDE* 41/*GW*5 31). The understanding (*Verständigung*) that leads to the definition marks a *finis,* a goal, which is at the same time the end of speaking and the end of dialogue. Through this process, hermeneutic openness is put into play.

In dialogical dialectics, by contrast, the process unfolds in exactly the opposite way, since its provisional nature leads not to an irrevocable definition but to a conversation that in its open indeterminacy, as a question, always demands a response. The interpretation that the dialectician suggests makes further interpretations possible, on the basis of the openness that it preserves. Thus dialectics achieves a speaking that is endlessly prepared to find its motivation, its justification, and its foundation in the response of the other. In the way in which Gadamer takes it up, Platonic dialectics lives from the participation of the other and is supported at each step by the possibility of assuring the other's agreement.

Notes

1. Otto Pöggeler, *Schritte zu einer hermeneutischen Philosophie* (Freiburg/Munich: Alber, 1994), 497. See also the judgment by Werner Beierwaltes, "Rezension zu *Gesammelte Werke* 5 und 6," *Philosophy and History* 20 (1987): 120–122.

2. Strauss, by contrast, thinks of the relation between the Greeks and the moderns as an opposition. See Hans-Georg Gadamer, "Philosophizing in Opposition: Strauss and Voegelin on Communication and Science," in Peter Emberley and Barry Cooper, eds., *Faith and Political Philosophy. The Correspondence between Leo Strauss and Eric Voegelin, 1934–1964* (University Park: Pennsylvania State University Press, 1993), 249–259.

3. Hans-Georg Gadamer, "Die Gegenwartsbedeutung der griechischen Philosophie" (1972), in Gadamer, *Hermeneutische Entwürfe. Vorträge und Aufsätze* (Tübingen: Mohr Siebeck, 2000), 97–111, 99. Gadamer's reading of the Greeks is problematized, though, by Yvon Lafrance, "Notre rapport à la pensée grecque: 'Gadamer ou Schleiermacher?'" in Catherine Collobert, ed., *L'avenir de la philosophie est-il grec?* (Montréal: Fides, 2001), 44–54; see in the same volume, François Renaud, "L'appropriation

de la philosophie grecque chez Hans-Georg Gadamer," 79–96; see also Renaud, "Gadamers Rückgang auf die Griechen," in Andrzej Przylebski, ed., *Das Erbe Gadamers* (Frankfurt a.M.: Peter Lang, 2006), 95–118. On this topic see also Günter Figal, "Platonforschung und hermeneutische Philosophie," in Thomas A. Szlezák and Karl-Heinz Stanzel, eds., *Platonisches Philosophieren. Zehn Vorträge zu Ehren von Hans Joachim Krämer* (Hildesheim: Olms, 2001), 19–29, 26.

4. Gadamer, "Die griechische Philosophie und das moderne Denken" (1978), in *Griechische Philosophie II, GW6*, 3–8, 3. For an overview of his interest in the Greeks see the interview with Glenn Most, "'Die Griechen, unsere Lehrer.' Ein Interview mit Glenn Most," *Internationale Zeitschrift für Philosophie* 1 (1994): 139–149.

5. It is sufficient to mention the philosophers and philologists of ancient languages with whom Gadamer was connected: next to Paul Friedländer there were especially Werner Jaeger, Julius Stenzel, Karl Reinhardt, Kurt Riezler, Bruno Snell, and Kurt von Fritz. After 1960, Gadamer followed closely the studies published in the United States on Greek philosophy.

6. See in this volume chapter 4, part 4.

7. Gadamer, "Die Sprache der Metaphysik" (1968), *GW3* 229–237; "Heidegger und die Sprache" (1990), *GW10* 14–30. See Ingrid Scheibler, "Gadamer's Appropriation of Heidegger: Language and the Achievement of Continuity," *Études phénoménologiques* 26 (1997): 59–89, 66–67.

8. For Gadamer it is always important to reconstruct or destructure the history of a concept, since only from that point can we begin to philosophize once more. See on this topic *TM* 428–429/*GW1* 432–433; "Begriffsgeschichte als Philosophie" (1970), *GW2* 77–91; "Die Begriffsgeschichte und die Sprache der Philosophie" (1971), *GW4* 78–94. See on this Reiner Wiehl, "Begriffsbestimmung und Begriffsgeschichte: Zum Verhältnis von Phänomenologie, Dialektik und Hermeneutik," in Rüdiger Bubner, Konrad Cramer, and Reiner Wiehl, *Hermeneutik und Dialektik* (Tübingen: Mohr, 1970), 1:167–213; see also Wiehl, "Die philosophische Hermeneutik Hans-Georg Gadamers jenseits von Erkenntnistheorie und Existenzphilosophie," in *Das Erbe Gadamers*, 33–63, 44ff.

9. See in this volume chapter 8, part 9.

10. See in this volume chapter 9, part 2.

11. See also Heidegger's positive commentary on Gadamer's discussion of "twisting out" in a letter to Gadamer from December 2, 1971 (published incomplete in Hans-Georg Gadamer and Jürgen Habermas, *Das Erbe Hegels* (Frankfurt/M.: Suhkramp, 1979), Nachwort, 89–94; Gadamer, *Das Erbe Hegels, GW4* 476–483.

12. On this topic, see also André Laks, "Gadamer et les présocratiques," in Jean-Claude Gens, Pavlos Kontos, and Pierre Rodrigo, *Gadamer et les Grecs* (Paris: Vrin, 2004), 13–29.

13. Parmenides, VS Fr B 6, 1–3. The pre-Socratic fragments are cited according to the version by Hermann Diels and Walther Kranz, *Die Fragmente der Vorsokratiker*, 7th ed., vols. 1–3 (Berlin: Weidmann, 1954).

14. Parmenides, VS Fr B 8, 50–65.

15. Parmenides, VS Fr B 6, 1–2.

16. Parmenides, VS Fr B 6, 4–7.

17. See Karl Reinhardt, "*Parmenides und die Geschichte der griechischen Philosophie* (Frankfurt/M: Klostermann, 1977). The essays by Gadamer on Heraclitus follow those on Parmenides in the volume *Plato im Dialog* (*GW7*). I should also draw attention to the two reviews that Gadamer devoted to Reinhardt: Gadamer, "Schein und Sein. Zum Tode von Karl Reinhardt" (1958), *GW6* 278–288; "Die Krise des Helden. Zum Gedenken an Karl Reinhardt nach zehn Jahren" (1966), *GW6* 285–291; see also his portrait in *PA* 127–134 and *PL* 151–160.

18. Heraclitus, VS Fr B 10, 1–2.

19. Georg Wilhelm Friedrich Hegel, *Vorlesungen über die Geschichte der Philosophie I*, vol. 18 of *Werke* (Frankfurt/M: Suhrkamp, 1986), 320. See Gadamer, "Vom Anfang bei Heraklit" (1974), *GW6*

232–241, 232 (reprinted with the title "Zur Überlieferung Heraklits," in Gadamer, *Der Anfang des Wissens* [Stuttgart: Reclam, 1999], 17–34, 17); "Hegel und Heraklit," (1990), *GW7* 32–42, 32.

20. Heraklit, VS Fr B 48.

21. Heraklit, VS Fr B 64. See also Heidegger's interpretation of Heraclitus in Martin Heidegger, "Logos (Heraklit Fragment 50)," in Heidegger, *Vorträge und Aufsätze, GA 7*, ed. Friedrich-Wilhelm von Hermann (Frankfurt/M: Klostermann, 2000), 211–234. For a comparison between Heidegger and Gadamer in this regard, see Hans Ruin, "Einheit in der Differenz—Differenz in der Einheit. Heraklit und die Wahrheit der Hermeneutik," in Günter Figal, Jean Grondin, and Dennis J. Schmidt, eds., *Hermeneutische Wege* (Tübingen: Mohr Siebeck, 2000), 87–106.

22. Heraklit, VS Fr B 89.

23. On the proximity of sleep and death, see also Gadamer, "Goethe und Heraklit" (1999), in *Hermeneutische Entwürfe* (Tübingen: Mohr Siebeck, 2000), 234–237.

24. Heraklit, VS Fr B 101; Gadamer, "Hegel und Heraklit," *GW7* 40; "Heraklit-Studien," *GW7* 83.

25. See Plato, *Phaedo* 96a–99b, *Plato,* 83–85. See Mark Painter, "Phaedo 99d–101d: Socrates and Gadamer's 'Second Way,'" *Southwestern Philosophical Review* 14 (1998): 179–186.

26. *Phaedo,* 99e; *Plato,* 86. Gadamer himself translated this text in Platon, *Texte zur Ideenlehre,* ed. and trans. Hans-Georg Gadamer (Frankfurt/M: Klostermann, 1978), 21.

27. For a portrait of Socrates, see Günter Figal, *Sokrates* (Munich: Beck, 1995). See also Francis J. Ambrosio, "The Figure of Socrates in Gadamer's Philosophical Hermeneutics," in Lewis E. Hahn, ed., *The Philosophy of Hans-Georg Gadamer* (LaSalle, Ill.: Open Court, 1997), 259–273. See Gadamer, "Sokrates und das Göttliche," in *Sokrates. Gestalt und Idee,* ed. Herbert Kessler (Heiterheim: Graue Edition, 1993), 97–108.

28. See in this volume chapter 9, part 4.

29. Reale is right in this sense to identify Gadamer as the "Platonist" of the last century. See Giovanni Reale, "Gadamer, ein grosser Platoniker des 20. Jahrhunderts," in Günter Figal, ed., *Begegnungen mit Hans-Georg Gadamer* (Stuttgart: Reclam, 2000), 92–104, 92.

30. The limits of Heidegger's interpretation of Plato are shown, for example, by Alain Boutot, in *Heidegger et Platon. Le problème du nihilisme* (Paris: PUF, 1987); one should also think of Heidegger's negative conception of dialectics as "appearance." See Martin Heidegger, *Die Grundbegriffe der Metaphysik. Welt—Endlichkeit—Einsamkeit, GA 29/30,* ed. Friedrich-Wilhelm von Herrmann (Frankfurt/M: Klostermann, 1992), 306.

31. The Tübingen School, whose most significant representatives are Konrad Gaiser, Hans Joachim Krämer, Heinz Happ, and more recently Thomas Alexander Szlezák, whose interpretations concur with those of Giovanni Reale and Maurizio Migliori, see Plato's actual doctrines in the "unwritten" teachings that were passed down in the Academy and that can be reconstructed on the basis of a few witnesses, including Aristotle. The result is a systematic and heavily mathematical philosophy. Gadamer turns his focus, by contrast, to the Socratic Plato, although he was also interested in the indirect tradition, not least because of its implications for the relation of orality to writing (see in this volume chapter 8, part 2). From this starting point he saw the "royal way" for interpretations of Plato to pursue. See Gadamer, "Platos ungeschriebene Dialektik" (1968), *GW6* 129–153, 133. For Gadamer's final position on the Tübingen School see his introduction to the volume: Giuseppe Girgenti, ed., *La nuova interpretazione di Platone* (Milan: Rusconi, 1998), 19–23.

32. Gadamer, "Schleiermacher als Platoniker" (1969), *GW4* 374–383, 374–376. See on this P. Christopher Smith, "H.-G. Gadamer's Interpretation of Plato," *Journal of the British Society for Phenomenology* 12 (1981): 211–230; Charles L. Griswold, "Gadamer and the Interpretation of Plato," *Ancient Philosophy* 1 (1981): 171–178; White has expressed a critical view, see Nicholas P. White, "Observations and Questions about Hans-Georg Gadamer's Interpretation of Plato," in Charles L. Griswold, ed., *Platonic Writings—Platonic Readings* (New York and London: Routledge, 1988), 247–257; Francois Renaud, *Die Resokratisierung Platons. Die platonische Hermeneutik Hans-Georg Gadamers* (Sankt

Augustin: Academia, 1999). See also James Risser, "Gadamer's Plato and the Task of Philosophy," in Mirko Wischke and Michael Hofer, eds., *Gadamer verstehen—Understanding Gadamer* (Darmstadt: Wissenschaftliche Buchgesellschaft, 2003), 87–100.

33. Renouncing the theory of two worlds in Plato implies a rethinking of the entire Western tradition. Zuckert states this clearly: "Gadamer asks his readers to reconsider and reconceive their understanding of the entire Western tradition." See Catherine H. Zuckert, "Hermeneutics in Practice: Gadamer on Ancient Philosophy," in *The Cambridge Companion to Gadamer*, ed. Robert J. Dostal (Cambridge: Cambridge University Press, 2002), 200–224, 219f; see also Zuckert, *Postmodern Platos: Nietzsche, Heidegger, Gadamer, Strauss, Derrida* (Chicago/London: University of Chicago Press, 1996), 70–103.

34. See Gadamer, "Zur Vorgeschichte der Metaphysik" (1950), *GW6* 9–29.

35. The dialogue Socrates leads, in the ingenious way Plato portrays him—see "Plato als Porträtist" (1988), *GW7* 228–257—is the model of philosophizing itself, because the reader gets drawn into the process of question and answer and loses their own apparent superiority. For Gadamer this means: "To philosophize *with* Plato, not just to criticize Plato, that is the task" (*RPJ* 32/*GW2* 501). See Stepan Spinka, "'Plato im Dialog.' Hans-Georg Gadamer als Interpret der platonischen Dialektik," in Wischke and Hofer, *Gadamer verstehen—Understanding Gadamer*, 120–137.

36. See P. Christopher Smith, *Hermeneutics and Human Finitude: Toward a Theory of Ethical Understanding* (New York: Fordham University Press, 1991), 144–145.

37. Gadamer has a negative image of sophistry that one need not share.

38. Gadamer, "Zur Vorgeschichte der Metaphysik," *GW6* 21.

39. Gadamer, "Zur Vorgeschichte der Metaphysik," *GW6*, 23.

40. The idea here is nothing other than the question that opens the investigation. Gadamer takes over Natorp's conception of the idea as the starting point. See Paul Natorp, *Platons Ideenlehre. Eine Einführung in den Idealismus* (1902) (Hamburg: Meiner, 1994), 150–163. See also Paulette Kidder, "Gadamer and the Platonic Eidos," *Philosophy Today* 39 (1995): 83–92.

41. See in this volume chapter 8, part 6.

42. See in this volume chapter 9, parts 3–4.

43. See Plato, *Philebus*, 23b–27b, *Plato*, as well as Gadamer, *PDE* 112–125/*GW5* 94–107.

44. Gadamer owes Klein a great deal on this point, which is decisive for his philosophy. See Jacob Klein, "Die griechische Logistik und die Entstehung der Algebra," in *Quellen und Studien zur Geschichte der Mathematik, Astronomie und Physik*, Abteilung B: *Studien*, vol. 3, 1st book, (Berlin: Julius Springer, 1934), 18–105, and second book, Berlin 1936, 122–235; reprinted in English: *Greek Mathematical Thought and the Origin of the Algebra*, trans. Winfree J. Smith and Eva Brann (Cambridge, Mass.: MIT Press, 1968), 68 and 70. See Burt Hopkins, "Klein and Gadamer on the Arithmos-Structure of Platonic Eidetic Numbers," *Philosophy Today* 52 (2008): 151–157.

45. The concept of the *logos* stems from mathematics and is called "relation": the number, like the *logos*, too, is a weave, a weaving of relations. See Gadamer, "Mathematik und Dialektik bei Plato" (1982), *GW7* 290–312.

46. Aristotle uses the term *dyas*, "dyad" or "twoness," in order to describe Plato's philosophy; but the term does not appear at all in his works and is thus counted as a key concept of Plato's "unwritten teaching." See Aristotle, *Metaphysica*, 987b 25.

47. The concept of the "dyad," which is decisive for Gadamer's philosophy, has received very little attention until now; the brief essay by Prufer represents an exception. See Thomas Prufer, "A Thought or Two on Gadamer's Plato," in Hahn, *The Philosophy of Hans-Georg Gadamer*, 549–551; see also Gadamer, "Reply to Thomas Prufer, 552–554.

48. On this point Plato could be criticized for accepting what Hegel calls "bad infinity." See in this volume chapter 9, part 4.

49. It is important to note that Gadamer's first publication deals with pleasure, whereas the last deals with pain: see the small, posthumously published book *Schmerz. Einschätzungen aus medizinischer, philosophischer und therapeutischer Sicht* (Heidelberg: Winter, 2004).

50. See in this volume chapter 8, part 7.

51. Against this conception, however, see Christopher Gill, "Critical Response to the Hermeneutic Approach from an Analytic Perspective," in Giovanni Reale and Samuel Scolnicov, eds., *New Images of Plato: Dialogues on the Idea of the Good* (Sankt Augustin: Academia Verlag, 2002), 211–222, esp. 213–219.

52. See also Gadamer, "Hegel's Philosophy and Its Aftereffects Today," *RAS* 21–37/*VZW* 32–53.

53. The lecture was given in Naples under the title "Hegel und die Hermeneutik." See in this volume chapter 1, part 11. See also Gadamer, "The Heritage of Hegel" (*RAS* 42/*GW*4 467).

54. Martin Heidegger, "Hegel and the Greeks," in *Pathmarks*, ed. William McNeill (Cambridge: Cambridge University Press, 1998), 323–336; "Hegel und die Griechen," in *Wegmarken*, 427–444.

55. For a comparative study see Merold Westphal, "Hegel and Gadamer," in Brice R. Wachterhauser, ed., *Hermeneutics and Modern Philosophy* (Albany: SUNY Press, 1986), 65–86; see also Theodore Kiesel, "Hegel and Hermeneutics," in Frederick G. Weiss, ed., *Beyond Epistemology* (The Hague: Nijhoff, 1974), 197–220.

56. Hegel, Phänomenologie des Geistes, 43; Phenomenology of Spirit, 37.

57. Hegel, Phänomenologie des Geistes, 43–44; Phenomenology of Spirit, 38.

58. Georg Wilhelm Friedrich Hegel, *Wissenschaft der Logic*. Erster Band, *Gesammelte Werke*, vol. 21, ed. Friedrich Hogemann and Walter Jaeschke (Hamburg: Felix Meiner, 1984), 10.

59. On the speculative dialectic of the word for Gadamer, see in this volume chapter 8, part 4.

60. See in this volume chapter 9, part 4. See also James Risser, "In the Shadow of Hegel: Infinite Dialogue in Gadamer's Hermeneutics," *Research in Phenomenology* 32 (2002): 86–102.

61. Gadamer returned to this topic more and more into his later years, and held his last seminar in Naples in 1997 on it.

62. Gadamer, "Die sokratische Frage und Aristoteles, *GW*7 373–380. See Jean Grondin, "Gadamers sokratische Destruktion der griechischen Philosophie," in Grondin, *Der Sinn für Hermeneutik* (Darmstadt: Wissenschaftliche Buchgesellschaft, 1994), 54–70, 69. See also Jamey Findling, "Gadamer and the Platonic Contribution to Practical Philosophy," in *Internationales Jahrbuch für Hermeneutik* 4 (2005): 125–139.

63. See Aristotle, *Analytica priora*, 46a 31–b 19.

64. See Gadamer, "Die sokratische Frage und Aristoteles," *GW*7 377; "Aristoteles und die imperativische Ethik," *GW*7 388.

8 The Horizon of Dialogue

Language is a uni-versal and by no means a completed whole. (*LL* 20/*GW8* 402)

The conversation, that we are, [is] one that never ends. No word is the last word, just as no word is the first. (*DD* 96/*GW10* 140)

Both speakers agreeing so fully that no foundation is required, is to converse without presuppositions. (*LL* 23/*GW8* 406)

1. The Forgetting of Language in the Western Tradition: Plato, Augustine, Humboldt

When Gadamer wrote the last part of *Truth and Method,* language had not yet reached the leading role on the philosophical stage that it would later come to have. The "linguistic turn" of the twentieth century, the point at which the most varied of philosophical currents run together, had not yet occurred. These currents go from logical positivism to Wittgenstein, from American pragmatism to structuralism and psychoanalysis, from Heidegger to the transcendental pragmatism of Apel and Habermas, from Merleau-Ponty to Derrida's deconstruction. Philosophical hermeneutics contributes as well. But at that time even Gadamer could not imagine that his "turn"—the "ontological turn of hermeneutics guided by language"—would have corresponded to the "linguistic turn." In a note to the last edition of *Truth and Method* he wrote: "I am not unaware that the 'linguistic turn,' of which I knew nothing in the early 50s, recognized the same thing" (*TM* 487/*GW2* 421; RPJ 41/*GW2* 4).

How did the reflection on language manifest itself in Germany during the early sixties? Wittgenstein was virtually unknown. Analytic philosophy, which had gradually gained the upper hand in North America, was associated with the positivism of the Vienna Circle and had been ostracized in Germany. In Husserl's phenomenology the role of language was secondary, and this perspective radically changed only with Heidegger. Gadamer knew, for the most part, the essays linking language and poetry that Heidegger had written since 1935, and certainly he found inspiration in them. Nevertheless it should not be forgotten that *On the Way to Language* did not appear until 1959, when *Truth and Method* was already in print. Just as he did not mention Heidegger in the sections on aesthetics in the book, the section on language does not mention him either.[1] Still there are moments in the book when Heidegger's formulations can be heard unmistakably, beginning with the *Kehre* or "turn," which Gadamer instead refers to as the *Wendung,* or "turning." Clearly he wants to distance himself from Heidegger, who left hermeneutics behind in order to turn to the mystery of language. Heidegger's turn, for Gadamer, is a return to the early hermeneutics of *Geworfenheit,* or "thrownness." Gadamer's turning, by contrast, takes place on the terrain of philosophical hermeneutics.[2]

In German philosophy, language is, however, anything but an unexplored field. For the present context it suffices to mention Ernst Cassirer, Hans Lipps, Johannes Lohmann, Julius Stenzel, and above all Richard Hönigswald. These are names that Gadamer often mentions.[3] They all point to the great tradition of the philosophy of language in Germany that is linked to Hamann, Herder, and, especially, Wilhelm von Humboldt. Gadamer belongs to this tradition. Nevertheless, the somewhat forced synthesis in part 3 of *Truth and Method* contains many elements that seem questionable and unsatisfactory. Many of the theoretical arguments have a rudimentary character. It is therefore no coincidence that this third part, in contrast to the other two, has received comparatively little response. And it is also no coincidence that Gadamer, in subsequent decades, frequently returned to this part of the book, turning language into the guiding theme of the last phase of his philosophy.

In *Truth and Method* a long discussion of language in the Western tradition occupies nearly half of part 3 (*TM* 405–438/*GW1* 409–460). Gadamer proceeds from the question: what happened to language in the history of philosophy? His firm answer is that language has been completely forgotten and repressed, so that one must speak of a "forgetting of language" (*TM* 418/*GW1* 422). If, for Heidegger, the Western tradition is characterized by a forgetting of Being, then for Gadamer it stands under the sign of a forgetting of language. For both, Plato is the one primarily responsible.

What does the "forgetting of language" mean? It means that the innermost link between language and thought has been severed. As a result, thinking appears independent of language, and language gets demoted to the status of a mere tool of thought. This instrumental grasp of language, according to which words are nothing but signs for things and ideas that exist autonomously, is the implicit presupposition of the whole of Western philosophical reflection. According to Gadamer, ancient Greek philosophy refuses to recognize the constitutive role of language in the enactment of thought, and thus aspires to disclose to thought a realm beyond language (*TM* 417/*GW1* 421–422). Since Plato, the essence of language has been hidden here.

Gadamer's reading of Plato concentrates on only the *Cratylus,* which for Gadamer is the paradigmatic, "fundamental statement of Greek thought on language" (*TM* 405/ *GW1* 409). In this dialogue two theories of language are set against each other: the first by Cratylus, for whom a natural similarity exists between a name and a thing, and the second by Hermogenes, for whom words are only conventional labels. Although Plato claims that both views are unsustainable, he does not move beyond them. Plato's error, according to Gadamer, is that he tries to prove that the supposed "correctness" of words is no guarantee of their "truth"; hence it becomes important to know things *without words* (*TM* 407/*GW1* 411). As dim reflections of the light of the ideas, words block our ability to press forward to the truth of beings. Gadamer also criticizes the Platonic theory of ideas, which had been developed in order to counter the Sophists' misuse of language. He comes to the somewhat surprising view "that Plato's discovery of the ideas conceals the true nature of language even more than the theories of the Sophists" (*TM* 408/*GW1* 412). Plato on this account even interprets dialectics as the liberation of thought from language. What the essence of language really obscures, however, is the metaphysical model of the "similarity" between the original and the copy. Plato measures the word by the idea. However much the word can resemble the idea, it will never actually be the idea. The question becomes one of *mímesis*: the word is not a more or less correct imitation—if this were so, the world of names would be a doubling of the real world. Considered more closely, the word is a representation of what is taken to be worth revealing about a thing; as such, the word will always be right. In fact, it will not only be "right," it will also be "true." Regarding this truth of the word, it is legitimate to speak of "an *absolute perfection of the word*" (*TM* 410/*GW1* 415).

The critique of Plato, and especially his noetic concealment of language, gives Gadamer the opportunity to develop his thesis about the truth of the word and to distance his own position from any notion that the name is a sign.[4] Starting from the *Cratylus,* the name for Plato loses all power of presentation, and becomes reduced to a "*mere sign*" or even a "*number*" (*TM* 412/*GW1* 416). With this move the premises of that fateful decision were put in place that would lead to a view of language as an ideal system of signs (*TM* 414/*GW1* 422). Yet if we remember all that Gadamer owes to Platonic dialectics, we must wonder about his somewhat questionable critique. It makes Plato appear, as if according to a Heideggerian yardstick, as the representative of a metaphysics of domination, aimed at constructing an ideal language with which Being, "as absolutely available objectivity," can be calculated and controlled (*TM* 414/*GW1* 418).

As we have seen, Gadamer elsewhere offers a completely different image of Plato,[5] and for this reason he later abandons the critique of the *Cratylus.* In one of his last essays he writes: "If Plato has no concept of 'language' that corresponds exactly to ours, it does not prevent his entire thinking from being grounded in language, specifically on the *logoi*" (*LL* 49/*GW8* 435). The so-called flight into the *logoi*, reported in the *Phaedo,* is viewed as an "epochal turn" in philosophy, even as the "beginning of philosophy" (*GR* 311/*GW7* 335).[6]

For Gadamer, Augustine's *verbum interior* marks the only exception to the forgetting of language in the Western tradition. This interpretation contradicts the standard image of a conventionalist Augustine, which one encounters for example at the beginning of Wittgenstein's *Philosophical Investigations*. Gadamer does not refer to Augustine's *De magistro* in his argument, but rather to *De trinitate* (*TM* 422/*GW1* 424).[7] A closer look shows, however, that it is not Augustine but Aquinas who is the most frequently cited author in this section, which Gadamer significantly entitles "Language and Verbum" (*TM* 418–428/*GW*1 422–431).

In Gadamer's interpretation, the Christian notion of *incarnation* plays a central role. Christian theology opens up a new perspective with its referral to the prologue to the Gospel of St. John. Creation happens through the word of God. In contrast to the Greek *logos*, the Christian *logos* achieves its spirituality when it becomes "flesh" (*TM* 418/*GW*1 423). Far from a diminution or depreciation, incarnation is a full and essential realization of God, but its consequences are not only theological. According to Gadamer, incarnation sheds light on the miracle of language. In order to understand this we must follow Augustine, who moves in the opposite direction: he calls on language in order to penetrate the mystery of incarnation. For this reason he takes up the distinction from the Stoics between *lógos endiáthetos* and *lógos prophorikós*, inner and outer *logos*. The former is the inner space of thinking, while the latter is pure externality. Augustine sees an "analogy" between the inner and the outer word, though he does not reverse the relationship between inner and outer (*TM* 422/*GW*1 424). Fundamental theological reasons prevent him from making this reversal: the *verbum* as such is not to be confused with the *Verbum* chosen by God for his revelation. The same holds true for the inner human word that precedes the outer one. The "true" and original word—the mirror of God's word—is the inner word that "lies in the heart" (*verbum in corde*).[8] The intimate, purely intellectual and universal word is independent from any outer form. Augustine's contribution, according to Gadamer, was to "situate the problem of language, too, entirely within inner thought" (*TM* 420/*GW*1 424). Through incarnation, one comes to the discovery of the inner word of thinking. But Gadamer asks, not without reason, "whether we are not here using the unintelligible to explain the unintelligible" (*TM* 421/*GW*1 425). For what is this "inner word" that seems to lie before and beyond language?

In order to find a way out of this impasse Gadamer turns to Thomas Aquinas, who designated the inner word as a *forma excogitata*, which means "the subject matter thought through to the end" (*TM* 422/*GW*1 426). The processual character of the inner word emerges in this "thinking to the end," and indicates that discursivity to which finite human understanding is condemned. Here an opposition seems to form between *noûs* and *diánoia*, between intuition and discursivity. What would the processual character of the human word have in common with the procession of the divine word? Even in the process of human thought there is no change, no "transition from potentiality into action, but an emergence *ut actus ex actu*" from act to act (*TM* 424/*GW*1 428). The word comes to light in the same moment in which the knowledge of the thing occurs—not later. For Aquinas "the word is like a mirror in which the thing is seen" (*TM* 425/*GW*1 429). Yet the distinction remains between the divine and the human word: whereas the former springs from a single act of intuition, the latter is the result of a movement of thought that searches for the word as it thinks the matter through to the end (*TM* 425/*GW*1 429). Thus the human word is dispersed and incomplete, for the "word of human thought is directed toward the thing, but it cannot contain it as a whole within itself" (*TM* 425/*GW*1 429).

The first result of this discussion with Scholastic theology is the discovery that the word "*is not formed by a reflective act*" (*TM* 426/*GW*1 430). Gadamer will later say that speaking is a self-forgetting action. The second result is the discovery of the "event character" of language (*TM* 427/*GW*1 430–431). As the divine word promulgates itself ever anew in the *kérygma,* it can be said that the meaning of the human word belongs to the event character itself (*TM* 427/*GW*1 430).

The dialogue with Aquinas leads Gadamer to recognize that the unreflected formation of the word is one and the same as the formation of the thing in the concept. Much less clear is the role of Augustine's *verbum interior.* For what is this inner word supposed to be? Since it is audible neither to the other nor to oneself, it runs the risk of disappearing in the indefinite realm of inwardness. It is reasonable to ask if it is really a word at all. Even the weaker formulation of an "inner conversation"—which follows from an Augustinian reading of Plato—does not resolve the problem.

The attempt to locate the universality of hermeneutics in the *verbum interior* can have grave consequences.[9] In particular, it allows the specter of the subject to reappear, one that does not need to speak to itself and is therefore not self-conscious. This inner dialogue would be inarticulate and inaudible, and would be reduced in the end to a monologue, or better: to the immediacy of a self-presence that dispenses with all linguistic mediation. It would bring about a relapse into an instrumental conception of language in which the outer, expressed word is only secondary, derivative, and incomplete. The priority accorded to the *verbum interior* is really a way of returning the word, even if only the inner word, to reason, and thereby elevating reason, pure and cleansed, above language. Nothing could be further from hermeneutics. It is precisely this problematic return to Augustine that reveals one of the limits of Gadamer's reflections on language.[10] This is also chosen in the difficulty of resolving the tension between the doctrine of the *verbum interior* and other aspects of philosophical hermeneutics, above all the centrality of dialogue. The question of the limits of language is rather different. The *verbum interior* should not be confused with the unsaid. The limit is the limit of what is said, the spoken or expressed word that points toward the unsaid, and it is such only because it can always be said again and again differently. Hermeneutics begins where the said word arises and the voice of the other becomes audible.

Gadamer's analysis of Humboldt in the section entitled "Language as Experience of the World," also occurs in the shadow of Heidegger (*TM* 438–456/*GW*1 442–460). Since phenomenology had neglected the role played by language in the world, it falls to hermeneutics to reveal this role. But what should actually be explored is not so much *language in the world* as, in a radical reversal, *the world in language.*

Humboldt had already accomplished this reversal. The diversity of language, in other words the self-articulation of language in the forms of human discourse, is a phenomenon that Humboldt investigated more intensively than anyone else. He was able to grasp individuality without losing sight of universality: the poles between which the circle of language unfolds. According to Gadamer, however, Humboldt's contribution was above all that he had seen in each language "a particular view of the world" (*TM* 440/*GW1* 444). As he follows Humboldt's lead, Gadamer will be able to uncover *the fundamental and originary linguisticality of the human experience of the world.*

In Gadamer's reception he also raises objections against Humboldt that take up Heidegger's critique and can be summarized in three main points. The first rests on the old prejudice against philosophy of language and linguistics. Humboldt's limitation, even though he is recognized as the creator of modern philosophy of language and linguistics, supposedly lay in his approach. He came to language as a philologist and not as a speaker, and thus he treated language as an object of research (*TM* 439/*GW1* 443). A similar charge could of course be made against Gadamer and even against Heidegger—moreover, Humboldt knew very well about the dangers of objectifying language. The second objection is that Humboldt's notion of "mental power" diminishes the connection between language and thinking to the formalism of a competency, specifically to the ability to form the world in language's *enérgeia* (*TM* 439/*GW1* 444). The third objection is connected to the second: Humboldt proceeds from the *"metaphysics of individuality"* initially developed by Leibniz. As a result he thinks of a subject that structures the world in front of him through language. This world, in turn, becomes the "object of language" (*TM* 439/*GW1* 444).[11]

If we look more closely, however, we can see that without language no world would exist for the subject to act upon. The conventional relationship between language and world should be reversed, since language is the primordial foundation for the subject's activity. To be sure, with this reversal Gadamer has simply paraphrased what Humboldt had already said. The world is the world only through language, and on the other hand there is language only insofar as the world articulates itself in language. With this in mind we can understand what Gadamer means when he writes: "man's being-in-the-world is primordially linguistic" (*TM* 443/*GW1* 447). To clarify this further, Gadamer distinguishes between world (*Welt*) and environment (*Umwelt*) (*TM* 443/*GW1* 447). The world is linguistically constituted only through our "freedom from environment" (*TM* 444/*GW1* 448). Here the question of the world in itself disappears (*TM* 447/*GW1* 451). This is because there can be no standpoint outside the human world of language, from which the world in itself can be grasped. And the "world" is nothing other than the totality of linguistic human experience as it is structured by different languages. The world lies in these linguistic perspectives, or better: the world is their open totality. The linguistic experience of the world transcends all relativism in such a view, because it encompasses every in-itself and so reveals itself to be "absolute" (*TM* 450/*GW1* 454). The fundamental relationship between language and world therefore does not mean that the world becomes the object of language, but rather that the horizon of language always already embraces everything that is and everything that we are.

2. Writing and the Voice of the Other: Listening to Derrida

Gadamer's *Truth and Method* carries out the turn to language using the model of writing rather than orality. Though he claims otherwise, Gadamer begins with textual interpretation in order to return to dialogue and from there to reach the universality of language (*TM* 383–389/*GW1* 387–393). This path is necessary because history is transmitted in the "medium" of language; in other words, language is the happening of history. Here is where the linguistic character of understanding emerges, which is "*the concretion of historically effected consciousness*" (*TM* 389/*GW1* 393). It is true of course that there are "fragments of the past"; but what tradition hands down to us as spoken, or better, as written, is quite another matter (*GW8* 260). Inasmuch as writing transcends all finite determination, anyone can participate in the transmission of the past, provided he can read. Historically effective consciousness is a consciousness that reads (*TM* 389–395/*GW1* 393–399).

Yet what is the relationship between orality and writing? What is the place of the voice? And what role does the text play? Gadamer's complex position on these questions changed over the years, especially as a result of his debate with Derrida, which also led to Gadamer's distancing himself from Plato. The position can be summarized in the thesis of an inseparable connection between the oral and the written: "In truth there is no real opposition. What is written must be read and therefore all that is written is 'subordinated to the voice.'"[12]

Gadamer does not share Plato's "one-sided" condemnation of writing in the *Phaedrus* and in the excursus of the *Seventh Letter*.[13] He takes Plato's argument about the peculiar "weakness" of all written language to be an "ironic exaggeration." Nor does he accept the thought, expressed in the *Protagoras,* that written language is resistant to dialogue (*TM* 393/*GW1* 396).[14] For Gadamer the text *speaks* in responding to the questions a reader puts to it. He does not give up the idea that the text is a partner in a dialogue. Hermeneutics itself is just this "coming into conversation with the text" (*TM* 368/*GW1* 374). Cognizant of the asymmetry between a written and an oral dialogue, when an embodied other is present, Gadamer nevertheless emphasizes the *continuity* between the oral and the written. The boundaries are fluid: writing is voicelike and can be made oral again at any time; the oral, to the extent that it is language, can always potentially be written, or is always "destined for writing," as Gadamer put it in his 1983 essay "Unterwegs zur Schrift?" (*GW7* 258–269). Put otherwise: the oral is potentially always already in the written, and the written is always already potentially in the oral.

The transition from the oral to the written occurs through *reading*. Here the distance from Derrida becomes apparent. *Lécture,* reading, becomes a paradigm that is implicitly opposed to *écriture,* writing. And it is no coincidence that the paradigm of reading, which is described as letting-speak or giving-voice-to, is ultimately expanded so far that it coincides with hermeneutics.[15] "What is writing, if it is not read?" (*DD* 97/*GW10* 141) Gadamer posed this question to Derrida. "Writing is a phenomenon of language only insofar as it is read" (*GW8* 264). Writing is just as voicelike (*stimmlich*) as speech is potentially writing (*schriftfähig*). How can one avoid vocalizing writing while reading, or articulating it with the voice?

In 1981 Gadamer published an essay with the programmatic and significant title "Voice and Language" (*GW8* 258–270). Here he answers Derrida's objections and develops his own conception of the *voice,* which comes to play a key role in the debate between hermeneutics and deconstruction.[16] The voice is, to a certain extent, an attempt to build a bridge to *écriture.* If writing is not an "image of the voice," then the voice is not an image of writing (*GR* 388/*GW10* 159). But what do articulated voice and the writing have in common?

Plato had already asked this question in the *Philebus,* which becomes decisive for dialectics because it concerns the relation between the one and the many (*Philebus* 14c–18d). Both the sounds articulated by the voice and the letters of the alphabet are given as examples. In the end it becomes clear that both, far from being mere examples, are precisely what reveal the unity of the many and the multiplicity of the one in the *lógos.* The voice reveals our incompleteness and finitude, because we cannot master it. One is thrown back on the *méson,* the "midpoint" of language, its middle or center, particularly in relation to those "elements," articulated sounds and written signs, that mark the limits of an otherwise unlimited continuum and so enable both speaking and writing. Both are constants that open up a "field of play" (*Spielraum*). Despite its expansiveness, it is bound to the *articuli,* the boundaries carved into the boundlessness of phonic and graphic material (*GW8* 259). Articulation is therefore the reciprocal relation of voice and writing, a relation that sheds light on the transition that occurs in reading. In contrast to every natural form of expression, speaking and writing amount to a coming to agreement in what is held in common, beginning with the communal space of play of the letters and the articulated sounds in any language.

Nevertheless the voice for Gadamer has "both the first and the last word," and this is where his distance from Derrida becomes visible (*LL* 34/*GW8* 419). But this position should not be confused with giving priority to the voice. The voice for hermeneutics is the continuous unity of speaking, whereas writing is characterized by the difference of interruption. It is "a phase in the event of understanding," which is fixed in the text (*DD* 21–51, 30/*GW2* 330–360, 341). Yet this fixity is not permanent, and the text becomes that "between" which interrupts the continuity of the voice.[17] This relates to the figure of the interpreter, who as *inter-pres* is the interlocutor. The "eminent text" of literature is no exception (*DD* 40/*GW2* 351). It demands to have its word heard; no less than other texts it demands to be given a voice. In the circular continuity of the voice the text stands for discontinuity. To the extent that philosophical hermeneutics emphasizes unity over difference, continuity over discontinuity, it favors the voice.

If in Derrida's wake we have no choice but to rethink writing, the voice also becomes problematic. Next to *Ousia and grammē* it is above all the book *Speech and Phenomena* from the 1960s that powerfully impressed Gadamer, as he himself pointed out (*GR* 377/*GW*10 149). Derrida had "rightfully criticized Husserl in this book," by putting into question the self-conscious *cogito* that assumes it can think without signs (*LL* 33/*GW*8 418). Though he partially agrees with Derrida, Gadamer also expresses his skepticism. He accepts Derrida's critique of Western metaphysics for its "logocentricity," though it might better be called its "monologocentricity." Yet Gadamer rejects Derrida's condemnation of the voice and, more precisely, the link that Derrida sees between the *voice* and the *self-presence* of consciousness (*DD* 112/*GW*2 371).[18] Even though Gadamer never mounts a full-scale critique, his view is easy to summarize. The voice, so readily denounced for its presumed metaphysics of presence, is the phenomenological voice, the "spiritual flesh" that continues to be present to itself but hears itself in the absence of world.[19] It is not clear why this should be so, for the voice both in its empirical embodiment and in its relation to articulation, that is, to writing. Just as much as writing, the voice would have to be a form of exile for the self-presence of consciousness. For hermeneutics, in other words, difference is carved into voice. The possibility that what is evoked may regain a voice in no way eliminates the reference to its absence (*DD* 112–113/*GW*2 371–372). This reference is the space of difference in the voice. The hermeneutic voice is in the first place *the voice of the other*, the voice I hear before I hear my own. This voice carries the otherness of the you into what would otherwise be only the identity of self-presence.[20] Nor should it be forgotten that presence is also *simultaneously* an absence, for hermeneutics as for deconstruction; it is never a pure, full, and completed presence that is immediately given without past or future. Presence is the presence of an absence, regardless of whether it is spoken by the voice or manifested in writing.

It remains an open question whether the hermeneutic voice can be accused of relying on the metaphysics of presence, or whether, by contrast, deconstruction, with its critique of phenomenology, itself succumbs to an objectivistic conception of presence understood mainly as permanence. Certainly Gadamer, as Derrida argued, was guided by the intention to let the voice emerge from its relative obscurity. At the same time, Gadamer's overall aim was not to assign a central position to the voice, but to emphasize the co-belonging of voice and writing through articulation.

Considering the importance of the voice, it is no wonder that hermeneutics proves to be a philosophy of listening or hearing.[21] The power of sight, which has been privileged throughout the entire philosophical tradition, is now contrasted to the power of hearing. To be sure, Herder had already reversed the hierarchy of the senses in the eighteenth century. But Gadamer takes his cue directly from Aristotle, who had already clearly prioritized the sense of hearing.[22] While the other senses offer access to only their own specific domains, hearing is "an avenue to the whole" as it participates in the linguistic experience of the world (*TM* 462/*GW*1 466). The claim of universality for hermeneutics finds its legitimacy here (*RPJ* 28/*GW*2 497). As the sense of language, hearing is the hermeneutic sense par excellence. "The art of understanding is certainly above all else the art of listening" (*GW*10 274). Already in *Truth and Method* the motif of hearing—*hören*—resonates audibly in the German word for belonging: *Zugehörig-keit*. The interpreter belongs to what is interpreted: he who is addressed *belongs*, is *zugehörig*, to what has been spoken to him. He cannot refuse to hear. Gadamer frequently returned to this theme, even in his last years, as in the untranslated essay from 1998 entitled "On Hearing" ("Über das Hören"). He links the inseparable connection between hearing and understanding to the moment of opening freely to the dimension of the other. This opening lies at the basis of every human relationship.[23]

3. In the Beginning Was the Question: Against the Analytic

In this way the *openness* of hermeneutic consciousness takes on more defined contours. Openness can be attributed to the one who *listens to the voice of the other*. The situation of every speaker, inasmuch as he or she speaks, is from the beginning the situation of being spoken to. One might say: in the beginning is the question. This condition further determines the primordial linguisticality of our being-in-the-world. But hermeneutics, which follows Plato's dialectics, rejects every inception and every beginning. Hence even this beginning should not be turned into an abstract absolute. If there is a beginning for hermeneutics it always lies in the middle of dialogical praxis, where every question is a response and every response is a question—and so on to infinity.

Nevertheless, within the circularity of this dialectical movement we should speak in a Socratic sense of the *"hermeneutic priority of the question"* (*TM* 362/*GW1* 368).[24] It is the knowledge of not-knowing that justifies this priority. He who believes he knows does not need to question. Conversely, he who is capable of questioning knows that he does not know—and as the Platonic dialogues show, asking questions is much more difficult than giving answers. "Actually, the secret of the question contains the miracle of thinking" (*GR* 392/*GW10* 162). The question reveals the openness of possibility, an aporetic hovering between "this way or that way." At this stage a distinction is required, a distinction (*Unterscheidung*) that is always a decision (*Entscheidung*). Accordingly, "questioning . . . is more a passion than an action," something that happens to us rather than something actively undertaken (*TM* 366/*GW1* 372). One does not pose questions. Instead, questions occur to us, they present themselves; they arise and force themselves on us. There is no method that can compel questioning to come forward. The only one who knows how to question is the one who lets himself or herself be called into question by being pulled up short by the other's question, which breaks and disorients. The priority of the question is the priority of the otherness of the you.

The priority of the question is also legitimized by everyday practice, as for example in the *logic of question and answer*. What happens when one tries to understand what is being said in everyday language? One refers back to the horizon from which the question has emerged. Here lies one of the most important principles of hermeneutics: *the utterance is always understood as an answer to a question* (*TM* 370/*GW1* 375; *RAS*

98–99/*VZW* 102–103). Understanding takes place in the move from the answer back to the question it answers—or so says Gadamer, invoking the work of R. G. Collingwood (1889–1943).²⁵ "Questioning" is another way of saying "understanding" (*TM* 370/*GW*1 379–380). Referring back to the horizon of the question, the motivational context of the dia-logue from which speech emerges has a theoretical scope that should not be overlooked.²⁶ Here the contrast between *hermeneutic* and *analytic philosophy* comes into focus more sharply.

When hermeneutics returns to the motivating questions behind assertions, it is not following an artificial procedure but simply making available for reflection a process already embedded in everyday practice. If a person does not understand a question that has been put to them, then they are forced to ask. The process is not at all artificial. On the contrary: "It is very artificial to imagine that assertions fall from the sky and that they can be submitted to analysis without considering why they were said and in what way they are answers to something" (*RAS* 99/*VZW* 103). It is artificial to take assertions to be autonomous and to detach them from their motivational context, as analytic philosophy does. Hermeneutics challenges the presumed autonomy of assertions. The assertion is just *one* among the infinite multiplicity of speech forms, and moreover it is both a *derivative* and a *secondary* form. Aristotle was already well aware of this, when he distinguished between *lógos semantikós* and *lógos apophantikós*.²⁷ All utterances are semantic, that is, they mean something; by contrast not all are apophantic; that is, the alternative between truth and falsity does hold for all. For example, a prayer is not an apophantic utterance. In our everyday communication utterances are simply semantic—and it would be truly strange if everything that is said were examined as if it could be verified. The apophantic logos is derived by logical abstraction from the semantic. That is why it is considered secondary, as Heidegger remarked (*BT* 144–150/*SZ* 209). In contrast to Heidegger, Gadamer accepts the legitimacy of apophantic logic, even in its final analytic version, and thus he overcomes the dichotomy between the authentic and the inauthentic. On the other hand, analytic philosophy, where "the different dimensions of speech are only covered from a particular aspect," should recognize that it is a logical curtailment of language (*EH* 166/*UVG* 204), and, without severing its semantic roots, it should grant both space and right of the plurality of human *logoi*.

In this way the question of the autonomy of the assertion takes on broader contours; it reveals itself to be an ethical and a political question as well. One should uncover the motives that have led to the dominance of the assertion: supported by the ideal of method, it is the supremacy of modern science that underwrites this dominance. At least since Galileo, method has proceeded by abstraction, isolation, and experiment, in order to dominate and control (*GW*2 186). The assertion is the formalized object that can be fully controlled. Although science can govern assertions, it cannot govern its own ends, beginning with the practical application of technology. Technology does not allow itself to be dominated, and science does not limit itself—their limits are ultimately left to our political abilities (*GW2* 192–193). Here it should be asked whether the unlimited use of knowledge in the form of assertions does not come at too high a price.

4. The Speculative Dialectics of the Word

"It is hermeneutics to know how much remains unsaid whenever something is said" (*GR* 417/*GL* 286). To move from what is said back to the unsaid is called *speculation*. Gadamer takes up the speculative movement of language in the penultimate chapter of *Truth and Method*, which introduces the universality of the hermeneutic experience. What does "speculative" mean? (*TM* 456–474/*GW1* 460–478) The etymology of the word points to *speculum*, a mirror that can reflect an image. Besides the mystery of the mirror, a "speculative" writer in eighteenth-century German philosophy was some-one who reflects without surrendering to the concrete immediacy of appearances. The more recent meaning of the word stems from Hegel's "speculative proposition," which, as has been shown, is introduced in the *Phenomenology of Spirit*.[28]

Gadamer returns to this meaning from Hegel, but alters it somewhat and expands it to encompass language altogether. The movement of language for him is always spec-ulative, because whatever is said mirrors in its finitude the infinitude of the unsaid and, from within its limits, points toward the horizon of the infinite. This movement, however, does not occur in the case of an assertion that is supposedly independent and detached from its horizon, which asserts its identity through the erasure of every dif-ference that might call forth the reference to another. The assertion is the sliding back into what is merely finite. In our everyday use of language: "what is said combines with the infinity of what is unsaid in one unified meaning and ensures that it is understood in this way . . . Someone who speaks is behaving speculatively when his words do not reflect beings, but express a relation to the whole of being" (*TM* 469/*GW1* 473). Every word bursts forth, as if from the middle of a totality, in virtue of which is it a word at all. One could refer to Humboldt here, for according to him every word "resonates with and presupposes the entire language."[29] Here Gadamer sees the "dialectic of the word," which is ultimately the dialectic of the finite and the infinite. The word in its finitude evokes the infinitude of what is unsaid, but without being able to say it. Thus the word is no "casual imperfection," but an irrevocable witness to our finitude (*TM* 458/*GW1* 462).

At this point Gadamer distances himself from Hegel, for whom the speculative movement of the proposition should be expressed in the dialectical presentation, which is the way speculative movement shows itself, or better, demonstrates itself. Hegel introduces here a distinction between the speculative and the dialectical. By ab-stracting the reflexive relations of conceptual determinations from language, he brings this relation, by way of dialectical mediation, to absolute knowledge. For Gadamer, by contrast, the speculative is always dialectical. As a result, we can speak of a *speculative dialectic of language*. It is this dialectic that unfolds from the "middle" (*Mitte*) where all hermeneutic experience occurs.Gadamer takes the beginning away from Hegel. Since every word bursts forth from the "medium" of language, which is also the medium of historically effected consciousness, hermeneutics does not have the problem of the beginning. It recognizes the radical finitude provoked by this middle or medium (*TM* 472/*GW1* 476).[30] Since it proceeds in its speculative truth from the event of the word, hermeneutic dialectics differs from metaphysical dialectics in its awareness of the constitutive and never-ending openness of this event.

5. Being, Understanding, Language

In the last subsection of *Truth and Method,* which concerns the universal aspect of hermeneutics, Gadamer addresses the meaning of "the turn" from Being to language with one of his most famous and widely quoted sentences: "*Being that can be understood is language*" (*TM* 474/*GW1* 478). This is also, however, among Gadamer's most misunderstood statements, and has by now a reception history of its own. The interpretation by Gianni Vattimo, the translator of *Truth and Method* into Italian, has been influential. He reads this line as an identification of Being with language and his reading makes it possible to turn hermeneutics into a "weak ontology."[31] In this way, the decisive and far-reaching question arises about *hermeneutics as philosophy.*

It is significant that Vattimo interprets this sentence as a "translation" of a passage from *Being and Time* (*BT* 270–271/*SZ* 301–302). Gadamer's discourse is measured against Heidegger's discourse on the authenticity of being, while also invoking the well-known metaphor of language as the "house of Being."[32] But this metaphor never occurs in Gadamer's work. Not so much the house of Being, language is, for Gadamer, the home of mankind that is often far too cramped (*EE* 172–173) The mother tongue, for Gadamer, is the most familiar place of being-with-oneself, but starting from an even more fundamental uncanniness.[33] For language appears so "uncannily near" (*unheimlich nahe*) that it belongs among the "most mysterious questions that man ponders" (*TM* 378/*GW1* 383). To be sure, the most well known version of hermeneutics is the most urbanized one, which emphasizes the familiar. But to this should be added the more unsettling version, the one that emphasizes uncanniness, where we are not so much at home. The fleeting and ephemeral home that language offers us is not easily separated from the more substantial homelessness that defines our finitude in language, one that exists even prior to our finitude in the world. On this point Gadamer's later hermeneutics appears almost to overlap with Derrida's deconstruction.

Yet what is this more primordial uncanniness, if not the resistance of Being to language? Indeed, Gadamer does not at all identify Being and language. In a retrospective interview conducted in 1996 he clearly warns: "But no, I have never meant and never said that everything is language" (*GR* 417/*GL* 286). This "is" marks both identity and difference here; it differentiates this sentence from a tautology, and turns it into a speculative sentence in which *Being* unfolds in the predicate *language,* where it is understood but not exhausted. For the way in which something is shown in language belongs to its Being but does not exhaust it. So it is, on the one hand, that "the word is a word only because of what comes to language in it," and on the other hand, "that which comes into language is not something that is pre-given before language; rather, the word gives it its own determinateness" (*TM* 475/*GW1* 479).

In Gadamer's self-interpretation the relative clause between the two commas—"that can be understood"—should not be read as a supplement but rather as a "delimitation" (*GR* 417/*GL* 286). It does not say that Being is language and that it can also, in addition, be understood. The middle term is decisive, namely, *understanding* (*PH* 103/*GW8* 1–8,7). Thus the sentence could be rewritten in this way: "*Being, insofar as it . . .*" or "*Being, within the limits in which* it can be understood, is language." Being that gives itself *to be understood* is language. For Gadamer, "understanding itself has a fundamental connection with language" (*TM* 395–396/*GW1* 399). Being that makes itself understandable *for us* is that way because it exists in language, and precisely this "understandability" is what concerns hermeneutics. If we proceed from understanding, the question of language for hermeneutics becomes unavoidable: "*language is the universal medium in which understanding occurs*" (*TM* 389/*GW1* 399).

6. The Limits of Language

The relationship between Being and language already points to the limits of language. The hermeneutic experience of language that follows the speculative movement turns out to be an *experience of the limits of language*. This theme was already mentioned in *Truth and Method* (*TM* 402/*GW1* 406). Furthermore, in the 1980s it became truly central to Gadamer, especially in the essay "The Boundaries of Language" (1985), which marks a turning point in Gadamer's self-critical reflections (*LL* 9–17/*GW8* 350–361).

The "boundaries" should not be seen as imperfections of language, measured in relation to the perfection of reason. Then what are these "boundaries?" They can be experienced phenomenologically in what is prior to language, alongside language, and beyond language. Needless to say, it is clear that these border regions are defined by their striving to become language. The striving is for linguisticality, for the virtuality of what is not yet said but what awaits fulfillment in the linguistic event, and yet will likely run up against these limits of the latter.[34] If on the one hand the primacy of verbal language is asserted here, into which all other "languages" could be translated, on the other hand the constitutive limits are also emphasized.

Gadamer summarizes the hermeneutic experience of the boundaries of language as the *search for the right word*. The "right word" is by definition never right—that would mean it is the appropriate, fitting word for a pre-given object. On the contrary, our experience of its boundaries demonstrates that language is anything but an instrument of domination and calculation. In all speech, however forgetful of itself it may be, we experience the boundary of the spoken and, specularly, the understood word. This is how Gadamer describes the experience of the boundary:

Finally, the deepest of the problems that essentially belongs to the boundary of language should be indicated. I feel it only dimly, although in other areas—I am thinking of psychoanalysis—it already plays an important role. It is the awareness that every speaker has in each moment when he seeks the right word—and this word is the one that reaches the other—the awareness that he never completely finds it. What reaches the other through language, what has been said in words, always overshoots or falls wide of what is meant or intended. An undying desire for the right word—that is what constitutes actual life and the essence of language. Here there appears a close connection between the unrealizable nature of this desire, this *désir* (Lacan), and the fact that our own human existence fades away in time and with death. (*LL* 17/*GW8* 361)

The experience of the boundaries of language is thus the experience of the boundaries of our existence and our finitude. The search for the right word appears to be an endless task. On the other hand, it is the word that always carries us *above* and *beyond* ourselves. In order to elucidate this, Gadamer recalls Rilke's angel, that is, the possibility surrounded by a limit and evoked as an angel: "Above, beyond us, / the angel plays."[35] The word that we bring forth has always already caught up with us, is always already beyond us.

An important essay from 1971 also explores this theme. The essay, entitled "On the Truth of the Word," was rewritten several times and did not appear in print until 1993 with its publication in volume eight of Gadamer's collected works (*SR* 135–155/ *GW8* 37–57). Hermeneutic truth is bound to language because the world is there for us, and we for the world, only in language. When Gadamer takes up the question of the "truth of the word," he means the word—as a singular word and not plural words—in the multiplicity of its forms: it can be a simple "yes," or what you might say in making a promise—"You have my word on it!"—or it can be "the Word" in the Prologue to the Gospel of St. John (*SR* 135/*GW8* 37). Before it can be understood in the sense of an objective genitive, "the truth of the word" points to a more subjective genitive. It is the word that reveals the truth as it "comes out" before we can reflect and confirm it to be the true or "right" word. Just as he had spoken of the "ontological valence" of the image, now Gadamer speaks of the "ontological valence" of the word.[36] The world attains Being for us only in the *universal* "Da," or "there," of the word that constitutes the wonder of language (*SR* 152/*GW8* 54). Whereas Being (*Sein*) comes to exist in the word, or *Dasein* in the word, we too are called by the word to this "Da," we come alive to Being, we are awakened to it. In the "Da" of the word we are anamnetically drawn out of the forgetting of language and awakened to Being. Here lies the wonder. Yet what lies ready in this "Da" points at the same time to what escapes its grasp. The presence of the universal "Da" in the word is therefore also an absence. The word always already rises beyond the "Da," always already transcends itself. Hermeneutics cannot overlook the play of presence and absence in the existence or *Dasein* of the word; by colliding with the boundaries of the "Da," it reveals itself to be a hermeneutics of language and its boundaries. Such a hermeneutics constantly points to that which is not yet there in the "Da,"—and what always remains beyond it. The transcendence of language determines the movement of hermeneutics as always having to go beyond itself. Habermas is justified in his observation that hermeneutics promotes "the tendency to self-transcendence immanent in the praxis of language."[37] However, this point in no way puts into question the non-transcendental nature of the "dialogue, that we are," within which everything can be said differently.

7. The Dialogue That We Are

"Language [*Sprache*] is dialogue [*Gespräch*]" (*GW8* 369). Gadamer formulates this thesis as early as *Plato's Dialectical Ethics*, returning to it in *Truth and Method*, and taking it up again in his late works (*PDE* 35–65/*GW5* 27–48; *TM* 446/*GW1* 449; *GW2* 207; *GW8* 360). The hermeneutics of language unfolds as a hermeneutics of dialogue. If language arises from the openness of a historical language and realizes itself as individual speech, which for its part is always a speaking *for* or *with* the other, then the *existence of language lies in dialogue*. In its simplicity, this is the secret core of Gadamer's philosophy, which, both in its theoretical reach and its practical intention, is a *philosophy of dialogue*.

At the basis of this thesis there lies, however, a philosophical motivation that should not be overlooked. Gadamer offers here a radical interpretation of this verse from Hölderlin: "Since we have been a conversation."[38] This line does not mean only that we simply participate in dialogue. We are always already in dialogue and speak out of its flow, or out of its unending flow. Even more so: *we are dialogue*. Each of us is not only in a dialogue, but according to our most intimate nature we are ourselves dialogue. For dialogue is our *ubi consistam*, it is the hermeneutic universe in which we breathe, in which we live.

But what does it mean that dialogue is an unending flow? Every word opens up to an endless number of possible further words, of response that it calls for and requires (*GW8* 38). Since it speculatively reflects the unspoken, no spoken word can be the last word. On the basis of this virtuality, every word points toward the openness in which we speak further. Thus it can be said that "speaking takes place in the element of the 'dialogue'" (*GW2* 198). The endlessness opened up by the virtuality of the word is the endlessness of our speaking with each other. It follows that the dialogue has "an inner endlessness and no end" (*GW2* 152).

To be sure, the dialogue can be interrupted for many reasons: one might have nothing more to say, become irritated, or not want to continue speaking. But for hermeneutics the interruption is only a pause that implies a continuation. Arising from the primordial, inner endlessness of the dialogue, an interruption from outside might occur, but it in no way disturbs the endless openness. According to Gadamer, even the limit case of the soul's inner dialogue with itself is *endless* (*TM* 547–548/ *GW2* 200–201). Here one comes across one of the most significant points of dissonance between hermeneutics and deconstruction: whereas Derrida accentuates the creativity of the *interruption,* Gadamer focuses—beyond all interruption—on the endless, or better, *the uninterrupted dialogue.*[39] This adjective, actually suggested by Derrida, seems more appropriate for describing Gadamer's dialogue.[40] But even if the dialogue continues endlessly, it is discontinuous, that is, ending and endless at the same time. Rather than endless, we might say from the perspective of interruption that dialogue is *un-interrupted.*

Here arises the *unlimited readiness for dialogue* that distinguishes hermeneutics. Such readiness is philosophically justified by a trust in language and its ability to communalize. This does not mean that dialogue will always succeed. On the contrary: agreement is never certain, and understanding is never perfect. The dialogue cannot succeed if by success we mean closure, or self-enclosure within a wordless, ultimate consensus. The dialogue never closes. Of course this is not to say that we never reach a successful accord within dialogue's potential endlessness. But when can we say that a dialogue has succeeded? A dialogue is certainly not successful only when we have learned something new. Success is reached, rather, when we come across something in the other that we have not met before in our experience of the world. Something changes, and changes us. The dialogue possesses a "transformative power."[41] This power is not a matter of more information. What counts in dialogue is the encounter with the other. Dialogue succeeds when the other has changed because of the self, and the self has changed because of the other. "Dialogue transforms both."[42] After the dialogue one is no longer the same person as before. Paradoxically, a dialogue succeeds all the more, the less it comes to a close: the more the disagreements come to light, the more misunderstandings and nonunderstandings appear anew. Hence, the dialogue does not conclude if the word, which the I addresses to the you and the you to the I, leads to a new openness, from which, through new questions and answers, the dialogue can go further (*GR* 393/*GW*10 162).

On the other hand, dialogue for Gadamer also responds to the fundamental disposition of life, fundamental insofar as it is abyssal, namely, anxiety. Driven out of one's own narrowness and into the always alien expanse—as Schelling had already said—the I takes a distance from itself. In this centrifugal movement, the I runs up against the boundary of the other, the you, and loses its center. Yet it is precisely the you who makes it possible for the I to find its center again. Only when the center has been given away to the other, when it turns to the you, can the I recuperate its focus and restore its balance. This paradoxical event occurs in dialogue, where the center of the I is restored each and every time in the collision with the you. And each time, obviously, the center is never the same but always different: it differs through time, through language, in dialogue. In the encounter with the you, *the I always understands itself differently.*

To recuperate here means to heal. To be concerned with oneself does not mean to withdraw into oneself, but to care for the other. And conversely, one can heal especially—as Gadamer often emphasized—through the word of dialogue.[43] The word heals better than any kind of medication—above all, the word of a friend. Here appears the immediate proximity of dialogue and friendship, the guiding thread that Gadamer followed from the beginning to the end of his path of thought. In the *philía*, where one's own limits are recognized, one recognizes in the other, in the friend, "an increase of being, self-esteem and the richness of life."[44]

All of this, however, is underappreciated in a time that seems to be character-ized by the "*incapacity for a conversation.*"[45] Today all forms of everyday dialogue are impoverished. Gadamer reviews the phenomenology of these forms, from pedagogi-cal discussions to business negotiations to therapeutic dialogue.[46] In psychoanalytic therapy, the inability to dialogue that manifests itself is a "disturbance" to be healed. But in everyday dialogue, this inability, which is not transparent to itself, takes on the "normal" form of blaming the other. In this way, for example, we say: "There is no talking to you." This inability is then traced back to both the inability to listen and the inability to speak. People forget how to speak when the shared language has been exhausted and reduced to terminology, a frequent experience in the monological condition of today's society.[47] But in every dialogue, even the least successful, the I is elevated beyond its limitations by the encounter with the word from the you. The you is the lever that the I needs, even for a dialogue with itself.[48] The I experiences its own limits in the strangeness of the you, who is also always familiar, just as the I, in the transcending movement of language, is always already beyond itself, thanks to the you, and with the you in the shared word. The "right" word proves here to be the word that reaches the you, that is heard and then answered by the you as if it were his or her own. In the word that has become communal, that resonates when it is uttered by the you, the I finds a home—a home that, however, because of the irrevocable homelessness of language, always remains fleeting. Gadamer takes up a Hegelian expression again when he says that speaking with one another is *to make oneself at home with the other.*

8. Understanding, Interpreting, Translating: Where Hermeneutics Is Misunderstood

If we consider the four decades of its reception history, it is surprising to note that philosophical hermeneutics has so often been misunderstood in its attempt within philosophy to give voice to the question of understanding. There are two misunder-standings above all that need to be addressed.

The first is contained in the charge that understanding, according to hermeneu-tics, would be an appropriation of the other. The charge is aimed at the furor, "the fury of understanding" that supposedly animates hermeneutics, as well as the conciliatory intention that would presumably guide its movements.[49] Philosophical hermeneutics seems to claim that it could and should understand in a complete way, that it could and should reconcile and harmonize. Understanding in hermeneutics would, from this view, be self-evident and taken for granted. If this were so, however, hermeneutics would have no reason to exist, since it exists in order to raise the philosophical question of understanding.

In following the Heideggerian view that understanding is the fundamental enactment of human existence,[50] Gadamer maintains that *"agreement . . . is more primordial than misunderstanding."*[51] This "agreement" is a matter neither of glib optimism nor of simply adopting an ethical task. On the contrary, with this thesis Gadamer describes in phenomenological terms the practice of speaking and understanding. A *more originary understanding* involves nothing other than bringing into harmony the common language that communalizes. One who speaks in a historical language—and in doing so speaks for the other and with the other—assents (*Zustimmung*) even before any accord has been reached, by being ready to attune one's voice to the voice (*Stimme*) of the other, articulating oneself in the meaningful sounds of the common language. In short, whoever speaks has already agreed to share what is common and communicable with the speakers of that language, binding them to past, present, and future speakers. Even before any agreement with oneself, one is already in agreement with the other: speaking is thus a "mutual agreement." Gadamer interprets the *synthéke* of Aristotle in this sense:[52] "The concept of 'synthéke,' of mutual agreement, suggests in the first place the view that language forms itself in the being with one another" (*LL* 12/*GW8* 354). This agreement is the *prelude of language,* and sets in motion the further play of agreement and disagreement. Such a prelude cannot be avoided: every speaker must enter into the play of language, accepting the preexisting communality that language offers us. To speak means, then, to articulate further the commonalities of the world articulated in language. The spoken is further shared in speaking, and this communication can be communicated further. This is the reality of human communication, that is, of dialogue.[53]

Yet the flow of dialogue can be interrupted and agreement can also turn into disagreement. In this context Gadamer speaks of a "stumbling block" (*TM* 270/*GW1* 272). Almost completely overlooked by the reception, the "stumbling block" is a key concept for hermeneutics, because it clarifies the movement of understanding (*GR* 93/*GW2* 184). Without it, one might assume that understanding is self-generated. In order to delineate the concept of a stumbling block more precisely, Gadamer returns to Greek philosophy: "The Greeks had a very beautiful word for what brings our understanding to a standstill, they called it the *atopon.* That actually means: the unplaceable, whatever cannot be brought into the schematism of our horizon of understanding and therefore causes us to halt" (*GR* 93/*GW2* 185). The *átopon* is whatever provokes uneasiness and irritation, what seems strange to us, uncanny and alien. In the Platonic dialogues it is Socrates who is *átopos,* the philosopher who, being out of place, puts into question the order of the *pólis* and points to the externality of an *ou-tópos,* a beyond place to come.[54] For hermeneutics, the *átopon* is the incomprehensible that breaks in on what once understood, and almost entirely forgotten, was taken for granted as self-evident.

The *átopon* strikes what is seemingly familiar and suddenly puts into question the commonality of our words.[55] The incomprehensible, which is still placeless, makes way for both nonunderstanding and misunderstanding. This does not, however, prevent attempts to continue to interpret in order to reestablish agreement—without excluding disagreement.

The second misunderstanding in the reception concerns the connection between *understanding* and *interpretation*. There is a widespread belief that understanding and interpretation are the same in hermeneutics, and the idea has actually provoked numerous criticisms. Can one really say, however, that "understanding" and "interpretation" are synonymous for hermeneutics? Certainly not, and the proof of this would be to read the texts in light of Gadamer's complex reflections on understanding. To this end a third term needs to be considered: *translation*. Gadamer follows Schleiermacher, who tries to show that nonunderstanding and misunderstanding are not limited to the interpretation of texts, but jeopardize understanding in all discourse.[56] It is precisely on this issue that hermeneutics becomes a universal question. Gadamer's intention is to rediscover the hidden connection between interpretation and understanding. But connection does not mean identification. With his emphasis on understanding, through which he underlines our fundamental linguisticality, Gadamer in no way claims that all understanding is an interpretation, as if we—and this would indeed be a strange and untenable thesis—would actively interpret each moment of our everyday understanding. On the contrary, although he insists on the continuity of understanding, interpretation, and translation—a continuity that is constituted by the thread of nonunderstanding and misunderstanding that runs through them—he does not neglect their differences, which prove to be quantitative, not qualitative: different degrees of intensity (*TM* 389–390/*GW1* 391). Where understanding occurs, there is not translation or interpretation but speech (*TM* 386/*GW1* 388), and understanding a language means to live in it. To understand a language "does not involve an interpretive process; it is an accomplishment of life" (*TM* 385/*GW1* 388). There can be *an understanding without interpretation*—indeed, this happens normally in every dialogue. However, since nonunderstanding and misunderstanding are always lurking in every dialogue, understanding can always be interrupted and requires the between, or *inter-*, of an interpretation, an explicative interpretation. This interpretation is not separate from understanding, but rather the development of the understanding, its "conditions of fulfillment"—as Heidegger had already suggested in *Being and Time* (*BT* 143/*SZ*153). Interpretation unfolds in the *medium* of language and should be understood as a further linguistic articulation of understanding, one that is possible at any time:

> This is also true in those cases when there is immediate understanding and no explicit interpretation is undertaken. For in these cases, too, interpretation must be possible. But this means that interpretation is contained potentially within the understanding process. It simply makes the understanding explicit. Thus interpretation is not a means through which understanding is achieved; rather, it enters into the content of what is understood. (*TM* 398/*GW1* 402)

An interpretation, which like any performance is a concretion of sense, can be called a success when "it too disappears again as an interpretation and preserves its truth in the immediacy of understanding" (*TM* 400/*GW1* 404). The extreme case of "translation" is marked by its greater degree of strangeness, which of course also exists in understanding and in interpretation but is unavoidable in translation. Gadamer gives the example of a dialogue in two different languages. In this case the recourse to translation is the self-incapacitation (*Selbstentmündigung*) of the speakers, who admit to their own incapacitation and are forced to make use of the artificiality of a translation (*TM* 384/*GW1* 388). Pushed toward interpretation, of which it is a "fulfillment," the translation can be described as "highlighting" (*TM* 386/*GW1* 389). If the interpretation is, however, an explicit development of the understanding, the translation is an explicit, albeit "artificial," development. The "despair of translation," which might capture the "letter but not the spirit" of an utterance, would thus stem from the requirement that the translator must convey the "unity of viewpoint that a sentence possesses," without however being able to get it right (*GR* 106/*GW2* 197). In this very traditional and not very hermeneutic sense, translation understood in a strictly interlinguistic way is not so much an extreme case, but rather a peculiar case and a deviation from the norm of intralinguistic dialogue. Even in his much later works, Gadamer will retain this negative view of translation and treat it as merely an artificial mediation of meaning that can be brought back to life only in dialogue. Translation, and even more the work of simultaneous translation, "is merely a vestige of living conversation, even if mediated, split, broken" (*GW8* 348).

9. Play and Dialogue: The Encounter with Wittgenstein

The paradigm of play is taken up again on the penultimate page of *Truth and Method*, only this time with respect not to art but to language: "*Language games* exist where we, as learners—and when do we cease to be that?—rise to the understanding of the world" (*TM* 490/*GW1* 493). It seems as if Wittgenstein could have written these words. Gadamer himself addresses this surprising convergence in the introduction to the second edition of *Truth and Method* from 1965 (*TM* xxxvi/*GW2* 446).[57] We should therefore assume that Gadamer read Wittgenstein's principal works, including the *Tractatus* and the *Philosophical Investigations,* sometime between 1960 and 1965, perhaps as early as the last months of 1959. At any rate his 1963 essay on "The Phenomenological Movement" contains what are probably Gadamer's most significant comments on Wittgenstein. Above all, in the final part of that essay, the "language game" is recognized as the common denominator of all the more recent philosophies, especially those that do without an "ultimate foundation," after which for example Husserl sought (*PH* 172–177/*GW3* 142–146). This convergence, which reveals itself to be an important encounter up until his last writings, is surprising because Wittgenstein was almost completely unknown in Germany at the beginning of the 1960s. Gadamer appears to have been one of the first to read him productively there. Thirty years later, in 1990, he declared:

"The name of Wittgenstein is today one of the great names in the philosophy of our century" (*GW8* 343).

But what unites and what divides these two philosophers? For Gadamer, the importance of the encounter was evident. He had worked for some time on a phenomenology of play, which had clarified more and more for him the post-metaphysical implications of this concept. The encounter with Wittgenstein strengthened Gadamer in his belief that it is "play" which puts metaphysics into question. Wittgenstein's position encouraged him to take this paradigm, which he had already applied to art, and extend it to language as a whole, seeing the reciprocity of play especially in the universality of language, or better, in dialogue (RPJ 41–42/*GW2* 5–6). It was, in other words, Wittgenstein who showed Gadamer a path toward overcoming metaphysics that differed from Heidegger's. The language of metaphysics is, as has been shown, still language.[58] Even petrified concepts reveal—as soon as they are integrated into living speech, into the web of language games and continue to "work" there—the lines of their own overcoming.[59] Gadamer does not find the convergence between himself and Wittgenstein in the *Tractatus,* which refers all sentences to a "propositional logic." Rather, he finds confirmation in the *Philosophical Investigations,* especially in Wittgenstein's "pragmatics of language," the new vision of language as public practice and shared action, and in the argument against private language.[60] Precisely because language is always "public," it is always *communal* and necessarily dialogical. The argument against private language is another way of emphasizing the priority of the dialogue (*GW8* 369; *LL* 45/*GW8* 432). For Gadamer, as for Wittgenstein, speaking involves mutual agreement at the middle point of the word, which is what "grounds" commonality, but this should not be confused with what is universally valid: "Even children's games are of such a nature that we cannot go behind their established rules with any kind of superior knowing" (*PH* 175/*GW3* 144). This has an explosive impact on the concept of the "concept," which, lost in the families of language games, loses its sharp contours, but gains the productivity of indeterminacy (*PH* 175/*GW3* 144; *GR* 385/*GW10* 156).

Yet despite their proximity the distance between Wittgenstein and Gadamer should not be overlooked, especially in their different views on the relationship between language and philosophy. For Wittgenstein, philosophy is a *critique of language,* a form of therapy that would lead to the dissolution of philosophical problems.[61] For Gadamer, by contrast, hermeneutics is a *listening to language,* which in no way leads to a cathartic release from philosophy. The differences between them extend to their reflections on language. Gadamer expresses his doubts about the term "use," which points to a much too instrumental view of language for him, and he also writes against the term "rule," which seems too reductive in view of the complexity of speaking.[62]

Gadamer in his later work sees play more and more clearly as the binding element between nonverbal and verbal communication: from the language of animals to the language we use with animals to learning language, when children and adults "join together in play" (*LL* 14/*GW8* 356). Play is already the prelinguistic dialogue from which the linguistic dialogue proceeds. As the structural relation between play and the dialogue comes into view, the "medial" character of play (*Spielen*) emerges, which, since it is always a playing-with (*Mit-Spielen*), reveals an activity that borders on passivity. As a consequence, the rigid dichotomy between the subject and the object disappears. The speaker moves beyond his subjectivity by submitting to the interactive play of language, which always already points to the "beyond" of the other. And he opens himself up to the other's wanting-to-say, by declining and conjugating himself with the other's word, which thereby becomes communal.[63]

Here Gadamer distances himself not only from Wittgenstein, but also from Heidegger. For Wittgenstein, the perspectives of the speakers dominate. On the basis of their competence, that is, their operational skills with rules, they can move within the grammar of the game. Speakers play the game, and speaking is "part of an activity" in which a remnant of subjectivity emerges.[64] In Gadamer's view, the speaker's perspective is overcome by the common perspective of the language game. However, this does not result in the hypostasis of language. In this way, Gadamer's position should also be distinguished from Heidegger's, since, for Gadamer, it is not language that speaks; it is rather the speakers. Whereas for Wittgenstein the subject retains mastery, for Heidegger it is language. Gadamer's position between the two reflects the "medial" character of play, which casts light on the active process, which is nonetheless undergone, of dialogue.

10. The Diversity of Languages and the Future of Europe

For Gadamer, dialogue takes on even broader contours. The dialogue is not only between the I and the you, but also involves a *dialogue between languages*. The topic of diversity, which is already discussed in *Truth and Method* in the confrontation with Humboldt, becomes increasingly important for both philosophical and political reflection in Gadamer's later works, where his attention turns more and more to the future of the *European oikoumene*. The most important text for this issue is the 1990 essay on "The Diversity of Languages and the Understanding of the World" (*GW8* 339–349).

If the story of the Tower of Babel (Gen. 11:4–9) disturbs us even today, it is because we are still seduced by the idea of constructing a unique language in which human hubris could takes shape: "The Tower of Babel repeats, in a form distorted until it is upside down, the problem of unity and multiplicity. Here, unity is the danger, and multiplicity is its overcoming" (*GW8* 340). But what does this tower represent in our contemporary world? Gadamer has no doubts about the answer given by the history of the West: the tower is science. As the product of logic's power of abstraction, it rises up and is strengthened, too, by the language of mathematics, so that it rejects any foundation in common language. Yet a common language does not cease to differentiate itself into a multiplicity of historical, individual languages. Neither rationalization nor bureaucracy—in the sense articulated by Max Weber—will solve this problem by constructing some empty, mechanical unity. Thus the chimera of an artificial language should give way to the dialogue of languages, which is the only way to discover the value of every individual language—because "in each language everything can be said" (*GW10* 270). This insight helps us to resist the temptation to force onto others the world sedimented in our own particular language, as if it were purely and simply *the* world.

Dialogue is the way to preserve diversity in a culturally richer unity. The languages of Europe speak against monological unity and bear witness to the model of a unity articulated in differences. Because of the destinal eccentricity that, from the beginning, has inhabited Europe and pointed it toward dialogue, Europe's *oikoumene* has been forced to experience, throughout its history, such a unity as always different, differentiated, and decentered.

Precisely at this point Gadamer sees Europe as a "true training ground" for coexistence, in a confined space, of different peoples, cultures, religions, and denominations (*EPH* 234/*EE* 31). As a result of the upheavals and traumas that have characterized it for centuries, Europe has the privilege and the task of learning how to respect the other in its otherness (*EPH* 234/*EE* 30). In "The Diversity of Europe: Inheritance and Future," Gadamer writes not only of other people, but also of the other: it is the you who demands to be respected, but it is also the other "whom we meet at first as the other," that is, in that otherness which nature, for instance, has for us (*EPH* 232–233/ *EE* 28–29). What today makes Europe significant, promising and momentous, is the privilege of respecting others or the other. This frequently disregarded task is imposed upon us now more urgently than ever in its universality. From this Gadamer draws his conviction that the European question is linked to the "future of humanity as a whole" (*EPH* 234/*EE* 31).[65] "To live with an other, to live as the other of the other": for a long time, this has been Europe's task (*EPH* 234/*EE* 31). It is a matter of both an "ethical" and a "political" task, which has been posed to the individual, peoples, and states. In this sense, Europe anticipates the future of the globalized world. And the "new Babel," in its productivity, requires that the free spaces of human cohabitation are not only respected but also lived—all the more so where foreignness is most present (*GW8* 343).

Gadamer's emphasis on the other, the foreign, and the different does not at all weaken his demand that we build on what we share *in common*. Even if it is true that we encounter ourselves in the other, and above all in what distinguishes the other from us, nevertheless we should still recognize in and with the other what we have in common (*EPH* 219/*EE* 124–125). Above all, Gadamer calls on us to strengthen the web of community and to care for a shared future (*EE* 135). The question of Europe and its future is tied closely to the question of community, or rather, to the urgency of a new community. This latter point is very complex, because European identity is today more nonidentical with itself than ever. But precisely the creative experience of foreignness, which constitutes the heart of Europe's eccentric identity, constitutes one final opportunity. We should begin from Europe's peripheries and margins, which are at the same time places of failure as well as borders where horizons might be opened. The new community that arises against the backdrop of Europe will not be able to invoke an empty, abstract universality—even for Hegel the Europeans had "concrete universality" as their principle and character. Instead, Europe will have to repostulate the difference that is part of the European heritage, that difference that denies self-identity and forces it to shape itself again and again in difference. The heritage of Europe promises, from this new perspective, a future in which the culture of the self, in the plurality of differences, will also become a culture of the other.

Yet how does Gadamer understand the European heritage? For him, the European heritage is like a work of art, a "successful attempt to unite what is falling apart," a work of art hovering between the dangers of the "character of the past" and the opening toward utopia. It is the impossible possibility of rebuilding a world in harmony through being-with-one-another, of recreating it in poetry and in art, even among the ruins of the prosaic (*EE* 65, 74/*GW8* 208, 213). The reconstruction must occur among these ruins—the ruins of Europe, but especially of Germany—yet this reconstruction is specifically entrusted to philosophy: Europe's future, according to Gadamer, is intimately bound up with the future of philosophy. Still, the teachers Gadamer recommends are not contemporary philosophers, but instead Plato and Hegel: the poet-philosopher and the Swabian professor who took up the word of philosophy from its European past and gave it a universal resonance (*EE* 163–165).

11. Paul Celan: Between Poem and Dialogue

For philosophical hermeneutics there is already a place where one can live with the other as the other of the other. That place is poetry. But how would dialogue harmonize with the singularity of poetry? After his encounter with Paul Celan, perhaps the most important poet on his path of thinking, Gadamer came to the idea of the *dialogue of the poem*.

In the slender book from 1967, *Who Am I and Who Are You?* Gadamer explores Celan's cycle of poems *Breath-Crystal*. Beyond this book, which Heidegger valued even more than *Truth and Method*, Gadamer also wrote a number of essays and collected them in 1990 under the title *Poem and Dialogue*.[66] But *Who Am I and Who Are You?* is at the same time the most widely criticized of Gadamer's works. And the criticisms are certainly justified, for the most part, since Gadamer fails to read Celan as part of the Jewish tradition, and he fails to take him for what he was and wanted to be: the poet of the *Shoah*. Here we should also note that this book, one of the first on Celan, was published in a time when, despite having won the Büchner Prize in 1960 in Germany, Celan was not well known. It is further true that Gadamer chose Celan as his chief witness for hermeneutical dialogue and thus universalized the question asked by Celan's poetry: "Who am I and who are you?"

Gadamer frequently refers to Celan, also in autobiographical contexts. In particular he recalls Celan in order to juxtapose his poetic language with the philosophical language of Hegel, and in this way to examine the relationship between poetry and philosophy (*GR* 37–38/*GW2* 493. He deals with this topic in the 1977 essay on "Poetry and Philosophy" (*RB* 131–139/*GW8* 232–239). According to Gadamer, in their distance from ordinary language one finds the proximity of poetry and philosophy, but such a proximity divides itself into two extremes: the extreme of a word that sublates itself into a concept, in contrast to a word that stands for itself. In ordinary language, which tends to forget itself, the word passes into what is said, or fades away into the unsayable. In poetic language, however, the word stands "there in itself," and does not withdraw from the said (*RB* 107/*GW8* 72). With an etymological figure borrowed from Heidegger, Gadamer frequently accentuates the *dictation* (*Diktat*) of poetry (*Dichtung*).[67] The poetic word is "all word" and, as language in a "preeminent sense," must be taken "at its word."[68] In order to explain this further, Gadamer introduces a simile from Valery: ordinary language is like small change, whereas poetic language is like a gold coin, whose value corresponds to its imprint.[69]

This significance is especially true for lyric poetry, which Gadamer—like Hegel—prefers above other art forms (*GW8* 58–69). Gadamer sees in Celan's hermetic poetry an extreme and paradigmatic case in the context of contemporary literature. Celan's poetry is a "message in a bottle," a kind of cryptogram.[70] Deciphering, reading, and listening mark the rhythm of the hermeneutic work that aims to give voice to those almost illegible signs. In order to reach its destination, the poetic message must be *read*, just as a piece of music must be performed—reading means allowing the text to speak, and so it is also always an interpretive act.[71]

For Gadamer, the close proximity between writing poetry (*dichten*) and interpreting (*deuten*) now comes to light (*GW8* 18–24). To interpret means to put oneself in the service of the poetic text, in order to draw out what the text itself already shows. An interpretation is successful when it retreats and disappears into a new experience of the poem (*GC* 147/*WBI* 156). The interpretive word interprets only what the poetic word points to. Thus interpretation is always a pointing- to something: here the interpretive word demonstrates its poetic vocation. Yet the poetic word, to the extent that it points- to something, is itself an interpretative word. Writing poetry and interpreting are equally primordial. They are joined in the pointing (*deuten*) beyond themselves and toward what is other than themselves: "Neither the interpreter nor the poet possesses artistic legitimacy—both are always already exceeded by that which actually is where a poem is. They both pursue a point that points into the open" (*GW8* 23–24). Celan's poetry is an interpretive act, which is a way of pointing to something and an interpretation of it, because it is a reflection on poetry that is at work within poetry itself. For Celan, poetry is a "turn of breath" (*Atemwende*). For Gadamer, it suggests "the breath-like transition and reversal between inhalation and exhalation . . . where the poem's breath-crystal falls like a single snowflake into its pure form" (*GC* 143/*WBI* 152). The crystal stands still in the breath, which as the life-breath belongs to all. It is from here that, in its uniqueness, it is raised to universality. It is not "my poem" but "your incontrovertible witness," because it comes from the language of the you, that dialogical place which, despite its uniqueness, is universal because it is itself the place where language occurs (*GC* 113/*WBI* 124).

The universality of such witnessing emerges all the more plainly from the *dialogue* that the *poem* opens. Gadamer sees the poem as the place where the fundamental question arises: "Who am I and who are you?" The simplest answer is that the "I" is that of the poet and the "you" is that of the reader. But for Gadamer this is not at all the case. Although the "I" is often taken to be the poet, this "I" is the "I-form," which encompasses both the "I" of the poet and anyone's "I."[72] The "you" for its part is the "you-form," that listens to the word of the I, the privileged dialogue partner of the poetic message, the you of the I, regardless of whether it is directed to the you as absolute other, as lover, or as one's own soul (*GC* 109/*WBI* 120). In this way the question "who am I and who are you?" gains a completely new meaning. To begin with, "I" and "you" are neither fundamentally different nor defined once and for all: "I" and "you" are interdependent, and are even in a certain sense interchangeable. Your "I" can enter into my "I," and your "you" can enter into my "you." "To enter into" means here to take on the forms of the I or the you and to recognize oneself in these forms. The poles of the I and the you remain open, and this openness is the invitation that the poem offers to the reader: to join in the dialogue. This invitation is confirmed in the possibility that is offered to the reader to take up, from his or her perspective, the role of the I as well as the role of the you. The I and the you from the dialogue opened by the poem are *absolute*. The you is the you of the absolute dialogue partner and the I is the absolute I of the poet. The you and I, in their absoluteness, translate the humanity of the I and the you into a universal language. This is how the poet gives voice to the destiny of all. It allows the reader to be the I that the poet is, because the poet is the I who we all are (*EPH* 81/*GW9* 366).

Both question and answer, of the I to the you and the you to the I, the poetic word is the right word that, sought after desperately, offers protection and dwelling to both.[73] Our basic experience as temporal beings is that everything slips away from us. By contrast, the poetic word in its "da," or "there-ness," brings the transitory quality of time to a standstill. In the poetic word the nearness, the intimate familiarity is "da," "there," where we can dwell, where the situation becomes homely: "The poetic word, by being there, bears witness to our being."[74]

Gadamer addresses in this way the distinction between the poem and the dialogue. Since it does not pass away, the poetic word is, in contrast to the dialogical word, not processual (*GW9* 335–346). Our entire Being extends and unfolds between these two poles of language: the flow of dialogue and the crystal of poetry (*GW9* 338–339). The poetic word, because it *prescribes* the poetic dictation to the text, is in its crystalline form more fully "text" than any other word. On the other hand, every spoken word—and this constitutes the priority of writing over speech—is always only an attempt to allow the text of the poetic dictation to speak. Poem and dialogue reveal themselves in this way as extreme opposites: "The poem gains existence as 'literature,' the dialogue lives on the pleasure of the moment" (*GW9* 339).

Thanks to the inexhaustibility of their meanings, both are endless, though in different ways. The dialogue is infinite in the word that, in the horizontal *endlessness* of *speaking-with-one-another,* asks for further possible answers; the poem is infinite in the assertive word whose meaning is vertically inexhaustible.[75] Even prior to any dialogical process, the poetic word founds community in its universality. The poem is the "refrain of the soul," the refrain in which I and you discover that they are the "same soul," reaching an agreement, that is, being attuned to the whole song to which the poem is an invitation.[76]

The poem proves to be dialogical in its very nature. In response to the question, "Who am I and who are you?" it answers by holding the question open, which allows no final answer. Rather, the question—as question—constitutes its own answer (*GC* 26/*WBI* 39). To ask, "who am I and who are you?" is a way of being the other of the other.

12. Ritual and the Reciprocity of Language

To linger in art means to contemplate or to participate, which indicates the close connections between art, festival, and language. In this context the paradigm of *play* becomes more and more important in the last phase of Gadamer's philosophy. Play not only illuminates art, festival, and language, but also sheds light on ritual, that phenomenon of human existence which is just as immemorial as it is difficult to grasp. Its multiplicity of forms and relevance, for Gadamer, go far beyond what has previously been recognized. The important essay of 1992, "Towards a Phenomenology of Ritual and Language," is dedicated to the discussion of this topic.[77]

In this essay Gadamer corrects himself. He admits that his focus to date had been too much on language and too little on the "lifeworld," where one encounters action no less than language. This change of direction brings him to the limit of the "prelinguistic," the site where the frequently reiterated comparison between animal language and human language takes place. It is difficult to speak of "ritual" with regard to the behavior of animals and their ways of understanding each other, because nature prescribes animal behavior. As a result these forms of behavior are natural and specific: they vary according to species. With human beings, by contrast, socially transformed rites vary within the species itself; rites take different forms in different cultures. Where, then, lies the specific difference? Where is the border between the animal and the human? One could easily offer an answer by accepting again the Kantian distinction between natural conditioning and freedom, or the old dualism of nature and mind. Contrary to the conventional view, Aristotle was not responsible for this; rather, it is with Aristotle that we should begin anew and with his definition of the soul as the *enteléchia* of the body.

For this reason Gadamer introduces the distinction between being *together-with* (*Mitsamt*) and *with-one-another* (*Miteinander*), which is only a logical distinction; considered ontologically, one is interwoven with the other (*LL* 24–34/*GW8* 407–419).

Despite the connection of the preposition *with*, the distinction lies between these two expressions: between the mere together-with and the with-one-another, which involves *reciprocity*, mutuality. Nevertheless, this border is fluid and the together-with bears the with-one-another on the basis of its natural determinacy. Human behavior is never free of natural drives, and it is perhaps in the interweaving of the together-with and the with-one-another that one should locate the specificity of humanity. Rituality occurs in the life forms that the together-with opens, and only in that sense do they participate in the with-one-another of language. To put it another way, the ritual belongs to speaking, yet it is not really speaking, but acting. Where speaking crosses into ritual, it becomes action. From this perspective the particular feature of human language can be better grasped. It comes to light in the shared trait of showing and naming, in the distance of any speaker from what is here and now, and also from oneself, pointing in the direction of a meaning that, if it cannot be proved, is already the opening of a new space for the self and the other. This space is where the community of the world articulates itself.

Nonetheless, speaking has a ritualistic character, and thus it participates in rituals. This is shown in polite forms of speech, but also in religious ceremonies or the celebration of a festival where rituality dominates and language more or less defers to ritual. The play-space of one's role is limited here, and everyone plays their respective roles. It is thus a matter of play, but one that is different from the play of dialogue. Ritual play, which is always already linguistic, nevertheless takes place in the together-with of collectivity, whereas linguistic play, which is always already ritual, occurs by contrast in the with-one-another of community. The difference is this: together-with is the becoming part of a collectivity, and with-one-another is the invitation to become a speaker in the reciprocal community of dialogue.

In regard to this reciprocity Gadamer turns to Plato's concept of *methéxis*, in order to show what is not only a sharing, but also a participation and co-participation. The reciprocity of language, in which there is neither a first nor a last word, unfolds from a single "presuppositionless" element. Gadamer calls it, following Plato, the *hikanón*, that is, the communal word on which and in which the speakers agree in order to renew the dialogue (*LL* 23/*GW8* 405).[78] The participation plays itself out not only in the infinite play of question and answer, but also in the binding community of language that communalizes and, furthermore, in the universal linguistic constitution of human life.

Notes

1. See chapter 3, part 3, of the present volume.
2. See chapter 4, part 5, of the present volume.
3. The importance of Hönigswald and his groundbreaking 1937 work on the philosophy of language has yet to be appropriately recognized (see *TM* 404/*GW1* 408). See Richard Hönigswald, *Philos-*

ophie und Sprache. Problemkritik und System (1937) (Darmstadt: Wissenschaftliche Buchgesellschaft, 1970).

4. See chapter 5 in this volume.

5. See chapter 7, parts 5 and 6, in the present volume.

6. *GR* 311; *GW*7 335. See also Gadamer, *Der Anfang der Philosophie* (Stuttgart: Reclam, 1996), 72.

7. Augustine, *De Trinitate*, XV, 10–15.

8. Augustine, *De Trinitate*, XV, X, 19.

9. See esp. Jean Grondin, "Gadamer und Augustinus: Zum Ursprung des hermeneutischen Universalitätsanspruchs," in his *Der Sinn für Hermeneutik* (Darmstadt: Wissenschaftliche Buchgesellschaft, 1994), 24–39.

10. After *Truth and Method* Gadamer seldom returns to Augustine, and when he does so it is only to repeat the position he had already taken there.

11. Similarly, Heidegger writes that Humboldt's ideas speak the language of a metaphysics that belongs to his era, a language whose basis was established by Leibniz. He writes that Humboldt's ideas "speak the language of the metaphysics of his time, a language in which Leibniz' philosophy plays a decisive role." Heidegger, *On the Way to Language*, trans. Peter D. Hertz (New York: Harper Collins, 1971), 119/*Unterwegs zur Sprache* (Stuttgart: Klett-Cotta, 2007), 238.

12. Gadamer, "Reply to James Risser," in *The Philosophy of Hans-Georg Gadamer*, ed. Lewis E. Hahn (Chicago and La Salle: Open Court, 1997), 403–404, 403.

13. Gadamer, "Unterwegs zur Schrift?" *GW*7 228–269; *Phaedrus* 274b–278e/*Plato* 525–555; *Seventh Letter* 341c, 344c/*Plato* 1659, 1661.

14. *Protagoras* 329a/*Plato* 762.

15. See in this volume chapter 3, part 11, and chapter 14, part 2.

16. See Donatella Di Cesare, "Die Verborgenheit der Stimme: Gadamer zwischen Platon und Derrida," *Internationales Jahrbuch für Hermeneutik* 5 (2006): 325–345.

17. See James Risser, "Reading the Text," in Hugh J. Silverman, ed., *Gadamer and Hermeneutics* (New York and London: Routledge, 1991), 93–105, 102–105.

18. See Rudolf Bernet, "Differenz und Anwesenheit: Derridas und Husserls Phänomenologie der Sprache, der Zeit, der Geschichte," in Ernst Wolfgang Orth, ed., *Phänomenologische Forschungen: Studien zur neueren französischen Philosophie* (Freiburg: Alber, 1986), 88–98.

19. Jacques Derrida, *Speech and Phenomena and Other Essays on Husserl's Theory of Signs*, ed. David B. Allison (Evanston, Ill.: Northwestern University Press, 1973), 59.

20. As Brice R. Wachterhauser observes: "there is no 'pure' alinguistic intuition of the self, but, according to Gadamer, all self-knowledge is linguistically mediated. . . . Gadamer would argue that even the philosophical attempts to locate and describe the essential core of selfhood, the transcendental ego, failed to come up with an ahistorical metalanguage of the self." Brice R. Wachterhauser, "Must We Be What We Say? Gadamer on Truth in the Human Sciences," in Wachterhauser, ed., *Hermeneutics and Modern Philosophy* (Albany: SUNY Press, 1986), 219–240, 230. See also chapter 5, part 2, of the present volume.

21. Riedel wrote of an "acroamatic" dimension of hermeneutics, referring to the Greek word for listening, *akroâsthai*: Manfred Riedel, *Hören auf die Sprache: Die akroamatische Dimension der Hermeneutik* (Frankfurt/M: Suhrkamp, 1990), 163–176.

22. Aristotle, *Of the Senses*, 473a 3; *Metaphysics*, 980b 23–25.

23. "Über das Hören," in *Hermeneutische Entwürfe. Vorträge und Aufsätze* (Tübingen: Mohr Siebeck, 2000), 48–55, 51.

24. See Thomas Schwarz Wentzer, "Das Diskrimen der Frage," in *Hermeneutische Wege: Hans-Georg Gadamer zum Hundertsten*, ed. Günter Figal, Jean Grondin, and Dennis J. Schmidt (Tübingen: Mohr Siebeck, 2000), 219–240.

25. Terry J. Diffey, "Some Thoughts on the Relationship between Gadamer and Collingwood," *Philosophical Inquiry* 20 (1988): 1–12.

26. In this context Gadamer discusses the theme of "occasionality," which he dealt with in the section on aesthetics. See chapter 2, part 7, in the present volume. "Occasional expressions" are those whose meaning is fulfilled only by the *occasion*, the occasion in which they are used. But "occasional" does not mean "accidental." All that is spoken appears occasionally, because it refers back to the context of its origin. Gadamer's position, which is a development of Lipps's position, comes close here to Austin's pragmatism. Hans Lipps, *Untersuchungen zur hermeneutischen Logik* (Frankfurt/M: Klostermann, 1976); John L. Austin, *How to Do Things with Words* (Cambridge, Mass.: Harvard University Press, 1962).

27. See *On Interpretation*, 17, 1–4.

28. See chapter 7, part 6, in this volume.

29. See Wilhelm von Humboldt, "Über das vergleichende Sprachstudium," in his *Gesammelte Schriften*, ed. A. Leitzmann (Berlin: Behr [reprint, Berlin: De Gruyter, 1968]), 4:1–35.

30. For Gadamer, observes Wright, "language is a center (*Mitte*), not an end (*telos*). It is a medium (*Mitte*), not a ground (*arche*)." Kathleen Wright, "Gadamer: The Speculative Structure of Language," in Wachterhauser, *Hermeneutics and Modern Philosophy*, 193–218, 204; Rod Coltman, "Gadamer, Hegel, and the Middle of Language," *Philosophy Today* 40 (1996): 151–159.

31. See in this volume chapter 10, part 6.

32. See Heidegger, from "The Letter on 'Humanism,'" 217, and "The Way to Language," in *On the Way to Language*, 135; *Brief über den "Humanismus,"* in *Wegmarken*, 313–364, 333; "Aus einem Gespräch von der Sprache," in *Unterwegs zur Sprache*, 112.

33. See Gadamer, "Heimat und Sprache" (1992), GW8 366–372. See also Gadamer, "Leben ist Einkehr in die Sprache. Gedanken über Sprache und Literatur," *Universitas* 10 (1993): 922–926.

34. See Deborah Cook, "Reflections on Gadamer's Notion of *Sprachlichkeit*," *Philosophy and Literature* 10 (1986): 84–92.

35. Gadamer, "Intendimento e rischio," *Archivio di Filosofia* 1–2, ed. Enrico Pastelli (1961): 75–82, 82. In a somewhat revised form this essay appeared as "Zur Problematik des Selbstverständnisses: Ein hermeneutischer Beitrag zur Frage der Entmythologisierung," GW2 121–132. For Gadamer's thoughts on Rilke, see "Mythopoetische Umkehrung in Rilkes *Duineser Elegien*," and "Rilkes Deutung des Daseins: Zu dem Buch von Romano Guardini," GW9 289–305 and 271–281. On the connection between language and freedom, see Dennis J. Schmidt, "What We Cannot Say: On Language and Freedom," in Schmidt, *Lyrical and Ethical Subjects*, 77–90. See *Selected Poetry of Rainer Maria Rilke*, ed. and trans. Stephen Mitchell (New York: Random House, 1982), 170.

36. See chapter 3, part 2, of the present volume.

37. Jürgen Habermas, *Zur Logik der Sozialwissenschaften*, 5th ed. (Frankfurt/M: Suhrkamp, 1986), 273.

38. Friedrich Hölderlin, "Friedensfeier," in Hölderlin, *Sämtliche Werke und Briefe*, ed. Jochen Schmidt (Frankfurt/M: Deutscher Klassiker Verlag, 1992), 1, 341.

39. See chapter 10, part 4, of the present volume.

40. Jacques Derrida, "Rams: Uninterrupted Dialogue—Between Two Infinities, the Poem," in *Sovereignties in Question: The Poetics of Paul Celan* (New York: Fordham University Press 2005), 135–163; "Der ununterbrochene Dialog: Zwischen zwei Unendlichkeiten, das Gedicht," in Jacques Derrida and Hans-Georg Gadamer, *Der ununterbrochene Dialog*, ed. and intro. Martin Gessmann (Frankfurt/M: Suhrkamp, 2004), 7–50.

41. Gadamer, "The Incapacity for Conversation," *Continental Philosophy Review* 39, no. 4 (2006): 351–359, 355; "Die Unfähigkeit zum Gespräch," GW2 211.

42. "Sprache und Verstehen," GW2 188. See Claude Thérien, "Gadamer et la phénoménologie du dialogue," *Laval théologique et philosophique* 53 (1997): 167–180.

43. See chapter 6, part 4, and chapter 9, part 5, of the present volume.

44. "Freundschaft und Selbsterkenntnis: Zur Rolle der Freundschaft in der griechischen Ethik," *GW7* 403. The original version of this still untranslated essay on friendship and self-knowledge in Greek ethics was written in 1928. However, it did not appear in print until 1985 (*GW7* 396–406). In 1999 Gadamer published "Freundschaft und Solidarität," in *Hermeneutische Entwürfe,* 56–65. See also an essay from 1970: "Isolation as a Symptom of Self-Alienation," *PT* 103–113.

45. "The Incapacity for Conversation," *Continental Philosophy Review* 39, no. 4 (2006): 351–359 *GW2* 207–215.

46. "The Incapacity for Conversation," 356; *GW2* 213.

47. "The Incapacity for Conversation," 357–358; *GW2* 214–215.

48. "Schreiben und Reden" (1983), *GW10* 354.

49. Jochen Hörisch, *Die Wut des Verstehens: Zur Kritik der Hermeneutik* (Frankfurt/M: Suhrkamp, 1988).

50. See chapter 5, part 1, of the present volume.

51. This thesis, which also appears in *Truth and Method,* is subsequently developed in *GR* 96; *GW2* 187; *LL* 12/*GW8* 354.

52. Aristotle, "On Interpretation," 16 a 19.

53. Wittgenstein offers a similar thought: human beings "agree in the *language* they use. That is not agreement in opinions but in forms of life." *Philosophical Investigations,* trans. G. E. M. Anscombe (Oxford: Blackwell, 1997), #241, 88.

54. See chapter 6, part 5, of the present volume.

55. Donatella Di Cesare, "*Átopos:* Die Hermeneutik und der Ausser-Ort des Verstehens," in *Das Erbe Gadamers,* ed. Andrzej Przylebski (Frankfurt/M: Peter Lang, 2006), 85–94.

56. See chapter 4, part 2, of the present volume.

57. From this point on, Gadamer often returned to his encounter with Wittgenstein. See, for example, *GW2* 507; *GW8* 149; *GW10* 107 and 347.

58. Living language is thus always recuperated in its fundamental metaphoricity. See Gadamer, *TM* 432/*GW1* 436–437. See also Joel Weinsheimer, "Gadamer's Metaphorical Hermeneutics," in *Gadamer and Hermeneutics,* ed. Hugh J. Silverman, Continental Philosophy 4 (New York and London: Routledge, 1991), 181–201; James Risser, "Die Metaphorik des Sprechens," in Figal, Grondin, and Schmidt, *Hermeneutische Wege,* 177–190.

59. See Gadamer, *GW2* 248 and *GW2* 507; *GW10* 156 and 349. See also chapter 7, part 2, of the present volume. See Ulrich Arnswald, "On the Certainty of Uncertainty: Language Games and Forms of Life in Gadamer and Wittgenstein," in Jeff Malpas, Ulrich Arnswald, and Jens Kertscher, eds., *Gadamer's Century. Essays in Honor of Hans-Georg Gadamer* (Cambridge, Mass. and London: MIT Press, 2002), 25–44. A new approach to this issue can be found in Chris Lawn, *Wittgenstein and Gadamer: Towards a Post-Analytic Philosophy of Language* (London: Continuum, 2004).

60. See *PH* 175/*GW3* 144; *GW8* 343.

61. *GW2* 429 and *PH* 177/*GW3* 146.

62. *GR* 384/*GW10* 157, 275.

63. See chapter 9, part 7, in the present volume.

64. Wittgenstein, *Philosophical Investigations,* #23, 11.

65. See "Europa und die Oikoumene," *GW10* 271.

66. See also "Im Schatten des Nihilismus: Was muss der Leser wissen?" *GW9* 367–382. This essay is not included in *Gadamer on Celan.*

67. "From Word to Concept: The Task of Hermeneutics as Philosophy," *GR* 115; *GW9* 337; *GW8* 251; *GW10* 140. [Trans. note: The German word for poetry, *Dichtung,* is etymologically related to the Latin *dictum.*]

68. "On the Contribution of Poetry to the Search for Truth," *RB* 105–115, 106/*GW8* 72; "Philosophy and Poetry," *RB* 139/*GW8*, 239.

69. "Philosophy and Poetry," 132–133; *GW8* 233; *GW8* 19; *GW8* 59; *GW9* 62. See also Christopher Lawn, "Gadamer on Poetic and Everyday Language," *Philosophy and Literature* 25 (2001): 113–126.

70. Paul Celan, "Ansprache anlässlich der Entgegennahme des Literaturpreises der Freien Hansestadt Bremen," in *Ansprachen bei der Verleihung des Bremer Literaturpreises an Paul Celan* (Stuttgart: Deutsche Verlags-Anstalt, 1958), 10–11; trans. Robert Kelly as "Address on Acceptance of the Prize for Literature of the Free Hanseatic City of Bremen," *Origin*, 3rd series, no. 15 (1969): 16–17.

71. "Lesen ist wie Übersetzen," *GW8* 279–285; "Der 'eminente Text' und seine Wahrheit" (1986), *GW8* 286–295, 287–288.

72. See Gadamer, "Hilde Domin, Lied der Ermutigung II," *GW9* 320–322, 321.

73. *GC* 104/*WBI* 115; "Hilde Domin, Dichterin der Rückkehr," *GW9* 323–328; "Heimat und *Sprache*," *GW8* 366–372. See James Risser, "Poetic Dwelling in Gadamer's Hermeneutics," *Philosophy Today* 38 (1994): 369–379; Bruce Krajewski, "Gadamer's Aesthetics in Practice in *Wer bin ich und wer bist du?*" in *Maps and Mirrors: Topologies of Art and Politics*, ed. Steve Martinot (Evanston, Ill.: Northwestern University Press, 2001), 16–27.

74. "On the Contribution of Poetry to the Search for Truth," RB 115/*GW8* 79. Alejandro A. Vallega, "On the Tactility of Words: Gadamer's Reading of Paul Celan's *Atemkristall*," *Internationales Jahrbuch für Hermeneutik* 2 (2004): 99–121.

75. See Gadamer, "On the Truth of the Word," in *The Specter of Relativism: Truth, Dialogue, and Phronesis in Philosophical Hermeneutics*, ed. Lawrence K. Schmidt (Evanston, Ill.: Northwestern University Press, 1995), 135–155, 135–136; "To What Extent Does Language Perform Thought?" *TM* 552–553; "Von der Wahrheit des Wortes," *GW8* 37–38; "Wie weit schreibt Sprache das Denken vor?" *GW2* 206.

76. "Hölderlin and George," *EPH* 93–109, 104–105; *GW9* 229–244, 241; also "Gedicht und Gespräch," *GW9* 337–338, 344.

77. "Towards a Phenomenology of Ritual and Language," trans. Lawrence K. Schmidt and Monika Reuss, in *Language and Linguisticality in Gadamer's Hermeneutics*, ed. Lawrence K. Schmidt (Lanham, Md.: Lexington Books, 2000), 19–50; *GW8* 400–440. See Richard Palmer, "Gadamer's Recent Work on Language and Philosophy: On 'Zur Phänomenologie von Ritual und Sprache,'" *Continental Philosophy Review* 33 (2000): 381–393; Palmer, "Ritual, Rightness and Truth in Two Late Works of Hans-Georg Gadamer," in Hahn, *The Philosophy of Hans-Georg Gadamer*, 529–547.

78. See *Phaedo* 101e 1.

9 Hermeneutics as Philosophy

> Philosophy never really finds it necessary to justify its existence, since whoever would contest it is also engaging in the process of reflection that one calls philosophy. (*IG* 171/ *GW7* 223)

> I didn't dare to use the pretentious word "philosophy" with respect to myself, and tried to apply it only attributively. (*GW10* 199)

1. Children and the Future of Philosophy

What role does philosophy play today? What will be its future? Who is the philosopher in the age of technology? Gadamer was asked these questions more and more frequently, above all in his last years. This was because many saw him as the last philosopher, with whom a great century came to an end. He was conscious of the need to justify philosophy, and answered such questions in numerous essays and interviews. On these occasions he also made clear how hermeneutics should be understood *as* philosophy.

In contrast to others, Gadamer never believed in the "end" of philosophy. Of course it is undeniable that the scientific and technological age is deeply anti-philosophical. In the meantime it has become customary to ask what philosophy is good for. Everywhere we can see that philosophy has fallen into disrepute.

> We live in an age that would as soon count philosophy among the theological relics of a bygone age or that suspects nothing so much of having a dependence upon secret or unconscious interests as the ideal of pure theory and of knowledge for the sake of knowledge alone. (*RAS* 139/*VZW* 110)

The passion for philosophy seems only to be an "irresponsible flight into a world of fading dreams" (*RAS* 139/*VZW* 110). In an epoch marked by acceleration, do we still have time for leisurely and unproductive speculation about unsolvable problems?

The old prejudices against philosophy have consolidated and intensified since, beginning with Galileo, experimental science based on mathematical methods imposed itself with unprecedented success. The new concept of science not only narrowed philosophy, which for the Greeks was the highest "science," but undermined its identity and forced it into permanent "self-defense" (*RAS* 6/*HE* 15). The systematic philosophical constructions of the last centuries have become merely unsuccessful attempts to reconcile the inheritance of metaphysics with modern science. The "rapid demise of the Hegelian empire of absolute Spirit" only confirms for Gadamer that metaphysics has exhausted itself and that science has moved to the center of human knowledge (*RAS* 111/*VZW* 140).

The split between science and philosophy appears to have lead to mutual exclusion. But what becomes of philosophy then? Should it not adapt to the successful model of rigorous science and disguise itself as theory of science? "Philosophy or Theory of Science?"—Gadamer formulated this alternative in a 1974 essay.[1] The question primarily concerns science. Despite all of our expectations, science can offer us only an endless process of the investigation of nature, yet no orientation in the world—in a world that has become "ever more strange because it has been all too changed by ourselves" (*RAS* 20/*VZW* 25). The perception of this new alienation does not mean, of course, that philosophy should be relegated to a private sphere. The very limits of science prevent this. It is not only a matter of the will to control every area of life, without however being able to eliminate that strange phenomenon of death. The paradox lies rather in this: on the one hand the authority of science frees us from the responsibility of decision, which now appears objective; on the other hand science itself proves to be incapable of assuming responsibility, because it is unable to give an account of the importance it has gained for human life—it suffices here to think about genetic manipulation or global warming. In the moment when science must justify itself beyond its own procedures, it is already forced to go beyond itself; it is already philosophy (ibid. 162/138–139). As soon as science, in order to legitimize itself, switches from formalized terminology back to everyday language and its web of language games, science not only shows that it needs a foundation, but it also legitimizes philosophy and the flight into the *logoi* defended from Plato to Hegel.

Surely no one can hold the view the philosophy might regain the role it had in the past, and integrate all of our knowledge into a unified image. Nevertheless Gadamer was convinced that philosophy should continue to intervene in the work of the sciences, and that it must begin with technically rationalized life. Philosophy should not be brought too close to art, even if the great authors of the nineteenth century—it is enough to mention the name of Dostoevsky—assumed a philosophical task for themselves (ibid. 19/24).[2] Philosophy is not only "the expression of life," for it cannot escape the labor of the concept.

Even in the age of science we cannot do without philosophy, because it is obviously more than merely a phase of the human journey. Drawing on Kant, Gadamer puts forward the thesis that philosophy is a "natural inclination of humans."[3] It does not come and go—it does not reach an end. Philosophy is a characteristic trait that marks humans just as much as the knowledge of death. Philosophy is nothing other than this thought of a beyond (*RAS* 140/*VZW* 114). This "beyond" is already contained in the name of metaphysics. It was Socrates who first pointed in this direction and gave philosophy the meaning it has even today. He brought philosophy to the people and transformed it from the investigation of nature into a restless, untiring dialogue about the knowledge of oneself that is always a not-knowing. Precisely this is the value that hermeneutics seeks as philosophy.

Since it is a natural inclination, philosophy cannot be a profession. Here lies its weakness, which is however at the same time its strength. What would a professional philosopher look like? It is an illusion to believe that there can be experts who ask questions and who can find the appropriate answers to them. The philosophy professor is not necessarily wiser than others; indeed she is not even necessarily wise. Nothing can protect her from error. What distinguishes her from others is her knowledge of the tradition, which should enable her to formulate more easily the questions everyone wants to ask. Her responsibility consists in this ability and in the influence she can exert as teacher and as model.[4] But philosophy is not a specialized form of knowledge, for everyone philosophizes—no matter how unconsciously. Even children ask questions about the future, about death, and about happiness. "A child is a bit of a philosopher, a philosopher is a bit of a child."[5] This guarantees the future of philosophy.

2. Taking Leave of Metaphysics

Yet what is the relation between hermeneutics and philosophy's past, particularly metaphysics? The answer to this question is necessary to determine the place of hermeneutics within the constellation of contemporary philosophy. The difficulty, however, is that Gadamer never really clarified this relation. This has given rise to numerous misunderstandings. But a clarification would surely have entailed an explicit distantiation from Heidegger and the question of Being.

Hermeneutics is not metaphysics, and it does not aim to be. Yet at the same time hermeneutics is not *anti-metaphysical*—as for example Heidegger's philosophy understands itself. Hermeneutics conceives of itself even less as a *post-metaphysical* philosophy, for it does not share the worry about the overcoming of metaphysics that has passed from Heidegger to many contemporary philosophies, from Derrida's deconstruction to Rorty's neo-pragmatism and Vattimo's "weak thought." Hence, it would be pointless to look for Gadamer's writings on metaphysics or the question of its overcoming.[6] What characterizes the attitude of hermeneutics towards Being is its *non-metaphysical* quality.

As with most philosophers after Heidegger, Gadamer speaks of "ontology" rather than of "metaphysics." *Truth and Method* ends with an ontological turn, which takes place following the guiding idea of language. But with this turn, hermeneutics distances itself at the same time from ontology altogether. For ontology is the *logos* that wants to say what Being is. But since Being cannot be grasped in an immediate intuition, hermeneutics will understand it, since Being is always linguistically mediated, as an infinite process in which *per definitionem* there can be no last word. With this turn, hermeneutics radicalizes Heidegger's fundamental ontology. *There is no Being without the understanding of Being.* If that is so, then ontology must recover itself in hermeneutics—which means at the same time reestablish itself, as if after an illness, but also retreat or revoke itself. To put it differently: *ontology necessarily becomes hermeneutics.*

Hermeneutics draws all the consequences from this and from the outset gives up all metaphysical aspirations.[7] Hermeneutics does not ask the question of Being because it has already become the question of understanding. Therefore, hermeneutics looks away from Being. While it admits that it cannot do anything but understand Being, hermeneutics is aware of its ties to understanding and aware of its finitude.

3. The Hermeneutics of Finitude

It is less a farewell to Being than the attention to understanding that drives hermeneutics to the limits of finitude. Finitude always already affects understanding. In this sense, hermeneutics is a *philosophy of finitude.* By declaring itself to be the heir of phenomenology and the Heideggerian analytic of *Dasein,* hermeneutics reveals a trait that it has in common with many contemporary philosophies. Since it is conscious of the danger that finitude could now take the place of the absolute, it does not hesitate to recognize itself as finite. In short: a *philosophy of finitude* brings with it the unavoidable transition to the *finitude of philosophy.* As a philosophy of finitude, hermeneutics unfolds by trying to understand the forms in which finitude manifests itself. On the other hand, however, it is finitude that defines and determines understanding, that is, the manner of its philosophizing. From this it follows that a philosophy of finitude, which knows itself to be finite, can be nothing other than hermeneutic.

Such a radicalization of finitude, which thereby becomes the standard for philosophy, brings forth an equally radical transformation of philosophy. At this point philosophy, which adopts the form and condition of its thinking from the finite, recognizes itself as finite and thus knows that it, without renouncing universality, can only think itself at the limit of its own, inappropriable, finitude.

The concept of the *limit,* of the border and the end, traverses the entirety of hermeneutics and constitutes its guiding thread.[8] Consciousness of the limit—not so much to have a limit but rather to be a limit—is what defines human finitude.[9] As a result, to experience means to perceive the limits of one's own finitude.[10] The limit is perceived as the site where understanding becomes nonunderstanding (and self-understanding is no exception to this), where interpretation carries the trace of finitude in itself and demands further interpretations, where knowledge never attains the in-itself of things, where time withdraws and is no longer available, indeed is even "already at the end," where every day we are overwhelmed by sleep and stand constantly menaced by death. There is no experience that can avoid running up against a limit in some way. To live means to experience one limit after another, between the limits of birth and death. In this context Gadamer cites a fragment by Alcmaeon of Croton: "Human beings perish because they are not able to join their beginning to their end."[11] The fatefully determined linearity of humans separates them from the perfect circularity of nature, in which the beginning and the end coincide.[12] In light of this transitoriness the end is not the aim, the conclusion does not bring the achievement of the goal, and finality founders on mortality. Finitude is not completion.

Language tells us this, for it is the trace of our finitude, the middle point, the "medium" or the *méson* on which we as finite beings depend. But finitude does not mean merely mortality, temporality, and linguisticality. The appeal to finitude in hermeneutics should not be misunderstood and interpreted as a belated version of existentialist positions. It is rather a matter of the questions asked by hermeneutics, not coincidentally, in a world made increasingly uniform by the ever-increasing breakdown of spatial and temporal limits. Paradoxically it is technology itself that, eager to overcome one limit after another, determines the collision with the limit that enables finitude in all its incomprehensibility to resurface from contemporary amnesia. The illusion of limitlessness only increases our disappointment at the limit, and insufferance only makes our suffering more acute. It is hence here that hermeneutics interrogates itself on the limits of finitude, which can no longer be understood as privation.

4. Between Plato and Hegel: Reclaiming the Infinite

By radically thinking finitude as position and not as privation, hermeneutics reveals its debt to Heidegger. Both Heidegger and Gadamer know that they are the inheritors of pre-Socratic philosophy, in which the finite is valued as perfect and the infinite as imperfect. Already in Christianity, however, the peripety of the finite in the history of thought becomes inescapable. The infinite is the sovereignly perfect absolute, in front of which the finite is destined, for centuries and through unlimited variations, to remain secondary and derivate—at least until Kant, who, pointing to the limits of reason, legitimizes finitude in epistemology. As Heidegger makes clear, the repercussions are also ontological. The limit becomes the condition of unlimited knowledge, the possibility of transcendence itself. Where there is a limit, there is also transcendence. For transcendence is overcoming: what transcends points beyond experience, beyond the limit of the ontic in the direction of the ontological. It is precisely in Kant that Heidegger indicates in finitude the place from which ontology arises.[13] For Heidegger, to think of finitude in a radical way means to think of finitude as the source of a new ontology. Even if human finitude is a daily revelation, it must be seen in its essential primordiality. To put it differently: finitude is bound up with the end, with the Being-towards-death of *Dasein*. Only when *Dasein* recognizes that it *"exists finitely,"* can it make a decision for the end that is its own most authentic possibility (BT 378/329). Here lies for Heidegger the finite temporality of *Dasein*, which is only "da" or "there," that is, it exists, because it understands and because each being, insofar as it understands, is enabled to come into Being; Being, too, only occurs as such in this finitude. Ontology happens as *Dasein*. For finite *Dasein*, to exist means to understand and to understand means to transcend. *Dasein* is always a *beyond*. Yet the beyond does not move toward the infinite, for Heidegger it redefines the finite each and every time. What is, always has a limit, and Being as such is always finite.[14] In light of this originary finitude, the infinite is denied.

This negation of the infinite raises many problems. For the "royal road" to finitude that Heidegger opened appears to be a dead end. If finitude is originary, then it has originary consequences for Being, which is indeed finite for Heidegger. Nevertheless, this finitude always remains secondary to Being. Of course it could—at the limit—take leave of Being. But the difficulty would still remain because finitude would now involve a relation to negated infinity. Will originary finitude not claim to be a new absolute, which gathers into itself also the attributes of the infinite? How can the finite be preserved as finite, without reverting into an infinite? How can a philosophy of finitude do without the infinite?

This is the question that Gadamer asks, though not explicitly. The distance between both philosophers here should not be overlooked: for Heidegger the finite negates the infinite, whereas Gadamer recuperates this negated infinite. For hermeneutics the infinite lies in the "beyond," since *Dasein* moves forward in understanding from finitude to finitude in the infinite. It is, therefore, not so much a farewell to Being as it is the way indicated by understanding that clarifies the hermeneutic need to interpret finitude in the light of an infinite that is still possible and can therefore never be extinguished. This amounts to an *infinitely finite finitude*.

Most symptomatic of the differences between the two philosophers are their differing attitudes toward finitude, but also toward the final end, the most extreme limit of death. Gadamer's reflections on death take shape in his interpretation of Plato's *Phaedo*, which goes back to 1973, develop further in the essay on "Death as a Question" from 1975, and lead finally to the short work on "The Experience of Death" from 1983.[15] Gadamer does not share Heidegger's Being-towards-death, because for him there is neither authenticity nor appropriation in the relation with the final end. Death is the unexpected, unforeseeable event, which cannot be appropriated. Death is the incomprehensible par excellence.[16] To think of death would mean to think of one's own no-longer-being. Accordingly, the human thought of death experiences a "defeat," which Gadamer however reverses: "The inconceivability of death is the highest triumph of life" (*GW4* 172). No one can think of no longer being. From this there emerges the antinomy of death and thought, which for philosophical hermeneutics already makes the question of death philosophically impossible. Since thought refuses to think its own not-being, it transforms not-being into a future life. In this way, thought supports life in its continual self-overcoming. The impossibility of thinking the end is subsequently translated into the freedom of thinking the possibility of a beyond. Gadamer here draws on Simmel, and speaks of the "transcendence of life" (*GW4* 168). Whoever lives cannot accept dying. This forgetting of death, which for Heidegger merges with the forgetting of Being, is interpreted in hermeneutics by contrast as the necessity of the finite that demands the possibility of the infinite, that is the beyond opened by dialogue—even after death.[17] Insofar as it is destined to be an infinite dialogue, it is not surprising that hermeneutics, in its eschatological aspirations, declines itself again in the word and conjugates itself in the dialogue. Precisely at the most extreme limit, hermeneutics speaks of the reciprocal connection of the finite and the infinite. Thinking, revealing the *aporia* of the finite and the infinite, makes such a connection emerge: if it is true that thinking is finite, then it is just as true that it cannot think its own not-being and so it transforms it into being other, or overcomes it in a beyond, and in this way manifests its vocation to the infinite.

Gadamer recuperates the infinite after Heidegger without suppressing finitude. Gadamer finds support for this in Hegel's bad infinity and Plato's indeterminate dyad.[18] Hegel's infinity is the one of consciousness that, in its dialogue with itself, by saying "I" to itself, is already divided in itself.[19] This "inner difference," this self-differentiation of the undifferentiated, is the *infinite* that self-consciousness shares with life. Despite its finitude, life will always remain infinitely exposed to the question that extends beyond it, just as consciousness that asks about, thinks about, and reflects on itself will always be open in an infinite dialogue. The end in bad infinity is an end that is always beyond and to come. Owing to the negative side that makes this infinity the accomplice of finitude, there is no conclusion, and the dialectic is destined to aporetic openness.

Here Hegel draws on Plato and in this light refers the self-differentiation of the undifferentiated to the indeterminate dyad. Hermeneutics asserts its need to hold onto the infinite with the help of Plato's reading of the negative infinite in its connections with not-being, that is, with being-other. In the same breath in which the "not" becomes the cipher of difference, the infinite turns out to be the undifferentiated in its undefined self-differentiation. With every differentiation, the "is" simultaneously expresses the "is not." The presence of the identical announces the absence of the different. "Is" can be said only insofar as "is not" is also implied (*HW* 84/*GW*3 245). The infinite and the finite call forth each other reciprocally: the finite cannot avoid evoking the infinite, and, for its part, the infinite cannot avoid articulating and declining itself in the finite. Being must compromise itself with not-Being, in order to come into Being, to become understandable, and to become sayable in the interweaving of identity and difference, the one and many, the finite and the infinite. Therefore Being is not finite, but defined, that is, interwoven with the infinite of not-Being in the *logos*. Once again, *logos* takes on here a paradigmatic importance for Gadamer.

By recuperating the infinite in this way, hermeneutics can hold fast to the limit of finitude. But holding fast does not mean coming to a standstill: hermeneutics is not an asceticism of the limit (*TM* 99/*GW*1 105).[20] Here it follows Kant's gesture, which, to a more conscious reason, indicates the limit that could be transcended. For hermeneutics, conversely, finite and infinite are correlated and should not be grasped statically.[21] At this point, again, Gadamer's distance from Heidegger can be seen. The finitude of hermeneutics must not negate the infinite in order to posit itself; indeed it demands it as the possibility of an impossibility, a *beyond*. Yet hermeneutics interprets this *beyond* in a new way, as a being-further that is at the same time a being-other.

5. Being Hermeneutical: On Vigilance

In hermeneutics the limit is an inception, because it opens the beyond that is the play-space of the other and with the other. Each encounter with truth is also an encounter with ourselves, whereby "encounter" means above all to run up against own limits, so that one is forced to go beyond them. It is no coincidence that Gadamer, in order to explain this, repeatedly comes to speak of *play*. Considered closely, it is play that, traversing hermeneutics, puts metaphysics into play. Even more so: the phenomenology of play presents itself as an alternative to all ontology or to any discourse on Being that claims to be final and fundamental. Play is the paradigm for the interpretation of the *beyond* that characterizes both understanding and life, or indeed, that reveals their reciprocal connection. The seal of finitude is imprinted in the "transcendence of play," and "to play" means not only "to elevate," but also "to bestow permanence" (*RB* 46/*GW8* 137). These expressions mean not so much to keep or to hold onto; rather they refer to a movement that goes beyond one's own life. Life is, specifically, not only living further; it is surviving in the sense of a living beyond oneself.

For hermeneutics, the beyond is a way of describing human existence that is always an existence at the limit. This means that there is no-limit situation; instead the limit itself is the situation of human beings that are *Grenzgänger*, wanderers on the edge between this side and the other, destined to remain at the boundary, at the mercy of the boundary (*EH* 67/*GW4* 293). But what constitutes the step beyond?

Whoever takes part in a game, and does this in order to hold on to existence in its transitoriness, in order to go beyond themselves, lingers in the game. This lingering shows an affinity to *theorein*, which means to be drawn in, taken in, and captured.[22] The condition of someone who takes part in a game is to be outside themselves. According to the perspective of rationalism, this "being-outside-oneself"—in contrast to being with oneself—has a privative and negative connotation. For hermeneutics, the opposite is the case.

To be hermeneutic means to be outside oneself. Culture emerges in this distance from oneself, in the sense of "seeing with the eyes of the other."[23] All of the experiences bound up with this are characterized by a devoted attentiveness or an attentive devotion, which ultimately coincide with hermeneutics. This is *vigilance* (*Wachsamkeit*), which hermeneutics substitutes for the concept of consciousness in the philosophical tradition.[24] Only if one is attentive and vigilant can one be ready for the step beyond oneself and outside of oneself. This step requires a turning away from oneself, which is also a forgetting of oneself. Paradoxically, the forgetting of oneself means here precisely to be wakeful and vigilant. For only if one can distance oneself from oneself in order to reach out toward the other, does one then become completely enthralled and absorbed by the other—and only then is one really with oneself. To stay by oneself, to withdraw into oneself, means by contrast: no longer being with oneself. Caring about oneself is nothing other than caring for or about the other (*EH* 147/*GW4* 183–184). The life that closes in on itself and stops at the limit is the kind of life that can go no further beyond itself. To be outside oneself, to tarry with others, is therefore a way of saying that one is alive.

The model of full self-presence and of perfect self-transparency, which corresponds to the Greek concept of the *noûs* or the modern concept of ideal subjectivity, reveals its entire eccentricity in hermeneutics. To be in oneself means to be outside oneself, that is, to be in the other. In order to be with oneself, one must be with others and one needs others. The *beyond* is to be read here as *other*. Far from being an asceticism at the limit, hermeneutics is a theory of ecstatic absorption in the other. The instance of the beyond translates into the passage beyond the limit and moving toward the other.

6. The Limit That Is the Other

The new conception introduced by hermeneutics, and over against Heidegger, is that of the limit as other. Although it is often repeated that Being for Heidegger is always *Being-with*, *Dasein* remains absolutely alone in its thrownness. Here the other is lacking, and the limit proves to be an insurmountable wall. If *Dasein* goes beyond itself, it is precisely not toward the other; rather it turns toward itself and toward authentic self-appropriation.

Gadamer questions this way of grasping the finitude of *Dasein* as "thrownness," because he directs his attention to the other and to the absence of the other. In his essay on "Subjectivity and Intersubjectivity, Subject and Person," from 1975, he writes:

> In any case Heidegger's answer seemed to me to give short shrift to the phenomenon I was concerned with. It is not only that everyone is in principle limited. What I was concerned with was why I experience my own limitation through the encounter with the Other, and why I must always learn to experience anew if I am ever to be in a position to surpass my limits.[25]

By encountering the other, one's own finitude becomes perceptible.[26] Only when the limit is perceived and understood as other, and not as one's own limit that can be appropriated, but rather as the limit of the other, which refers and turns toward the other, then the limit is open and becomes the opening point of newer possibilities.

In order to clarify this point, Gadamer draws on the myth about the nature of love as it is narrated in Plato's *Symposium*.[27] According to the myth, humans were originally spherical and therefore perfect. But because of human pride, the gods cut them in half. Since then, everyone has been merely a fragment: a countermark, a *sýmbolon*, divided into "two out of one."[28] Here the two of the indeterminate dyad reappear, and point to the infinite concealed in every fragment, despite its finitude. As a fragment, the human being will always remain dependent on the other. This means that finitude is defined by the other, not in the sense that it would be closed and confined by the other, but conversely, in the sense that the other in their infinite being-other forces us to transcend our limits. Independent of how she or he is experienced, whether as a stranger, an enemy, or an opponent, it is still the other who pushes us beyond the limit.

Even if the limit points to the other, nevertheless the other is not only the limit. He or she is not only the completion, compensation, or other fragment of the symbol. Much more than this, the other is the encounter and the participation in the encounter that overcomes finitude and opens the way to the infinite.

7. The Infinite Dialogue

Yet what is this infinitude? And how is the question of the infinite connected to the insurmountable finitude of the one who is asking the question? Is there a way of showing philosophy the connection of the finite and the infinite, and in doing so to strengthen it? The hermeneutical way—as Gadamer does not tire of repeating—is *the way of language*.[29]

It is surely true that language is the trace of our finitude. If there were not a word that originally discloses finitude, then there would also be no finitude. But this means that language is finite precisely because it is open. The finitude disclosed by the word is that of a "middle," such as the opening of a mouth that begins to speak. All of our understanding, our speaking, and our existing lie in this openness, in the midst of the becoming of history and language. It is in the everydayness of the now that both the finitude of every spoken and every understood word, as well as the finitude of the speaker who must rely on the word, are experienced. In this way there arises the unquenched and unquenchable desire for another word, which would give voice each time to what is unsaid and not understood. But this is possible only because the word in its finite presence evokes the absent infinitude of what still remains to be said and what lets itself be said.[30] The limit of every word is thus always the beginning of something infinitely new. For every word demands another word—in an infinite dialogue. The other is the possibility of overcoming finitude because his or her word, which is received, understood, and repeated, in the mystery of an identity that differs, becomes a communal word. Finitude is overcome in this way; indeed it is already beyond itself in the word of the other, since this word also discloses the access to the *infinite of the dialogue.*

In this sense the other is not only the limit. The transition to the infinite is possible only *with the other,* in the encounter and during the participation in the encounter. The finite word, which is always shared since it arises from the middle, the shared center, is the opening limit that initiates the free play of the other, with the other, the infinitude of the dialogue. As the Greek term *méson* suggests, what lies in the center, in the openness of the encounter, is also what is shared, what is shared with one another. Once again, Gadamer names this point of transition from the finite to the infinite using Plato's term *hikanón*. In contrast to the technical concept of the "unconditioned," which belongs to the logic of mathematical proof, the "unconditional" feature of Platonic dialectics is the necessary limit to reciprocal understanding. Thus the *hikanón* is the point at which the speakers agree, in order to begin the infinite play of question and answer, the infinitude of the dialogue, in the reciprocity of their participation.

In this moment, in which hermeneutics follows the path of language, it renounces as philosophy any *ultimate foundation*. For wherever one insists on an ultimate foundation, language must be ignored, and wherever language is admitted, the ultimate foundation must be renounced. How could the claim for an ultimate foundation, the idea of the system, the principle, the founding, the derivation, be brought into harmony with language, in which there is neither a first nor a last word—but only reciprocity? The unconditional is here the *hikanón*, the finite and limited point of encounter of the shared word, which, through reciprocity, opens participation to the infinite of the dialogue.

With its dialectical interweaving of the *logos*, hermeneutics reveals the possibility of the reciprocal participation of the finite and the infinite, with which the one can be read in light of the other. In this *logos*, this dialogue without end, hermeneutics recognizes itself again and adopts the dialogue as the form of its own philosophizing. Hermeneutics is this *infinite dialogue*.

In this way hermeneutics also defines its position *as* philosophy. Here, too, it follows a suggestion from Plato. In the myth of the winged chariot narrated in the *Phaedrus*, finitude and the destiny of the human soul are described.[31] As in the nocturnal ascent of the stars, human souls proceed on winged chariots led by the gods. They continue until the limit of the firmament, until the site of the beyond where the hyperuranium is disclosed and the true, immutable, perennial forms of Being can be contemplated. Whereas the gods give themselves over fully to this vision, the human souls are troubled by it. After having cast a fleeting *glance*, in the confusion they lose their wings and, separated from the "plain of truth," from *alétheia*, of which they retain only a vague memory, they fall back to earth. In the exile of finitude only a few souls can regain their wings and elevate themselves, even only briefly, to truth.[32] These are the human souls who have chosen and have loved *sophia*. The gods, who have stayed behind in the celestial vault and from there continue to gaze on the truth, do not philosophize. With this myth Plato describes the path of philosophy, which is an exclusively human path between heaven and earth. Hermeneutics follows this path, and so situates itself in the middle between the one and the dyad, the finite and the infinite. Although it knows itself as finite, it does not renounce the infinite. It consigns itself to the opening of an aporetic dialectic where, not having said the first word, it also does not claim to say the last.

Notes

1. Gadamer, "Philosophie oder Wissenschaftstheorie?" (1974), *VZW* 125–149; "Philosophy or Theory of Science?" in *Reason in the Age of Science*, trans. Frederick G. Lawrence (Cambridge, Mass.: MIT Press, 1981), 151–170.

2. See "Über die Naturanlage des Menschen zur Philosophie," 118–119; "On the Natural Inclination of Human Beings Toward Philosophy" 147.

3. Immanuel Kant, "Prolegomena zu einer jeden künftigen Metaphysik, die als Wissenschaft wird auftreten können," in *Werkausgabe*, Band V, hrsg. von Wilhelm Weischedel (Frankfurt am Main: Suhrkamp, 1978), A 48, 141; Prolegomena to Any Future Metaphysics, trans. Gary Hatfield (Cambridge: Cambridge University Press, 1997), A 48, 141.

4. See Gadamer, "Über die politische Inkompetenz der Philosophie" (1992/1993), in *Hermeneutische Entwürfe. Vorträge und Aufsätze* (Tübingen: Mohr Siebeck, 2000), 38; "On the Political Incompetence of Philosophy," in *The Heidegger Case: On Philosophy and Politics*, ed. Tom Rockmore and Joseph Margolis (Philadelphia: Temple University Press, 1992), 364-9, 366.

5. See Gadamer, "Cent'anni senza solitudine," interview with Donatella Di Cesare, in *Corriere della sera*, February 7, 2000.

6. In the few essays where he refers to metaphysics, Gadamer deals either with the question of metaphysics for Heidegger or the question of the language of metaphysics (see chapter 7, part 2, in this volume).

7. It is important to keep in mind how far Gadamer's hermeneutics is from all nihilistic consequences, but also from positions that aim at a rehabilitation of metaphysics. See Reiner Wiehl, "Heidegger, Gadamer, und die Möglichkeit einer Ontologie heute," in Wiehl, *Metaphysik und Erfahrung* (Frankfurt/M: Suhrkamp, 1996), 127-154.

8. This is probably why Gadamer never devoted a single essay to the topic of finitude.

9. See chapter 5, part 12, in this volume.

10. See Gadamer, "Dialogues in Capri" in *Religion*, ed. Jacques Derrida and Gianni Vattimo (Stanford, Calif.: Stanford University Press, 1996), 205-206.

11. Alcmaeon of Croton, VS 24 A 1, 3.

12. Gadamer, "Über leere und erfullte Zeit," GW4 144-145; "Concerning Empty and Ful-filled Time" in *Martin Heidegger in Europe and America*, ed. E. G. Ballard and C. E. Scott (The Hague: Martinus Nijhoff, 1973), 86.

13. See Heidegger, *Kant und das Problem der Metaphysik*. GA 3, hrsg. von Friedrich-Wilhelm von Herrmann (Frankfurt am Main: Klostermann, 1991); Kant and the Problem of Metaphysics, trans. Richard Taft (Indianapolis: Indiana University Press, 1997).

14. See Heidegger, "Was ist Metaphysik?" in *Wegmarken*, 120; "What is Metaphysics?" in *Pathmarks*, ed. William McNeill (Cambridge: Cambridge University Press, 1998), 95.

15. See Gadamer, "Die Unsterblichkeitsbeweise in Platos ›Phaidon‹" (1973), GW6 187-200; "The Proofs of Immortality in Plato's *Phaedo*," in *Dialogue and Dialectic: Eight Hermeneutical Studies on Plato*, trans. and ed. P. Christopher Smith (New Haven, Conn.: Yale University Press, 1980),187-200; "Der Tod als Frage," (1975), GW4 161-172; "Die Erfahrung des Todes" (1983), GW4 288-294. "The Experience of Death," in *The Enigma of Health: The Art of Healing in a Scientific Age*, trans. J. Gaiger and N. Walker (Stanford, Calif.: Stanford University Press, 1996), 288-294.

16. For more on this topic, see Donatella Di Cesare, "*Savoir vivre—savoir mourir*. Der Tod als Grenze zwischen Heidegger und Gadamer," in Günter Figal and Hans Helmuth Gander, eds., *Dimensionen des Hermeneutischen—Heidegger und Gadamer* (Frankfurt am Main: Klostermann 2005), 73-87.

17. This was emphasized by Derrida in his commemorative address.

18. Bruns reads the dyad in a similar way. See Gerald L. Bruns, "The Hermeneutical Anarchist: *Phronesis*, Rhetoric, and the Experience of Art," in *Gadamer's Century: Essays in Honor of Hans-Georg Gadamer* (Cambridge, Mass.: MIT Press, 2002), 45-76, 52.

19. See Gadamer, "Die Dialektik des Selbstbewußtseins" (1973), GW3 47-64; "Hegel's Dialectic of Self-Consciousness," in *Hegel's Dialectic: Five Hermeneutical Studies*, trans. P. Christopher Smith (New Haven, Conn.: Yale University Press, 1976), 47-64, as well as Hegel, *Phenomenology of Spirit*, trans. A. V. Miller (Oxford: Oxford University Press, 1977), 104-105. See also Robert B. Pippin, "Gadamer's Hegel," in Robert J. Dostal, ed., *The Cambridge Companion to Gadamer* (Cambridge:

Cambridge University Press, 2002), 225–238, 230 (this same essay is published again in *Gadamer's Century*, 217–238).

20. See "Die phänomenologische Bewegung," *GW3* 141; "The Phenomenological Movement," trans. David E. Linge, in *Philosophical Hermeneutics* (Berkeley: University of California Press, 1976), 134–135.

21. The question of finitude is interpreted in a similar way by Ruggenini: see Mario Ruggenini, "Wahrheit und Endlichkeit," in Ingeborg Schüssler and Alexandre Schild, eds., *Genos. Phenomenologie et hermeneutique* (Lausanne, Payot, 2000), 175–189.

22. See chapter 3, part 9, and chapter 6, part 3, in this volume.

23. See chapter 2, part 2, in this volume.

24. See chapter 5, part 5, in this volume.

25. Gadamer, "Subjektivität und Intersubjektivität, Subjekt und Person" (1975), *GW10* 87–99, 98; "Subjectivity and Intersubjectivity; Subject and Person," in *Continental Philosophy Review* 33, no. 3 (2000): 275–287, 285.

26. See chapter 8, part 8, in this volume.

27. Gadamer, "Die Aktualität des Schönen," *GW8* 122–123; "The Relevance of the Beautiful," in *The Relevance of the Beautiful and Other Essays*, ed. and intro. Robert Bernasconi and trans. Nicholas Walker (Cambridge: Cambridge University Press, 1986), 31.

28. Plato, *Symposium*, 191d.

29. See Gadamer, *WM*, *GW1* 460–463/*TM* 456–460; "Die Natur der Sache und die Sprache der Dinge" (1960), *GW2* 71; "The Nature of Things and the Language of Things," in *Philosophical Hermeneutics*, ed. and trans. David E. Linge (Berkeley: University of California Press, 1976), 75; "Das Erbe Hegels," *GW4* 480 "The Heritage of Hegel," in *Reason in the Age of Science*, trans. Frederick G. Lawrence (Cambridge, Mass.: MIT Press. 1981), 56.

30. See chapter 8, part 4, of this volume; see Gadamer, "Wie weit schreibt Sprache das Denken?" *GW2* 206.

31. Plato, *Phaedrus*, 243e–257b.

32. See Gadamer, "Die Aktualität des Schönen," *GW8* 106. "The Relevance of the Beautiful," 15.

10 Keeping the Dialogue Going

One must seek to understand the other, and that means that one has to believe that one could be in the wrong. (*DD* 119/*GW10* 130)

It would be a poor hermeneuticist who thought he could have, or had to have, the last word. (*TM* 581/*GW2* 478)

1. When a Philosophy Becomes *Koiné*

Following the publication of *Truth and Method,* hermeneutics moved quickly into the spotlight on the philosophical scene. Gadamer's work found great resonance, insofar as it was soon recognized as one of the most significant contributions to twentieth-century philosophy, which is evinced by the numerous reviews from the 1960s onward.[1] The widespread enthusiasm with which it was received in Europe, as well as in North America, gives a sense of its potential, which extends far beyond the horizon of philosophy.

Yet the publication of *Truth and Method,* which for Gadamer himself was still a *work in progress,* also marked the beginning of the complex history of the effects of hermeneutics. When put to the test, hermeneutics has consistently shown that, depending on the focus of one's position, it can be understood differently. The success of hermeneutics can largely be attributed to its flexibility, as well as to its readiness to confront even the sharpest critiques and the harshest attacks. Thus all attempts to put the validity of hermeneutics into question, even when they actually identified problematic central points, came to nothing and quickly passed into oblivion.

The case of the Italian legal scholar Emilio Betti (1890–1968) is exemplary. His *Allgemeine Theorie der Interpretation,* which mainly reviews the development of the discipline until Dilthey, seeks to establish hermeneutics as a normative aesthetic doctrine that would provide rules and principles in order to guarantee the *objectivity* of method.[2] According to Betti, from philology to historiography, from theology to legal practice, a universally valid interpretation would always be necessary. Betti's polemic against Bultmann and Heidegger arises from this position: both compromise the objectivity of hermeneutics, since they conceive of understanding as a determination of existence. His vehement attack on Gadamer is simply a consequence of this critique. Betti accuses Gadamer of making prejudice the "condition" of understanding, and through his theory of application, confusing the objective "meaning" of texts with their "significance" for the interpreter. In this way, for Betti, Gadamer misses the actual goal of establishing the meaning of the text in the way in which it was intended by the *mens auctoris*. Yet for Gadamer this general theory of interpretation would never be able to deliver on what it promises, that is, a hermeneutics that could guarantee positive objectivity. In the foreword to the second edition of *Truth and Method* from 1965, Gadamer defends his own hermeneutics as a philosophy that seeks to be neither a method nor a reflection on method. The technical question, "How should we understand?" is always preceded by the philosophical question, "How is understanding possible?" (*TM* xxvii–xxxviii/*GW*2 441)

The objection raised by Betti was taken up again by the literary critic Eric Donald Hirsch (b. 1928). His work, *Validity in Interpretation,* represents the first significant confrontation with hermeneutics in the United States.[3] Yet Hirsch narrows the breadth that understanding had acquired for human existence and again reduces it to a methodical process of textual interpretation. According to Hirsch, philosophical hermeneutics is untenable because it fails to deliver valid objective criteria. For Hirsch, the "original meaning," which coincides with the author's intention, must be differentiated from the "significance"—in other words, from the relation between the original meaning and the multiple meanings derived by the readers. Whereas criticism seeks the text's significance, interpretation should aim for textual meaning. In order to avoid the contradictions that allegedly weaken hermeneutics, which proceed for example from an "identity" that is not actually an identity and a "repetition" that is not actually a repetition, one should always presuppose a self-identical textual meaning that varies only according to the situation of the reader. According to Hirsch, this is what Gadamer actually means to say, or "should have meant by the concept of *Horizontverschmelzung.*"[4] Beyond the difficulties that Hirsch seems to have had with the new hermeneutic concept of "identity," his distance from Gadamer is already marked by his conception of understanding, which for Gadamer "is never a subjective relation to a given 'object' but to the history of its effect; in other words, understanding belongs to the being of that which is understood" (*TM* xxviii/*GW*2 441).[5] By forcefully bending circularity into linearity, Hirsch lets himself be led by a concept of truth derived from a realistic epistemology, and, not by chance, he seeks a marriage between hermeneutics and the falsification theory of Karl Popper. In light of the history of effects, however, it must be admitted that today very little remains in the humanities of the search for a method, undertaken by Hirsch and Betti, that could ascertain objective textual meaning.

By contrast, the influence of philosophical hermeneutics on literary studies has steadily increased over time. Gadamer's philosophy had already gained considerable significance in the 1960s. After a brief period when it was marginalized by the stronger interest in French structuralism, it was rejuvenated in the 1990s in American departments of comparative literature, in part because of the growing philosophical vocation in the humanities.

One of the most interesting results of hermeneutics in this area is represented by the "Constance School," which was initiated by Hans Robert Jauss (1921–97) with his "aesthetics of reception."[6] Already in his famous 1967 essay, "Literaturgeschichte als Provokation der Literaturwissenschaft" ("Literary History as a Provocation to Literary Studies"), Jauss draws on Gadamer's "history of effects" in order to formulate the thesis that literary historiography arises from the interaction of text and reader, and should be conceived according to this dialogical model.[7] A literary work is, accordingly, not a historical fact but rather an event that requires "reception" in order to reach its true existence. This new hermeneutic paradigm does not prevent Jauss, however, from raising critical objections against Gadamer—the most important of which involves the concept of the "classical"[8]—and in this way to distinguish his position from Gadamer's. For example, Jauss develops the argument that the text determines our "horizon of expectations," and from that point controls the further reading process. For Gadamer, by contrast, the text is limited to giving an impetus; otherwise the text should be considered a transhistorical structure. It is not the text that controls the change of horizon, but the reverse: the event of understanding is the uncontrollable way in which the horizon changes. Wolfgang Iser (1926–2007) also belongs to the "Constance School," and he developed a phenomenology of reading on the basis of the phenomenological aesthetics of Roman Ingarden (1893–1970).[9] Gadamer's influence on musical studies should also be recognized, in particular on Carl Dahlhaus (1928–1989), who can be seen as the most important music theorist of the second half of the twentieth century. In his numerous writings, Dahlhaus frequently referred to Gadamer and developed many hermeneutic theses with his conception of music. Only the time interval is understood differently by Dahlhaus, since the tunings of the past should become for him a constitutive moment of the performance.

Whereas the first critical objections against *Truth and Method* came from within, and above all from those who argued for a return to traditional hermeneutics, there were also attacks from without, as for example the one by Hans Albert (b. 1921). In 1968 he published his *Traktat über kritische Vernunft*, which directed, in a very questionable way, Popper's falsification theory against hermeneutics, even though Popper himself had directed his work against analytic trends.[10] Albert has recently returned to his polemic, which beyond Gadamer also criticizes Habermas, Heidegger, and all of German thought back to Hegel.[11] Albert accuses hermeneutics of wanting to expand textual analysis as far as knowledge of reality in general, and in this way to bring about a break between science and philosophy, whereby the latter would fall into a dangerous proximity to theology. Without too much difficulty, Gadamer replied that for hermeneutics, too, "there is only one 'logic of scientific investigation'"—but this is not the main point, since the main issues to consider are selective and epistemological, practical viewpoints that in each case determine the research in advance. A theory of science that neglects these will end in complete irrationalism, precisely for the sake of rationalism (*TM* 563/*GW3* 453). Albert's accusation against Gadamer is clearly unjustified, as has been shown by the recent developments in American theory of science, especially those arising from the contextualism of the paradigm theory of Thomas S. Kuhn (1922–96), who recognized in hermeneutics an important ally against neo-positivism.[12]

From Protestant theology in the twentieth century there arose the "new hermeneutics," which was initiated in the 1950s by Ernst Fuchs (1903–83) and developed further in different ways by Gerhard Ebeling (1912–2001), Eugen Biser (b. 1918), Günter Stachel (b. 1922), and Eberhard Jüngel (b. 1934).[13] What is characteristic of this movement, which draws on Heidegger as well as the Marburg theology of Bultmann and Barth, is the meaning that the word of God acquires when it becomes the event of revelation.[14] *Truth and Method* consolidated the theoretical core of this approach and thereby inspired further reflections on language. In any case, the debate around Gadamer's hermeneutics in the theological area remained relatively limited, whether because of the anti-dogmatic potential of hermeneutics or because its religious dimension was hidden for a long time. Philosophical hermeneutics represented a problem more than a possibility for both Protestant and Catholic theology—perhaps because theology still wavers between its metaphysical inheritance and the obsessive fear of relativism. In recent years, however, theology's hermeneutic interest has become more persistent and deeper, as in for example the essays published in 2002 in the comprehensive collection entitled *Between the Human and the Divine*.[15]

Beyond theology and literary studies, hermeneutics has had important consequences not only for the philosophy of law but also for judicial practice, as the works of Franz Wieacker (1908–94), Fritz Rittner (b. 1921), Ronald Dworkin (b. 1931), and Joachim Hruschka (b. 1935) reveal.[16] The relevance of the dialogue model for the relation between legal texts and their interpreters has above all been underlined by Giuseppe Zaccaria (b. 1947).[17] The important consequences of philosophical hermeneutics in the area of historiography should also be mentioned, where Gadamer's privileged interlocutor, Reinhart Koselleck (1923–2006), applied hermeneutical theses in an original manner.[18] For his part Gadamer always kept open the debate with the "Historical School," in particular with Erich Rothacker (1888–1965), the theorist of "conceptual history" and the founder of the Archiv für Begriffsgeschichte in Bonn. After Rothacker, the direction of the Archiv went to Gadamer and Joachim Ritter (1903–74), an important representative of Neo-Aristotelianism.[19] In the course of these debates philosophical hermeneutics has left clear and numerous traces on the historiography of philosophy, too, especially in Germany.

But it is probably impossible to sketch an overview, in just a few strokes, of all the multifaceted developments that have been promoted or inspired by hermeneutics. This counts not only for contemporary philosophy, which has been decisively marked by hermeneutics, but also for the overall cultural life of recent decades, in which hermeneutics continually played a leading role. It is sufficient to mention here the most important debates between philosophical hermeneutics and Habermas's ideology critique, Rorty's neo-pragmatism, Derrida's deconstruction, and Vattimo's "weak thought." The impressive bibliography that has been gathered in the process sheds considerable light on the complex and multilayered phenomenon of this reception.[20] What is remarkable are the numerous *Festschriften* or collected volumes dedicated to Gadamer's philosophy—since 2000 alone more than twenty have appeared. The volume published by Hahn for the Library of Living Philosophers in 1997 represents a significant recognition and a kind of official investiture. In addition, however, there are also a number of recently published collections that offer a useful perspective on the many remarkable changes in the history of the effects of hermeneutics. In these the more traditional themes that were discussed into the 1980s recede into the background, such as the self-understanding of the humanities, the conception of history and the relation to historicism, and all the classical hermeneutic questions about the history of hermeneutics, including its influences on other areas, from literary criticism to sociology. On the one hand, the polemics between hermeneutics and the ideology critique have waned, whereas the debate between hermeneutics and deconstruction, particularly after Derrida's passing, has been taken further and rethought anew.[21] Unchanged is the attention to practical philosophy, which remains, along with aesthetics, an unavoidable theoretical core. But what has gained prominence in recent decades is the reflection on language, the difficult and often misunderstood question of understanding, the relation of hermeneutics to Greek philosophy, the issue of politics and the concept of utopia, the debate with the theory of science, and the problem of the philosophical status of hermeneutics. In the process Gadamer's interpretations of Plato and Hegel have acquired more visible contours, and while the connection of hermeneutics to phenomenology has been more strongly emphasized, its relation to Heidegger at the same time appears in a new light.

An important recent development is the interest that analytic philosophy in North America has shown in hermeneutics. With this an omission has been corrected on both sides, for both should have reflected on their proximity, starting from the *linguistic turn*.[22] Thus David C. Hoy emphasized the affinity between Gadamer's hermeneutics and the *principle of charity* that for Donald Davidson (1917–2003) guides benevolent interpretation.[23] Whereas the relation between Gadamer and Davidson, but also between Davidson and Heidegger, is the topic of an essay by Jeff Malpas in the collection *Gadamer's Century*, the attention of analytic philosophers has concentrated above all on the question of understanding.[24] John McDowell (b. 1942), whose relationship to Gadamer's philosophy had already become visible in the 1994 book *Mind and World*, has also contributed an important recent essay in this context that more clearly emphasizes the connection.[25] The opening of analytic philosophy to hermeneutics proceeds together with a rediscovery of Hegel and the entirety of classical philosophy.[26] It is surely of some importance that analytic philosophy has chosen philosophical hermeneutics, from all of continental philosophy, as its chief interlocutor.

Even though it has been criticized repeatedly, and frequently from quite opposite directions, Gadamer's philosophical hermeneutics has maintained a dominant position within continental philosophy. Already in an essay from 1985, Vattimo had called hermeneutics in this sense the philosophical *koiné* or common language of recent decades.[27] If the hub around which debates had turned in the 1950s and 1960s was Marxism, and structuralism in the 1970s, in the 1980s the central position had been taken by philosophical hermeneutics. Often the very different currents of European thought flowed together in hermeneutics, which through the increasingly urgent confrontation with analytic philosophy was forced to recognize itself as the new *koiné*. Vattimo's claim, which gave rise to many discussions, clearly testifies to the destiny of hermeneutics.

From this destiny, however, it is necessary to emphasize one particular trait. Philosophical hermeneutics has had less a centrifugal than a centripetal impact on contemporary culture. It has exercised a strong power of attraction, rather than radiating out and spreading itself around. But this has also led to persistent backlashes against hermeneutics.[28] Its effects have called forth or inspired positions that could not be characterized as "hermeneutic" from their original starting points, but perhaps rather from their convergence with Gadamer's original project—a convergence that, however, in the following developments has often proven to be a divergence. It should suffice here to mention the related hermeneutic phenomenology of Paul Ricoeur (1913–2005).[29]

Against this background, of course, the question arises whether a philosophy can ever be a *koiné*, and what constitutes the price that hermeneutics would have to pay for that status. In today's linguistic usage, "hermeneutics" has certainly become a synonym for "continental philosophy." As much as this role of "standing for" continental philosophy has undoubtedly brought advantages, it has also brought great disadvantages—first and above all the charge, too often misused and too extreme, of vagueness.[30] Hermeneutics has not had nearly as much difficulty with the attacks as with the positive acceptance it has encountered. From the debates with Habermas, Rorty, and Derrida, hermeneutics has gone forward strengthened.[31] By contrast, what has weakened hermeneutics is precisely its expansion to a *koiné*, a kind of common idiom, which can easily be instrumentalized because it has been robbed of nearly all its semantic density, and ultimately comes close to the terminology that Gadamer often equated with metaphysics. From this tendency there has emerged, especially after Gadamer's passing, the clear necessity to reinterpret philosophical hermeneutics.[32] It is not a matter of abandoning the key questions of hermeneutics, but on the contrary, of discovering them anew and strengthening them in their theoretical core.

2. Hermeneutics and the Critique of Ideology

In a long research article entitled "Zur Logik der Sozialwissenschaften" published in the 1967 *Philosophische Rundschau*, Jürgen Habermas took a position on Gadamer's philosophy for the first time.[33] With this article a debate began between hermeneutics and ideology critique, which lasted only a brief while and was heavily marked by the *Zeitgeist* of the late 1960s. Nevertheless the debate had important consequences for both the critique of ideology and hermeneutics. Gadamer responded with an essay entitled "Rhetorik, Hermeneutik und Ideologiekritik. Metakritische Erörterungen zu *Wahrheit und Methode*."[34] Soon other representatives from both parties entered the discussion, including Albrecht Wellmer, Karl-Otto Apel, and Rüdiger Bubner. Habermas developed his position further in the work "Der Universalitätsanspruch der Hermeneutik," from 1970, to which Gadamer responded with his "Replik," one year later.[35]

Habermas comes from the Frankfurt School but was for a long time in contact with Gadamer, who in 1961 had secured a position for him in Heidelberg as an assistant professor. Habermas's intention was to develop an emancipatory critique of ideology, which had as a point of reference Freudian psychoanalysis and Marxist thought. Against the objectivist positivism that dominates sociology, he seeks a linguistic theoretical foundation for the social sciences. Social action is not organized according to the model of atomistic and causally, interactively effective centers of force; rather, it is carried out according to linguistic schemes that guide the interaction. Habermas finds support in the later Wittgenstein, who succeeded in reaching beyond the phenomenological lifeworld to recognize linguistically constituted "life forms" articulated in a multiplicity of "language games." Insofar as it converges with the practice of language games, social action turns out to be communicative action.[36] Yet for Habermas, who emphasizes the commonalities more than the differences, it is necessary to dissolve the "monadic structures" of language games in which every actor would otherwise remain imprisoned. Thus the accent must be placed on the connections between the language games, or better, on their "translation."[37] With the aim of overcoming the remnants of positivism that he found in Wittgenstein's conception, Habermas appeals to the hermeneutic starting point. In order to tear down the grammatical limits, it is not at all necessary to leave everyday language behind, by for example following the path of Noam Chomsky; it suffices, following Humboldt, to take up Gadamer's teaching. Hermeneutics has shown that language can always transcend itself; in this it discloses the self-reflexive potential of reason.[38] The hermeneutic experience is nothing other than the movement by which reason escapes the coercion of language and, on the other hand, gets articulated as linguistic. Everything that is said can always be said differently: therein lies the universality of reason. By simultaneously reflecting and negating the limits of language, reason asserts itself each time in the act of translation. The limit case of translation between languages shows the kind of reflection that also takes place within the same language, where the horizons are open and the forms are dynamic. Wittgenstein had not seen that the application of rules is also an interpretation, that linguistic spheres are "porous" to the inner and the outer. Thus he had neglected historicity, which decisively marks translation. As a historical process translation is not only horizontal but also vertical, because it runs through generations and epochs. Whoever proceeds from the hermeneutic situation of dialogue cannot ignore the "openness" of language. By reaching back to Gadamer's "great critique" of the self-understanding of the humanities, which also affects the "false consciousness" of its practitioners, Habermas ultimately becomes the authority that speaks for the claim of hermeneutics to universality.[39]

In light of this basic solidarity, the controversial topics between hermeneutics and the critique of ideology have only a secondary importance, for they refer either to misunderstandings or to insufficiently clarified points. In general the controversy involves three areas of debate. The first revolves around the concept of "tradition," which Gadamer had subjected to critical reflection without presumably finding the proper balance between authority and reason. This goes together with a kind of "prejudice" that Gadamer's displays toward prejudices and a discrediting of the Enlightenment. Yet even though some of the formulations in *Truth and Method* may sound excessive, Gadamer never sought to obscure reason. His aim was rather to show that reason, far from being sovereign, is situated in tradition and gets worked out in history.[40] Habermas himself recognizes this when he elaborates: "One is tempted to use Gadamer against himself," in order to defend the right of reflection.[41]

Further, Habermas accuses hermeneutics of "linguistic idealism."[42] This means, according to Habermas, not seeing the outer limits of language, which is everything that cannot be said, as well as the inner limits, namely the web that every language weaves around every speaker. If the first part of this accusation is simply unjustified, the second part by contrast bears considerable weight for the hermeneutic debate.[43] "Language is *also* a medium of domination and social power," runs the thesis by Habermas.[44] Language is, therefore, *ideological,* because it reflects "interests." But this conclusion is reached only thanks to the hermeneutic investigation of the relation between language and speaker, that is, the dialogue whose conflict-laden character Habermas justifiably underlines. With this sharpening of the conflict hermeneutics is radicalized, it becomes ideology critique—without, however, ceasing to be hermeneutics.

In order to unmask the power relations at work in language, and thereby to underline the constraining role of consensus, Habermas mobilizes both ideology critique and psychoanalysis. In his third criticism, he questions the dichotomy of truth and method and shows the possibility of a methodical understanding that, "behind the back of language," returns to the false individual or social consciousness and, in the name of undistorted communicative relations, subjects it to critical reflection.[45] Psychoanalysis and ideology critique become the proof of a methodizing and objectifying understanding in the area of the social sciences.[46] Indeed, Gadamer—in contrast to Ricoeur—does not consider the scientific status of these disciplines and emphasizes rather their openly hermeneutic character.[47] For Gadamer it is important to defend the distinction between truth and method in order to turn against the thesis, which has become widespread in modernity, that there could be no truth outside of method.[48] Nevertheless he also draws attention to another point: the transposition of the psychoanalytic model to social critique.[49] The therapeutic dialogue takes place between a patient, who subjects himself to an asymmetrical relationship in order to regain his balance, and a psychoanalyst, who is responsible for this but who is "never analyzed to the end."[50] It would therefore be quite dangerous to transpose this schema, which arises through "voluntary submission," onto all areas of social life. This would resemble the attempt to turn every speaker into a patient, who is emancipated, either voluntarily or against their will, from the troubles and pressures of communication, and who in this way would be elevated by "metahermeneutics" to a rational and more self-transparent form of consciousness. This questionable transposition, which Habermas however does not insist upon, indicates in any case another more far-reaching and more complex question, whose answer forms the watershed between both philosophers. Whereas the psychoanalytic dialogue is, for Habermas, the extreme case that puts the *universality of hermeneutics* in question, Gadamer sees only an individual case in it, since it is linguistically performed and thus influenced by a *preliminary agreement,* in the sense that it proceeds from the play of language that no speaker can escape.[51] Language, according to Gadamer, is "the game in which we all play."[52] But agreement does not mean consensus—as was already shown. And understanding means neither accepting necessarily nor approving. This is the equation that Habermas mistakenly employs. To speak a language means to be enmeshed in the web of language, but not held captive; to this extent, language is no ideological prison. If language is seen as a prison, then it becomes an autonomous power over and above the speaker. In the process the reflexive ability of the speaker is overvalued, who, in order to avoid all forms of blindness seems to gain an external perspective in which he, according to the model of the Enlightenment, would be emancipated from "the rhetorically produced consensus."[53] Philosophical hermeneutics, which lies at the dividing line between the rhetorical and the hermeneutic aspects of linguisticality, raises to consciousness the position of the speaker in relation to language, and thereby opens the path to a reflection made possible by the speculative structure of language. Although in its transcendence it can reveal new and further possibilities, reflection based on language can never reach a "complete, idealistic transparency of meaning."[54] This does not exclude, however, that hermeneutics also begins with the agreement of language and then aims for an approval that—according to Apel—should be seen as the regulative ideal of an infinite dialogue.[55] Habermas called this ideal the "anticipation of the good life," which is common to all and gets articulated through the play of forces in the dialogue through which the community is constituted. Habermas himself, in the 1980s, will put the basic hermeneutic category of "linguistic agreement" once again into play, and derives the *telos* that guides his "discourse ethics" from this: "This underlying agreement, which unites us before the fact and in the light of which every actually attained agreement can be criticized, grounds the hermeneutic utopia of universal and unlimited dialogue in a commonly inhabited lifeworld."[56] The debate between hermeneutics and ideology critique was not without repercussions.[57] Gadamer will in the future pay more attention to unfolding the critical potential of hermeneutics. To be sure, reflection cannot bring us out of tradition, but tradition, and particularly the one from which the drive to emancipation emerges, needs critical questioning in order to be understood. In an important passage in his "Replik," Gadamer writes: "Philosophical hermeneutics [. . .] thus no longer serves to overcome certain difficulties of understanding, as might occur with texts or in dialogue with other people, but what it strives for is, as Habermas calls it, a 'critical reflexive knowledge.'"[58] The agreement that authorizes the continuity of tradition will at the same time legitimize its change. Even revolution is not absolute and hence abstract change, but a kind of confrontation with tradition. Similarly, complete agreement can also be read as "revolutionary solidarity."[59]

This debate also leaves its mark in Habermas's thought. Clearly, since 1970 psychoanalysis no longer represents the paradigm of a critical theory of society. By contrast, Habermas develops in his *Theorie des kommunikativen Handelns* a "discourse ethics," which brings to light, under many aspects, the debt he owes to the hermeneutic dialogue. What binds Gadamer and Habermas further to each other, even after their debate, is the concept of "solidarity," whereby what is common is made possible in language. It is the thesis of Richard J. Bernstein (b. 1932) that philosophical hermeneutics contains a political critique, confirmed by the role of *phrónesis* or practical wisdom. Bernstein perceives here an influence exercised by ideology critique.[60]

Habermas himself insisted on this point in his *laudatio* of 1979, which has become known by the title "Hans-Georg Gadamer. Die Urbanisierung der Heideggerschen Provinz" ("The Urbanization of the Heideggerian Province").[61] Habermas can be credited with having emphasized the emancipatory potential of hermeneutics, which he happens to share with Vattimo; yet he still did not see this potential in its "thinking in utopias," principally because he had neglected the role of Plato in hermeneutics. With the authority of a voice that can hardly be contradicted, he had at the same time contributed to putting Gadamer in Heidegger's shadows—despite his connection to Hegel and the substantial differences between Heidegger's "turn to the mysticism of Being" and Gadamer's "humanism."[62] But in this approach by Habermas there lies a problem that goes beyond Gadamer's hermeneutics and concerns the difficult relation of German philosophy to its history and its identity.

3. Hermeneutics and Neo-Pragmatism

After 1968 Gadamer taught at various American universities. At first his work was far more received by literary scholars, theologians, and legal scholars than in philosophy departments, where analytic philosophy dominated. But Gadamer never sought to avoid the debate with analytic philosophy and was searching there, too, for possible ways to build bridges.[63] The contemporary constellation in the United States seemed entirely favorable for the arrival of hermeneutics. On the one hand North American thought can look back on a solid tradition of pragmatism, and on the other hand analytic philosophy has been in crisis for a long time. It is thus not surprising that hermeneutics would find its preferred interlocutor in the neo-pragmatist Richard Rorty (1931–2007), who was just in the process of stepping down from his position at Princeton University, one of the strongholds of mainstream analytic philosophy. His 1979 book, *Philosophy and the Mirror of Nature*, confirmed Rorty's departure from analytic philosophy. He declared the era of systematic philosophy at an end and sought to open a new epoch in which philosophy would be a struggle against "normalization," that is, it would be hermeneutics.

Rorty's argument becomes clearer in light of the numerous common features shared by American pragmatism and continental hermeneutics. Both William James (1842–1910) and, especially, John Dewey (1859–1952) begin with the need to overcome the epistemological perspective that has become mired in the modern division between subject and object. By contrast they promote connections with the lifeworld, in which the self forms itself with others and with the world. Reciprocity becomes the cipher of this new concept of truth. Art plays a significant role for them; as an event that reveals truth it can far more substantially transform existence than the abstract assertions of truth by science. Pragmatism agrees with hermeneutics that reason must be stripped of its claim to absoluteness. Reason is, for pragmatism too, always concrete and historical.[64]

In his renewal of the pragmatic tradition, through which he begins a critique of analytic philosophy, Rorty draws explicitly on Gadamer's hermeneutics. This undeniable proximity is accompanied, however, by a distance between them, which can be explained for the most part on the basis of the American philosopher's background.[65] Yet precisely for this reason Rorty's access to hermeneutics opens the way to new and original developments.

According to Rorty, hermeneutics gives a twofold answer to the questions about the future of philosophy: it says no to "epistemology" and yes to "education or self-formation" (*Bildung*). Epistemology, for him, is in a broader sense a kind of foundationalism, since it postulates the necessity of providing an ultimate epistemological basis for philosophy. In a narrower sense it is the *normal science,* as Kuhn had conceived it, that is, a complex of methods and contents that develop within dominant "paradigms." As against such foundationalism, hermeneutics offers a clear alternative. Rorty finds confirmation for this in the critique Gadamer launched against Husserl's concept of "ultimate foundation."[66] At the same time, however, hermeneutics is entirely prepared to dialogue with epistemology as "normal discourse," and thus to show its ability not only to let various "normal" discourses interact, but also to open itself to "abnormal" discourses, that is, to such discourses that are articulated in alternative paradigms and are incommensurable with the dominant paradigm.[67] As normal discourse supposedly needs the abnormal, this latter is always "reactive" or "parasitical." Such a sharp distinction seems to yield more than one difficulty—both for hermeneutics and for philosophy in general. For either hermeneutics identifies with abnormal discourse, whereby it would make room for a systematic philosophy involved with normal discourse, or it would admit, in just as dangerous a way, the articulation of a normal discourse, which can however be elevated to a foundational discourse.

If hermeneutics renounces an ultimate foundation, this occurs because from the very outset it renounces an understanding based on a pre-given vocabulary that can adequately translate all discourses. For a post-foundationalist philosophy, however, the problem of *understanding* the multiplicity of paradigms still arises. With this Rorty touches on a key question for hermeneutics and comes very close to Gadamer's position. Far from being a matter of appropriation and subjugation, understanding rather shows respect for the vocabulary in which the incommensurability of the other is articulated. Understanding as suggested by hermeneutics is, according to Rorty, "more like getting acquainted with a person than like following a demonstration."[68]

The theme of a "dialogue," and "dialogue" with partners who are different and incommensurable, is developed further on the basis of the hermeneutic concept of *Bildung*.[69] Rorty translates this complex and multilayered German word not with "education," but with "edification." "Edification" for him does not mean the knowledge of what is "out there"; rather it means to form oneself and others, so that edification should be taken as the "reinterpretation" of our familiar environment. Accordingly, edification is not necessarily constructive: "For edifying discourse is *supposed* to be abnormal, to take us out of our old selves by the power of strangeness, to aid us in becoming new beings."[70] It would be a mistake, however, to understand "edification" as "a structure erected upon foundations." For edification is for its part "dialogue."[71] Although Rorty indicates a way out of epistemology, his answer is not a foundationalist one, since it points to the possibility of leaving the dialogue endlessly open.

On this point Gadamer would agree with Rorty and probably also subscribe to his interpretation of *Bildung*. But he would have doubts about Rorty's way of reading the concept of *wirkungsgeschichtliches Bewusstsein,* or "effective historical consciousness." Whereas Derrida thought he could sense the residue of a metaphysics of consciousness in this concept, Rorty want to find the basic principle of neo-pragmatism in it:

> Gadamer develops his notion of *wirkungsgeschichtliches Bewusstsein* (the sort of consciousness of the past which changes us) to characterize an attitude interested not so much in what is out there in the world, or in what happened in history, as in what we can get out of nature and history for our own uses.[72]

Obviously, in this way of reading, *wirkungsgeschichtliches Bewusstsein* is not oriented toward an interpretation of the past. But under the sign of free self-determination, it decides on the usefulness of the past for the present and the future. Rorty distorts Gadamer's concept not so much because he projects it into the future, but because he introduces the criterion of usefulness, which is of course central to pragmatism, but alien to hermeneutics.

Rorty's philosophical project aims at a radical "deontologization" of hermeneutics that does not coincide with a dismissal of its metaphysical remnants. For him, it is much more a question of turning our gaze away from Being and toward language, or better, toward dialogue as the site where a common experience of truth is possible in a non-foundationalist manner. With this emphasis on the post-metaphysical outcome of hermeneutics, Rorty's contribution opens new perspectives for continental philosophy.

4. Hermeneutics and Deconstruction

The first meeting between Gadamer and Derrida took place at the Goethe Institut in Paris April 25–27, 1981. The aim was a public debate between the main representatives of continental philosophy. But both participants and witnesses were unanimous in speaking of the event as a dialogue between the deaf, and the proceedings published a little later in Germany and France seem to confirm this impression.[73] Nevertheless this "improbable debate"—as Philippe Forget defined it—was epoch-making. The 1989 American edition, entitled *Dialogue and Deconstruction: The Gadamer-Derrida-Encounter,* contains new essays by philosophers from both sides.[74]

The legitimate question of the *difference* between hermeneutics and deconstruction was left open, even after the Paris meeting. Not coincidentally the debate continued primarily in North America, where the proximity of both philosophical currents led to doubts about whether truly different positions could be identified behind the different labels.[75] The common provenance of hermeneutics and deconstruction is entirely evident in Europe.[76] Both follow the way opened by Heidegger, engage with Hegel, and ceaselessly return, even if on different paths, to Greek philosophy. Their commonalities are also reflected in the themes they share. It is sufficient to think of the significance of art, especially literature and poetry.[77] Nonetheless hermeneutics and deconstruction represent various philosophical alternatives and demand that this difference be illuminated. Thus the question developed in the North American context in the 1980s has still lost none of its relevance: *How hermeneutic is deconstruction and how deconstructive is hermeneutics?*

Regarding the two protagonists, it seems that the debate at first left deeper traces in Gadamer's thinking, since he accepted Derrida's challenge and changed his positions, or made them more precise, in several essays: "Destruktion und Dekonstruktion" from 1985, "Frühromantik, Hermeneutik, Dekonstruktion" from 1987, "Dekonstruktion und Hermeneutik" from 1988, and "Hermeneutik auf der Spur" from 1994.[78] In these essays Gadamer clearly expressed how seriously he took the debate and revealed, above all, his esteem for the French philosopher. He recognized in Derrida one of the most important figures he had encountered since the publication of *Truth and Method:*

Back in the 1960s, when I had finished up my own project in philosophical hermeneutics and offered it to the public, I paused to take a look at the world around me. At that time, two important things struck me, in addition to the works of the later Wittgenstein. The first of these was that I met the poet Paul Celan, in whose late works I began to immerse myself. The other was the fact that Derrida's essay, *"Ousia et Grammè,"* published in the *Festschrift for Beaufret,* came into my hands, followed

later by the several important books that Derrida published in 1967 which I immediately began to study. (*GR* 377/*GW10* 149)

Derrida for his part only occasionally engaged hermeneutics, and when he did it
was especially to emphasize the difference between his deconstruction and hermeneutics.[79] But one year after Gadamer's death, on February 15, 2003, Derrida gave a memorial address in Heidelberg entitled "Rams: The Uninterrupted Dialogue between Two
Infinites, the Poem."[80] From the "strange interruption" of that time in Paris, Derrida
returned to the "uninterrupted dialogue," that "encounter" or "clash" between two
rams, alluding to the thread of the poem that bound them. He welcomed the word "dialogue" in his vocabulary in order to announce an unexpected interpretation: that "improbable debate" had been "successful," contrary to what most believed—and precisely
because of the interruption, which had not been an "original misunderstanding," but
"an *epoché* that made one hold one's breath, withhold judgment or conclusion."[81] Thus
it had left behind a living and provocative trace that promised more than one future.
In returning to the uninterrupted dialogue Derrida renews the topic of "interruption,"
which already arose during the Paris encounter, but which had afterward remained in
the shadows. He pointed, even if only indirectly, less to the proverbial opposition between orality and writing and more to the *question of understanding,* that motif which
had guided the debate and which could still illuminate the distance and the nearness
between both philosophies. For in the topic of understanding it becomes clear how
hermeneutics begins with unity and deconstruction proceeds from *difference.*

When Gadamer held his opening address in Paris, which was published subsequently with the title "Text und Interpretation," he seemed most concerned to distinguish himself from French philosophy in general and deconstruction in particular
through the conception of the "text" (*GR* 156–191/*GW2* 330–360).[82] He advocated the
need to give voice to the text again, in order to highlight its "unity of meaning" and
to lead it back to the dialogue from which it originally sprang.[83] His unquestionable
reversions to the "language of metaphysics"—Gadamer spoke for example of the "task
of understanding"—contributed to the fact that his remarks must have sounded like
a provocation to Derrida's ears. Gadamer reached his culmination when he spoke of
"the goodwill to try to understand one another," and with these words provoked the
discussion (*GR* 174/*GW2* 343).[84]

It is not surprising that on the next day Derrida responded with three short questions that aimed to call into question the entirety of hermeneutics and converge in
a single goal. Behind the efforts of hermeneutics to understand the other, behind its
"appeal to goodwill," is concealed Nietzsche's "will to power."[85] Already with his first
question, Derrida charges hermeneutics with a relapse into metaphysics. The will to
understand, which precedes every concrete interaction between speakers, suggests for
Derrida the outlines of an ethical axiom that would equate Gadamer's good will to
understand with Kant's "good will." Would not the good will to understand, which

s as axiomatic and unconditioned as the "absolute value" of Kant's will, amount to a new version of metaphysical "subjectivity," which would, following Heidegger's expressed suspicions, amount to a domination of Being? With a second question Derrida appeals to psychoanalysis, which is of course a borderline case, but nevertheless paradigmatic for abandoning "good will" and so bears witness to the failure of the 'living dialogue." Habermas had already recognized a problematic limit in psychoanalysis and expressed his doubts about whether it could be integrated into a general hermeneutics. For his part, Derrida emphasized that psychoanalytic discourse would even explode the broad interpretative context that Gadamer suggested. To this extent it calls for a kind of productive interpretation that would at first require a rupture. Derrida's third, philosophically decisive question turned around this concept of the rupture, or better, the interruption. What came under discussion here was what Gadamer called "understanding." One would have to ask, according to Derrida, whether the condition of understanding would be not the limitless readiness for dialogue, the continuous relation to the other, but instead the "the interruption of rapport, a certain rapport of interruption, the suspending of all mediation."[86] With this the suspicion of deconstruction overtakes the hermeneutic dialogue. Deconstruction seems to offer an alternative view because it prefers the interruption, protects disunity, preserves the difference and the otherness of the other, which cannot be appropriated, as well as the impossibility of understanding.

Gadamer responded with an equally brief paper entitled "Und dennoch: Macht des Guten Willens."[87] He lets the contradictions in Derrida's position appear by using the classic argument against the skeptics. "I am finding it difficult to understand these questions that have been addressed to me. But I will make an effort, as anyone would do who wants to understand another person or be understood by the other" (*DD* 55/*TI* 59). However, this "effort" has nothing to do with metaphysics or with Kant's "good will." Gadamer would much rather draw on the Platonic Socrates, who explains in the *Gorgias* that it would be better to be refuted than to refute.[88] This principle, in which hermeneutics recognizes itself again, is however not an ethical instance. "*Even immoral beings try to understand one another*" (*DD* 55/*TI* 59). Thus it is a matter of a phenomenological position describing the everyday practices of speaking and understanding. Whoever opens their mouth to speak would like to be understood—unless he or she wants to hide something. Derrida and Nietzsche do not constitute exceptions: "both speak and write in order to be understood" (*DD* 57/*TI* 61).[89] But this in no way means that nonunderstanding and misunderstanding could be eliminated. Gadamer agrees with Derrida that there is no unbroken understanding. The psychoanalytic dialogue, which aims to understand not what the speaker wants to say, but what he or she does not want to say, is an extreme manifestation of such a *break*.

Then where does the distance lie between Gadamer and Derrida, if not in the need for the interruption? For hermeneutics the interruption is not something fundamental and originary, because the prelude of language always takes precedence. Thus interruption already writes itself into the constellation of language; it is difference that inscribes this unity. Here hermeneutics shows its proximity to the critique of ideology.[90] A still greater distance from deconstruction is shown in the conception of the rupture. Even where the rupture is more noticeable and the collision more violent, as in the work of art and above all in the poetic text, hermeneutics takes up this collision but does not strengthen it, just as it also does not deepen it. Rather it acts in the reverse way: for hermeneutics the interruption opens the dialogue, but does not close it off. Though it may know that the rupture never heals, that nonunderstanding is never eliminated, hermeneutics gives itself over to an infinite dialogue.[91] This is, by the way, the position that Gadamer also takes up in the debate with Derrida. One year after the encounter in Paris, Gadamer writes: "Whoever wants me to take deconstruction to heart and insists on difference stands at the beginning of a conversation, not at its end" (*DD* 113/*GW*2 372).

The distance between hermeneutics and deconstruction, in other words, lies not in the good will to understand but in understanding itself, in the way in which understanding follows either from the *unity* of the *uninterrupted dialogue* or from the *difference* of the *interruption*. For Gadamer, one perspective points to the other. After Heidegger's attempt to dismantle the language of metaphysics there are for Gadamer only two ways, or perhaps one common path, that could still lead into the openness of philosophical experience: the path of hermeneutics, which goes from dialectics back to dialogue, and the path of deconstruction, which in *écriture* causes the laceration of metaphysics.[92]

In his memorial speech, "Béliers," Derrida returns to the topic of interruption, which this time refers to a final interruption, the separation of life and death. What will become of the dialogue after death has stamped its seal on it? Will there still be a dialogue after death? The dialogue continues, according to Derrida, and follows the traces in those who survive, who in the future will allow the voice of the dead friend to be heard. The promise and the obligation find their expression in the verse of the poet who brought the two philosophers together: Paul Celan. *The world is gone, I must carry you.*[93] The topic of death interweaves itself here with the topic of dialogue, but also with the topic of the poem. Two works by Gadamer stand in the background: *Poem and Conversation* and *Who Am I and Who Are You?* The death of the other is the "world after the end of the world."[94] The surviving one remains alone, robbed of the world of the other, remains in the world outside of the world, responsible alone and thereby determined to carry both the other and his or her world further. As Heidegger had pointed to the nearness of "thinking" (*Denken*) to "thanking" (*Danken*), Derrida draws together "thinking" (*penser*) and "weighing" (*peser*). In order to think and to weigh, also in the sense of bearing a weight, one must therefore carry, carry within oneself and on oneself. Yet

> *To carry* now no longer has the meaning of "to comprise" [*comporter*], to include, to comprehend in the self, but rather *to carry oneself for bear oneself toward* [*se porter*

vers] the infinite inappropriability of the other, toward the encounter with its absolute transcendence in the very inside of me, that is to say, in me outside of me.[95]

It means, above all, to transmit and translate what is untranslatable, what will remain as such, as an irreducible surplus, if that remainder of "unreadability" will be preserved which hermeneutics has made possible and which makes hermeneutics possible. The obligation of deconstruction consists of *carrying* hermeneutics, and in the process to perceive what is common to them and to preserve the remainder of the difference. Unity and difference, difference and unity, offer in return the uncanny secret of their elusive reference. Between two infinities, Celan is the *tertium datur*, more than the point of convergence, a point of new orientation.

5. Hermeneutics or Nihilism?

The unique history of hermeneutics in Italy began with the translation of *Truth and Method*, which Gianni Vattimo published in 1972.[96] Gadamer is read, studied, and reviewed, and his thought finds such widespread resonance that it is almost seen as the result of the indigenous philosophical tradition. But more than anywhere else, hermeneutics in Italy essentially becomes the *koiné* of philosophy, with all the advantages and the disadvantages that this brings. It delivers a shared idiom for many and various voices, whereby it becomes difficult in this polyphony to find a common tone in which such vastly different philosophical projects could be harmonized.[97]

Hermeneutics fits into a many-sided and eclectic horizon in Italy. Its acceptance has been encouraged by historicism, which since Benedetto Croce (1866–1952) has deliberately aimed to do justice to the individual and the differentiated character of historical reality. Yet hermeneutics finds a fruitful ground above all in the humanistic tradition, which already with Vico had contributed to a rediscovery of rhetoric. This strong affinity also explains why the phenomenological components of hermeneutics at first remained hidden. The enormous spread of Heidegger's philosophy, which found easy entry within existentialism, led to a certain antagonism toward phenomenology. Heidegger opened the door for Gadamer, so to speak. But we should nevertheless ask how advantageous this was for Gadamer. "Heidegger and Gadamer" is the formula that gained quick acceptance and became questionable interpretive cipher for Gadamer's philosophy.

A key role in the reception of hermeneutics in Italy was played by Luigi Pareyson (1918–91). Far more influenced by the Christian tradition than by Greek philosophy, Pareyson saw in Fichte and Schelling a possible corrective to Hegel, whereas his existentialism brought him much closer to Jaspers than to Heidegger. These features alone make visible the distance separating him from Gadamer.

Certainly there is no lack of contact points. In his 1971 work, *Verita e interpretazione*, Pareyson emphasizes that the original relation to Being is necessarily hermeneutic, which appears above all in art.[98] By highlighting the irreplaceability of the person in order to have access to truth, however, Pareyson at the same time emphasizes the strongly personal character of truth. According to him, hermeneutic truth unfolds in an endless series of interpretations that, to be sure, do not reciprocally relativize each other, yet nevertheless cannot claim the absoluteness that remains reserved only for its inexhaustible source. If truth is such, then every interpretative experience turns out to be an experience of freedom. This is the thesis that underlies his posthumous book from 1995, *Ontologia della libertà*.[99] His distance from Gadamer becomes clearly visible here: Pareyson places the accent on *interpreting*, which comes about as "congeniality," whereas Gadamer accents *understanding*, which results primarily from a "collision." Moreover, the historical character of truth, which for philosophical hermeneutics is irrevocable, is increasingly passed over in silence by Pareyson, until it tragically becomes silent in the immemorial that is the source of mythos. "Ontological and personal" thought, concerned with the question of salvation, declines itself in this source, in a hermeneutics of Christianity as the founding myth of modernity.

This obvious difference between Gadamer and Pareyson determines the fate of philosophical hermeneutics in Italy, for most of the representatives of hermeneutics come from the Pareyson school, and almost all of them rely on him in an unmediated way.

Isolated and emblematic is the figure of Valerio Verra (1928–2001), who, as a student of Pareyson, was nevertheless strongly influenced by Gadamer. Already in 1963, Verra wrote a balanced and insightful review of *Truth and Method,* and at the same time explicitly showed his support.[100] Verra devoted significant essays to philosophical hermeneutics: from the early ones on the question of the consciousness of effective history to the later, in which he compares Gadamer's aesthetics to Kant's and Hegel's and thereby shows how far hermeneutics is from any relativization of truth. Nonetheless his interpretations, which remain close to the texts and take Plato and Hegel as reference points, have to this day found only limited resonance.

The "urbanization of the Heideggerian province," which in the meantime has become almost a continent, took place toward the end of the 1970s in a complex context. The renewal of Marxism, which was to be freed from its Enlightenment inheritance as well as from the systematic and closed thinking of Hegel, found a new starting point in Nietzsche's critique of modern subjectivity and in Heidegger's destruction of metaphysics. With the "crisis of reason," which the Frankfurt School had warned of for years, the debate began about postmodernity.

The protagonist of this debate is Gianni Vattimo (b. 1936), who, as the student of Pareyson, Löwith, and Gadamer, lastingly influenced the impact of hermeneutics into Italy. He is to be thanked not only for his excellent translation of *Truth and Method,* but also for the resounding success of this work.[101]

Though he was an original interpreter of philosophical hermeneutics, Vattimo also developed his own philosophy, with references primarily to Nietzsche and Heidegger. In the extent to which he, over time, more clearly emphasized his distance from Gadamer's hermeneutics, Vattimo's philosophy emerged as an independent project. After 1983 his philosophy takes the name *pensiero debole,* or "weak thought."

"Nihilism" became his key term. The history of Being, which for the Heidegger of *Being and Time* had suffered the most extreme transformation into the *mè ón*, in other words, the negation into that not-being which is the nothing, is welcomed by Vattimo in its decline. Weak thought, which is conscious of this "weakening" of Being, takes it up and sees in nihilism "the only path possible for ontology."[102] Embracing this declining Being, which, groundless, hermeneutically gives itself in becoming, in the transitory forms of history and language, weak thought in turn plays itself out in an infinite play of interpretations. In light of the identification of Being and language, Vattimo reads hermeneutics as "the ontology of the decline of Being," or as the "ontology of actuality"—if the contemporary age is the "age of nihilism."[103] In this way, weak ontology moves in Nietzsche's wake and recognizes itself again in that "complete" nihilism that determines, after the disappearance of all values, that it no longer possesses the truth, that truth is given only in the infinite perspectival effects of interpretations. The conquest of truth would accordingly be "a *path leading away from the real* as the immediate pressure of the given, the incontrovertible imposition of the in itself."[104] Nietzsche's perspectivism plays a decisive role here and sets in motion a philosophy of interpretation—in Vattimo's recuperation of the famous saying, "there are no facts, only interpretations." At the same time, Pareyson's influence should not be underestimated. This is true both for the breadth of the interpretation and for the meaning that Christianity has in Vattimo's later philosophy. In a hermeneutics that is attentive not so much to the meaning of Being but to its history, and is thus prepared to recognize its own event character and its own provenance, Christianity, read in light of the present, reveals itself to be that interpretative event from which hermeneutics itself emerges. The birth of the *verbum*, which takes the place of the "death of God," leads the way to the nihilistic process of the weakening of God's Being, that downgrading which initiates the "secularization" of Being. The Christian *kénosis* is thus for Vattimo the origin and fate of hermeneutics as nihilistic ontology, which in taking up, even promoting, the weakening of God's Being retains support only through *caritas*. This religious outcome should not be misunderstood. Aesthetic experience finds a new voice that was already central in the first phase of Vattimo's thought.[105] In late modernity, for Vattimo, art, recognizing itself in its truth claim as secularized religion, can help religion to free itself of its dogmatic content.

But what remains here of Gadamer's philosophical hermeneutics? Weak thought is a particular reworking of hermeneutics—but not only that. Here one must guard against confusion: *hermeneutics is not nihilism*. It is also important to hold these two terms apart from each other in the future, in order both to do justice to Vattimo's philosophical contribution and to bring clarity to the debate about hermeneutics, which could have further positive effects for the debate between continental and analytic philosophy.

As hard as one may try, it is impossible to find the word "nihilism" in Gadamer's writings.[106] But it is even more important that a "hermeneutic ontology" represents a kind of *contradictio in adjecto*, since hermeneutics has taken leave of ontology as *logos*, which wants to say what Being is.[107] Thus in hermeneutics there is no longer the concern for Being, and just as little the thought of "overcoming" that Vattimo takes from Heidegger. If this absence of Being and the concern for Being is taken into account, then Gadamer's hermeneutics is nearer to Derrida's deconstruction. And if hermeneutics does not speak of Being, then it speaks even less of nothingness. The path of philosophical hermeneutics is in these ways exactly opposite to nihilism and its "me-ontology," or the study of non-being: hermeneutics reads *mè ón* in Plato's sense as *ouk ésti*. From the abyss of nothingness, hermeneutics rethinks the Being of nothing as being other; the transformation that occurs is *from Being to alterity*. The lack of any tragic accent in hermeneutics is simply further confirmation of this change. Not coincidentally, Vattimo senses in hermeneutics the disappearance of that tragic element which still marked Heidegger's ontology, in a vision of history and language that is all too "irenic" for him. Hermeneutics leaves behind the negativity of a limit that is nothing and silence, in order to turn to the beyond of the other. In the consciousness of the limit, and in the instance of the beyond, that "religious comportment" of hermeneutics becomes visible, which Gadamer consistently summarized with the famous title from a discourse of Kierkegaard's: "On what is edifying in the thought that against God one is always wrong" (GR371/GW10 70).

What weak thought undoubtedly does have in common with philosophical hermeneutics is the rejection of the *ultimate foundation* of philosophy. But the way in which this rejection is conceived again shows an important difference, which goes by the name of Nietzsche. While Vattimo separates hermeneutics from phenomenology, he gives considerable space to Nietzsche's philosophy of interpretation. Accordingly, he conceives of hermeneutics as a "philosophy of interpretation." Yet *hermeneutics is not a philosophy of interpretation* and hermeneutics has never understood itself as such. This is probably the greatest misunderstanding that still burdens the reception of hermeneutics.[108] The question that Gadamer asks is that of *understanding*—not the question of *interpretation*. Understanding is not interpretation; interpretation is rather a borderline case of understanding.[109] Wherever understanding is replaced by interpretation, there Nietzsche's influence makes itself felt.

Gadamer stands just as far from Nietzsche as he stands close to Plato and Hegel. How can this distance be explained? Here it is not question of an aversion, but rather of philosophical motivation. Gadamer sees in Nietzsche's hermeneutic radicalism the reverse side of Cartesian metaphysics, since a truth that does not exist, or no longer exists, is still the absolute truth of the *fundamentum inconcussum*. Measured by the absoluteness of this truth, everything else will appear as mere interpretation and become relativized to a perspective. Here lies the complicity of metaphysics and nihilism, which hermeneutics cannot accept. Correspondingly, it also does not accept the resignation that takes the lack of absolute values and fixed positions as characteristic of our age. To see a collapse of all support in the lack of an ultimate foundation of truth is, rather, the indication of intellectual arrogance, another form of the will to power.[110]

But even if it puts metaphysics at stake and rejects the claims of science, which forgets its roots in finitude, hermeneutics does not therefore deliver itself over to the swindle of a perspectivism in which everything is indifferent. Philosophical hermeneutics does not give up on truth. In no way does it abandon every support. For hermeneutics the support is not simply found in the other, in the otherness that cannot be appropriated, but in the Being with the other.

6. A Hermeneutics of the Other: New Perspectives

In an essay devoted to Gadamer's philosophy in 2002, Charles Taylor (b. 1931) writes: "The great challenge of this century . . . is that of understanding the other," and he adds that precisely on this issue "Gadamer has made a tremendous contribution to twentieth-century thought."[111] Yet for some decades, the way in which hermeneutics has from the beginning conceived itself as the *understanding of the other* has been sharply and to some extent vehemently disputed.

An important part of the debate in continental philosophy, marked by the "thought of difference," has energetically argued for the right of the individual to his or her otherness. Hence otherness has been advanced as an ethical category, whose recognition and respect are strongly promoted. But such a focus on alterity is a *novum* in Western philosophy. As is well known, the difference between the one and the other has been seen by most philosophers as merely accidental, and thus not as important for reflection. In this sense the question of the possibility of the radical otherness of the other has distinguished twentieth-century thought.[112] On this everyone would probably agree. What is problematic, however, is to determine where and how the question of the other was first raised. Already here opinions would begin to differ. For those who represent the thought of difference, and who above all connect it with more recent French philosophy, the invention of the other has an unquestionable origin, namely, phenomenology. The question of the knowability of the other first arose in the phenomenological investigations of Husserl, who was one of the first philosophers to deal with the topic of intersubjectivity. With this claim, though, other sources are put aside, beginning with the Jewish tradition, which was heavily influenced not only by the "philosophers of dialogue," Buber and Rosenzweig, but also by Levinas, if not also by Derrida. What is neglected and forgotten by this view, however, is also the source of hermeneutics, indeed even the hermeneutics of Schleiermacher.

Undeniably, hermeneutics raises the question of understanding for the first time in philosophy. As with the question of the other, so the question of understanding had previously had no philosophical relevance. Presumably the one question belongs with the other. In any case hermeneutics unfolds with the guiding question of understanding, which in a discontinuous continuity provides the background in which the question of the otherness of the other becomes unavoidable. Yet hermeneutics still faces the objection that it seeks, in the process of understanding, to reduce the difference of the other to identity. Thus understanding would conceal the "destruction of the individual by the universal."[113] Even the simple repetition of what one has heard would be, secretly or not according to this view, under pressure to conform. Understanding would basically mean wanting-to-understand. Unmasked as the last version of the metaphysics of will, the hermeneutic project, in which the attempt to reach understanding would always amount to a consensus and thereby to the reduction of the other to oneself, should be rejected out of hand. *The misunderstood understanding of hermeneutics is reduced*—perhaps violently?—to an act of violence. Seen in this way, hermeneutics—as the basic tenor of its critics could by summarized—would dispense with every ethical dimension.

This diametrical opposition between philosophical hermeneutics and the thought of alterity, however, seems quite conspicuous and questionable, as if the one would exclude and would have to exclude the other. Such an opposition, which is scarcely motivated by philosophical concerns, can perhaps be explained by the strategic need that forces the thought of alterity to gain in profile by emphasizing the break with hermeneutics. To this end the philosophical hermeneutics of Gadamer is presented as the last, suspicious version of the old way of thinking. The suspicion is fed by the proximity of philosophical hermeneutics to Plato, Hegel, and not least to Heidegger. But what is decisive is the, more or less conscious, emphatic demand to free oneself from German philosophy, to break with it forever, to a certain extent repress it, and only to save phenomenology from it. Not coincidentally, hermeneutics is accepted in this context only insofar as it can be brought back to its phenomenological roots.

In following this strategy several themes are ignored or even passed over in silence, while at the same time the accent is placed upon a few, mostly extrapolated, formulations. These allegedly show that hermeneutic understanding would involve the appropriation of the other, the integration, inclusion, and finally even the very incorporation of what is radically foreign. Animated by the frenzy of understanding, hermeneutics would strive to make the nonunderstandable understandable, the ungraspable graspable and intelligible; it would simply conquer and overwhelm the foreign, bracket out the different and seek to force it into a consensus or into a pseudo-dialogue.

"Beyond Meaning and Understanding": thus reads a chapter in the volume *Vielstimmigkeit der Rede* (*The Polyphony of Discourse*), the last in the four-volume *Studien zur Phänomenologie des Fremden* (*Studies on the Phenomenology of the Foreign*) by Bernhard Waldenfels (b. 1934). In this chapter Waldenfels critically confronts Gadamer's hermeneutics. The fundamental critique he levels against hermeneutics is: "Is the foreign allowed to be conquered on the basis of hermeneutics, or is it likely to put hermeneutics itself into question?"[114] Following Schleiermacher, Gadamer would consider the "overcoming of foreignness" as the "actual task" of hermeneutics. In this overcoming, in this movement from the foreign to one's own, one would have to discern a moderate Hegelianism. Similar to Derrida, Waldenfels thinks he recognizes a "will to meaning" in the presumed hermeneutic "usurping" of the foreign.[115] Although he admits that the foreign is more than a moment for hermeneutics that must be overcome, Waldenfels nevertheless aims to bring into effect that "anti-hermeneutic counter-force," which would arise from the "incursions of the incomprehensible" and would as such provoke hermeneutics. Without this counter-force, hermeneutics would circle around itself and, searching for the "original form" of the dialogue, or for the "true dialogue," would simply only validate itself.[116] Against the "generally ordered understanding of hermeneutics," which already as a fore-understanding wants to incorporate or eliminate each new claim by the foreign, Waldenfels returns to Levinas's "asymmetry," which is meant to interrupt the dialectical tension between the claim and the response. The dialogue begins differently for Levinas than for Gadamer; it does not begin with the "common." "The much-proclaimed 'dialogue that we are'"—Waldenfels asserts—"comes from the distance of the stranger, whose claim precedes every partnership."[117]

It would be doing an injustice not only to Gadamer, however, but also to Schleiermacher to claim that the foreign would be *sublated*. Waldenfels's view, according to which the incomprehensible is "an indissoluble limit that shifts but never lets itself be extinguished," has already been very clearly formulated by Schleiermacher as well as by Humboldt.[118] It is certain, for Schleiermacher, that "non-understanding never wants to dissolve itself completely."[119] Perhaps even more clearly, Humboldt emphasizes: "Thus all understanding is always at the same time non-understanding, all assent in thought and feeling is at the same time a dissent."[120] Since Humboldt and Schleiermacher, who not by chance took a very critical position toward Hegel, understanding has no longer been valued as self-evident, since it is influenced from the outset by nonunderstanding and misunderstanding. This significant and controversial legacy of the hermeneutic tradition should not be disavowed. Within the phenomenological lifeworld Gadamer follows the way to language opened by hermeneutics, and it is precisely language that is the watershed that distinguishes his perspective on dialogue from that of Waldenfels.

From a hermeneutic standpoint one can support without hesitation the statement by Levinas: "The other remains infinitely transcendent, infinitely foreign."[121] The question for hermeneutics, however, is the question of the *foreign*. What is meant by the "foreign"? Is it the original, radical, absolute foreign? The *absolute* foreign is endangered by the silence that threatens every absolute. It remains inarticulate and inarticulable—beyond human language, beyond hermeneutics. It is certainly not the case that hermeneutics undercuts the understanding of the foreign. Rather, it develops its conception of the foreign on the basis of the understanding. Once more, language offers the starting point for this movement. To this extent the priority for hermeneutics is not the foreign, but the common linguisticality of understanding. The foreign can emerge as such only in relation to what is held in common; the foreign can show itself only on the basis of linguistic unity. Foreignness has duration, relative to this unity. The absolutely foreign cannot be spoken of hermeneutically, since this would have the position of something entirely inadequate. For hermeneutics the foreign is always relative—it steps forward wherever there is already an access, wherever linguisticality is already common. Foreignness is the difference of the unintelligible that breaks in on what has already been understood and taken as self-evident, in order to initiate the movement of understanding once again.[122] Thus the foreign is discovered in each understanding. The foreign is, however, not an absolute quantity. The foreign is always relatively foreign, and as such it is *the unintelligible of the other*. The relativity of foreignness, however, is in no way the subjugation of the foreign to understanding. Foreignness is not obtained by understanding; it remains unobtainable in understanding. The charge from those who want to give priority to the foreign as a radical provocation is, therefore, unwarranted.[123] Despite all criticisms, philosophical hermeneutics does appear to open a play-space in which the other as feminine, masculine, or neuter can intervene as an unexpected, extraordinary event.[124]

As hermeneutics can be brought into a productive dialogue with deconstruction, however, so it can be shaken, provoked, and spurred on by a phenomenological starting point that places the accent on foreignness. The "sting of the foreign" can drive hermeneutics to be at home in a world it never believed in, to get to know this world further through the other and with the other.[125] It is certain in any case that a future hermeneutics cannot ignore the revised accentuation that has been introduced by the phenomenology of the foreign. The problem for hermeneutics is the *return (Rückkehr)*. As long as hermeneutics remains bound up with Heidegger's legacy, it will hardly be able to escape the temptation to return to the origin and thereby to follow the movement from one's own to the foreign and, through the foreign, to return to one's own. The simple abandonment of the return would, on the other hand, end in the swindle of nihilism. Yet the urbanization of the province enables for hermeneutics an opening to the globalized world, from which the movement toward the other and the return can be thought anew.

For hermeneutics, though, the other in their otherness can be recognized only from the starting point of linguistic commonality. Thus it takes its point of departure from the communal.[126] It should not be forgotten that hermeneutics limits itself to describing the everyday practice of speaking and understanding phenomenologically. Hence it is not a question of striving, making an effort, having a task or even a duty in a moral sense. Here at first an ethical and political dimension is lacking. For language is the articulation of our world. Only on the basis of this linguistic community can an ethics and a politics be erected: "The commonality between the partners is so very strong that the point is no longer the fact that I think this and you think that, but rather it involves *the shared interpretation of the world which makes moral and social solidarity possible*" (GR 96/GW2 188). Hermeneutics has never campaigned for consensus and reconciliation. The "agreement" from which all speakers proceed is the harmony of a common language. For speaking is always a *coming-to-agreement*. The other is already recognized here: even before every agreement with oneself, each speaker comes to an agreement with the other. Hence, to speak means to articulate the linguistic commonality further and otherwise. That does not prevent language, however, in its always open movement between familiarity and foreignness, understanding and nonunderstanding, from offering not only the starting point but also the paradigm of an ethics, a politics, or justice, which can be thought on the basis of its hospitable, common, and nevertheless differentiating in-between. This in-between is the space for the other and with the other, the undetermined of hermeneutic truth, and the finite meeting point of common words, which opens participation in the infinitude of the dialogue.

Timeline

February 11, 1900	Hans-Georg Gadamer is born in Marburg.
October 1902	The family moves to Breslau.
1907–18	HGG attends the school *Zum Heiligen Geist* (Holy Ghost).
1918–19	Registered at the University in Breslau. HGG listens to the lectures in philosophy by Richard Hönigswald.
October 1919	HGG continues his studies at the University of Marburg and attends, among others, lectures on art history (by Richard Hamann), Romance studies (by Ernst Robert Curtius), and philosophy (by Paul Natorp and Nicolai Hartmann).
April–September 1921	HGG studies for a semester in Munich, where he hears the name of Heidegger for the first time in a seminar given by Moritz Geiger.
May 17, 1922	Completion of the dissertation with Natorp. Title: "The Essence of Pleasure according to the Platonic Dialogues."
August 1922	HGG falls victim to polio and must spend many months in isolation.
April 20, 1923	Marriage to Frida Kratz.
April–July 1923	HGG spends the summer semester in Freiburg, where he attends courses taught by Martin Heidegger and meets Edmund Husserl.
1924	First publication: "On the Idea of a System in Philosophy." Discussion of the *Metaphysics of Knowledge* by Nicolai Hartmann.
October 1924	Gadamer follows Heidegger and returns to Marburg.
1925–1927	HGG studies classical philology with Paul Friedländer.
July 20, 1927	State examinations in classical philology.

February 23, 1929	Habilitation in philosophy with Martin Heidegger. Title: "Interpretation of Plato's 'Philebus.'"
July 10–12, 1930	On the invitation of Paul Friedländer, HGG participates in the famous conference of classical philologists in Naumburg (and also meets Werner Jaeger).
1931	The revised version of his habilitation is published by Meiner. Title: *Plato's Dialectical Ethics.*
1933	Hitler seizes power.
April 21, 1933	Martin Heidegger becomes rector of the University of Freiburg and officially announces his involvement with National Socialism.
1933–1937	HGG receives a teaching contract for "Ethics and Aesthetics" at the University of Marburg. Substitute positions in Kiel and Marburg.
January 24, 1934	Lecture on "Plato and the Poets" for the Society of the Friends of the Humanistic Gymnasium in Marburg, whose chairman was Rudolf Bultmann.
June 30, 1934	Röhm-Putsch. Hitler has the leader of the SA murdered and takes over the position himself.
April 1935	The National Socialist League of University Teachers (Dozentenbund) rejects Gadamer's application for the title of an unofficial assistant professor.
1936	In the summer semester Gadamer gives the lecture course on "Art and History," which later becomes the basis of *Truth and Method*
April 20, 1927	HGG becomes assistant professor of philosophy at the University of Marburg.
November 9, 1938	*Kristallnacht.* The universities in Germany are emptied by the emigration of the Jews.
January 1, 1939	HGG becomes associate professor of philosophy at the University of Leipzig.
September 1, 1939	Germany attacks Poland. The Second World War begins.
May 10, 1940	The Wehrmacht marches into Holland, Belgium, and France. HGG visits Karl Jaspers, who is in Heidelberg under house arrest.
June 22, 1941	Hitler orders the attack on the Soviet Union. The mass extermination of the Jews in Europe begins.

February 2, 1943	German capitulation in Stalingrad.
December 4, 1943	The center of Leipzig is completely destroyed by the Allies' bombing attacks.
June 6, 1944	Allied landing in Normandy. HGG hears the news from a woman student.
May 8, 1945	Capitulation of Leipzig.
January 21, 1946	HGG becomes the rector of the University of Leipzig, which has been reopened by the Russian occupying forces. Rector's speech: "On the Primordiality of Science."
October 1, 1948	Resettlement in the Western zone, where HGG is called to the University of Frankfurt.
March 30– April 9, 1948	Travels to Argentina, where he takes part in the first international philosophy congress after the war. HGG meets Löwith and Kuhn again.
September 2, 1949	HGG accepts the position as professor of philosophy at the University of Heidelberg.
June 1950	Moves to Heidelberg. Second marriage begins, to Käte Lekebusch.
May 27, 1951	Accepted into the Heidelberg Academy of Sciences.
1953	With Helmut Kuhn, HGG founds the journal *Philosophische Rundschau.*
November 19–30, 1957	Lectures in Leuven: "On the Problem of Historical Consciousness."
1960	*Truth and Method.* HGG is elected as the chairman of the General German Society for Philosophy (Allgemeine Deutsche Gesellschaft für Philosophie)
1961	Lecture tour in Italy (Milan and Rome). Meeting with Emilio Betti.
February 14, 1968	Retirement. But HGG continues his teaching activities.
1968–1988	HGG gives lectures and seminars at several universities in the United States.
February 11, 1970	Two-volume *Festschrift: Hermeneutik und Dialektik.* Debate with Habermas.
1971	Publication of the book *Hegels Dialektik* (*Hegel's Dialectic: Five Hermeneutical Studies*). HGG becomes knighted to the order, "Pour le merite," and wins both the *Bundesverdienstkreuzes* (the Federal Cross of Merit) and the Reuchlin Prize from the city of Pforzheim.

September 1972	Participation in the Celan Colloquium at the Goethe Institut in Paris. One year later publishes the book *Wer bin Ich und wer bist Du?* (*Gadamer on Celan: "Who Am I and Who Are You?" and Other Essays*).
December 16, 1976	In response to the death of Martin Heidegger, HGG holds the memorial address in Freiburg, "Being, Spirit, God," which later in 1983 appears in the book *Heideggers Wege* (*Heidegger's Ways*).
June 13, 1979	Hegel Prize from the city of Stuttgart. Jürgen Habermas gives the laudation, "Die Urbanisierung der Heideggerschen Provinz" ("The Urbanization of the Heideggerian Province").
April 25–27, 1981	Encounter with Jacques Derrida at the Goethe Institut in Paris.
May 2–9, 1981	First seminar at the Istituto Italiano per gli Studi filosofici in Naples, where HGG will return to almost every year until 1997.
November 12, 1981	Honorary doctorate at MacMaster University in Hamilton, Canada.
1982	Travels to Poland. HGG visits Breslau for the first time since the war.
1985	Publication of the *Gesammelte Werke* (*Collected Works*) begins with the publisher Mohr Siebeck in Tübingen.
May 25, 1986	Participation in Messkirch in the symposium for the Martin Heidegger Society (HGG remains an honorary member until his death). Lecture: "Der eine Weg Martin Heideggers" ("The One Way of Martin Heidegger")
June 15, 1986	Karl Jaspers Prize.
July 1989	First hermeneutics meeting organized in Heidelberg by North American philosophers.
November 9, 1989	Fall of the Berlin Wall, which leads to Germany's reunification one year later on October 3, 1990.
October 20, 1993	First trip to the new German states. Ceremonial address at the University of Leipzig.
February 11, 1995	The tenth and final volume of the *Collected Works* appears, entitled *Hermeneutik im Rückblick* (*Hermeneutics in Review*). Antonio Feltrinelli Prize of the Accademia dei Lincei in Rome.
February 12, 1996	Honorary doctorate from the University of Breslau (Wroclav). In the same year HGG receives the honorary doctorate from the University of Leipzig.
1997	In the United States a volume of the Library of Living Philosophers series dedicated to HGG appears.

March 27, 1997	Travels to Prague, where HGG receives an honorary doctorate.
June 24, 1999	Honorary doctorate from the University of Marburg.
February 11, 2000	A celebration in Gadamer's honor is organized by the city of Heidelberg and held at the university. Among the participants are Habermas, Rorty, Theunissen, Vattimo. Publication of HGG's last volume: *Hermeneutische Entwuerfe* (*Hermeneutic Sketches*). His students dedicate two *Festschriften* to HGG: *Hermeneutische Wege* (*Hermeneutic Ways*), published by Mohr Siebeck, and *Begegnungen mit Hans-Georg Gadamer* (*Encounters with Hans-Georg Gadamer*), published by Reclam.
July 7, 2000	Honorary doctorate from the University of Saint Petersburg.
March 13, 2002	HGG dies in a university clinic in Heidelberg.

Notes

1. See Helmut Kuhn, "Wahrheit und geschichtliches Verstehen. Bemerkungen zu Hans-Georg Gadamers philosophischer Hermeneutik," *Historische Zeitschrift* 193, no. 2 (1961): 376–389; Joseph Möller, "Wahrheit und Methode," *Theologische Quartalsschrift* 5 (1961): 467–471; Helmut Ogiermann, "Wahrheit und Methode," *Scholastik* 27 (1961): 403–406; Oskar Becker, "Zur Fragwürdigkeit der Transzendierung der ästhetischen Dimension der Kunst," *Philosophische Rundschau* 10 (1962): 225–238; Alphonse De Waehlens, "Sur une herméneutique de l'herméneutique," *Revue philosophique de Louvain* 60 (1962): 573–591; Heinz Kimmerle, "Hermeneutische Theorie oder ontologische Hermeneutik," *Zeitschrift für Theologie und Kirche* 59 (1962): 114–130; Karl-Otto Apel, "Wahrheit und Methode," *Hegel-Studien* 2 (1963): 314–322; Walter Hellebrand, "Der Zeitbogen," *Archiv für Rechts- und Sozialphilosophie* 49 (1963): 57–76; Otto Pöggeler, "Wahrheit und Methode," *Philosophischer Literaturanzeiger* 1 (1963): 6–16; Franz Wieacker, "Notizen zur Rechtshistorischen Hermeneutik," in *Nachrichten der Akademie der Wissenschaften zu Göttingen* (Göttingen: Vandenhoeck & Ruprecht, 1963), 1–22; Johannes Lohmann, "Wahrheit und Methode," *Gnomon* 37 (1965): 709–718; Klaus Dockhorn, "Hans-Georg Gadamer: Wahrheit und Methode," *Göttingen Gelehrte Anzeigen* 218 (1966): 169–206; Helmut Ogiermann, "Wahrheit und Methode (Zweite Auflage)," *Theologie und Philosophie* 14 (1966): 450–451. Of particular resonance was the review by Pannenberg, who claimed that Gadamer had fallen back into a Hegelian perspective: see Wolfhart Pannenberg, "Hermeneutik und Universalgeschichte," *Zeitschrift für Theologie und Kirche* 60 (1963): 90–121, reprinted in Hans-Georg Gadamer and Gottfried Boehm, *Die Hermeneutik und die Wissenschaften* (Frankfurt/M: Suhrkamp, 1978), 283–319.

2. See Emilio Betti, *Allgemeine Auslegungslehre als Methodik der Geisteswissenschaften* (Tübingen: Mohr, 1962). Betti published a summary of his theory in German as an open polemic against Gadamer: Emilio Betti, *Die Hermeneutik als allgemeine Methodik der Geisteswissenschaften* (Tübingen: Mohr, 1962).

3. Eric D. Hirsch, *Validity in Interpretation* (New Haven, Conn., and London: Yale University Press, 1967).

4. Hirsch, *Validity in Interpretation*, 255.

5. Gadamer, "Foreword to the Second Edition," *GW*2 441/*TM* xxxi.

6. Hans Robert Jauss, *Ästhetische Erfahrung und literarische Hermeneutik* (Munich: Wilhelm Fink, 1977); *Aesthetic Experience and Literary Hermeneutics,* trans. Michael Shaw (Minneapolis: University of Minnesota Press, 1982).

7. See Hans Robert Jauss, "Literaturgeschichte als Provokation der Literaturwissenschaft," in Rainer Warning, ed., *Rezeptionsästhetik* (Munich: Fink, 1994), 126–162; "Literary History as a Challenge to Literary Theory," in *Towards an Aesthetic of Reception,* trans. Timothy Bahti (Minneapolis: University of Minnesota Press, 1982).

8. See chapter 5, part 5, in this volume.

9. See Wolfgang Iser, *Der Akt des Lesens. Theorie ästhetischer Wirkung* (Munich: Fink, 1976); *The Act of Reading: A Theory of Aesthetic Response* (Baltimore and London: Johns Hopkins University Press, 1978. See Nicholas Davey, "Art's Enigma: Adorno, Gadamer and Iser on Interpretation," in Mirko Wischke and Michel Hofer, eds., *Gadamer verstehen/Understanding Gadamer* (Darmstadt: Wissenschaftliche Buchgesellschaft, 2003), 232–247.

10. See Hans Albert, *Traktat über kritische Vernunft* (1968), 5th ed. (Tübingen: Mohr Siebeck, 1991).

11. See Hans Albert, *Kritik der reinen Hermeneutik* (Tübingen: Mohr Siebeck, 1994).

12. See Thomas S. Kuhn, *The Structure of Scientific Revolutions* (Chicago: University of Chicago Press, 1962).

13. See Ernst Fuchs, *Hermeneutik* (1954), 4th ed. (Tübingen: Mohr, 1970); See also James M. Robinson, ed., *Die neue Hermeneutik* (Zürich: Zwingli, 1965). See also Hans-Josef Jeanrond, *Text und Interpretation als Kategorien theologischen Denkens* (Tübingen: Mohr Siebeck, 1986). Interesting comparisons between Gadamer's philosophical hermeneutics and Wittgenstein's linguistic-philosophical positions in relation to the New Testament are in Anthony C. Thiselton, *The Two Horizons: New Testament Hermeneutics and Philosophical Description with Special Reference to Heidegger, Bultmann, Gadamer and Wittgenstein* (Grand Rapids, Mich.: W. B. Eerdmans, 1980), 330–427. A defense of hermeneutics, particularly in regard to its productivity for theology, is by Bernd Jochen Hilberath, *Theologie zwischen Tradition und Kritik. Die philosophische Hermeneutik Hans-Georg Gadamers als Herausforderung des theologischen Selbstverständnisses* (Düsseldorf: Patmos, 1978). See also Charles Richard Ringa, *Gadamer's Dialogical Hermeneutics: The Hermeneutics of Bultmann, of the New Testament Sociologists, and of the Social Theologians in Dialogue with Gadamer's Hermeneutic* (Heidelberg: Winter, 1999). On a connection between hermeneutics and homilectics, see Jeffrey Francis Bullock, *Preaching with a Cupped Ear: Hans-Georg Gadamer's Philosophical Hermeneutics as Postmodern World* (New York: Peter Lang, 1000), 77–120. See also Fred Lawrence, "Gadamer, the Hermeneutic Revolution, and Theology," in Robert J. Dostal, ed., *The Cambridge Companion to Gadamer* (Cambridge: Cambridge University Press, 2002), 167–200, 188–189. A reading of Gadamer's hermeneutics from a theological standpoint has also been recently developed by Philippe Eberhard, *The Middle Voice in Gadamer's Hermeneutics* (Tübingen: Mohr Siebeck, 2004); on hermeneutics and theology, see esp. 172–215.

14. On Gadamer and Bultmann, see Thomas Ommen, "Bultmann and Gadamer: The Role of Faith in Theological Hermeneutics," *Thought* 59 (1984): 348–359; Jean Grondin, "Gadamer und Bultmann," in Wischke and Hofer, *Gadamer verstehen—Understanding Gadamer,* 186–208.

15. See Andre Wiercinski, ed., *Between the Human and the Divine: Philosophical and Theological Hermeneutics* (Toronto: Hermeneutic Press, 2002).

16. On Gadamer and Dworkin, see Kenneth Henley, "Protestant Hermeneutics and the Rule of Law: Gadamer and Dworkin," *Ratio-Juris* 3 (1990): 14–27.

17. See Giuseppe Zaccaria, *Ermeneutica e giurisprudenza. I fondamenti filosofici nella teoria di Hans-Georg Gadamer* (Milan: Giuffre, 1984).

18. See Reinhart Koselleck and Hans-Georg Gadamer, *Sprache und Hermeneutik. Eine Rede und eine Antwort* (Heidelberg: Manutius, 2000). See Reinhart Koselleck, *Vergangene Zukunft. Zur Se-*

mantik geschichtlicher Zeiten (Frankfurt/M: Suhrkamp, 1989). See also Koselleck, *Zeitschichten Studien zur Historik* (Frankfurt/M: Suhrkamp, 2000), with a contribution from Gadamer.

19. See Gadamer "Hermeneutik und Historismus" (1965), *GW2* 387–424, 398–399/*TM* 541–542. See also in this volume chapter 6, part 1.

20. Gadamer himself tries to take stock of this in his "Afterword to the Third Edition," *GW2* 449–478/*TM* 551–579; "Zwischen Phänomenologie und Dialektik—Versuch einer Selbstkritik," *GW2* 3–23.

21. In contrast, a discussion of the relation between philosophical hermeneutics and "weak thought" remains to be developed. See part 6 in this chapter.

22. Already in 1970 Tugendhat had expressed the desirability of a debate between hermeneutics, understood from its phenomenological roots, and linguistic analysis. See Ernst Tugendhat, "Phänomenologie und Sprachanalyse," in Rüdiger Bubner, Konrad Cramer, and Reiner Wiehl, eds., *Hermeneutik und Dialektik* (Tübingen: Mohr, 1970), 2:3–23.

23. See David C. Hoy, "Post-Cartesian Interpretation: Hans-Georg Gadamer and Donald Davidson," in Lewis E. Hahn, ed., *The Philosophy of Hans-Georg Gadamer* (Chicago: Open Court, 1997), 111–128. See also Karsten R. Steuber, "Understanding Truth and Objectivity: A Dialogue between Donald Davidson and Hans-Georg Gadamer," in Brice R. Wachterhauser, ed., *Hermeneutics and Truth* (Evanston, Ill.: Northwestern University Press, 1994), 148–171; Joel Weinsheimer, "Charity Militant: Gadamer, Davidson, and Post-Critical Hermeneutics," in *Revue international de philosophie* 54 (2000): 405–422; Bjorn Torgrim Ramberg, "Interpretation and Understanding in Gadamer and Davidson," in Carlos G. Prado, ed., *A House Divided: Comparing Analytic and Continental Philosophy* (Amherst, N.Y.: Humanity Books, 2003), 213–234.

24. See Jeff Malpas, "Gadamer, Davidson, and the Ground of Understanding," in Jeff Malpas, Ulrich Arnswald, and Jens Kertscher, eds., *Gadamer's Century: Essays in Honor of Hans-Georg Gadamer* (Cambridge, Mass.: MIT Press, 2002), 195–215. Davidson himself, who studied with Jaeger, has written on his relation to Gadamer in an essay on Plato's "Philebus." See Donald Davidson, "Gadamer and Plato's 'Philebus,'" in Hahn, *The Philosophy of Hans-Georg Gadamer*, 421–432. It must be underlined here, however, that "interpretation" for Davidson is a much more comprehensive concept that at times risks becoming too unspecific. Not coincidentally Davidson speaks of "radical interpretation," though he often does not distinguish between understanding and interpretation. See Donald Davidson, "Radical Interpretation," in Davidson, *Inquiries into Truth and Interpretation* (1984), 2nd ed. (Oxford and New York: Oxford University Press, 2001), 125–139. On this topic, see this chapter, part 5.

25. John McDowell, "Gadamer and Davidson on Understanding and Relativism," in *Gadamer's Century*, 173–194; McDowell, *Mind and World* (Cambridge: Cambridge University Press, 1994). A very informative contribution is the one by Alasdair MacIntyre, "On Not Having the Last Word: Thoughts on Our Debts to Gadamer," in *Gadamer's Century*, 157–172; see also his response to *Truth and Method* in MacIntyre, "Context of Interpretation: Reflections on Hans-Georg Gadamer's *Truth and Method*," in *Boston University Journal* 24 (1976): 41–46.

26. Rorty's case in this respect is characteristic. See part 3 of this chapter.

27. See Gianni Vattimo, *Beyond Interpretation: The Meaning of Hermeneutics for Philosophy*, trans. David Webb (Stanford, Calif.: Stanford University Press, 1998).

28. Especially the situation in Italy has been exemplary for this. See part 5 in this chapter.

29. See Gary E. Aylesworth, "Dialogue, Text, Narrative: Confronting Gadamer and Ricoeur," in Hugh J. Silverman, ed., *Gadamer and Hermeneutics* (New York: Routledge, 1991), 63–81; see also James Di Censo, *Hermeneutics and the Disclosure of Truth: A Study in the Work of Heidegger, Gadamer and Ricoeur* (Charlottesville: University Press of Virginia, 1990).

30. See Andrzej Przylebski, "Die Grenzen der hermeneutischen Vernunft. Über die vermeintlichen und wirklichen Begrenzungen der Hermeneutik Gadamers," in Wolfram Hogrebe, ed., *Grenzen und Grenzüberschreitungen. XIX Deutscher Kongress für Philosophie* (Bonn: Sinclair, 2002), 221–226.

31. Direct attacks have had little influence, as for example the one by Heinrich Rombach, *Welt und Gegenwelt. Umdenken über die Wirklichkeit. Die philosophische Hermeneutik* (Basel: Herder, 1983), who refers to a "hermetics" that is much more originary than hermeneutics, or the indirect critique by Luhmann, concerning the question of understanding. See Niklas Luhmann, *Soziale Systeme. Grundriss einer allgemeinenTheorie* (1987) (Frankfurt/M: Suhrkamp, 2000); see on this Jaromir Brejdak, "Der hermeneutische und der differentielle Begriff des Verstehens: Gadamer—*Luhmann*," in Andrzej Przylebski, ed., *Das Erbe Gadamers* (Frankfurt am Main: Peter Lang, 2006), 227–245.

32. Günter Figal has raised this very question, see Günter Figal, "Philosophische Hermeneutik—hermeneutische Philosophie," in Günter Figal, Jean Grondin, and Dennis J. Schmidt, *Hermeneutische Wege* (Tübingen: Mohr Siebeck 2000), 335–344; cf. also Figal, "Gadamer im Kontext. Zur Gestalt und den Perspektiven philosophischer Hermeneutik," in Wischke and Hofer, *Gadamer verstehen/Understanding Gadamer*, 141–156. Figal's most recent book can also be understood as an answer to this question, cf. *Gegenständlichkeit. Das Hermeneutische und die Philosophie* (Tübingen: Mohr Siebeck, 2006). On this topic, see also Donatella Di Cesare, "Re-interpreting Hermeneutics: U-topias from the Continent," *Philosophy Today* 49 (2005): 325–332.

33. See Jürgen Habermas, "Zu Gadamer's *Wahrheit und Methode*," in Karl-Otto Apel, ed., *Hermeneutik und Ideologiekritik* (Frankfurt am Main: Suhrkamp, 1971), 45–56; "A Review of Gadamer's Truth and Method," in *Understanding and Social Inquiry*, ed. and trans. Fred R. Dallmayr and Thomas A. McCarthy (Notre Dame, Ind.: University of Notre Dame Press, 1977), 335–363. This research report was later republished: Jürgen Habermas, *Zur Logik der Sozialwissenschaften* (1970), 5th expanded ed. (Frankfurt/M: Suhrkamp, 1982), 331–366; *On the Logic of the Social Sciences* (Cambridge, Mass.: MIT Press, 1988), 143–171.

34. Gadamer, "Rhetorik, Hermeneutik und Ideologiekritik," *GW2* 232–250; "Rhetoric, Hermeneutics, and Ideology-Critique," trans. G. B. Hess and R. E. Palmer, in *Rhetoric and Hermeneutics in Our Time: A Reader*, ed. Walter Jost and Michael J. Hyde (New Haven, Conn.: Yale University Press, 1997), 313–334.

35. The debate included representatives of both ways of thinking, such as Karl-Otto Apel, Claus von Bormann, Rüdiger Bubner, and Hans-Joachim Giegel, and has been collected in the volume by Karl-Otto Apel, ed., *Hermeneutik und Ideologiekritik*.

36. See Habermas, *Zur Logik der Sozialwissenschaften* (Frankfurt am Main: Suhrkamp, 1970), 240ff.; *On the Logic of the Social Sciences* (Cambridge, Mass.: MIT Press, 1988), 206–207. Habermas contributed substantially to making Wittgenstein known in Germany.

37. Habermas, *Zur Logik der Sozialwissenschaften*, 272; *On the Logic of the Social Sciences*, 179.

38. See chapter 7, part 6, in this volume.

39. Habermas, *Zur Logik der Sozialwissenschaften*, 284; *On the Logic of the Social Sciences*, 163.

40. See chapter 5, parts 3–5, in this volume.

41. Habermas, *Zur Logik der Sozialwissenschaften*, 305; *On the Logic of the Social Sciences*, 170.

42. Habermas, *Zur Logik der Sozialwissenschaften*, 309; *On the Logic of the Social Sciences*, 174.

43. See chapter 8, part 6, in this volume.

44. Habermas, *Zur Logik der Sozialwissenschaften*, 307; *On the Logic of the Social Sciences*, 172.

45. Habermas, *Zur Logik der Sozialwissenschaften*, 309; *On the Logic of the Social Sciences*, 174.

46. Habermas, *Zur Logic der Sozialwissenschaften*, 342; *On the Logic of the Social Sciences*, 188.

47. See Paul Ricoeur, *De l'interpretation. Essai sur Freud* (Paris, 1965); Paul Ricoeur, *Freud and Philosophy: An Essay on Interpretation*, trans. Denis Savage (New Haven, Conn.: Yale University Press, 1970).

48. See Gadamer, "Rhetorik, Hermeneutik und Ideologiekritik," *GW2* 238; "Rhetoric, Hermeneutics, and Ideology-Critique," 320.

49. See Gadamer, "Replik zu 'Hermeneutik und Ideologiekritik'" (1971), *GW2* 251–275, 257–259.

50. Gadamer, "Replik zu 'Hermeneutik und Ideologiekritik," *GW2* 272.

51. See chapter 8, part 8, in this volume. Gadamer draws explicitly here on Jacques Lacan and the interpretation of Lacan by Lang: Helmut Lang, *Die Sprache und das Unbewusste. Jacques Lacans Grundlegung der Psychoanalyse* (Frankfurt/M: Suhrkamp, 1973).

52. Gadamer, "Rhetorik, Hermeneutik und Ideologiekritik," *GW*2 243; "Rhetoric, Hermeneutics, and Ideology-Critique," 325.

53. Habermas, *Zur Logik der Sozialwissenschaften*, 334; *On the Logic of the Social Sciences*, 174.

54. Gadamer, "Replik zu 'Hermeneutik und Ideologiekritik,'" *GW*2 265.

55. See Gadamer, "Replik zu 'Hermeneutik und Ideologiekritik,'" *GW*2 272. See also Karl-Otto Apel, *Transformation der Philosophie*, 2 vols., vol. 1: *Sprachanalytik, Semiotik, Hermeneutik*; vol. 2: *Das Apriori der Kommunikationsgemeinschaft* (Frankfurt/M: Suhrkamp, 1973), as well as more recently: Apel, "Regulative Ideas or Truth Happening? An Attempt to Answer the Question of the Conditions of the Possibility of Valid Understanding," in Hahn, *The Philosophy of Hans-Georg Gadamer*, 67–94.

56. Jürgen Habermas, *Theorie des kommunikativen Handelns*, vol. 1: *Handlungsrationalität und gesellschaftliche Rationalisierung* (Frankfurt/M: Suhrkamp, 1981), 193; *Theory of Communicative Action*, vol. 1: Reason and the Rationalization of Society, trans. Thomas McCarthy (Boston: Beacon Press, 1984), 134.

57. For more on this debate, see Demetrius Teigas, *Knowledge and Hermeneutic Understanding A Study of the Habermas-Gadamer Debate* (Lewisburg, Pa.: Bucknell University Press, 1995); see also Dieter Misgeld, "Critical Theory and Hermeneutics: The Debate between Habermas and Gadamer," in John O'Neill, ed., *On Critical Theory* (New York: Sabury Press, 1976), 164–183; Michael Kelley, ed., *Hermeneutics and Critical Theory in Ethics and Politics* (Cambridge, Mass., and London: MIT Press, 1990); Tuan A. Nuyen, "Critique of Ideology: Hermeneutics or Critical Theory? (Gadamer-Habermas)," in *Human Studies* 17 (1994): 419–432; Alan How, *The Habermas-Gadamer Debate and the Nature of the Social* (Brookfield, Vt.: Averbury, 1995); Jose Maria Aguirre Oraa, *Raison critique ou raison herméneutique? Une analyse de la controverse entre Habermas et Gadamer* (Paris: Éditions du Cerf, 1998); Austin Harrington, "Some Problems with Gadamer's and Habermas' Dialogical Model of Sociological Understanding," *Journal for the Theory of Social Behaviour* 29 (1999): 371–384; David Ingram, "Jürgen Habermas and Hans-Georg Gadamer," in Robert C. Solomon and David Sherman, eds., *The Blackwell Guide to Continental Philosophy* (Malden and Oxford: Blackwell, 2003), 219–242.

58. Gadamer, "Replik zu 'Hermeneutik und Ideologiekritik,'" *GW*2 254.

59. Gadamer, "Replik zu 'Hermeneutik und Ideologiekritik,'" *GW*2 269. Warnke's criticism, according to which hermeneutics disallow revolutionary practice, cannot be sustained; on the contrary, Warnke understands revolution in much too abstract a way. See Georgia Warnke, *Gadamer: Hermeneutics, Tradition, and Reason* (Stanford, Calif.: Stanford University Press, 1987).

60. In a letter to Bernstein, Gadamer acknowledged this influence only slightly and with particular emphasis on Plato. See Richard J. Bernstein, *Beyond Objectivism and Relativism: Science, Hermeneutics, and Praxis* (Philadelphia: University of Pennsylvania Press, 1986), 58–93. See also the more recent essay: Richard J. Bernstein, "The Constellation of Hermeneutics, Critical Theory and Deconstruction," in Dostal, *The Cambridge Companion to Gadamer*, 267–282.

61. See Jürgen Habermas, "Urbanisierung der Heideggerschen Provinz," reprinted in Habermas, *Philosophisch-politische Profile*, 3rd exp. ed. (Frankfurt/M: Suhrkamp, 1981), 392–401; "Hans-Georg Gadamer: Urbanizing the Heideggerian Province," in *Philosophical-Political Profiles*, trans. F. Lawrence (Cambridge, Mass.: MIT Press, 1983), 189–197.

62. Habermas, "Urbanisierung der Heideggerschen Provinz," 397; "Hans-Georg Gadamer: Urbanizing the Heideggerian Province," 193.

63. See Gadamer, "Mit der Sprache denken," *GW*10 347.

64. On Gadamer and James, see Paul Fairfield, "Truth without Methodologism: Gadamer and James," in *American Catholic Quarterly* 67 (1993): 285–298; on Gadamer and Dewey, see also Victor

Kestenbaum, "Meaning on the Model of Truth: Dewey and Gadamer on Habit and Vorurteil," *Journal of Speculative Philosophy* 6 (1992): 25–66; Lawrence K. Schmidt, "Participation and Ritual: Dewey and Gadamer on Language," in Lawrence K. Schmidt, ed., *Language and Linguisticality in Gadamer's Hermeneutics* (Lanham, Md.: Lexington Books, 2000), 127–142.

65. See the lecture Rorty gave in Heidelberg on Gadamer's one-hundredth birthday, entitled in English "Being That Can Be Understood Is Language," in Bruce Krajewski, ed., *Gadamer's Repercussions: Reconsidering Philosophical Hermeneutics* (Berkeley: University of California Press, 2004), 21–29, 26. See Georgia Warnke, "Hermeneutics and the Social Sciences: A Gadamerian Critique of Rorty," *Inquiry* 28 (1986): 355–361; see also Steve Bouma-Prediger, "Rorty's Pragmatism and Gadamer's Hermeneutics," *Journal of the American Academy of Religion* 57 (1989): 313–324.

66. See chapter 4, part 4, in this volume.

67. Richard Rorty, *Philosophy and the Mirror of Nature* (Princeton, N.J.: Princeton University Press, 1979), 320.

68. Rorty, *Philosophy and the Mirror of Nature*, 319. See also Rorty, "Questioning," *Bochumer Philosophisches Jahrbuch* 2 (1997): 243–252; "On Hans-Georg Gadamer and the Philosophical Conversation," *London Review of Books* 22, no. 6 (2000): 23–25.

69. See chapter 2, part 3, in this volume.

70. Rorty, *Philosophy and the Mirror of Nature*, 360.

71. Rorty, *Philosophy and the Mirror of Nature*, 319.

72. Rorty, *Philosophy and the Mirror of Nature*, 359.

73. See Philippe Forget, ed., *Text und Interpretation. Deutsch-französische Debatte (mit Beiträgen von Jacques Derrida, Philippe Forget, Manfred Frank, Hans-Georg Gadamer, Jean Greisch und Francois Laruelle* (Munich: Fink [UTB], 1984).

74. Diane P. Michelfelder and Richard E. Palmer, eds., *Dialogue and Deconstruction: The Gadamer-Derrida-Encounter* (Albany: SUNY Press, 1989). The volume includes essays by Fred Dallmayr, Josef Simon, James Risser, Charles Shepherdson, Gary B. Madison, Herman Rapaport, Donald G. Marshall, Richard Shusterman, David F. Krell, Robert Bernasconi, John Sallis, John D. Caputo, Neal Oxenhandler, and Gabe Eisenstein.

75. See Hugh J. Silverman and Don Ihde, eds., *Hermeneutics and Deconstruction* (Albany, SUNY Press, 1985); John D. Caputo, Alexander Nehamas, and Hugh Silverman, "Symposium: Hermeneutics and Deconstruction," *Journal of Philosophy* 83 (1986): 678–692. See also Graeme Nicholson, "Deconstruction or Dialogue," *Man and World* 19 (1986): 263–274; Ernst Behler, "Deconstruction versus Hermeneutics: Derrida and Gadamer on Text and Interpretation," *Southern Humanities Review* 21, no. 3 (1987): 201–223; Wayne J. Froman, "L'Écriture and Philosophical Hermeneutics," in Silverman, *Gadamer and Hermeneutics*, 136–148; Jean Grondin, "La définition derridienne de la déconstruction. Contribution au rapprochement de l'herméneutique et de la déconstruction," *Archives de Philosophie* 62 (1999): 5–16.

76. See Heinz Kimmerle, "Gadamer, Derrida und Kein Ende," *Allgemeine Zeitschrift fuer Philosophie* 16 (1991): 223–235; Toni Tholen, *Erfahrung und Interpretation. Der Streit zwischen Hermeneutik und Dekonstruktion* (Heidelberg: Winter, 1999); Rodolphe Gasché, "Deconstruction and Hermeneutics," in Nicholas Royle, ed., *Deconstructions: A User's Guide* (Houndmills: Palgrave, 2000), 137–150; Stephen Feldman, "Made for Each Other: The Interdependence of Deconstruction and Philosophical Hermeneutics," *Philosophy and Social Criticism* 26 (2000): 51–70. An important contribution to the discussion is contained in the book by Georg W. Bertram, *Hermeneutik und Dekonstruktion. Konturen einer Auseinandersetzung der Gegenwartsphilosophie* (Munich: Fink, 2002), esp. 9–23 and 219–221; see Bertram, "Sprache und Verstehen in Hermeneutik und Dekonstruktion," in Przylebski, *Das Erbe Gadamers*, 205–226; see also Fabian Stoermer, *Hermeneutik und Dekonstruktion der Erinnerung. Über Gadamer, Derrida und Hölderlin* (Munich: Fink, 2002); Zoran Jankovic insists on their common Heideggerian inheritance in *Au-delà du signe: Gadamer et Derrida. Le dépassement her-*

méneutique et deconstructiviste du Dasein (Paris: L'Harmattan, 2003); Emil Angehrn, *Interpretation und Dekonstruktion. Untersuchungen zur Hermeneutik* (Verbrück: Weilerswist, 2003). See also the volume *Déconstruction et herméneutique: dossier central,* issue 2 of *Cercle Herméneutique* (Le Cercle Herméneutique, 2004), 59–170 (with contributions from Guy Deniau, Natalie Depraz, Zoran Jakovic, Catherine Malabou, Vincent Houillon, and Donatella Di Cesare).

77. For a fuller discussion of this topic, see my article: Donatella Di Cesare, "Stars and Constellations: The Difference between Gadamer and Derrida," *Research in Phenomenology* 34 (2004): 73–102.

78. Gadamer, "Destruktion und Dekonstruktion," *GW2* 361–372; "Destruktion and Deconstruction," in *Dialogue and Deconstruction: The Gadamer-Derrida Encounter,* ed. Diane P. Michelfelder and Richard E. Palmer (Albany: SUNY Press, 1989), 102–113; "Frühromantik, Hermeneutik und Dekonstruktivismus," *GW10* 125–137; "Hermeneutics and Logocentrism," in *Dialogue and Deconstruction: The Gadamer-Derrida Encounter,* ed. and trans. Diane P. Michelfelder and Richard E. Palmer (Albany: SUNY Press, 1989), 125–137. "Dekonstruktion und Hermeneutik," *GW10* 138–147; "Letter to Dallmayr (1985)," in *Dialogue and Deconstruction,* 93–101. "Hermeneutik auf der Spur," *GW10* 148–174; "Hermeneutics Tracking the Trace [On Derrida]," in *The Gadamer Reader: A Bouquet of the Later Writings,* ed. Richard Palmer (Evanston, Ill.: Northwestern University Press, 2006), 372–406.

79. On the nature of "difference" for Derrida, see Rodolphe Gasché, *Inventions of Difference: On Jacques Derrida* (Cambridge, Mass.: Harvard University Press, 1994).

80. Derrida, "Rams. Uninterrupted Dialogue—Between Two Infinites, the Poem," in *Sovereignties in Question: The Poetics of Paul Celan,* ed. Thomas Dutoit and Outi Pasanen (New York: Fordham University Press, 2005), 135–164.

81. Derrida, "Rams," 136.

82. See chapter 8, part 2, of this book.

83. Gadamer, "Text und Interpretation," *GW2* 353; "Text and Interpretation," in *Dialogue and Deconstruction: The Gadamer- Derrida Encounter* (Albany: SUNY, 1989), 185.

84. Originally printed in Forget, *Text und Interpretation,* 38. It is important to emphasize here that, in the entire Gadamerian oeuvre, this expression appears only this one time. What remained neglected in the discussion, however, is among other issues the concept of the "text," which is interpreted differently by Gadamer and Derrida, since Gadamer proceeds from the unity of the text. Derrida takes aim at precisely this presupposed unity. See on this Rodolphe Gasché, *The Tain of the Mirror* (Cambridge, Mass.: Harvard University Press, 1989), 278–280.

85. Derrida's last statement at the Paris meeting revolved around Nietzsche. See Jacques Derrida, "Guter Wille zur Macht (II). Die Unterschriften interpretieren (Nietzsche/Heidegger)," in Forget, *Text und Interpretation,* 62–77; "Interpreting Signatures (Nietzsche/Heidegger): Two Questions," in *Dialogue and Deconstruction,* 58–71. The target of his polemic is Heidegger's interpretation, according to which Nietzsche would be the last metaphysician. For Derrida it was, on the contrary, Heidegger who remained chained to a logocentric metaphysics, because he consistently asked about Being and about the meaning of Being. Heidegger thus presumed to be able to hold Being in a *logos.*

86. Derrida, "Guter Wille zur Macht," in Forget, *Text und Interpretation,* 58; "Interpreting Signatures (Nietzsche/Heidegger): Two Questions," 53.

87. Gadamer, "Und dennoch: Macht des Guten Willens," in Forget, *Text und Interpretation,* 59–61; "Reply to Jacques Derrida," 55–57.

88. Plato, "Gorgias," 458a.

89. But Gadamer's attempt to derive Derrida's position from Nietzsche's is questionable. Gasché correctly warns of this: "Specters of Nietzsche," in Daniel O. Dahlstrom, ed., *The Proceedings of the Twentieth World Congress of Philosophy,* vol. 8, Contemporary Philosophy (Bowling Green: Philosophy Documentation Center, 2000), 183–193.

90. Gadamer draws on the "exceptional Derrida critique" by Habermas. See Gadamer, "Zwischen Phänomenologie und Dialektik. Versuch einer Selbstkritik," *GW2* 23. See Jürgen Habermas, *Der philosophische Diskurs der Moderne* (Frankfurt/M: Suhrkamp, 1985), 191ff; *The Philosophical Discourse of Modernity: Twelve Lectures,* trans. Frederick G. Lawrence (Cambridge, Mass: MIT Press, 1987), 198.

91. See chapter 8, part 7, in this volume.

92. See Gadamer, "Destruktion und Dekonstruktion," *GW2* 367–368; "Destruktion and Deconstruction," 108.

93. Paul Celan, "Grosse glühende Wölbung," in Celan, *Atemwende, Gesammelte Werke,* vol. 2, ed. Beda Allemann and Stefan Reichert with the assistance of Rolf Bücher (Frankfurt/M: Suhrkamp, 1986), 97.

94. Derrida, "Der ununterbrochene Dialog," 15; "Rams," 140.

95. Derrida, "Der ununterbrochene Dialog," 47–48; "Rams," 161.

96. The Italian translation is the first one in general.

97. The question remains relevant today. An overall view of Gadamer's reception in Italy is given in the important contribution by Valerio Verra, "Hans-Georg Gadamers hermeneutische Philosophie in Italien," *Heidelberger Jahrbücher* 34 (1990): 177–188. See also Reiner Wiehl, "Vielstimmige Hermeneutik in Italien," *Internationale Zeitschrift für Philosophie* 2 (1996): 286–292. The article reviews the volume *Beiträge zur Hermeneutik aus Italien,* ed. Franco Bianco (Freiburg and Munich: Alber, 1993). The unavoidable fragmentation of Italian hermeneutics also speaks, however, for its originality.

98. Luigi Pareyson, *Verita e interpretazione* (Milan: Mursia, 1971).

99. Luigi Pareyson, *Ontologia della liberta. Il male e la sofferenza* (Turin: Einaudi, 1995).

100. See Valerio Verra, "Hans-Georg Gadamer e l'ermeneutica filosofica," *Filosofia* (1963): 412–418.

101. Vattimo expressed his views very early. See Gianni Vattimo, "Estetica ed ermeneutica in Hans-Georg Gadamer," *Rivista di estetica* 8 (1963): 117–130, now in Vattimo, *Poesia e ontologia* (Milan: Mursia, 1967), 167–186.

102. Gianni Vattimo, *Aldi la del soggetto. Nietzsche, Heidegger e l'ermeneutica* (Milan: Feltrinelli, 1984), 71.

103. See chapter 8, part 5, in this volume.

104. Vattimo, *Beyond Interpretation,* 93.

105. See Gianni Vattimo, *Dopo la cristianita. Per un cristianesimo non religioso* (Milan: Garzanti, 2002). A similar starting point can be found in the book by Vaclav Umlauf, *Hermeneutik nach Gadamer* (Freiburg and Munich: Alber, 2007), which among other things does not contain what is stated in the title, since it deals with a religious-nihilistic reading of the most frequently considered topics in Gadamer's philosophy.

106. In the two or three cases where it appears, for example in the title "Im Schatten des Nihilismus" (*GW9* 367), it has a negative meaning.

107. See chapter 9, part 2, in this volume.

108. The analyses by Scholz aim at a much more comprehensive concept of interpretation, the "presumptive" character of interpretation. See Oliver R. Scholz, *Verstehen und Rationalität. Untersuchungen zu den Grundlagen der Hermeneutik und Sprachphilosophie* (Frankfurt am Main: Vittorio Klostermann, 2001), 147–249. Kraemer's more recent critique, which however contains productive initiatives, also relies on a much too comprehensive conception of interpretation. See Hans Kraemer, *Kritik der Hermeneutik. Interpretationsphilosophie und Realismus* (Munich: Beck, 2007).

109. See chapter 8, part 8, in this volume.

110. See Gadamer, "Nietzsche—der Antipode. Das Drama Zarathustras" (1984), *GW4* 448–462; "The Drama of Zarathustra," trans. T. Heilke, in *Nietzsche's New Seas,* ed. M. A. Gillespie and T. B. Strong (Chicago: University of Chicago Press, 1983), 220–231. On this topic, see Nicholas Davey, "A World of Hope and Optimism Despite Present Difficulties: Gadamer's Critique of Perspectivism,"

Man and World 23 (1990): 273–294. On Nietzsche and Gadamer, see also Johann Figl, "Nietzsche und die philosophische Hermeneutik des 20. Jahrhunderts. Mit besonderer Berücksichtigung Diltheys, Heideggers und Gadamers," *Nietzsche-Studien* 10/11 (1981–82): 408–430.

111. Charles Taylor, "Understanding the Other: A Gadamerian View on Conceptual Schemes," in *Gadamer's Century*, 279–297, 279.

112. See Nicole Ruchlak, "Alterität als hermeneutische Perspektive," in Hans-Martin Schönherr-Mann, ed., *Hermeneutik als Ethik* (Munich: Fink, 2004), 151–167; see also Ruchlak, *Das Gespräch mit dem Anderen. Perspektiven einer ethischen Hermeneutik* (Würzburg: Königshausen & Neumann, 2004). On the question of alterity in hermeneutics, see Robert Bernasconi, "'You Don't Know What I'm Talking About': Alterity and the Hermeneutical Ideal," in Lawrence K. Schmidt, ed., *The Specter of Relativism* (Evanston, Ill.: Northwestern University Press, 1995), 178–194; Lawrence K. Schmidt, "Respecting Others: The Hermeneutic Virtue," *Continental Philosophy Review* 33 (2000): 359–3791; see also Nicholas Davey, *Unquiet Understanding. Gadamer's Philosophical Hermeneutics* (Albany: SUNY, 2006), 179–180.

113. Robert Schurz, *Negative Hermeneutik. Zur sozialen Anthropologie des Nicht-Verstehens* (Opladen: WestdeutscherVerlag, 1995), 207.

114. Bernhard Waldenfels, *Vielstimmigkeit der Rede. Studien zur Phänomenologie des Fremden*, vol. 4 (Frankfurt/M: Suhrkamp, 1999), 67. On this, see Helmuth Vetter, *Philosophische Hermeneutik. Unterwegs zu Heidegger und Gadamer* (Frankfurt/M: Peter Lang, 2007), 148–149. Here is not the space to roll out the entire debate about the foreign, which has in the meantime widely branched out into various areas. An overview of the state of the discussion can be gathered from various perspectives: Iris Därmann, "Der Fremde zwischen den Fronten von Ethnologie und Philosophie," *Philosophische Rundschau* 43 (1996): 46–63; Herfried Münkler, ed., *Furcht und Faszination. Facetten der Fremdheit* (Berlin: Akademie Verlag,1997); Franz Martin Wimmer, "Fremde," in Christoph Wulff, ed., *Vom Menschen. Handbuch Historische Anthropologie* (Weinheim and Basel: Beltz, 1997), 1066–1078.

115. See Waldenfels, *Vielstimmigkeit der Rede*, 71–72. It is remarkable that almost all the citations Waldenfels uses from Gadamer are from *Truth and Method*.

116. Waldenfels, *Vielstimmigkeit der Rede*, 73; see also *Antwortregister* (Frankfurt/M: Suhrkamp, 1994), esp. 122–137.

117. Waldenfels, "Antwort auf das Fremde," in Bernhard Waldenfels and Iris Daermann, eds., *Der Anspruch des Anderen. Perspektiven phänomenologischer Ethik* (Munich: Fink, 1998), 35–49, 43.

118. Waldenfels, *Vielstimmigkeit der Rede*, 83.

119. Schleiermacher, *Hermeneutik und Kritik* (Frankfurt/M: Suhrkamp, 1977), 328; *Hermeneutics and Criticism, And Other Writings*, trans. and ed. Andrew Bowie (Cambridge: Cambridge University Press, 1998), 227.

120. Wilhelm von Humboldt, *Über die Verschiedenheit des menschlichen Sprachbaues*, ed. Donatella Di Cesare (Paderborn: Schöningh [UTB], 1998), 191; *On Language: On the Diversity of Human Language-Construction and Its Influence on the Mental Development Human Species*, trans. Peter Heath, Texts in German Philosophy (Cambridge: Cambridge University Press, 1999), 63. Translation modified.

121. Emmanuel Levinas, *Totality and Infinity: An Essay on Exteriority*, trans. Alphonso Lingis (Pittsburgh: Duquesne University Press, 1969), 194.

122. See the explanations of *átopon* in this volume, chapter 8, part 8.

123. See also Bertram, *Hermeneutik und Dekonstruktion*, 77.

124. There are few alternatives to this to be seen. See Werner Kogge, *Verstehen und Fremdheit in der philosophischen Hermeneutik. Heidegger und Gadamer* (Hildesheim: Olms, 2001), 156–157. I have tried in this volume to reconstruct the space for the other in the hermeneutics of infinite finitude.

125. See Bernhard Waldenfels, *Der Stachel des Fremden* (Frankfurt/M: Suhrkamp, 1998). New challenges also arise from the various contributions in the volume edited by Lorraine Code, *Feminist Interpretations of Hans-Georg Gadamer* (University Park: Pennsylvania State University Press, 2003).

126. On the concept of community, see Stephen Watson, "Interpretation, Dialogue and Friendship: On the Remainder of Community," *Research in Phenomenology* 26 (1996): 54–97; Thomas M. Alexander, "Eros and Understanding: Gadamer's Aesthetic Ontology of the Community," in Hahn, *The Philosophy of Hans Georg Gadamer*, 323–345; Donald Maier, "Community and Alterity: A Gadamerian Approach," *Philosophy in Contemporary World* 4 (1998): 26–33; James Risser, "Philosophical Hermeneutics and the Question of Community," in Charles Scott, ed., *Interrogating the Tradition: Hermeneutics and the History of Philosophy* (Albany: SUNY, 2000), 19–34.

Index of Names

Index of Terms

DONATELLA DI CESARE is Professor of Philosophy at the University of Rome "La Sapienza." She is author of *Grammatica dei tempi messianici* and *Ermerneutica della finitezza.*

NIALL KEANE is Lecturer in Philosophy at the University of Limerick.